International Association for the Evaluation of Educational Achievement

Science Achievement in the Middle School Years: IEA's Third International Mathematics and Science Study (TIMSS)

Albert E. Beaton
Michael O. Martin
Ina V.S. Mullis
Eugenio J. Gonzalez
Teresa A. Smith
Dana L. Kelly

November 1996

TIMSS International Study Center
Boston College
Chestnut Hill, MA, USA

Science Achievement in the Middle School Years: IEA's Third International Mathematics and Science Study / by Albert E. Beaton, Michael O. Martin, Ina V.S. Mullis, Eugenio J. Gonzalez, Teresa A. Smith, and Dana L. Kelly

Publisher: Center for the Study of Testing, Evaluation, and Educational Policy, Boston College.

Library of Congress Catalog Card Number: 96-71250

ISBN 1-889938-03-3

For more information about TIMSS contact:

TIMSS International Study Center
Center for the Study of Testing, Evaluation, and Educational Policy
Campion Hall
School of Education
Boston College
Chestnut Hill, MA 02167
United States

For information on ordering this report, write the above address or call +1-617-552-4521.

This report also is available on the World Wide Web:
http://wwwcsteep.bc.edu/timss

Funding for the international coordination of TIMSS is provided by the U.S. National Center for Education Statistics, the U.S. National Science Foundation, the IEA, and the Canadian government. Each participating country provides funding for the national implementation of TIMSS.

Printed and bound in the United States.

Contents

EXECUTIVE SUMMARY 1

INTRODUCTION 7

Which Countries Participated? 8

Table 1: Countries Participating in TIMSS 9

Table 2: Information About the Grades Tested 11

What Was the Nature of the Science Test? 12

How Do Country Characteristics Differ? 13

Table 3: Selected Demographic Characteristics of TIMSS Countries 14

Table 4: Public Expenditure on Education at Primary and Secondary Levels in TIMSS Countries 15

Figure 1: Centralization of Decision-Making Regarding Curriculum Syllabi 17

Figure 2: Centralization of Decision-Making Regarding Textbooks 18

Figure 3: Centralization of Decision-Making Regarding Examinations 19

CHAPTER 1 : INTERNATIONAL STUDENT ACHIEVEMENT IN SCIENCE 21

What Are the Overall Differences in Science Achievement? 21

Table 1.1: Distributions of Achievement in the Sciences - Upper Grade (Eighth Grade) 22

Figure 1.1: Multiple Comparisons of Achievement in the Sciences - Upper Grade (Eighth Grade) 23

Table 1.2: Distributions of Achievement in the Sciences - Lower Grade (Seventh Grade) 26

Figure 1.2: Multiple Comparisons of Achievement in the Sciences - Lower Grade (Seventh Grade) 27

What Are the Increases in Achievement Between the Lower and Upper Grades? 28

Table 1.3: Achievement Differences in the Sciences Between Lower and Upper Grades (Seventh and Eighth Grades) 29

What Are the Differences in Performance Compared to Three Marker Levels of International Science Achievement? 30

Table 1.4: Percentages of Students Achieving International Marker Levels in the Sciences - Upper Grade (Eighth Grade) 31

Table 1.5: Percentages of Students Achieving International Marker Levels in the Sciences - Lower Grade (Seventh Grade) 32

What Are the Gender Differences in Science Achievement? 33

Table 1.6: Gender Differences in Achievement in the Sciences - Upper Grade (Eighth Grade) 34

Table 1.7: Gender Differences in Achievement in the Sciences - Lower Grade (Seventh Grade) 35

What Are the Differences in Median Performance at Age 13? 36

Table 1.8: Median Achievement in the Sciences: 13-Year-Old Students 37

CHAPTER 2 : AVERAGE ACHIEVEMENT IN THE SCIENCE CONTENT AREAS 39

How Does Achievement Differ Across Science Content Areas? 39

Table 2.1: Average Percent Correct by Science Content Areas - Upper Grade (Eighth Grade) 41

Table 2.2: Average Percent Correct by Science Content Areas - Lower Grade (Seventh Grade) 42

Table 2.3: Profiles of Relative Performance in Science Content Areas - Lower and Upper Grades (Seventh and Eighth Grades) 44

What Are the Increases in Achievement Between the Lower and Upper Grades? 45

Figure 2.1: Difference in Average Percent Correct Between Lower and Upper Grades (Seventh and Eighth Grades) Overall and in Science Content Areas 46

What Are the Gender Differences in Achievement for the Content Areas? 49

Table 2.4: Average Percent Correct for Boys and Girls by Science Content Areas - Upper Grade (Eighth Grade) 50

Table 2.5: Average Percent Correct for Boys and Girls by Science Content Areas - Lower Grade (Seventh Grade) 52

CHAPTER 3 : PERFORMANCE ON ITEMS WITHIN EACH SCIENCE CONTENT AREA 55

What Have Students Learned About Earth Science? 55

Table 3.1: Percent Correct for Earth Science Example Items - Lower and Upper Grades (Seventh and Eighth Grades) 56

Figure 3.1: International Difficulty Map for Earth Science Example Items - Lower and Upper Grades (Seventh and Eighth Grades) 58

Earth Science Example Items 61

What Have Students Learned About Life Science? 64

Table 3.2: Percent Correct for Life Science Example Items - Lower and Upper Grades (Seventh and Eighth Grades) 66

Figure 3.2: International Difficulty Map for Life Science Example Items - Lower and Upper Grades (Seventh and Eighth Grades) 68

Life Science Example Items 69

What Have Students Learned About Physics? 72

Table 3.3: Percent Correct for Physics Example Items – Lower and Upper Grades (Seventh and Eighth Grades) 74

Figure 3.3: International Difficulty Map for Physics Example Items – Lower and Upper Grades (Seventh and Eighth Grades) 76

Physics Example Items 77

What Have Students Learned About Chemistry? 80

Table 3.4: Percent Correct for Chemistry Example Items – Lower and Upper Grades (Seventh and Eighth Grades) 82

Figure 3.4: International Difficulty Map for Chemistry Example Items – Lower and Upper Grades (Seventh and Eighth Grades) 84

Chemistry Example Items 85

What Have Students Learned About Environmental Issues and the Nature of Science? 87

Table 3.5: Percent Correct for Environmental Issues and the Nature of Science Example Items – Lower and Upper Grades (Seventh and Eighth Grades) 88

Figure 3.5: International Difficulty Map for Environmental Issues and the Nature of Science Example Items – Lower and Upper Grades (Seventh and Eighth Grades) 90

Environmental Issues and the Nature of Science Example Items 91

CHAPTER 4 : STUDENTS' BACKGROUNDS AND ATTITUDES TOWARDS THE SCIENCES 93

What Educational Resources Do Students Have in Their Homes? 93

Table 4.1: Students' Reports on Educational Aids in the Home: Dictionary, Study Desk/Table, and Computer – Upper Grade (Eighth Grade) 94

Table 4.2: Students' Reports on the Number of Books in the Home – Upper Grade (Eighth Grade) 95

Table 4.3: Students' Reports on the Highest Level of Education of Either Parent – Upper Grade (Eighth Grade) 97

Figure 4.1: Country Modifications to the Definitions of Educational Levels for Parents' Highest Level of Education 98

What Are the Academic Expectations of Students, Their Families, and Their Friends? 100

Table 4.4: Students' Reports on Whether They Agree or Strongly Agree That It is Important to Do Various Activities – Upper Grade (Eighth Grade) 102

Table 4.5 Students' Reports on Whether Their Mothers Agree or Strongly Agree That It is Important to Do Various Activities – Upper Grade (Eighth Grade) 103

Table 4.6: Students' Reports on Whether Their Friends Agree or Strongly Agree That It is Important to Do Various Activities – Upper Grade (Eighth Grade) 104

How Do Students Spend Their Out-of-School Time During the School Week? 105

Table 4.7: Students' Reports on How They Spend Their Daily Out-of-School Study Time – Upper Grade (Eighth Grade) 106

Table 4.8: Students' Reports on How They Spend Their Daily Leisure Time – Upper Grade (Eighth Grade) 107

Table 4.9: Students' Reports on Total Amount of Daily Out-of-School Study Time – Upper Grade (Eighth Grade) 108

Table 4.10: Students' Reports on the Hours Spent Each Day Watching Television and Videos – Upper Grade (Eighth Grade) 110

How Do Students Perceive Success in the Sciences? 111

Table 4.11: Students' Reports on Their Self-Perceptions About Usually Doing Well in the Sciences – Upper Grade (Eighth Grade) 112

Figure 4.2: Gender Differences In Students' Self-Perceptions About Usually Doing Well in the Sciences – Upper Grade (Eighth Grade) 113

Table 4.12: Students' Reports on Things Necessary to Do Well in the Sciences – Upper Grade (Eighth Grade) 117

Table 4.13: Students' Perceptions About the Need to Do Well in the Sciences to Get Their Desired Job – Upper Grade (Eighth Grade) 118

Table 4.14: Students' Perceptions About the Need to Do Well in the Sciences to Get Into Their Preferred University or Secondary School – Upper Grade (Eighth Grade) 119

Table 4.15: Students' Perceptions About the Need to Do Well in the Sciences to Please Their Parents – Upper Grade (Eighth Grade) 120

What Are Students' Attitudes Towards the Sciences? 121

Table 4.16: Students' Reports About Liking the Sciences – Upper Grade (Eighth Grade) 122

Figure 4.3: Gender Differences in Liking the Sciences – Upper Grade (Eighth Grade) 123

CHAPTER 5 : TEACHERS AND INSTRUCTION 125

Who Delivers Science Instruction? 126

Table 5.1: Requirements for Certification Held by the Majority of Lower- and Upper-Grade (Seventh- and Eighth-Grade) Teachers 128

Table 5.2: Teachers' Reports on Their Age and Gender – Upper Grade (Eighth Grade) 130

Table 5.3: Teachers' Reports on Their Years of Teaching Experience – Upper Grade (Eighth Grade) 131

What Are Teachers' Perceptions About Science? 133

Figure 5.1: Percent of Students Whose Science Teachers Agree or Strongly Agree with Statements About the Nature of Science and Science Teaching – Upper Grade (Eighth Grade) 134

Figure 5.2: Percent of Students Whose Science Teachers Think Particular Abilities Are Very Important for Students' Success in the Sciences in School – Upper Grade (Eighth Grade) 136

How Do Science Teachers Spend Their School-Related Time? 138

Table 5.4: Teachers' Reports on the Proportion of Their Formally Scheduled School Time Spent Teaching the Sciences - Upper Grade (Eighth Grade) 139

Table 5.5: Teachers' Reports on Average Number of Hours Integrated Science is Taught Weekly to Their Science Classes - Upper Grade (Eighth Grade) 140

Table 5.6: Average Number of Hours Students' Teachers Spend on Various School-Related Activities Outside the Formal School Day During the School Week - Upper Grade (Eighth Grade) 141

Table 5.7: Teachers' Reports on How Often They Meet with Other Teachers in Their Subject Area to Discuss and Plan Curriculum or Teaching Approaches - Upper Grade (Eighth Grade) 142

How Are Science Classes Organized? 143

Table 5.8: Teachers' Reports on Average Size of Science Class - Upper Grade (Eighth Grade) 144

Figure 5.3: Teachers' Reports About Classroom Organization During Science Lessons - Upper Grade (Eighth Grade) 146

What Activities Do Students Do in Their Science Lessons? 148

Table 5.9: Teachers' Reports on Their Main Sources of Written Information When Deciding Which Topics to Teach and How to Present a Topic - Upper Grade (Eighth Grade) 150

Figure 5.4: Teachers' Reports About Using a Textbook in Teaching Science - Upper Grade (Eighth Grade) 151

Table 5.10: Teachers' Reports on How Often They Ask Students to Do Reasoning Tasks - Upper Grade (Eighth Grade) 152

Table 5.11: Students' Reports on the Frequency with Which Their Teacher Gives a Demonstration of an Experiment - Upper Grade (Eighth Grade) 153

Table 5.12: Students' Reports on Frequency of Doing an Experiment or Practical Investigation in Science Class - Upper Grade (Eighth Grade) 154

Table 5.13: Students' Reports on Frequency of Using Things from Every Day Life in Solving Science Problems - Upper Grade (Eighth Grade) 155

How Are Calculators and Computers Used? 156

Table 5.14: Students' Reports on Having a Calculator and Computer in the Home - Upper Grade (Eighth Grade) 157

Table 5.15: Teachers' Reports on Frequency of Students' Use of Calculators in Science Class - Upper Grade (Eighth Grade) 158

Table 5.16: Teachers' Reports on Ways in Which Calculators Are Used At Least Once or Twice a Week - Upper Grade (Eighth Grade) 159

Table 5.17: Teachers' Reports on Frequency of Using Computers in Science Class to Solve Exercises or Problems - Upper Grade (Eighth Grade) 160

Table 5.18: Students' Reports on Frequency of Using Computers in Science Class - Upper Grade (Eighth Grade) 161

How Much Science Homework Are Students Assigned? ... 162

Table 5.19: Teachers' Reports About the Amount of Science Homework Assigned - Upper Grade (Eighth Grade) ... 163

Table 5.20: Teachers' Reports on Their Use of Students' Written Science Homework - Upper Grade (Eighth Grade) ... 164

What Assessment and Evaluation Procedures Do Teachers Use? ... 165

Table 5.21: Teachers' Reports on the Types of Assessment Given "Quite A Lot" or "A Great Deal" of Weight in Assessing Students' Work in Science Class - Upper Grade (Eighth Grade) ... 166

Table 5.22: Teachers' Reports on Ways Assessment Information Is Used "Quite A Lot" or "A Great Deal" - Upper Grade (Eighth Grade) ... 167

Table 5.23: Students' Reports on Frequency of Having a Quiz or Test in Their Science Lessons - Upper Grade (Eighth Grade) ... 168

APPENDIX A: OVERVIEW OF TIMSS PROCEDURES: SCIENCE ACHIEVEMENT RESULTS FOR SEVENTH- AND EIGHTH-GRADE STUDENTS ... A-1

History ... A-1

The Components of TIMSS ... A-1

Figure A.1: Countries Participating in Additional Components of TIMSS Testing ... A-4

Developing the TIMSS Science Test ... A-5

Figure A.2: The Three Aspects and Major Categories of the Science Framework ... A-6

Table A.1: Distribution of Science Items by Content Reporting Category and Performance Category ... A-7

TIMSS Test Design ... A-9

Sample Implementation and Participation Rates ... A-9

Table A.2: Coverage of TIMSS Target Population ... A-10

Table A.3: Coverage of 13-Year-Old Students ... A-12

Table A.4: School Participation Rates and Sample Sizes - Upper Grade (Eighth Grade) ... A-13

Table A.5: Student Participation Rates and Samples Sizes - Upper Grade (Eighth Grade) ... A-14

Table A.6: School Participation Rates and Sample Sizes - Lower Grade (Seventh Grade) ... A-15

Table A.7: Student Participation Rates and Samples Sizes - Lower Grade (Seventh Grade) ... A-16

Table A.8: Overall Participation Rates - Upper and Lower Grades (Eighth and Seventh Grades) ... A-17

Indicating Compliance with Sampling Guidelines in the Report ... A-18

Figure A.3: Countries Grouped for Reporting of Achievement According to Their Compliance with Guidelines for Sample Implementation and Participation Rates ... A-19

Data Collection ... A-20

Scoring the Free-Response Items A-21

Table A.9: TIMSS Within-Country Free-Response Coding Reliability Data for Population 2 Science Items A-22

Table A.10: Percent Exact Agreement for Coding of Science Items for International and Within-Country Reliability Studies A-24

Test Reliability A-25

Table A.11: Cronbach's Alpha Reliability Coefficients - TIMSS Science Test - Lower and Upper Grades (Seventh and Eighth Grades) A-26

Data Processing A-25

IRT Scaling and Data Analysis A-27

Estimating Sampling Error A-28

APPENDIX B: THE TEST-CURRICULUM MATCHING ANALYSIS B-1

Table B.1: Test-Curriculum Matching Analysis Results - Science - Upper Grade (Eighth Grade) B-3

Table B.2: Test-Curriculum Matching Analysis Results - Science - Lower Grade (Seventh Grade) B-4

Table B.3: Standard Errors for the Test-Curriculum Matching Analysis Results - Science - Upper Grade (Eighth Grade) B-7

Table B.4: Standard Errors for the Test-Curriculum Matching Analysis Results - Science - Lower Grade (Seventh Grade) B-8

APPENDIX C: SELECTED SCIENCE ACHIEVEMENT RESULTS FOR THE PHILIPPINES C-1

Table C.1: Philippines - Selected Achievement Results in the Sciences - Unweighted Data C-2

APPENDIX D: SELECTED SCIENCE ACHIEVEMENT RESULTS FOR DENMARK, SWEDEN, AND SWITZERLAND (GERMAN-SPEAKING) - EIGHTH GRADE D-1

Table D.1: Denmark - Selected Achievement Results in the Sciences D-2

Table D.2: Sweden - Selected Achievement Results in the Sciences D-3

Table D.3: Switzerland (German-Speaking) - Selected Achievement Results in the Sciences D-4

APPENDIX E: PERCENTILES AND STANDARD DEVIATIONS OF SCIENCE ACHIEVEMENT E-1

Table E.1: Percentiles of Achievement in the Sciences - Upper Grade (Eighth Grade) E-2

Table E.2: Percentiles of Achievement in the Sciences - Lower Grade (Seventh Grade) E-3

Table E. 3: Standard Deviations of Achievement in the Sciences - Upper Grade (Eighth Grade) E-4

Table E. 4: Standard Deviations of Achievement in the Sciences - Lower Grade (Seventh Grade) E-5

APPENDIX F: ACKNOWLEDGMENTS F-1

Executive Summary

Science

Since its inception in 1959, the International Association for the Evaluation of Educational Achievement (IEA) has conducted a series of international comparative studies designed to provide policy makers, educators, researchers, and practitioners with information about educational achievement and learning contexts. The Third International Mathematics and Science Study (TIMSS) is the largest and most ambitious of these studies ever undertaken.

The scope and complexity of TIMSS is enormous. Forty-five countries collected data in more than 30 different languages. Five grade levels were tested in the two subject areas, totaling more than half a million students tested around the world. The success of TIMSS depended on a collaborative effort between the research centers in each country responsible for implementing the steps of the project and the network of centers responsible for managing the across-country tasks such as training country representatives in standardized procedures, selecting comparable samples of schools and students, and conducting the various steps required for data processing and analysis. Including the administrators in the approximately 15,000 schools involved, many thousands of individuals around the world were involved in the data collection effort. Most countries collected their data in May and June of 1995, although those countries on a southern hemisphere schedule tested in late 1994, which was the end of their school year.

Five content dimensions were covered in the TIMSS science tests given to the middle-school students: earth science, life science, physics, chemistry and environmental issues and the nature of science. About one-fourth of the questions were in free-response format requiring students to generate and write their answers. These types of questions, some of which required extended responses, were allotted approximately one-third of the testing time. Chapter 3 of this report contains 25 example items illustrating the range of science concepts and processes addressed by the TIMSS test.

Because the home, school, and national contexts within which education takes place can play important roles in how students learn science, TIMSS collected extensive information about such background factors. The students who participated in TIMSS completed questionnaires about their home and school experiences related to learning science. Also, teachers and school administrators completed questionnaires about instructional practices. System-level information was provided by each participating country.

TIMSS was conducted with attention to quality at every step of the way. Rigorous procedures were designed specifically to translate the tests, and numerous regional training sessions were held in data collection and scoring procedures. Quality control monitors observed testing sessions, and sent reports back to the TIMSS International Study Center at Boston College. The samples of students selected for testing were scrutinized according to rigorous standards designed to prevent bias and ensure comparability. In this publication, the countries are grouped for reporting of achievement according to their compliance with the sampling guidelines and the level of their participation rates. Prior to analysis, the data from each country were subjected to exhaustive checks for adherence to the international formats as well as for within-country consistency and comparability across countries.

The results provided in this report describe students' science achievement at both the seventh and eighth grades. For most, but not all TIMSS countries, the two grades tested at the middle-school level represented the seventh and eighth years of formal schooling. Special emphasis is placed on the eighth-grade results, including selected information about students' background experiences and teachers' classroom practices in science. Results are reported for the 41 countries that completed all of the steps on the schedule necessary to appear in this report. The results for students in the third and fourth grades, and for those in their final year of secondary school will appear in subsequent reports.

The following sections summarize the major findings described in this report.

Students' Science Achievement

- Singapore was the top-performing country at both the eighth and seventh grades. The Czech Republic, Japan, and Korea also performed very well at both grades. Lower-performing countries included Colombia, Kuwait, and South Africa (see Tables 1.1 and 1.2; Figures 1.1 and 1.2).

- Perhaps the most striking finding was the large difference in average science achievement between the top-performing and bottom-performing countries. Despite this large difference, when countries were ordered by average achievement there were only small or negligible differences in achievement between each country and the one with the next-lowest average achievement. In some sense, at both grades, the results provide a chain of overlapping performances, where most countries had average achievement similar to a cluster of other countries, but from the beginning to the end of the chain there were substantial differences. For example, at both grades, average achievement in top-performing Singapore was comparable to or even exceeded performance for 95% of the students in the lowest-performing countries.

- In most countries and internationally, boys had significantly higher mean science achievement than girls at both the seventh and eighth grades. This is attributable mainly to significantly higher performance by boys in earth science, physics, and chemistry. In few countries were significant gender differences found in life science or environmental issues and the nature of science, although in life science one such difference favored girls in one country at the eighth grade.

- Compared to their overall performance in science, many countries did relatively better or worse in some content areas than they did in others. Consistent with the idea of countries having different emphases in curriculum, some countries performed better in life science, some performed better in physics, and others performed better in chemistry.

- Internationally, students had the most difficulty with the chemistry items. For example, an item that required students to explain how carbon dioxide fire extinguishers work was answered correctly by about half or fewer of both seventh- and eighth-grade students in many countries. Eighth-grade students, in general, performed better than seventh-grade students on this item, but in only four countries did 70% or more of eighth-grade students correctly explain the displacement of oxygen required for combustion – Austria, England, Singapore, and Sweden.

- A multiple-choice physics item requiring students to demonstrate knowledge of the earth's gravitational force acting on a falling apple was of similar international difficulty, with about half or fewer of the students in many countries selecting the correct response. Except in the Czech Republic and the Slovak Republic, where about three-quarters or more of students in both grades responded correctly, students' responses to this item indicated a common misconception internationally that gravity does not act on a stationary object when it is on the ground.

- One of the more difficult earth science items was an extended-response item requiring students to apply scientific principles and draw a diagram to explain the earth's water cycle. Internationally, about a third or fewer of both seventh- and eighth-grade students provided a completely correct response that included all three steps in the water cycle – evaporation, transportation, and precipitation. Performance on this item varied widely across countries, however, with percentages correct ranging from less than 10% in Lithuania and South Africa to 60% in Flemish-speaking Belgium.

Students' Attitudes Towards Science

- Even though the majority of eighth-graders in nearly every country indicated they liked science to some degree, clearly not all students feel positive about this subject area. Among countries where science is taught to eighth-grade students as a single subject, boys reported liking science more than did girls in England, Hong Kong, Japan, Kuwait, New Zealand, Norway, and Singapore. Where the major scientific disciplines are taught as separate subjects, the major gender differences were found in physical science, with boys expressing a liking for this content area more often than girls.

- In all except three countries, the majority of students agreed or strongly agreed that they did well in science or science subject areas – a perception that did not always coincide with the comparisons in achievement across countries on the TIMSS test. Interestingly, the exceptions included two of the higher-performing countries – Japan and Korea – where only 45% and 35% of the students, respectively, agreed or strongly agreed about doing well (the third was Hong Kong).

- In the majority of countries, for eighth-grade students, pleasing their parents and getting into their preferred university or secondary school were both stronger motivators for doing well in science than was getting their desired job.

Home Environment

Home factors were strongly related to science achievement in every country that participated in TIMSS.

- In every country, eighth-grade students who reported having more educational resources in the home had higher science achievement than those who reported little access to such resources. Strong positive relationships were found between science achievement and having study aids in the home, including a dictionary, a computer, and a study desk/table for the student's own use.

- The number of books in the home can be an indicator of a home environment that values and provides general academic support. In most TIMSS countries, the more books students reported in the home, the higher their science achievement.

- In every country, the pattern was for the eighth-grade students whose parents had more education to also have higher achievement in science.

- Beyond the one to two hours of daily television viewing reported by close to the majority of eighth graders in all participating countries, the amount of television students watched was negatively associated with science achievement.

- In most countries, eighth-graders reported spending as much out-of-school time each day in non-academic activities as they did in academic activities. Besides watching television, students reported spending several hours, on average, each day playing or talking with friends, and nearly two hours playing sports. (It should be noted, however, the time spent in these activities is not additive because students can talk with their friends at sporting events or while watching TV, for example.)

Instructional Contexts and Practices

In comparison to the positive relationships observed between science achievement and home factors, the relationships were less clear between achievement and various instructional variables, both within and across countries. Obviously, educational practices such as tracking and streaming can serve to systematically confound these relationships. Also, the interaction among instructional variables can be extremely complex and merits further study.

- The qualifications required for teaching certification were relatively uniform across countries. Most countries reported that four years of post-secondary education were required, even though there was a range from two to six years. Almost all countries reported that teaching practice was a requirement, as was an examination or evaluation.

- Teachers in most countries that teach integrated science reported that science classes typically meet for at least two hours a week, but less than three and one-half hours. At the extremes, less than two hours of in-class instruction was most common in Switzerland whereas three and one-half to five hours was most common in Singapore. The data, however, revealed no clear pattern across countries between the number of in-class instructional hours and science achievement.

- There was considerable variation in class-size across the TIMSS countries. In a number of countries, nearly all students (90% or more) were in classes of fewer than 30 students. At the other end of the spectrum, 89% of the students in Korea were in classes with more than 40 students. The TIMSS data showed different patterns of science achievement in relation to class size for different countries.

- Across countries, science teachers reported that working together as a class with the teacher teaching the whole class, and having students work individually with assistance from the teacher were the most frequently used instructional approaches. Working without teacher assistance was less common in most countries.

- In most participating countries, teachers reported using a textbook in teaching science for 95% or more of the students. Reasoning tasks were reported to be very common activities in science classes, with the majority of students in all countries being asked to do some type of science reasoning task in most or every science lesson. Using things from everyday life in solving science problems appears more common in countries where science is taught as an integrated subject than in countries where science is taught as separate subject areas.

- Demonstrations of experiments by the teacher were common in almost all countries where science is taught as an integrated subject, and were also common in chemistry and physics classes. In most countries with integrated science where students reported high frequencies of teacher demonstrations, there was also a high percentage of students that reported doing experiments or practical investigations in class. In countries where science is taught as separate subjects, according to students teachers performed demonstrations more frequently than students themselves did practical, hands-on work, particularly in physics and chemistry.

- Internationally, science teachers reported that most eighth-grade students were assigned science homework at least once a week, although most typically, the majority of students were assigned up to 30 minutes of homework once or twice a week. Student reports of the amount of time spent on science homework suggest higher levels of assigned homework.

- In some countries, students reported a lot of student assessment in their science classes, while in other countries there was apparently less reliance on quizzes or tests in science lessons. Of the countries where science is taught as an integrated subject more than half the students in Austria, Canada, Colombia, Cyprus, England, Hong Kong, Iran, Kuwait, Singapore, Spain, Thailand, and the United States reported having a quiz or test pretty often or almost always in their science lessons.

Introduction

SCIENCE

As the 21st century approaches, technology is having more and more impact on the daily lives of individuals throughout the world. It influences our receipt of news and information, how we spend our leisure time, and where we work. At an ever-increasing pace, technology also is becoming a major factor in determining the economic health of countries. To ensure their economic well-being, countries will need citizens prepared to participate in "brain-power" industries such as micro-electronics, computers, and telecommunications. The young adolescents of today will be seeking jobs in a global economy requiring levels of technical competence and flexible thinking that were required by only a few workers in the past. To make sensible decisions and participate effectively in a world transformed by the ability to exchange all types of information almost instantly, these students will need to be well educated in a number of core areas, especially mathematics and science.

The fact that skills in mathematics and science are so critical to economic progress in a technologically-based society has led countries to seek information about what their school-age populations know and can do in mathematics and science. There is interest in what concepts students understand, how well they can apply their knowledge to problem-solving situations, and whether they can communicate their understandings. Even more vital, countries are desirous of furthering their knowledge about what can be done to improve students' understanding of mathematical and scientific concepts, their ability to solve problems, and their attitudes toward learning.

The Third International Mathematics and Science Study (TIMSS) provided countries with a vehicle for investigating these issues while expanding their perspectives of what is possible beyond the confines of their national borders. It is the most ambitious and complex comparative education study in a series of such undertakings conducted during the past 37 years by the International Association for the Evaluation of Educational Achievement (IEA).[1] The main purpose of TIMSS was to focus on educational policies, practices, and outcomes in order to enhance mathematics and science learning within and across systems of education.

With its wealth of information covering more than half a million students at five grade levels in 15,000 schools and more than 40 countries around the world, TIMSS offers an unprecedented opportunity to examine similarities and differences in how mathematics and science education works and how well it works. The study used innovative testing approaches and collected extensive information about the contexts within which students learn mathematics and science.

[1] The previous IEA mathematics studies were conducted in 1964 and 1980-82, and the science studies in 1970-71 and 1983-84. For information about TIMSS procedures, see Appendix A.

The present report focuses on the science achievement of students in the two grades with the largest proportion of 13-year-olds – the seventh and eighth grades in most countries. Special emphasis is placed on the eighth-grade results, including selected information about students' background and classroom practices in teaching science.

All countries that participated in TIMSS were to test students in the two grades with the largest proportion of 13-year-olds in both mathematics and science. A companion report, *Mathematics Achievement in the Middle School Years: IEA's Third International Mathematics and Science Study (TIMSS),* [2] presents corresponding results about students' mathematics achievement.

Many TIMSS countries also tested the mathematics and science achievement of students in the two grades with the largest proportion of 9-year-olds (third and fourth grades in most countries) and of students in their final year of secondary education. Subsets of students, except the final-year students, also had the opportunity to participate in a "hands-on" performance assessment where they designed experiments and tested hypotheses. The results of these components of TIMSS will be presented in forthcoming reports.

Together with the achievement tests, TIMSS administered a broad array of background questionnaires. The data collected from students, teachers, and school principals, as well as the system-level information collected from the participating countries, provide an abundance of information for further study and research. TIMSS data make it possible to examine differences in current levels of performance in relation to a wide variety of variables associated with classroom, school, and national contexts within which education takes place.

Which Countries Participated?

TIMSS was very much a collaborative process among countries. Table 1 shows the 45 participating countries. Each participant designated a national center to conduct the activities of the study and a National Research Coordinator (NRC) to assume responsibility for the successful completion of these tasks.[3] For the sake of comparability, all testing was conducted at the end of the school year. The four countries on a Southern Hemisphere school schedule (Australia, Korea, New Zealand, and Singapore) tested in September through November of 1994, which was the end of the school year in the Southern Hemisphere. The remaining countries tested the mathematics and science achievement of their students at the end of the 1994-95 school year, most often in May and June of 1995. Because Argentina, Italy, and Indonesia were unable to complete the steps necessary to appear in this report, the tables throughout the

[2] Beaton, A.E., Mullis, I.V.S., Martin, M.O., Gonzalez, E.J., Kelly, D.L., Smith, T.A. (1996). *Mathematics Achievement in the Middle School Years: IEA's Third International Mathematics and Science Study (TIMSS).* Chestnut Hill, MA: Boston College.

[3] Appendix F lists the National Research Coordinators as well as the members of the TIMSS advisory committees.

Table 1

Countries Participating in TIMSS[1]

- Argentina
- Australia
- Austria
- Belgium *
- Bulgaria
- Canada
- Colombia
- Cyprus
- Czech Republic
- Denmark
- England
- France
- Germany
- Greece
- Hong Kong
- Hungary
- Iceland
- Indonesia
- Iran, Islamic Republic
- Ireland
- Israel
- Italy
- Japan
- Korea, Republic of
- Kuwait
- Latvia
- Lithuania
- Mexico
- Netherlands
- New Zealand
- Norway
- Philippines
- Portugal
- Romania
- Russian Federation
- Scotland
- Singapore
- Slovak Republic
- Slovenia
- South Africa
- Spain
- Sweden
- Switzerland
- Thailand
- United States

* The Flemish and French educational systems in Belgium participated separately.

1 Argentina, Italy, and Indonesia were unable to complete the steps necessary for their data to appear in this report. Because the characteristics of its school sample are not completely known, achievement results for the Philippines are presented in Appendix C. Mexico participated in the testing portion of TIMSS, but chose not to release its results at grades 7 and 8 in the international report.

report do not include data for these three countries. Results also are not presented for Mexico, which chose not to release its seventh- and eighth-grade results in the international reports.

Table 2 shows information about the lower and upper grades tested in each country, including the country names for those two grades and the years of formal schooling students in those grades had completed when they were tested for TIMSS. Table 2 reveals that for most, but not all, countries, the two grades tested represented the seventh and eighth years of formal schooling. Thus, solely for convenience, the report often refers to the upper grade tested as the eighth grade and the lower grade tested as the seventh grade. As a point of interest, a system-split (where the lower grade was in upper primary and the upper grade was in lower secondary) occurred in six countries: New Zealand, Norway, the Philippines, South Africa, Sweden, and Switzerland. Two countries, Israel and Kuwait, tested only at the upper grade.

Having valid and efficient samples in each country is crucial to the quality and success of any international comparative study. The accuracy of the survey results depends on the quality of the sampling information available, and particularly on the quality of the samples. TIMSS developed procedures and guidelines to ensure that the national samples were of the highest quality possible. Standards for coverage of the target population, participation rates, and the age of students were established, as were clearly documented procedures on how to obtain the national samples. For the most part, the national samples were drawn in accordance with the TIMSS standards, and achievement results can be compared with confidence. However, despite efforts to meet the TIMSS specifications, some countries did not do so. These countries are specially annotated and/or shown in separate sections of the tables in this report.[4]

[4] The TIMSS sampling requirements and the outcomes of the sampling procedures are described in Appendix A.

Table 2
Information About the Grades Tested

Country	Lower Grade: Country's Name for Lower Grade	Lower Grade: Years of Formal Schooling Including Lower Grade[1]	Upper Grade: Country's Name for Upper Grade	Upper Grade: Years of Formal Schooling Including Upper Grade[1]
[2] Australia	7 or 8	7 or 8	8 or 9	8 or 9
Austria	3. Klasse	7	4. Klasse	8
Belgium (Fl)	1A	7	2A & 2P	8
Belgium (Fr)	1A	7	2A & 2P	8
Bulgaria	7	7	8	8
Canada	7	7	8	8
Colombia	7	7	8	8
Cyprus	7	7	8	8
Czech Republic	7	7	8	8
Denmark	6	6	7	7
England	Year 8	8	Year 9	9
France	5ème	7	4ème (90%) or 4ème Technologique (10%)	8
Germany	7	7	8	8
Greece	Secondary 1	7	Secondary 2	8
Hong Kong	Secondary 1	7	Secondary 2	8
Hungary	7	7	8	8
Iceland	7	7	8	8
Iran, Islamic Rep.	7	7	8	8
Ireland	1st Year	7	2nd Year	8
Israel	–	–	8	8
Japan	1st Grade Lower Secondary	7	2nd Grade Lower Secondary	8
Korea, Republic of	1st Grade Middle School	7	2nd Grade Middle School	8
Kuwait	–	–	9	9
Latvia	7	7	8	8
Lithuania	7	7	8	8
Netherlands	Secondary 1	7	Secondary 2	8
[3,4] New Zealand	Form 2	7.5 - 8.5	Form 3	8.5 - 9.5
[3] Norway	6	6	7	7
[3] Philippines	Grade 6 Elementary	6	1st Year High School	7
Portugal	Grade 7	7	Grade 8	8
Romania	7	7	8	8
[5] Russian Federation	7	6 or 7	8	7 or 8
Scotland	Secondary 1	8	Secondary 2	9
Singapore	Secondary 1	7	Secondary 2	8
Slovak Republic	7	7	8	8
Slovenia	7	7	8	8
Spain	7 EGB	7	8 EGB	8
[3] South Africa	Standard 5	7	Standard 6	8
[3] Sweden	6	6	7	7
[3] Switzerland				
(German)	6	6	7	7
(French and Italian)	7	7	8	8
Thailand	Secondary 1	7	Secondary 2	8
United States	7	7	8	8

[1]Years of schooling based on the number of years children in the grade level have been in formal schooling, beginning with primary education (International Standard Classification of Education Level 1). Does not include preprimary education.

[2]Australia: Each state/territory has its own policy regarding age of entry to primary school. In 4 of the 8 states/territories students were sampled from grades 7 and 8; in the other four states/territories students were sampled from grades 8 and 9.

[3]Indicates that there is a system-split between the lower and upper grades. In Switzerland there is a system-split in 14 of 26 cantons.

[4]New Zealand: The majority of students begin primary school on or near their 5th birthday so the "years of formal schooling" vary.

[5]Russian Federation: 70% of students in the seventh grade have had 6 years of formal schooling; 70% in the eighth grade have had 7 years of formal schooling.

SOURCE: IEA Third International Mathematics and Science Study (TIMSS), 1994-95. Information provided by TIMSS National Research Coordinators.

What Was the Nature of the Science Test?

Together with the quality of the samples, the quality of the test also receives considerable scrutiny in any comparative study. All participants wish to ensure that the achievement items are appropriate for their students and reflect their current curriculum. Developing the TIMSS tests was a cooperative venture involving all of the NRCs during the entire process. Through a series of efforts, countries submitted items that were reviewed by science subject-matter specialists, and additional items were written to ensure that the desired science topics were covered adequately. Items were piloted, the results reviewed, and new items were written and piloted. The resulting TIMSS science test contained 135 items representing a range of science topics and skills.

The TIMSS curriculum frameworks described the content dimensions for the TIMSS tests as well as performance expectations (behaviors that might be expected of students in school science).[5] Five content areas are covered in the science test taken by seventh- and eighth-grade students. These areas and the percentage of the test items devoted to each include: earth science (16%), life science (30%), physics (30%), chemistry (14%), and environmental issues and the nature of science (10%). The performance expectations include: understanding simple information (40%); understanding complex information (29%); theorizing, analyzing, and solving problems (21%); using tools, routine procedures, and science processes (6%); and investigating the natural world (4%).

About one-fourth of the questions were in the free-response format, requiring students to generate and write their answers. These questions, some of which required extended responses, were allotted approximately one-third of the testing time. Responses to the free-response questions were evaluated to capture diagnostic information, and some were scored using procedures that permitted partial credit.[6] Chapter 3 of this report contains 25 example items illustrating the range of science concepts and processes addressed by the TIMSS test.

The TIMSS tests were prepared in English and translated into 30 additional languages using explicit guidelines and procedures. A series of verification checks were conducted to ensure the comparability of the translations.[7]

The tests were given so that no one student took all of the items, which would have required more than three hours. Instead, the test was assembled in eight booklets, each requiring 90 minutes to complete. Each student took only one booklet, and the items were rotated through the booklets so that each one was answered by a representative sample of students.

[5] Robitaille, D.F., McKnight, C.C., Schmidt, W.H., Britton, E.D., Raizen, S.A., and Nicol, C. (1993). *TIMSS Monograph No. 1: Curriculum Frameworks for Mathematics and Science*. Vancouver, B.C.: Pacific Educational Press.

[6] TIMSS scoring reliability studies within and across countries indicate that the percent of exact agreement for correctness scores averaged over 85%. For more details, see Appendix A.

[7] See Appendix A for more information about the translation procedures.

TIMSS conducted a Test-Curriculum Matching Analysis whereby countries examined the TIMSS test to identify items measuring topics not addressed in their curricula. The analysis showed that omitting such items for each country had little effect on the overall pattern of achievement results across all countries.[8]

How Do Country Characteristics Differ?

International studies of student achievement provide valuable comparative information about student performance and instructional practices. Along with the benefits of international studies, though, are challenges associated with comparing achievement across countries, cultures, and languages. In TIMSS, extensive efforts were made to attend to these issues through careful planning and documentation, cooperation among the participating countries, standardized procedures, and rigorous attention to quality control throughout.[9]

Beyond the integrity of the study procedures, the results of comparative studies such as TIMSS also need to be considered in light of the larger contexts in which students are educated and the kinds of system-wide factors that might influence students' opportunity to learn. A number of these factors are more fully described in *National Contexts for Mathematics and Science Education: An Encyclopedia of the Education Systems Participating in TIMSS*;[10] however, some selected demographic characteristics of the TIMSS countries are presented in Table 3. Table 4 contains information about public expenditure on education. The information in these two tables show that some of the TIMSS countries are densely populated and others are more rural, some are large and some small, and some expend considerably more resources on education than others. Although these factors do not necessarily determine high or low performance in science, they do provide a context for considering the difficulty of the educational task from country to country.

Describing students' educational opportunities also includes understanding the knowledge and skills that students are supposed to master. To help complete the picture of educational practices in the TIMSS countries, science and curriculum specialists within each country provided detailed categorizations of their curriculum guides, textbooks, and curricular materials. The initial results from this effort can be found

---

[8] Results of the Test-Curriculum Matching Analysis are presented in Appendix B.

[9] Appendix A contains an overview of the procedures used and cites a number of references providing details about TIMSS methodology.

[10] Robitaille D.F. (in press). *National Contexts for Mathematics and Science Education: An Encyclopedia of the Education Systems Participating in TIMSS.* Vancouver, B.C.: Pacific Educational Press.

Table 3

Selected Demographic Characteristics of TIMSS Countries

Country	Population Size (1,000) [1]	Area of Country (1000 Square Kilometers) [2]	Density (Population per Square Kilometer) [3]	Percentage of Population Living in Urban Areas	Life Expectancy [4]	Percent in Secondary School [5]
Australia	17843	7713	2.29	84.8	77	84
Austria	8028	84	95.28	55.5	77	107
Belgium	10116	31	330.40	96.9	76	103
Bulgaria	8435	111	76.39	70.1	71	68
Canada	29248	9976	2.90	76.7	78	88
Colombia	36330	1139	31.33	72.2	70	62
Cyprus	726	9	77.62	53.6	77	95
Czech Republic	10333	79	130.99	65.3	73	86
Denmark	5205	43	120.42	85.1	75	114
[6] England	48533	130	373.33	–	77	–
France	57928	552	104.56	72.8	78	106
Germany	81516	357	227.39	86.3	76	101
Greece	10426	132	78.63	64.7	78	99
[7] Hong Kong	6061	1	5691.35	94.8	78	98
Hungary	10261	93	110.03	64.2	70	81
Iceland	266	103	2.56	91.4	79	103
Iran	62550	1648	36.98	58.5	68	66
Ireland	3571	70	50.70	57.4	76	105
Israel	5383	21	252.14	90.5	77	87
Japan	124961	378	329.63	77.5	79	96
Korea, Republic of	44453	99	444.92	79.8	71	93
Kuwait	1620	18	80.42	96.8	76	60
Latvia	2547	65	40.09	72.6	68	87
Lithuania	3721	65	57.21	71.4	69	78
Netherlands	15381	37	409.30	88.9	78	93
New Zealand	3493	271	12.78	85.8	76	104
Norway	4337	324	13.31	73.0	78	116
Philippines	67038	300	218.83	53.1	65	79
Portugal	9902	92	106.95	35.2	75	81
Romania	22731	238	95.81	55.0	70	82
Russian Federation	148350	17075	8.70	73.2	64	88
[8] Scotland	5132	79	65.15	–	75	–
Singapore	2930	1	4635.48	100.0	75	84
Slovak Republic	5347	49	108.61	58.3	72	89
Slovenia	1989	20	97.14	62.7	74	85
South Africa	40539	1221	32.46	50.5	64	77
Spain	39143	505	77.43	76.3	77	113
Sweden	8781	450	19.38	83.1	78	99
Switzerland	6994	41	168.03	60.6	78	91
Thailand	58024	513	111.76	31.9	69	37
United States	260650	9809	27.56	76.0	77	97

[1]Estimates for 1994 based, in most cases, on a de facto definition. Refugees not permanently settled in the country of asylum are generally considered to be part of their country of origin.

[2]Area is the total surface area in square kilometers, comprising all land area and inland waters.

[3]Density is population per square kilometer of total surface area.

[4]Number of years a newborn infant would live if prevailing patterns of mortality at its birth were to stay the same throughout its life.

[5]Gross enrollment of all ages at the secondary level as a percentage of school-age children as defined by each country. This may be reported in excess of 100% if some pupils are younger or older than the country's standard range of secondary school age.

[6] Annual Abstract of Statistics 1995, and Office of National Statistics. All data are for 1993.

[7]Number for Secondary Enrollment is from Education Department (1985) Education Indicators for the Hong Kong Education System (unpublished document).

[8] Registrar General for Scotland Annual Report 1995 and Scottish Abstract of Statistics 1993.

(–) A dash indicates the data were unavailable.

SOURCE: The World Bank, Social Indicators of Development, 1996.

Table 4

Public Expenditure on Education at Primary and Secondary Levels[1] in TIMSS Countries

Country	Gross National Product per Capita (US Dollars)[2]	Gross National Product per Capita (Intl. Dollars)[3]	Public Expenditure on Education (Levels 1 & 2) as % of Gross National Product[4]	Public Expenditure on Education (Intl. Dollars per Capita)[5]
Australia	17980	19000	3.69	701
Austria	24950	20230	4.24	858
Belgium	22920	20450	3.70	757
Bulgaria	1160	4230	3.06	129
Canada	19570	21230	4.62	981
Colombia	1620	5970	2.83	169
[6] Cyprus	10380	–	3.60	–
Czech Republic	3210	7910	3.75	297
Denmark	28110	20800	4.80	998
[7] England	18410	18170	3.57	649
France	23470	19820	3.61	716
Germany	25580	19890	2.43	483
Greece	7710	11400	2.27	259
[8] Hong Kong	21650	23080	1.34	309
Hungary	3840	6310	4.31	272
Iceland	24590	18900	4.77	902
Iran	–	4650	3.93	183
Ireland	13630	14550	4.21	613
Israel	14410	15690	3.72	584
Japan	34360	21350	2.82	602
Korea, Republic of	8220	10540	3.43	362
Kuwait	19040	24500	3.46	848
Latvia	2290	5170	2.85	147
Lithuania	1350	3240	2.18	71
Netherlands	21970	18080	3.30	597
New Zealand	13190	16780	3.15	529
Norway	26480	21120	5.26	1111
Philippines	960	2800	1.78	50
Portugal	9370	12400	2.98	370
Romania	1230	2920	1.89	55
Russian Federation	2650	5260	–	–
[7] Scotland	18410	18170	3.57	649
Singapore	23360	21430	3.38	724
Slovak Republic	2230	6660	2.69	179
Slovenia	7140	–	4.20	–
South Africa	3010	–	5.12	–
Spain	13280	14040	3.17	445
Sweden	23630	17850	4.92	878
Switzerland	37180	24390	3.72	907
Thailand	2210	6870	3.00	206
United States	25860	25860	4.02	1040

[1] The levels of education are based on the International Standard Classification of Education. The duration of Primary (level 1) and Secondary (level 2) vary depending on the country.

[2] SOURCE: The World Bank Atlas, 1996. Estimates for 1994 at current market prices in U.S. dollars, calculated by the conversion method used for the World Bank Atlas.

[3] SOURCE: The World Bank Atlas, 1996. Converted at purchasing power parity (PPP). PPP is defined as number of units of a country's currency required to buy same amounts of goods and services in domestic market as one dollar would buy in the United States.

[4] SOURCE: UNESCO Statistical Yearbook, 1995. Calculated by multiplying the Public Expenditure on Education as a % of GNP by the percentage of public education expenditure on the first and second levels of education. Figures represent the most recent figures released.

[5] Calculated by multiplying the GNP per Capita (Intl. Dollars) column by Public Expenditure on Education.

[6] GNP per capita figure for Cyprus is for 1993.

[7] The figures for England and Scotland are for the United Kingdom.

[8] Calculated using Education Department (1985) Education Indicators for the Hong Kong Education System (unpublished document).

(–) A dash indicates the data were unavailable.

in two reports, entitled *Many Visions, Many Aims: A Cross-National Investigation of Curricular Intentions in School Mathematics* and *Many Visions, Many Aims: A Cross-National Investigation of Curricular Intentions in School Science.*[11]

Depending on the educational system, students' learning goals are commonly set at one of three main levels: the national or regional level, the school level, or the classroom level. Some countries are highly centralized, with the ministry of education (or highest authority in the system) having exclusive responsibility for making the major decisions governing the direction of education. In others, such decisions are made regionally or locally. Each approach has its strengths and weaknesses. Centralized decision-making can add coherence in curriculum coverage, but may constrain a school or teacher's flexibility in tailoring instruction to the different needs of students.

Figures 1, 2, and 3 show the degree of centralization in the TIMSS countries regarding decision-making about curriculum syllabi, textbooks, and examinations. Thirty of the TIMSS participants reported nationally-centralized decision-making about curriculum. Fewer countries reported nationally-centralized decision-making about textbooks, although 16 participants were in this category. Thirteen countries reported nationally-centralized decision-making about examinations. Regional decision-making about these three aspects of education does not appear very common among the TIMSS countries, with only a few countries reporting this level of decision-making for curriculum syllabi and textbooks, and none reporting it for examinations.

Most countries reported having centralized decision-making for one or two of the areas and "not centralized" decision-making for one or two of the areas. However, six countries – Bulgaria, Hong Kong, Lithuania, the Philippines, Romania, and Singapore – reported nationally-centralized decision-making for all three areas: curriculum syllabi, textbooks, and examinations. Six countries – Australia, Hungary, Iceland, Latvia, Scotland, and the United States – reported that decision-making is not centralized for any of these areas.

[11] Schmidt, W.H., McKnight, C.C., Valverde, G. A., Houang, R.T., and Wiley, D. E. (in press). *Many Visions, Many Aims: A Cross-National Investigation of Curricular Intentions in School Mathematics.* Dordrecht, the Netherlands: Kluwer Academic Publishers. Schmidt, Raizen, S.A., Britton, E.D., Bianchi, L.J., and Wolfe, R.G., (in press). *Many Visions, Many Aims: A Cross-National Investigation of Curricular Intentions in School Science.* Dordrecht, the Netherlands: Kluwer Academic Publishers.

Figure 1

Centralization of Decision-Making Regarding Curriculum Syllabi

Criteria

Countries are in the "Nationally Centralized" category regarding curriculum if the highest level of decision-making authority within the educational system (e.g., the ministry of education) has exclusive responsibility for or gives final approval of the syllabi for courses of study. If curriculum syllabi are determined at the regional level (e.g., state, province, territory), a country is in the "Regionally Centralized" Category. If syllabi for courses of study are not determined nationally or regionally, a country is in the "Not Centralized" category.

Nationally Centralized

Austria
Belgium (Fl)[1]
Belgium (Fr)[1]
Bulgaria
Colombia
Cyprus
Czech Republic
England
France
Greece
Hong Kong
Iran, Islamic Rep.
Ireland
Israel
Japan
Korea
Kuwait
Lithuania
New Zealand
Norway[2]
Philippines
Portugal
Romania
Singapore
Slovak Republic
Slovenia
South Africa
Spain[3]
Sweden[4]
Thailand

Regionally Centralized

Canada
Germany
Switzerland[5]

Not Centralized

Australia[6]
Denmark[7]
Hungary[8]
Iceland
Latvia
Netherlands[9]
Russian Federation
Scotland
United States

[1]Belgium: In Belgium, decision-making is centralized separately for the two educational systems.

[2]Norway: The National Agency of Education provides goals which schools are required to work towards. Schools have the freedom to implement the goals based on local concerns.

[3]Spain: Spain is now reforming to a regionally centralized system with high responsibility at the school level.

[4]Sweden: The National Agency of Education provides goals which schools are required to work towards. Schools have the freedom to implement the goals based on local concerns.

[5]Switzerland: Decision-making regarding curricula in upper secondary varies across cantons and types of education.

[6]Australia: Students tested in TIMSS were educated under a decentralized system. Reforms beginning in 1994 are introducing regionally centralized (state-determined) curriculum guidelines.

[7]Denmark: The Danish Parliament makes decisions governing the overall aim of education, and the Minister of Education sets the target, the central knowledge, and proficiency for each subject and the grades for teaching the subject. The local school administration can implement the subjects from guidelines from the Ministry; however, these are recommendations and are not mandatory.

[8]Hungary: Hungary is in the midst of changing from a highly centralized system to one in which local authorities and schools have more autonomy.

[9]Netherlands: The Ministry of Education sets core objectives (for subjects in primary education and in 'basic education' at lower secondary level) and goals/objectives (for subjects in the four student ability tracks in secondary education) which schools are required to work towards. Schools have the freedom, though, to decide how to reach these objectives.

SOURCE: IEA Third International Mathematics and Science Study (TIMSS), 1994-95. Information provided by TIMSS National Research Coordinators.

Figure 2

Centralization of Decision-Making Regarding Textbooks

Criteria

Countries are in the "Nationally Centralized" category regarding textbooks if the highest level of decision-making authority within the educational system (e.g., the ministry of education) has exclusive responsibility for determining the approved textbooks. If textbooks are selected from a regionally approved list (e.g., state, province, territory), a country is in the "Regionally Centralized" Category. If that decision-making body has less than exclusive repsonsibility for determining the approved textbooks, a country is in the "Not Centralized" category.

Nationally Centralized	Regionally Centralized	Not Centralized
Austria	Canada	Australia
Bulgaria	Germany	Belgium (Fl)
Cyprus	Japan	Belgium (Fr)
Greece	South Africa	Colombia
Hong Kong	Switzerland[2]	Czech Republic
Iran, Islamic Rep.		Denmark
Korea		England
Kuwait		France
Lithuania		Hungary[3]
Norway		Iceland
Philippines		Ireland
Romania		Israel
Singapore		Latvia
Slovenia		Netherlands
Spain[1]		New Zealand
Thailand		Portugal
		Russian Federation
		Scotland
		Slovak Republic
		Sweden
		United States

[1]Spain: Spain is now reforming to a regionally centralized system with high responsibility at the school level.
[2]Switzerland: Decision-making regarding textbooks in upper secondary varies across the cantons and the types of education.
[3]Hungary: Hungary is in the midst of changing from a highly centralized system to one in which local authorities and schools have more autonomy.

SOURCE: IEA Third International Mathematics and Science Study (TIMSS), 1994-95. Information provided by TIMSS National Research Coordinators.

Figure 3

Centralization of Decision-Making Regarding Examinations

Criteria

Countries are in the "Nationally Centralized" category regarding examinations if the highest level of decision-making authority within the educational system (e.g., the ministry of education) has exclusive responsibility for or gives final approval of the content of examinations. The notes explain during which school years the examinations are administered. If that decision-making body has less than exclusive responsibility for or final approval of the examination content, the country is in the "Not Centralized" category.

Nationally Centralized

Bulgaria
Denmark[1]
England[2]
Hong Kong[3]
Ireland[4]
Lithuania
Netherlands[5]
New Zealand[6]
Philippines[7]
Romania
Russian Federation[8]
Singapore[9]
South Africa

Not Centralized

Australia[10]
Austria
Belgium (Fl)
Belgium (Fr)
Canada
Colombia
Cyprus
Czech Republic
France
Germany[11]
Greece
Hungary
Iceland
Iran, Islamic Rep.
Israel[12]
Japan
Korea
Kuwait
Latvia[13]
Norway
Portugal
Scotland
Singapore
Slovak Republic
Slovenia[14]
Spain
Sweden[15]
Switzerland
Thailand
United States

[1]Denmark: Written examinations are set and marked centrally. The Ministry of Education sets the rules and framework for oral examinations. However, oral examinations are conducted by the pupil's own teacher, together with a teacher from another local school or an external (ministry-appointed) examiner.

[2]England: Centralized national curriculum assessments taken at Years 2, 6 and 9. Regionally centralized examinations taken at Years 11 and 13.

[3]Hong Kong: Centralized examination taken at Year 11.

[4]Ireland: Centralized examinations taken at Grade 9 and Grade 12.

[5]Netherlands: School-leaving examinations consisting of a centralized part and a school-bound part are taken in the final grades of the four student ability tracks in secondary education.

[6]New Zealand: Centralized examinations taken at Years 11, 12 and 13. Centralized national monitoring at Years 4 and 8.

[7]Philippines: Centralized examinations taken at Grade 6 and Year 10 (4th year high school).

[8]Russian Federation: Centralized examinations taken in Grades 9 and 11 in mathematics and Russian/literature.

[9]Singapore: Centralized examinations taken at Grades 6,10, and 12.

[10]Australia: Not centralized as a country, but low-stakes statewide population assessments are undertaken in most states at one or more of Grades 3, 5, 6 and 10. In most states, centralized examinations are taken at Grade 12.

[11]Germany: Not centralized as a country, but is centralized within 6 (of 16) federal states.

[12]Israel: Centralized examinations taken at the end of secondary school that affect opportunities for further education.

[13]Latvia: Centralized examinations taken at Grade 9 and Grade 12.

[14]Slovenia: Two-subject national examination taken after Grade 8 (end of compulsory education); five-subject externally-assessed baccalaureat after Grade 12 for everyone entering university.

[15]Sweden: There are no examinations in Sweden.

SOURCE: IEA Third International Mathematics and Science Study (TIMSS), 1994-95. Information provided by TIMSS National Research Coordinators.

Chapter 1

International Student Achievement in Science

What Are the Overall Differences in Science Achievement?

Chapter 1 summarizes achievement on the TIMSS science test for each of the participating countries. Comparisons are provided overall and by gender for the upper grade tested (often the eighth grade) and the lower grade tested (often the seventh grade), as well as for 13-year-olds.

Table 1.1 presents the mean (or average) achievement for 41 countries at the eighth grade.[1] The 25 countries shown by decreasing order of mean achievement in the upper part of the table were judged to have met the TIMSS requirements for testing a representative sample of students. Although all countries tried very hard to meet the TIMSS sampling requirements, several encountered resistance from schools and teachers and did not have participation rates of 85% or higher as specified in the TIMSS guidelines (i.e., Australia, Austria, Belgium (French), Bulgaria, the Netherlands, and Scotland). To provide a better curricular match, four countries (i.e., Colombia, Germany, Romania, and Slovenia) elected to test their seventh- and eighth-grade students even though that meant not testing the two grades with the most 13-year-olds and led to their students being somewhat older than those in the other countries. The countries in the remaining two categories encountered various degrees of difficulty in implementing the prescribed methods for sampling classrooms within schools. Because the Philippines did not document clearly its procedures for sampling schools, its achievement results are presented in Appendix C. A full discussion of the sampling procedures and outcomes for each country can be found in Appendix A.

To aid in interpretation, the table also contains the years of formal schooling and average age of the students. Equivalence of chronological age does not necessarily mean that students have received the same number of years of formal schooling or studied the same curriculum. Most notably, students in the three Scandinavian countries, Sweden, Norway, and Denmark, had fewer years of formal schooling than their counterparts in other countries,[2] and those in England, Scotland, New Zealand, and Kuwait had more. Countries with a high percentage of older students may have policies that include retaining students in lower grades.

The results reveal substantial differences in science achievement between the top- and bottom-performing countries, although the average achievement of most countries was somewhere in the middle ranges. The broad range of achievement both across

[1] TIMSS used item response theory (IRT) methods to summarize the achievement results for both grades on a scale with a mean of 500 and a standard deviation of 100. Scaling averages students' responses to the subsets of items they took in a way that accounts for differences in the difficulty of those items. It allows students' performance to be summarized on a common metric even though individual students responded to different items in the science test. For more detailed information, see the "IRT Scaling and Data Analysis" section of Appendix A.

[2] Achievement results for the eighth-grade students in Denmark and Sweden, as well as for the eighth-grade students in German-speaking schools in Switzerland are presented in Appendix D.

Table 1.1

Distributions of Achievement in the Sciences - Upper Grade (Eighth Grade*)

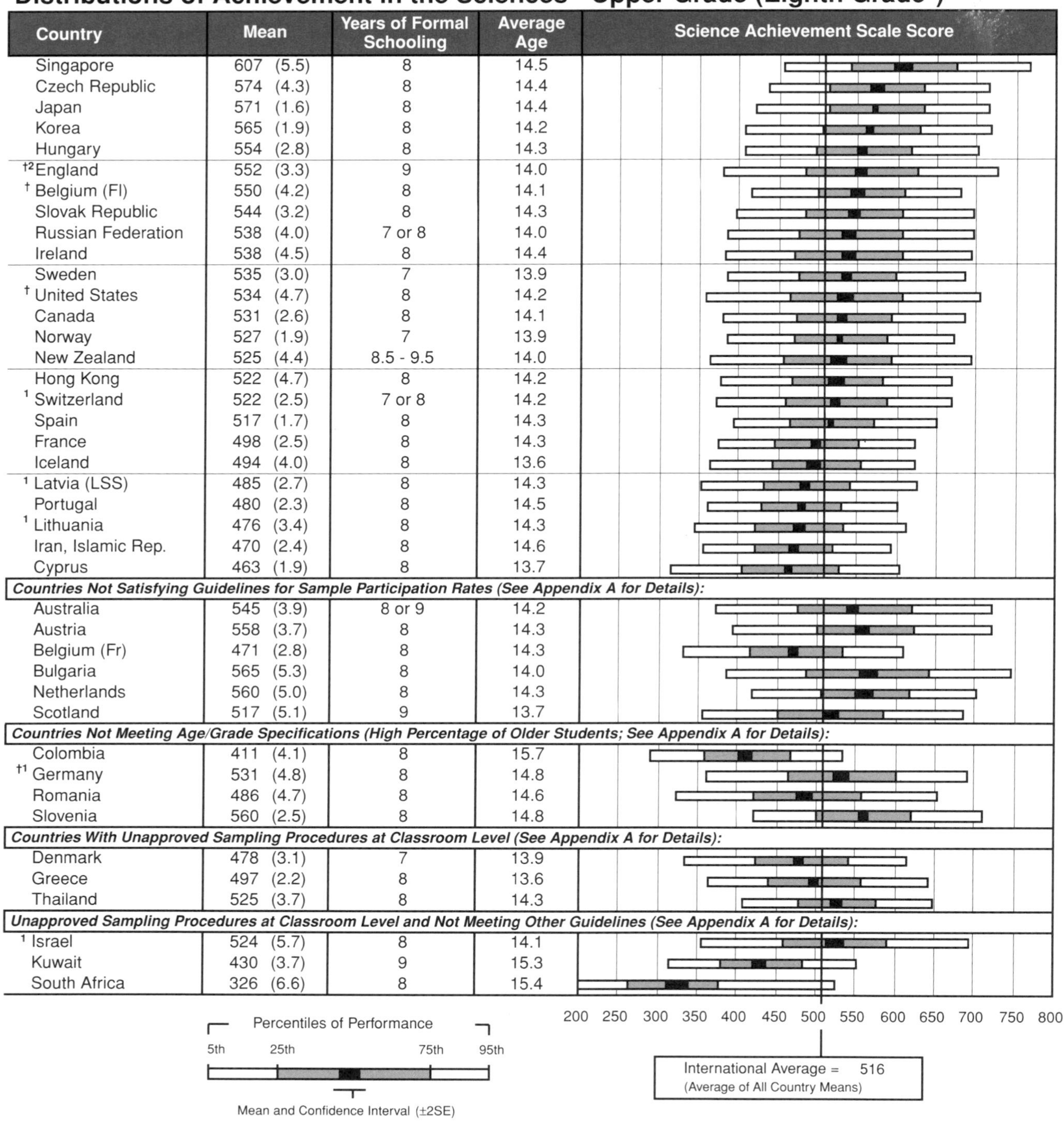

Country	Mean	Years of Formal Schooling	Average Age
Singapore	607 (5.5)	8	14.5
Czech Republic	574 (4.3)	8	14.4
Japan	571 (1.6)	8	14.4
Korea	565 (1.9)	8	14.2
Hungary	554 (2.8)	8	14.3
†2 England	552 (3.3)	9	14.0
† Belgium (Fl)	550 (4.2)	8	14.1
Slovak Republic	544 (3.2)	8	14.3
Russian Federation	538 (4.0)	7 or 8	14.0
Ireland	538 (4.5)	8	14.4
Sweden	535 (3.0)	7	13.9
† United States	534 (4.7)	8	14.2
Canada	531 (2.6)	8	14.1
Norway	527 (1.9)	7	13.9
New Zealand	525 (4.4)	8.5 - 9.5	14.0
Hong Kong	522 (4.7)	8	14.2
1 Switzerland	522 (2.5)	7 or 8	14.2
Spain	517 (1.7)	8	14.3
France	498 (2.5)	8	14.3
Iceland	494 (4.0)	8	13.6
1 Latvia (LSS)	485 (2.7)	8	14.3
Portugal	480 (2.3)	8	14.5
1 Lithuania	476 (3.4)	8	14.3
Iran, Islamic Rep.	470 (2.4)	8	14.6
Cyprus	463 (1.9)	8	13.7
Countries Not Satisfying Guidelines for Sample Participation Rates (See Appendix A for Details):			
Australia	545 (3.9)	8 or 9	14.2
Austria	558 (3.7)	8	14.3
Belgium (Fr)	471 (2.8)	8	14.3
Bulgaria	565 (5.3)	8	14.0
Netherlands	560 (5.0)	8	14.3
Scotland	517 (5.1)	9	13.7
Countries Not Meeting Age/Grade Specifications (High Percentage of Older Students; See Appendix A for Details):			
Colombia	411 (4.1)	8	15.7
†1 Germany	531 (4.8)	8	14.8
Romania	486 (4.7)	8	14.6
Slovenia	560 (2.5)	8	14.8
Countries With Unapproved Sampling Procedures at Classroom Level (See Appendix A for Details):			
Denmark	478 (3.1)	7	13.9
Greece	497 (2.2)	8	13.6
Thailand	525 (3.7)	8	14.3
Unapproved Sampling Procedures at Classroom Level and Not Meeting Other Guidelines (See Appendix A for Details):			
1 Israel	524 (5.7)	8	14.1
Kuwait	430 (3.7)	9	15.3
South Africa	326 (6.6)	8	15.4

*Eighth grade in most countries; see Table 2 for information about the grades tested in each country.
†Met guidelines for sample participation rates only after replacement schools were included (see Appendix A for details).
1 National Desired Population does not cover all of International Desired Population (see Table A.2). Because coverage falls below 65%, Latvia is annotated LSS for Latvian Speaking Schools only.
2 National Defined Population covers less than 90 percent of National Desired Population (see Table A.2).
( ) Standard errors appear in parentheses. Because results are rounded to the nearest whole number, some totals may appear inconsistent.

SOURCE: IEA Third International Mathematics and Science Study (TIMSS), 1994-95.

Figure 1.1

Multiple Comparisons of Achievement in the Sciences - Upper Grade (Eighth Grade*)

Instructions: Read ***across*** the row for a country to compare performance with the countries listed in the heading of the chart. The symbols indicate whether the mean achievement of the country in the row is significantly lower than that of the comparison country, significantly higher than that of the comparison country, or if there is no statistically significant difference between the two countries.[†]

Country	Singapore	Czech Republic	Japan	Korea	*Bulgaria*	*Netherlands*	*Slovenia*	*Austria*	Hungary	England	Belgium (Fl)	*Australia*	Slovak Republic	Russian Fed.	Ireland	Sweden	United States	*Germany*	Canada	Norway	New Zealand	*Thailand*	*Israel*	Hong Kong	Switzerland	*Scotland*	Spain	France	*Greece*	Iceland	*Romania*	Latvia (LSS)	Portugal	*Denmark*	Lithuania	*Belgium (Fr)*	Iran, Islamic Rep.	Cyprus	*Kuwait*	*Colombia*	*South Africa*
Singapore		▲	▲	▲	▲	▲	▲	▲	▲	▲	▲	▲	▲	▲	▲	▲	▲	▲	▲	▲	▲	▲	▲	▲	▲	▲	▲	▲	▲	▲	▲	▲	▲	▲	▲	▲	▲	▲	▲	▲	▲
Czech Republic	▼		●	●	●	●	●	●	▲	▲	▲	▲	▲	▲	▲	▲	▲	▲	▲	▲	▲	▲	▲	▲	▲	▲	▲	▲	▲	▲	▲	▲	▲	▲	▲	▲	▲	▲	▲	▲	▲
Japan	▼	●		●	●	●	▲	▲	▲	▲	▲	▲	▲	▲	▲	▲	▲	▲	▲	▲	▲	▲	▲	▲	▲	▲	▲	▲	▲	▲	▲	▲	▲	▲	▲	▲	▲	▲	▲	▲	▲
Korea	▼	●	●		●	●	●	●	▲	▲	●	▲	▲	▲	▲	▲	▲	▲	▲	▲	▲	▲	▲	▲	▲	▲	▲	▲	▲	▲	▲	▲	▲	▲	▲	▲	▲	▲	▲	▲	▲
Bulgaria	▼	●	●	●		●	●	●	●	●	●	●	▲	▲	▲	▲	▲	▲	▲	▲	▲	▲	▲	▲	▲	▲	▲	▲	▲	▲	▲	▲	▲	▲	▲	▲	▲	▲	▲	▲	▲
Netherlands	▼	●	●	●	●		●	●	●	●	●	●	●	▲	▲	▲	▲	▲	▲	▲	▲	▲	▲	▲	▲	▲	▲	▲	▲	▲	▲	▲	▲	▲	▲	▲	▲	▲	▲	▲	▲
Slovenia	▼	●	▼	●	●	●		●	●	●	●	▲	▲	▲	▲	▲	▲	▲	▲	▲	▲	▲	▲	▲	▲	▲	▲	▲	▲	▲	▲	▲	▲	▲	▲	▲	▲	▲	▲	▲	▲
Austria	▼	●	▼	●	●	●	●		●	●	●	●	●	▲	▲	▲	▲	▲	▲	▲	▲	▲	▲	▲	▲	▲	▲	▲	▲	▲	▲	▲	▲	▲	▲	▲	▲	▲	▲	▲	▲
Hungary	▼	▼	▼	▼	●	●	●	●		●	●	●	●	●	●	▲	▲	▲	▲	▲	▲	▲	▲	▲	▲	▲	▲	▲	▲	▲	▲	▲	▲	▲	▲	▲	▲	▲	▲	▲	▲
England	▼	▼	▼	▼	●	●	●	●	●		●	●	●	●	●	▲	●	▲	▲	▲	▲	▲	▲	▲	▲	▲	▲	▲	▲	▲	▲	▲	▲	▲	▲	▲	▲	▲	▲	▲	▲
Belgium (Fl)	▼	▼	▼	●	●	●	●	●	●	●		●	●	●	●	●	●	●	▲	▲	▲	▲	▲	▲	▲	▲	▲	▲	▲	▲	▲	▲	▲	▲	▲	▲	▲	▲	▲	▲	▲
Australia	▼	▼	▼	▼	●	●	▼	●	●	●	●		●	●	●	●	●	●	●	▲	▲	▲	●	▲	▲	▲	▲	▲	▲	▲	▲	▲	▲	▲	▲	▲	▲	▲	▲	▲	▲
Slovak Republic	▼	▼	▼	▼	▼	●	▼	●	●	●	●	●		●	●	●	●	●	▲	▲	▲	▲	●	▲	▲	▲	▲	▲	▲	▲	▲	▲	▲	▲	▲	▲	▲	▲	▲	▲	▲
Russian Fed.	▼	▼	▼	▼	▼	▼	▼	▼	●	●	●	●	●		●	●	●	●	●	●	●	●	●	●	▲	▲	▲	▲	▲	▲	▲	▲	▲	▲	▲	▲	▲	▲	▲	▲	▲
Ireland	▼	▼	▼	▼	▼	▼	▼	▼	●	●	●	●	●	●		●	●	●	●	●	●	●	●	●	●	●	▲	▲	▲	▲	▲	▲	▲	▲	▲	▲	▲	▲	▲	▲	▲
Sweden	▼	▼	▼	▼	▼	▼	▼	▼	▼	▼	●	●	●	●	●		●	●	●	●	●	●	●	●	▲	●	▲	▲	▲	▲	▲	▲	▲	▲	▲	▲	▲	▲	▲	▲	▲
United States	▼	▼	▼	▼	▼	▼	▼	▼	▼	●	●	●	●	●	●	●		●	●	●	●	●	●	●	●	●	▲	▲	▲	▲	▲	▲	▲	▲	▲	▲	▲	▲	▲	▲	▲
Germany	▼	▼	▼	▼	▼	▼	▼	▼	▼	▼	●	●	●	●	●	●	●		●	●	●	●	●	●	●	●	●	▲	▲	▲	▲	▲	▲	▲	▲	▲	▲	▲	▲	▲	▲
Canada	▼	▼	▼	▼	▼	▼	▼	▼	▼	▼	▼	●	▼	●	●	●	●	●		●	●	●	●	●	●	●	▲	▲	▲	▲	▲	▲	▲	▲	▲	▲	▲	▲	▲	▲	▲
Norway	▼	▼	▼	▼	▼	▼	▼	▼	▼	▼	▼	▼	▼	●	●	●	●	●	●		●	●	●	●	●	●	▲	▲	▲	▲	▲	▲	▲	▲	▲	▲	▲	▲	▲	▲	▲
New Zealand	▼	▼	▼	▼	▼	▼	▼	▼	▼	▼	▼	▼	▼	●	●	●	●	●	●	●		●	●	●	●	●	●	▲	▲	▲	▲	▲	▲	▲	▲	▲	▲	▲	▲	▲	▲
Thailand	▼	▼	▼	▼	▼	▼	▼	▼	▼	▼	▼	▼	▼	●	●	●	●	●	●	●	●		●	●	●	●	●	▲	▲	▲	▲	▲	▲	▲	▲	▲	▲	▲	▲	▲	▲
Israel	▼	▼	▼	▼	▼	▼	▼	▼	▼	▼	▼	●	●	●	●	●	●	●	●	●	●	●		●	●	●	●	▲	▲	▲	▲	▲	▲	▲	▲	▲	▲	▲	▲	▲	▲
Hong Kong	▼	▼	▼	▼	▼	▼	▼	▼	▼	▼	▼	▼	▼	●	●	●	●	●	●	●	●	●	●		●	●	●	▲	▲	▲	▲	▲	▲	▲	▲	▲	▲	▲	▲	▲	▲
Switzerland	▼	▼	▼	▼	▼	▼	▼	▼	▼	▼	▼	▼	▼	▼	●	▼	●	●	●	●	●	●	●	●		●	●	▲	▲	▲	▲	▲	▲	▲	▲	▲	▲	▲	▲	▲	▲
Scotland	▼	▼	▼	▼	▼	▼	▼	▼	▼	▼	▼	▼	▼	▼	●	●	●	●	●	●	●	●	●	●	●		●	▲	▲	▲	▲	▲	▲	▲	▲	▲	▲	▲	▲	▲	▲
Spain	▼	▼	▼	▼	▼	▼	▼	▼	▼	▼	▼	▼	▼	▼	▼	▼	▼	●	▼	▼	●	●	●	●	●	●		▲	▲	▲	▲	▲	▲	▲	▲	▲	▲	▲	▲	▲	▲
France	▼	▼	▼	▼	▼	▼	▼	▼	▼	▼	▼	▼	▼	▼	▼	▼	▼	▼	▼	▼	▼	▼	▼	▼	▼	▼	▼		●	●	●	▲	▲	▲	▲	▲	▲	▲	▲	▲	▲
Greece	▼	▼	▼	▼	▼	▼	▼	▼	▼	▼	▼	▼	▼	▼	▼	▼	▼	▼	▼	▼	▼	▼	▼	▼	▼	▼	▼	●		●	●	▲	▲	▲	▲	▲	▲	▲	▲	▲	▲
Iceland	▼	▼	▼	▼	▼	▼	▼	▼	▼	▼	▼	▼	▼	▼	▼	▼	▼	▼	▼	▼	▼	▼	▼	▼	▼	▼	▼	●	●		●	●	●	●	▲	▲	▲	▲	▲	▲	▲
Romania	▼	▼	▼	▼	▼	▼	▼	▼	▼	▼	▼	▼	▼	▼	▼	▼	▼	▼	▼	▼	▼	▼	▼	▼	▼	▼	▼	●	●	●		●	●	●	●	●	●	▲	▲	▲	▲
Latvia (LSS)	▼	▼	▼	▼	▼	▼	▼	▼	▼	▼	▼	▼	▼	▼	▼	▼	▼	▼	▼	▼	▼	▼	▼	▼	▼	▼	▼	▼	▼	●	●		●	●	●	▲	▲	▲	▲	▲	▲
Portugal	▼	▼	▼	▼	▼	▼	▼	▼	▼	▼	▼	▼	▼	▼	▼	▼	▼	▼	▼	▼	▼	▼	▼	▼	▼	▼	▼	▼	▼	●	●	●		●	●	●	●	▲	▲	▲	▲
Denmark	▼	▼	▼	▼	▼	▼	▼	▼	▼	▼	▼	▼	▼	▼	▼	▼	▼	▼	▼	▼	▼	▼	▼	▼	▼	▼	▼	▼	▼	●	●	●	●		●	●	●	▲	▲	▲	▲
Lithuania	▼	▼	▼	▼	▼	▼	▼	▼	▼	▼	▼	▼	▼	▼	▼	▼	▼	▼	▼	▼	▼	▼	▼	▼	▼	▼	▼	▼	▼	▼	●	●	●	●		●	●	▲	▲	▲	▲
Belgium (Fr)	▼	▼	▼	▼	▼	▼	▼	▼	▼	▼	▼	▼	▼	▼	▼	▼	▼	▼	▼	▼	▼	▼	▼	▼	▼	▼	▼	▼	▼	▼	●	▼	●	●	●		●	●	▲	▲	▲
Iran, Islamic Rep.	▼	▼	▼	▼	▼	▼	▼	▼	▼	▼	▼	▼	▼	▼	▼	▼	▼	▼	▼	▼	▼	▼	▼	▼	▼	▼	▼	▼	▼	▼	●	▼	●	●	●	●		●	▲	▲	▲
Cyprus	▼	▼	▼	▼	▼	▼	▼	▼	▼	▼	▼	▼	▼	▼	▼	▼	▼	▼	▼	▼	▼	▼	▼	▼	▼	▼	▼	▼	▼	▼	▼	▼	▼	▼	▼	●	●		▲	▲	▲
Kuwait	▼	▼	▼	▼	▼	▼	▼	▼	▼	▼	▼	▼	▼	▼	▼	▼	▼	▼	▼	▼	▼	▼	▼	▼	▼	▼	▼	▼	▼	▼	▼	▼	▼	▼	▼	▼	▼	▼		▲	▲
Colombia	▼	▼	▼	▼	▼	▼	▼	▼	▼	▼	▼	▼	▼	▼	▼	▼	▼	▼	▼	▼	▼	▼	▼	▼	▼	▼	▼	▼	▼	▼	▼	▼	▼	▼	▼	▼	▼	▼	▼		▲
South Africa	▼	▼	▼	▼	▼	▼	▼	▼	▼	▼	▼	▼	▼	▼	▼	▼	▼	▼	▼	▼	▼	▼	▼	▼	▼	▼	▼	▼	▼	▼	▼	▼	▼	▼	▼	▼	▼	▼	▼	▼	

Countries are ordered by mean achievement across the heading and down the rows.

Mean achievement significantly higher than comparison country

No statistically significant difference from comparison country

Mean achievement significantly lower than comparison country

*Eighth grade in most countries; see Table 2 for information about the grades tested in each country.

[†]Statistically significant at .05 level, adjusted for multiple comparisons.

Because coverage falls below 65%, Latvia is annotated LSS for Latvian Speaking Schools only.

Countries shown in italics did not satisfy one or more guidelines for sample participation rates, age/grade specifications, or classroom sampling procedures (see Appendix A for details).

SOURCE: IEA Third International Mathematics and Science Study (TIMSS), 1994-95.

and within countries is illustrated in Table 1.1 by a graphical representation of the distribution of student performance within each country. Achievement for each country is shown for the 25th and 75th percentiles as well as for the 5th and 95th percentiles.[3] Each percentile point indicates the percentages of students performing below and above that point on the scale. For example, 25% of the eighth-grade students in each country performed below the 25th percentile for that country, and 75% performed above the 25th percentile. The range between the 25th and 75th percentiles represents performance by the middle half of the students. In contrast, performance at the 5th and 95th percentiles represents the extremes in both lower and higher achievement. The dark boxes at the midpoints of the distributions show the 95% confidence intervals around the average achievement in each country.[4] These intervals can be compared to the international average of 516, which was derived by averaging across the means for each of the 41 participants shown in the table.[5] A number of countries had mean achievement well above or well below that level.

Considerable variation in student performance is observed between countries. For example, average performance in Singapore was comparable to or even exceeded performance at the 95th percentile in the lower-performing countries such as Colombia, Kuwait, and South Africa. The differences between the extremes in performance were also very large within most countries.

Figure 1.1 provides a method for making appropriate comparisons in overall mean achievement between countries.[6] This figure shows whether or not the differences in mean achievement between pairs of countries are statistically significant. Selecting a country of interest and reading across the table, a triangle pointing up indicates significantly higher performance than the country listed across the top, a dot indicates no significant difference in performance, and a triangle pointing down indicates significantly lower performance.

At the eighth grade, Singapore, with all triangles pointing up, had a significantly higher mean achievement than other participating countries. Other countries that performed very well included the Czech Republic, Japan, Korea, Bulgaria, the Netherlands, Slovenia, and Austria. These countries had performance levels similar to each other, although Japan had significantly higher performance than Slovenia and Austria. Interestingly, from the top-performing countries on down through the list of participants, the differences in performance from one country to the next was often negligible. For example, in addition to performing at about the same level as the other countries mentioned above, the Netherlands did not differ significantly from Hungary, England,

[3] Tables of the percentile values and standard deviations for all countries are presented in Appendix E.

[4] See the "IRT Scaling and Data Analysis" section of Appendix A for more details about calculating standard errors and confidence intervals for the TIMSS statistics.

[5] Because the Flemish and French educational systems in Belgium participated separately, their results are presented separately in the tables of this report.

[6] The significance tests in Figures 1.1 and 1.2 are based on a Bonferroni procedure for multiple comparisons that holds to 5% the probability of erroneously declaring the mean of one country to be different from another country.

Flemish-speaking Belgium, Australia, and the Slovak Republic. In turn, Hungary, while performing less well than Singapore, the Czech Republic, Japan, and Korea, performed at about the same level as Bulgaria, the Netherlands, Slovenia, Austria, England, Flemish-speaking Belgium, Australia, the Slovak Republic, the Russian Federation, and Ireland, and higher than all other countries.

Despite the small differences between adjacent countries when participants are ordered by performance, the differences between the top-performing and bottom-performing countries was very large. Because of this large range in performance, the pattern for a number of countries was one of having lower mean achievement than some countries, about the same mean achievement as other countries, and higher mean achievement than a third group. In contrast, Kuwait, Colombia, and South Africa performed less well than the other countries, with Colombia having significantly lower achievement than Kuwait, and South Africa having significantly lower achievement than Colombia.

Table 1.2 and Figure 1.2 present corresponding data for the seventh grade.[7] At the seventh grade there was no significant difference in mean science achievement among the seven top-performing countries – Singapore, Korea, the Czech Republic, Japan, Bulgaria, Slovenia, and Belgium (Flemish). The three lowest-performing countries were Lithuania, Colombia, and South Africa. However, students in Colombia performed less well than those in Lithuania, and students in South Africa below those in Colombia. For the remaining countries, performance rankings also tended to be similar, but not identical, to those found at the eighth grade.

Performance in eighth grade was naturally somewhat higher than that in seventh grade, since eighth-grade students have had one year more of schooling. The international average at the eighth grade (516) was 37 points higher than the international average of 479 at the seventh grade. Even though equivalent achievement increases cannot be assumed from grade to grade throughout schooling, this 37-point difference does provide a rough indication of grade-by-grade increases in science achievement during the middle years. By this gauge, the achievement differences across countries at both grades reflect several grade levels in learning between the higher- and lower-performing countries. A similarly large range in performance can be noted within most countries. There needs to be a further note of caution, however, in using growth from grade to grade as an indicator of achievement. The TIMSS scale measures achievement in science judged to be appropriate for seventh- and eighth-grade students around the world. Thus, higher performance does not mean students can do advanced high-school science, only that they are more proficient at middle-school science.

[7] Results are presented for 27 countries in the top portion of Table 1.2 because French-speaking Belgium and Scotland met the sampling requirements at this grade. Thirty-nine countries are presented in total because Kuwait and Israel tested only the eighth grade.

Table 1.2

Distributions of Achievement in the Sciences - Lower Grade (Seventh Grade*)

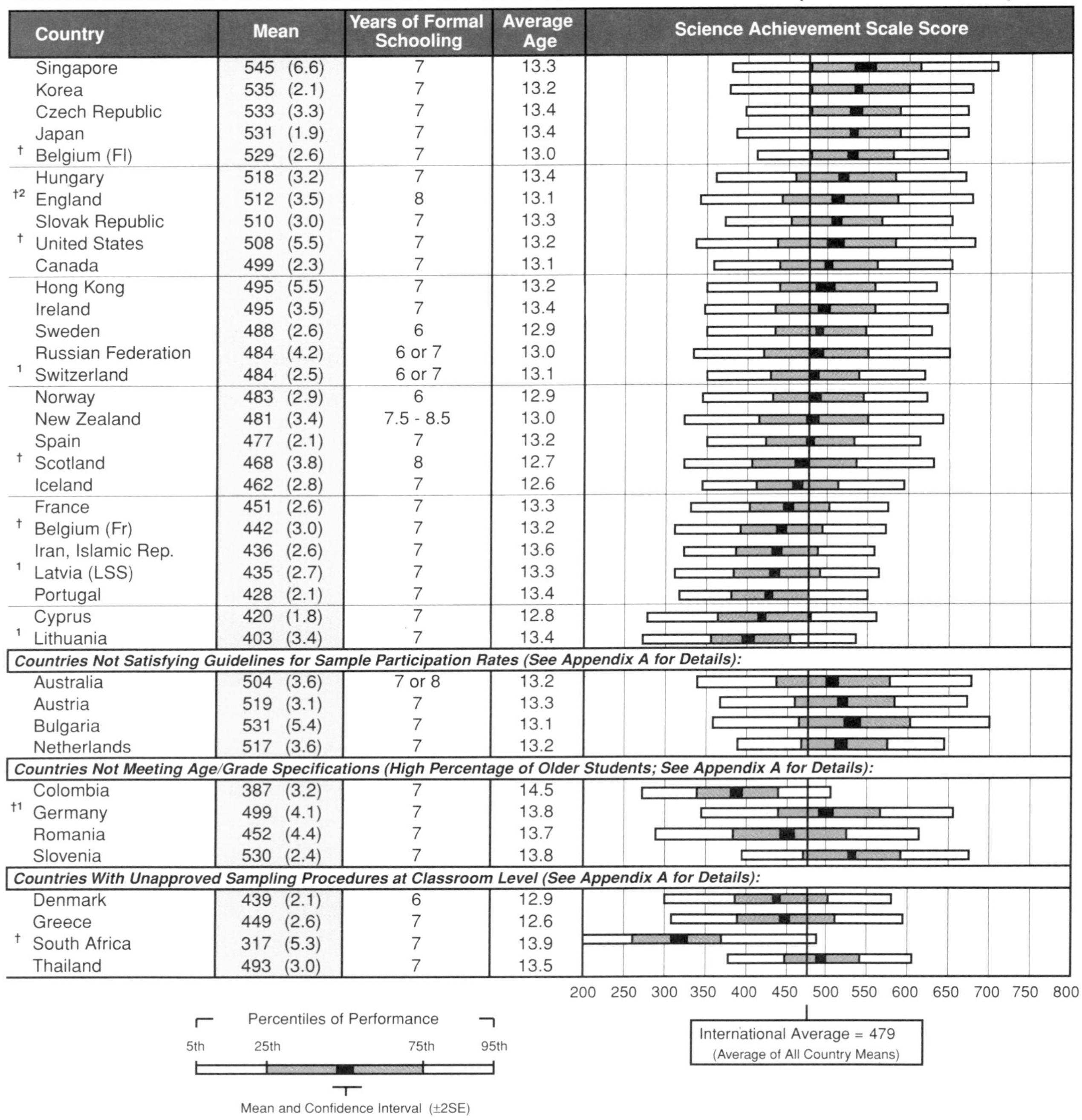

Country	Mean	Years of Formal Schooling	Average Age
Singapore	545 (6.6)	7	13.3
Korea	535 (2.1)	7	13.2
Czech Republic	533 (3.3)	7	13.4
Japan	531 (1.9)	7	13.4
† Belgium (Fl)	529 (2.6)	7	13.0
Hungary	518 (3.2)	7	13.4
†2 England	512 (3.5)	8	13.1
Slovak Republic	510 (3.0)	7	13.3
† United States	508 (5.5)	7	13.2
Canada	499 (2.3)	7	13.1
Hong Kong	495 (5.5)	7	13.2
Ireland	495 (3.5)	7	13.4
Sweden	488 (2.6)	6	12.9
Russian Federation	484 (4.2)	6 or 7	13.0
1 Switzerland	484 (2.5)	6 or 7	13.1
Norway	483 (2.9)	6	12.9
New Zealand	481 (3.4)	7.5 - 8.5	13.0
Spain	477 (2.1)	7	13.2
† Scotland	468 (3.8)	8	12.7
Iceland	462 (2.8)	7	12.6
France	451 (2.6)	7	13.3
† Belgium (Fr)	442 (3.0)	7	13.2
Iran, Islamic Rep.	436 (2.6)	7	13.6
1 Latvia (LSS)	435 (2.7)	7	13.3
Portugal	428 (2.1)	7	13.4
Cyprus	420 (1.8)	7	12.8
1 Lithuania	403 (3.4)	7	13.4
Countries Not Satisfying Guidelines for Sample Participation Rates (See Appendix A for Details):			
Australia	504 (3.6)	7 or 8	13.2
Austria	519 (3.1)	7	13.3
Bulgaria	531 (5.4)	7	13.1
Netherlands	517 (3.6)	7	13.2
Countries Not Meeting Age/Grade Specifications (High Percentage of Older Students; See Appendix A for Details):			
Colombia	387 (3.2)	7	14.5
†1 Germany	499 (4.1)	7	13.8
Romania	452 (4.4)	7	13.7
Slovenia	530 (2.4)	7	13.8
Countries With Unapproved Sampling Procedures at Classroom Level (See Appendix A for Details):			
Denmark	439 (2.1)	6	12.9
Greece	449 (2.6)	7	12.6
† South Africa	317 (5.3)	7	13.9
Thailand	493 (3.0)	7	13.5

*Seventh grade in most countries; see Table 2 for information about the grades tested in each country.

†Met guidelines for sample participation rates only after replacement schools were included (see Appendix A for details).

1National Desired Population does not cover all of International Desired Population (see Table A.2). Because coverage falls below 65%, Latvia is annotated LSS for Latvian Speaking Schools only.

2National Defined Population covers less than 90 percent of National Desired Population (see Table A.2).

( ) Standard errors appear in parentheses. Because results are rounded to the nearest whole number, some totals may appear inconsistent.

SOURCE: IEA Third International Mathematics and Science Study (TIMSS), 1994-95.

Figure 1.2

Multiple Comparisons of Achievement in the Sciences - Lower Grade (Seventh Grade*)

Instructions: Read ***across*** the row for a country to compare performance with the countries listed in the heading of the chart. The symbols indicate whether the mean achievement of the country in the row is significantly lower than that of the comparison country, significantly higher than that of the comparison country, or if there is no statistically significant difference between the two countries.[†]

Country	Singapore	Korea	Czech Republic	Japan	*Bulgaria*	*Slovenia*	Belgium (Fl)	*Austria*	Hungary	*Netherlands*	England	Slovak Republic	United States	*Australia*	*Germany*	Canada	Hong Kong	Ireland	*Thailand*	Sweden	Russian Fed.	Switzerland	Norway	New Zealand	Spain	Scotland	Iceland	*Romania*	France	*Greece*	Belgium (Fr)	*Denmark*	Iran, Islamic Rep.	Latvia (LSS)	Portugal	Cyprus	Lithuania	*Colombia*	*South Africa*
Singapore		●	●	●	●	●	●	▲	▲	▲	▲	▲	▲	▲	▲	▲	▲	▲	▲	▲	▲	▲	▲	▲	▲	▲	▲	▲	▲	▲	▲	▲	▲	▲	▲	▲	▲	▲	▲
Korea	●		●	●	●	●	●	▲	▲	▲	▲	▲	▲	▲	▲	▲	▲	▲	▲	▲	▲	▲	▲	▲	▲	▲	▲	▲	▲	▲	▲	▲	▲	▲	▲	▲	▲	▲	▲
Czech Republic	●	●		●	●	●	●	●	▲	●	▲	▲	▲	▲	▲	▲	▲	▲	▲	▲	▲	▲	▲	▲	▲	▲	▲	▲	▲	▲	▲	▲	▲	▲	▲	▲	▲	▲	▲
Japan	●	●	●		●	●	●	▲	▲	▲	▲	▲	▲	▲	▲	▲	▲	▲	▲	▲	▲	▲	▲	▲	▲	▲	▲	▲	▲	▲	▲	▲	▲	▲	▲	▲	▲	▲	▲
Bulgaria	●	●	●	●		●	●	●	●	●	●	▲	●	▲	▲	▲	▲	▲	▲	▲	▲	▲	▲	▲	▲	▲	▲	▲	▲	▲	▲	▲	▲	▲	▲	▲	▲	▲	▲
Slovenia	●	●	●	●	●		●	●	●	●	▲	▲	▲	▲	▲	▲	▲	▲	▲	▲	▲	▲	▲	▲	▲	▲	▲	▲	▲	▲	▲	▲	▲	▲	▲	▲	▲	▲	▲
Belgium (Fl)	●	●	●	●	●	●		●	●	●	▲	▲	▲	▲	▲	▲	▲	▲	▲	▲	▲	▲	▲	▲	▲	▲	▲	▲	▲	▲	▲	▲	▲	▲	▲	▲	▲	▲	▲
Austria	▼	▼	●	▼	●	●	●		●	●	●	●	●	●	▲	▲	▲	▲	▲	▲	▲	▲	▲	▲	▲	▲	▲	▲	▲	▲	▲	▲	▲	▲	▲	▲	▲	▲	▲
Hungary	▼	▼	▼	▼	●	●	●	●		●	●	●	●	●	▲	▲	▲	▲	▲	▲	▲	▲	▲	▲	▲	▲	▲	▲	▲	▲	▲	▲	▲	▲	▲	▲	▲	▲	▲
Netherlands	▼	▼	●	▼	●	●	●	●	●		●	●	●	●	▲	▲	▲	▲	▲	▲	▲	▲	▲	▲	▲	▲	▲	▲	▲	▲	▲	▲	▲	▲	▲	▲	▲	▲	▲
England	▼	▼	▼	▼	●	▼	▼	●	●	●		●	●	●	●	●	●	▲	▲	▲	▲	▲	▲	▲	▲	▲	▲	▲	▲	▲	▲	▲	▲	▲	▲	▲	▲	▲	▲
Slovak Republic	▼	▼	▼	▼	▼	▼	▼	●	●	●	●		●	●	●	●	●	●	▲	▲	▲	▲	▲	▲	▲	▲	▲	▲	▲	▲	▲	▲	▲	▲	▲	▲	▲	▲	▲
United States	▼	▼	▼	▼	●	▼	▼	●	●	●	●	●		●	●	●	●	●	●	▲	▲	▲	▲	▲	▲	▲	▲	▲	▲	▲	▲	▲	▲	▲	▲	▲	▲	▲	▲
Australia	▼	▼	▼	▼	▼	▼	▼	●	●	●	●	●	●		●	●	●	●	●	▲	▲	▲	▲	▲	▲	▲	▲	▲	▲	▲	▲	▲	▲	▲	▲	▲	▲	▲	▲
Germany	▼	▼	▼	▼	▼	▼	▼	▼	▼	▼	●	●	●	●		●	●	●	●	●	●	▲	▲	▲	▲	▲	▲	▲	▲	▲	▲	▲	▲	▲	▲	▲	▲	▲	▲
Canada	▼	▼	▼	▼	▼	▼	▼	▼	▼	▼	●	●	●	●	●		●	●	●	●	●	▲	▲	▲	▲	▲	▲	▲	▲	▲	▲	▲	▲	▲	▲	▲	▲	▲	▲
Hong Kong	▼	▼	▼	▼	▼	▼	▼	▼	▼	▼	●	●	●	●	●	●		●	●	●	●	●	●	●	●	▲	▲	▲	▲	▲	▲	▲	▲	▲	▲	▲	▲	▲	▲
Ireland	▼	▼	▼	▼	▼	▼	▼	▼	▼	▼	▼	●	●	●	●	●	●		●	●	●	●	●	●	▲	▲	▲	▲	▲	▲	▲	▲	▲	▲	▲	▲	▲	▲	▲
Thailand	▼	▼	▼	▼	▼	▼	▼	▼	▼	▼	▼	▼	●	●	●	●	●	●		●	●	●	●	●	▲	▲	▲	▲	▲	▲	▲	▲	▲	▲	▲	▲	▲	▲	▲
Sweden	▼	▼	▼	▼	▼	▼	▼	▼	▼	▼	▼	▼	▼	▼	●	●	●	●	●		●	●	●	●	▲	▲	▲	▲	▲	▲	▲	▲	▲	▲	▲	▲	▲	▲	▲
Russian Fed.	▼	▼	▼	▼	▼	▼	▼	▼	▼	▼	▼	▼	▼	▼	●	●	●	●	●	●		●	●	●	●	●	▲	▲	▲	▲	▲	▲	▲	▲	▲	▲	▲	▲	▲
Switzerland	▼	▼	▼	▼	▼	▼	▼	▼	▼	▼	▼	▼	▼	▼	▼	▼	●	●	●	●	●		●	●	●	▲	▲	▲	▲	▲	▲	▲	▲	▲	▲	▲	▲	▲	▲
Norway	▼	▼	▼	▼	▼	▼	▼	▼	▼	▼	▼	▼	▼	▼	▼	▼	●	●	●	●	●	●		●	●	●	▲	▲	▲	▲	▲	▲	▲	▲	▲	▲	▲	▲	▲
New Zealand	▼	▼	▼	▼	▼	▼	▼	▼	▼	▼	▼	▼	▼	▼	▼	▼	●	●	●	●	●	●	●		●	●	▲	▲	▲	▲	▲	▲	▲	▲	▲	▲	▲	▲	▲
Spain	▼	▼	▼	▼	▼	▼	▼	▼	▼	▼	▼	▼	▼	▼	▼	▼	●	▼	▼	▼	●	●	●	●		●	▲	▲	▲	▲	▲	▲	▲	▲	▲	▲	▲	▲	▲
Scotland	▼	▼	▼	▼	▼	▼	▼	▼	▼	▼	▼	▼	▼	▼	▼	▼	▼	▼	▼	▼	●	▼	●	●	●		●	●	▲	▲	▲	▲	▲	▲	▲	▲	▲	▲	▲
Iceland	▼	▼	▼	▼	▼	▼	▼	▼	▼	▼	▼	▼	▼	▼	▼	▼	▼	▼	▼	▼	▼	▼	▼	▼	▼	●		●	●	▲	▲	▲	▲	▲	▲	▲	▲	▲	▲
Romania	▼	▼	▼	▼	▼	▼	▼	▼	▼	▼	▼	▼	▼	▼	▼	▼	▼	▼	▼	▼	▼	▼	▼	▼	▼	●	●		●	●	●	●	●	▲	▲	▲	▲	▲	▲
France	▼	▼	▼	▼	▼	▼	▼	▼	▼	▼	▼	▼	▼	▼	▼	▼	▼	▼	▼	▼	▼	▼	▼	▼	▼	▼	●	●		●	●	▲	▲	▲	▲	▲	▲	▲	▲
Greece	▼	▼	▼	▼	▼	▼	▼	▼	▼	▼	▼	▼	▼	▼	▼	▼	▼	▼	▼	▼	▼	▼	▼	▼	▼	▼	▼	●	●		●	●	▲	▲	▲	▲	▲	▲	▲
Belgium (Fr)	▼	▼	▼	▼	▼	▼	▼	▼	▼	▼	▼	▼	▼	▼	▼	▼	▼	▼	▼	▼	▼	▼	▼	▼	▼	▼	▼	●	●	●		●	●	●	▲	▲	▲	▲	▲
Denmark	▼	▼	▼	▼	▼	▼	▼	▼	▼	▼	▼	▼	▼	▼	▼	▼	▼	▼	▼	▼	▼	▼	▼	▼	▼	▼	▼	●	▼	●	●		●	●	▲	▲	▲	▲	▲
Iran, Islamic Rep.	▼	▼	▼	▼	▼	▼	▼	▼	▼	▼	▼	▼	▼	▼	▼	▼	▼	▼	▼	▼	▼	▼	▼	▼	▼	▼	▼	●	▼	▼	●	●		●	●	▲	▲	▲	▲
Latvia (LSS)	▼	▼	▼	▼	▼	▼	▼	▼	▼	▼	▼	▼	▼	▼	▼	▼	▼	▼	▼	▼	▼	▼	▼	▼	▼	▼	▼	▼	▼	▼	●	●	●		●	▲	▲	▲	▲
Portugal	▼	▼	▼	▼	▼	▼	▼	▼	▼	▼	▼	▼	▼	▼	▼	▼	▼	▼	▼	▼	▼	▼	▼	▼	▼	▼	▼	▼	▼	▼	▼	▼	●	●		●	▲	▲	▲
Cyprus	▼	▼	▼	▼	▼	▼	▼	▼	▼	▼	▼	▼	▼	▼	▼	▼	▼	▼	▼	▼	▼	▼	▼	▼	▼	▼	▼	▼	▼	▼	▼	▼	▼	▼	●		▲	▲	▲
Lithuania	▼	▼	▼	▼	▼	▼	▼	▼	▼	▼	▼	▼	▼	▼	▼	▼	▼	▼	▼	▼	▼	▼	▼	▼	▼	▼	▼	▼	▼	▼	▼	▼	▼	▼	▼	▼		▲	▲
Colombia	▼	▼	▼	▼	▼	▼	▼	▼	▼	▼	▼	▼	▼	▼	▼	▼	▼	▼	▼	▼	▼	▼	▼	▼	▼	▼	▼	▼	▼	▼	▼	▼	▼	▼	▼	▼	▼		▲
South Africa	▼	▼	▼	▼	▼	▼	▼	▼	▼	▼	▼	▼	▼	▼	▼	▼	▼	▼	▼	▼	▼	▼	▼	▼	▼	▼	▼	▼	▼	▼	▼	▼	▼	▼	▼	▼	▼	▼	

Countries are ordered by mean achievement across the heading and down the rows.

Mean achievement significantly higher than comparison country

No statistically significant difference from comparison country

Mean achievement significantly lower than comparison country

*Seventh grade in most countries; see Table 2 for information about the grades tested in each country.
[†]Statistically significant at .05 level, adjusted for multiple comparisons.
Because coverage falls below 65%, Latvia is annotated LSS for Latvian Speaking Schools only.
Countries shown in italics did not satisfy one or more guidelines for sample participation rates, age/grade specifications, or classroom sampling procedures (see Appendix A for details).

SOURCE: IEA Third International Mathematics and Science Study (TIMSS), 1994-95.

What Are the Increases in Achievement Between the Lower and Upper Grades?

Table 1.3 presents the increases in mean achievement between the two grades tested in each TIMSS country. Countries in the upper portion of the table are shown in decreasing order by the amount of this between-grade difference. Increases in mean performance between the two grades ranged from a high of 73 points in Lithuania to 22 points in the Flemish-speaking part of Belgium[8] and a low of 9 points in South Africa.[9] This degree of increase can be compared to the difference of 37 points between the international average of 516 at eighth grade and that of 479 at seventh grade. Despite the larger increases in some countries compared to others, there is no obvious relationship between mean seventh-grade performance and the between-grade increase. That is, countries showing the highest performance at the seventh grade did not necessarily show either the largest or smallest increases in achievement at the eighth grade. Still, in general, countries with high mean performance in the seventh grade also had high mean performance in the eighth grade.

[8] Both educational systems in Belgium have policies whereby lower-performing sixth-grade students continue their study of the primary school curriculum and then re-enter the system as part of a vocational track in the eighth grade. Since these lower-performing students are not included in the seventh-grade results, but do compose about 10% of the sample at the eighth grade, this contributed to reduced performance differences between grades 7 and 8.

[9] In South Africa, there is no structural reason to explain the relatively small difference between seventh- and eighth-grade performance. However, in 1995, its education system was undergoing radical reorganization from 18 racially-divided systems into 9 provincial systems.

Table 1.3

Achievement Differences in the Sciences Between Lower and Upper Grades (Seventh and Eighth Grades*)

Country	Seventh Grade Mean	Eighth Grade Mean	Eighth-Seventh Difference
[1] Lithuania	403 (3.4)	476 (3.4)	73 (4.8)
Singapore	545 (6.6)	607 (5.5)	63 (8.6)
Russian Federation	484 (4.2)	538 (4.0)	54 (5.8)
Portugal	428 (2.1)	480 (2.3)	52 (3.1)
[1] Latvia (LSS)	435 (2.7)	485 (2.7)	50 (3.8)
† Scotland	468 (3.8)	517 (5.1)	49 (6.4)
Sweden	488 (2.6)	535 (3.0)	47 (3.9)
France	451 (2.6)	498 (2.5)	46 (3.6)
New Zealand	481 (3.4)	525 (4.4)	44 (5.5)
Norway	483 (2.9)	527 (1.9)	44 (3.5)
Cyprus	420 (1.8)	463 (1.9)	43 (2.7)
Ireland	495 (3.5)	538 (4.5)	43 (5.7)
Czech Republic	533 (3.3)	574 (4.3)	41 (5.4)
†[2] England	512 (3.5)	552 (3.3)	40 (4.8)
Japan	531 (1.9)	571 (1.6)	40 (2.5)
Spain	477 (2.1)	517 (1.7)	40 (2.7)
[1] Switzerland	484 (2.5)	522 (2.5)	38 (3.5)
Hungary	518 (3.2)	554 (2.8)	36 (4.2)
Slovak Republic	510 (3.0)	544 (3.2)	35 (4.4)
Iran, Islamic Rep.	436 (2.6)	470 (2.4)	33 (3.5)
Canada	499 (2.3)	531 (2.6)	32 (3.5)
Iceland	462 (2.8)	494 (4.0)	32 (4.9)
Korea	535 (2.1)	565 (1.9)	30 (2.9)
† Belgium (Fr)	442 (3.0)	471 (2.8)	29 (4.2)
Hong Kong	495 (5.5)	522 (4.7)	27 (7.2)
† United States	508 (5.5)	534 (4.7)	26 (7.2)
† Belgium (Fl)	529 (2.6)	550 (4.2)	22 (4.9)
Countries Not Satisfying Guidelines for Sample Participation Rates (See Appendix A for Details):			
Australia	504 (3.6)	545 (3.9)	40 (5.3)
Austria	519 (3.1)	558 (3.7)	39 (4.8)
Bulgaria	531 (5.4)	565 (5.3)	34 (7.6)
Netherlands	517 (3.6)	560 (5.0)	43 (6.1)
Countries Not Meeting Age/Grade Specifications (High Percentage of Older Students; See Appendix A for Details):			
Slovenia	530 (2.4)	560 (2.5)	30 (3.4)
Romania	452 (4.4)	486 (4.7)	34 (6.5)
†[1] Germany	499 (4.1)	531 (4.8)	32 (6.3)
Colombia	387 (3.2)	411 (4.1)	24 (5.2)
Countries With Unapproved Sampling Procedures at Classroom Level (See Appendix A for Details):			
Denmark	439 (2.1)	478 (3.1)	39 (3.8)
Greece	449 (2.6)	497 (2.2)	49 (3.4)
† South Africa	317 (5.3)	326 (6.6)	9 (8.5)
Thailand	493 (3.0)	525 (3.7)	33 (4.8)

-10 0 10 20 30 40 50 60 70 80 90

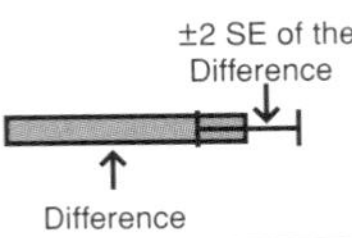

*Seventh and eighth grades in most countries; see Table 2 for infomation about the grades tested in each country.

†Met guidelines for sample participation rates only after replacement schools were included (see Appendix A for details).

[1]National Desired Population does not cover all of International Desired Population (see Table A.2). Because coverage falls below 65%, Latvia is annotated LSS for Latvian Speaking Schools only.

[2]National Defined Population covers less than 90 percent of National Desired Population (see Table A.2).

( ) Standard errors appear in parentheses. Because results are rounded to the nearest whole number, some differences may appear inconsistent.

SOURCE: IEA Third International Mathematics and Science Study (TIMSS), 1994-95.

What Are the Differences in Performance Compared to Three Marker Levels of International Science Achievement?

Tables 1.4 and 1.5 portray the performance of students in each TIMSS country in terms of international levels of achievement for the eighth and seventh grades, respectively. This method provides another useful comparison of student performance across countries by determining the percentage of students in each country reaching specific levels of performance. Since the TIMSS achievement tests do not have any pre-specified performance standards, three marker levels were chosen on the basis of the combined performance of all students at a grade level in the study – the Top 10%, the Top Quarter (25%), and the Top Half (50%). For example, Table 1.4 shows that 10% of all eighth graders in countries participating in the TIMSS study achieved at the level of 655 or better. This score point, then, was designated as the marker level for the Top 10%. Similarly, the Top Quarter marker level was determined as 592 and the Top Half marker level as 522. At the seventh grade, these marker levels are 615, 553 and 483, respectively.

If every country had the same distribution of high-, medium-, and low-performing students, then each country would be expected to have approximately 10% of its students reaching the Top 10% level, 25% reaching the Top Quarter level, and 50% reaching the Top Half level. Although no country achieved exactly this pattern, the distributions of eighth- and/or seventh-grade students in several countries were quite close. For example, 9%, 24%, and 49% of the seventh-grade students in the Russian Federation reached the corresponding levels. Similarly, percentages close to the international norm were noted at the eighth grade for New Zealand, Sweden, Scotland, and Israel. In contrast, in Singapore nearly one-third (31%) of the eighth-grade students and 24% of seventh-grade students reached the Top 10% level, approximately half or more reached the Top Quarter level (56% at the eighth grade and 48% at the seventh grade), and about three-quarters or more reached the Top Half level (82% at the eighth grade and 74% at the seventh grade).

It can be informative to look at performance at each marker level. For example, at the eighth grade, Norway, Switzerland, and Hong Kong did not quite attain the Top 10% level, with 7% of students reaching that level. However, performance in these countries approximated both the Top Quarter and Top Half levels. In comparison, eighth-grade students in Belgium (Flemish) attained approximately the Top 10% level (10%) and exceeded both the Top Quarter and Top Half levels (31% and 64%). This pattern for the Belgian (Flemish) students was even more pronounced at the seventh grade, with 73% of students reaching the Top Half level.

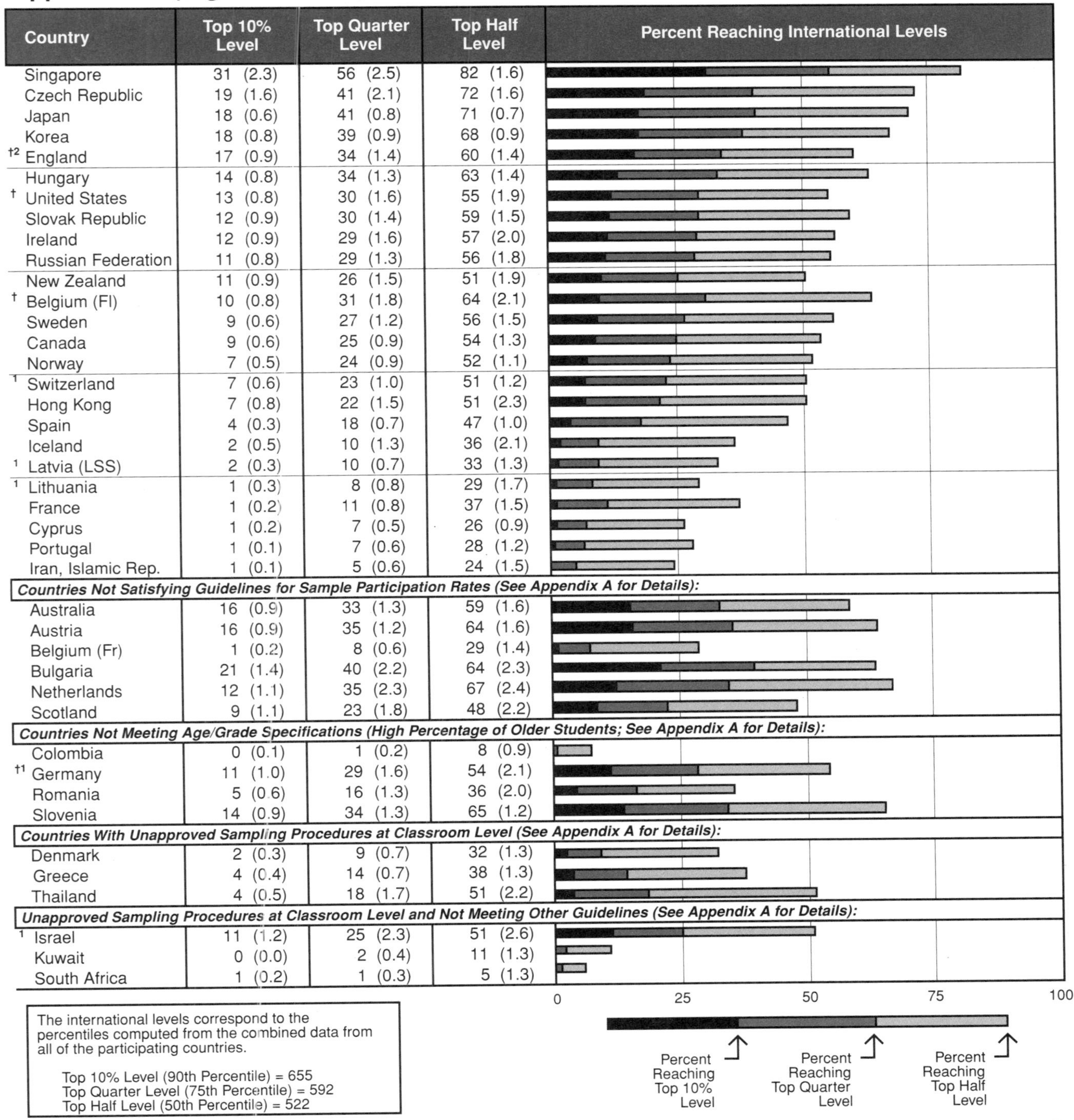

Table 1.4

Percentages of Students Achieving International Marker Levels in the Sciences Upper Grade (Eighth Grade*)

Country	Top 10% Level	Top Quarter Level	Top Half Level
Singapore	31 (2.3)	56 (2.5)	82 (1.6)
Czech Republic	19 (1.6)	41 (2.1)	72 (1.6)
Japan	18 (0.6)	41 (0.8)	71 (0.7)
Korea	18 (0.8)	39 (0.9)	68 (0.9)
[†2] England	17 (0.9)	34 (1.4)	60 (1.4)
Hungary	14 (0.8)	34 (1.3)	63 (1.4)
[†] United States	13 (0.8)	30 (1.6)	55 (1.9)
Slovak Republic	12 (0.9)	30 (1.4)	59 (1.5)
Ireland	12 (0.9)	29 (1.6)	57 (2.0)
Russian Federation	11 (0.8)	29 (1.3)	56 (1.8)
New Zealand	11 (0.9)	26 (1.5)	51 (1.9)
[†] Belgium (Fl)	10 (0.8)	31 (1.8)	64 (2.1)
Sweden	9 (0.6)	27 (1.2)	56 (1.5)
Canada	9 (0.6)	25 (0.9)	54 (1.3)
Norway	7 (0.5)	24 (0.9)	52 (1.1)
[1] Switzerland	7 (0.6)	23 (1.0)	51 (1.2)
Hong Kong	7 (0.8)	22 (1.5)	51 (2.3)
Spain	4 (0.3)	18 (0.7)	47 (1.0)
Iceland	2 (0.5)	10 (1.3)	36 (2.1)
[1] Latvia (LSS)	2 (0.3)	10 (0.7)	33 (1.3)
[1] Lithuania	1 (0.3)	8 (0.8)	29 (1.7)
France	1 (0.2)	11 (0.8)	37 (1.5)
Cyprus	1 (0.2)	7 (0.5)	26 (0.9)
Portugal	1 (0.1)	7 (0.6)	28 (1.2)
Iran, Islamic Rep.	1 (0.1)	5 (0.6)	24 (1.5)
Countries Not Satisfying Guidelines for Sample Participation Rates (See Appendix A for Details):			
Australia	16 (0.9)	33 (1.3)	59 (1.6)
Austria	16 (0.9)	35 (1.2)	64 (1.6)
Belgium (Fr)	1 (0.2)	8 (0.6)	29 (1.4)
Bulgaria	21 (1.4)	40 (2.2)	64 (2.3)
Netherlands	12 (1.1)	35 (2.3)	67 (2.4)
Scotland	9 (1.1)	23 (1.8)	48 (2.2)
Countries Not Meeting Age/Grade Specifications (High Percentage of Older Students; See Appendix A for Details):			
Colombia	0 (0.1)	1 (0.2)	8 (0.9)
[†1] Germany	11 (1.0)	29 (1.6)	54 (2.1)
Romania	5 (0.6)	16 (1.3)	36 (2.0)
Slovenia	14 (0.9)	34 (1.3)	65 (1.2)
Countries With Unapproved Sampling Procedures at Classroom Level (See Appendix A for Details):			
Denmark	2 (0.3)	9 (0.7)	32 (1.3)
Greece	4 (0.4)	14 (0.7)	38 (1.3)
Thailand	4 (0.5)	18 (1.7)	51 (2.2)
Unapproved Sampling Procedures at Classroom Level and Not Meeting Other Guidelines (See Appendix A for Details):			
[1] Israel	11 (1.2)	25 (2.3)	51 (2.6)
Kuwait	0 (0.0)	2 (0.4)	11 (1.3)
South Africa	1 (0.2)	1 (0.3)	5 (1.3)

The international levels correspond to the percentiles computed from the combined data from all of the participating countries.

Top 10% Level (90th Percentile) = 655
Top Quarter Level (75th Percentile) = 592
Top Half Level (50th Percentile) = 522

*Eighth grade in most countries; see Table 2 for information about the grades tested in each country.
[†]Met guidelines for sample participation rates only after replacement schools were included (see Appendix A for details).
[1]National Desired Population does not cover all of International Desired Population (see Table A.2). Because coverage falls below 65%, Latvia is annotated LSS for Latvian Speaking Schools only.
[2]National Defined Population covers less than 90 percent of National Desired Population (see Table A.2).
( ) Standard errors appear in parentheses. Because results are rounded to the nearest whole number, some differences may appear inconsistent.

SOURCE: IEA Third International Mathematics and Science Study (TIMSS), 1994-95.

Table 1.5

Percentages of Students Achieving International Marker Levels in the Sciences Lower Grade (Seventh Grade*)

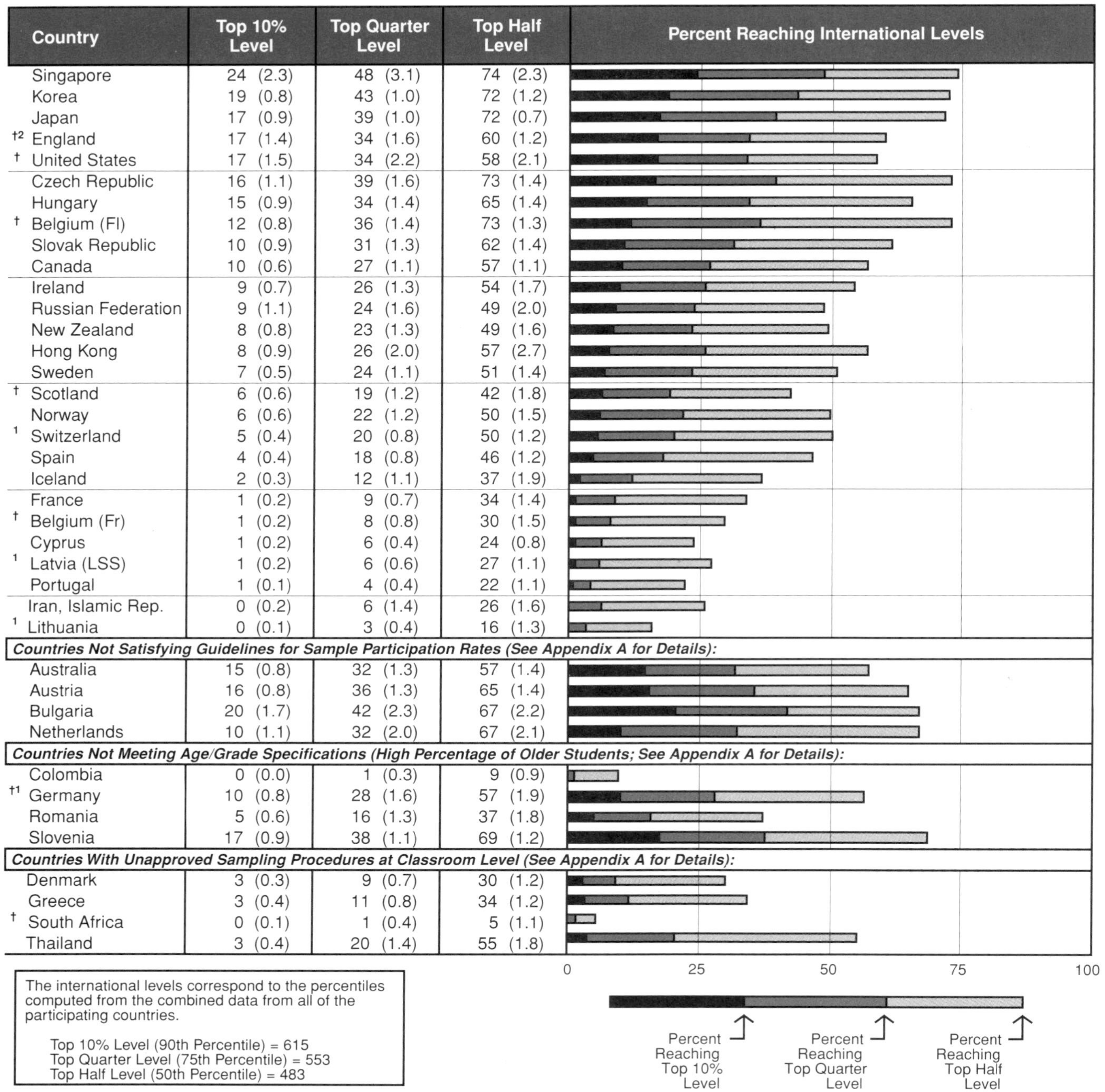

Country	Top 10% Level	Top Quarter Level	Top Half Level
Singapore	24 (2.3)	48 (3.1)	74 (2.3)
Korea	19 (0.8)	43 (1.0)	72 (1.2)
Japan	17 (0.9)	39 (1.0)	72 (0.7)
†2 England	17 (1.4)	34 (1.6)	60 (1.2)
† United States	17 (1.5)	34 (2.2)	58 (2.1)
Czech Republic	16 (1.1)	39 (1.6)	73 (1.4)
Hungary	15 (0.9)	34 (1.4)	65 (1.4)
† Belgium (Fl)	12 (0.8)	36 (1.4)	73 (1.3)
Slovak Republic	10 (0.9)	31 (1.3)	62 (1.4)
Canada	10 (0.6)	27 (1.1)	57 (1.1)
Ireland	9 (0.7)	26 (1.3)	54 (1.7)
Russian Federation	9 (1.1)	24 (1.6)	49 (2.0)
New Zealand	8 (0.8)	23 (1.3)	49 (1.6)
Hong Kong	8 (0.9)	26 (2.0)	57 (2.7)
Sweden	7 (0.5)	24 (1.1)	51 (1.4)
† Scotland	6 (0.6)	19 (1.2)	42 (1.8)
Norway	6 (0.6)	22 (1.2)	50 (1.5)
1 Switzerland	5 (0.4)	20 (0.8)	50 (1.2)
Spain	4 (0.4)	18 (0.8)	46 (1.2)
Iceland	2 (0.3)	12 (1.1)	37 (1.9)
France	1 (0.2)	9 (0.7)	34 (1.4)
† Belgium (Fr)	1 (0.2)	8 (0.8)	30 (1.5)
Cyprus	1 (0.2)	6 (0.4)	24 (0.8)
1 Latvia (LSS)	1 (0.2)	6 (0.6)	27 (1.1)
Portugal	1 (0.1)	4 (0.4)	22 (1.1)
Iran, Islamic Rep.	0 (0.2)	6 (1.4)	26 (1.6)
1 Lithuania	0 (0.1)	3 (0.4)	16 (1.3)
Countries Not Satisfying Guidelines for Sample Participation Rates (See Appendix A for Details):			
Australia	15 (0.8)	32 (1.3)	57 (1.4)
Austria	16 (0.8)	36 (1.3)	65 (1.4)
Bulgaria	20 (1.7)	42 (2.3)	67 (2.2)
Netherlands	10 (1.1)	32 (2.0)	67 (2.1)
Countries Not Meeting Age/Grade Specifications (High Percentage of Older Students; See Appendix A for Details):			
Colombia	0 (0.0)	1 (0.3)	9 (0.9)
†1 Germany	10 (0.8)	28 (1.6)	57 (1.9)
Romania	5 (0.6)	16 (1.3)	37 (1.8)
Slovenia	17 (0.9)	38 (1.1)	69 (1.2)
Countries With Unapproved Sampling Procedures at Classroom Level (See Appendix A for Details):			
Denmark	3 (0.3)	9 (0.7)	30 (1.2)
Greece	3 (0.4)	11 (0.8)	34 (1.2)
† South Africa	0 (0.1)	1 (0.4)	5 (1.1)
Thailand	3 (0.4)	20 (1.4)	55 (1.8)

The international levels correspond to the percentiles computed from the combined data from all of the participating countries.

Top 10% Level (90th Percentile) = 615
Top Quarter Level (75th Percentile) = 553
Top Half Level (50th Percentile) = 483

*Seventh grade in most countries; see Table 2 for information about the grades tested in each country.

†Met guidelines for sample participation rates only after replacement schools were included (see Appendix A for details).

1National Desired Population does not cover all of International Desired Population (see Table A.2). Because coverage falls below 65%, Latvia is annotated LSS for Latvian Speaking Schools only.

2National Defined Population covers less than 90 percent of National Desired Population (see Table A.2).

( ) Standard errors appear in parentheses. Because results are rounded to the nearest whole number, some differences may appear inconsistent.

SOURCE: IEA Third International Mathematics and Science Study (TIMSS), 1994-95.

What Are the Gender Differences in Science Achievement?

Tables 1.6 and 1.7 reveal that boys had significantly higher mean science achievement than girls at both the seventh and eighth grades internationally and in many countries. Each of the two tables, the first one for the eighth grade and the second for the seventh grade, presents mean science achievement separately for boys and girls for each country, as well as the difference between the means. Countries in the upper part of the tables are shown in increasing order of this gender difference. The visual representation of the gender difference for each country, shown by a bar, indicates the amount of the difference, whether the direction of the difference favored girls or boys, and whether or not the difference is statistically significant (indicated by a darkened bar).

In the eighth grade, statistically significant differences favoring boys ranged from 12 points in Canada to 33 points in Israel, with boys averaging 20 or more points higher than girls in 12 countries. For most of these countries, and many others, the seventh-grade gender differences were somewhat smaller. In only seven countries were there no statistically significant differences in science achievement between boys and girls in both grades – Cyprus, the United States, Singapore, Australia, Romania, Thailand, and South Africa. This finding of a pervasive difference favoring boys in science is substantially more pronounced than in the TIMSS mathematics results for seventh and eighth grades, which indicate an international pattern of gender differences favoring males but show few significant differences for individual countries.[10] The TIMSS findings, however, are very consistent with the results from the second IEA science study conducted in 1983-84. For 14-year-olds (or students in the grade with the most 14-year-olds) that study found standard score differences favoring boys in all 23 of the participating countries.[11]

[10] Beaton, A.E., Mullis, I.V.S., Martin, M.O., Gonzalez, E.J., Kelly, D.L., and Smith, T.A. (1996). *Mathematics Achievement in the Middle School Years: The IEA's Third International Mathematics and Science Study (TIMSS).* Chestnut Hill, MA: Boston College.

[11] Postlethwaite, T.N. and Wiley, D.E. (1992). *The IEA Study of Science II: Science Achievement in Twenty-Three Countries.* New York, NY: Pergamon Press.

Table 1.6

Gender Differences in Achievement in the Sciences - Upper Grade (Eighth Grade*)

Country	Boys' Mean	Girls' Mean	Difference Absolute Value
Cyprus	461 (2.2)	465 (2.7)	4 (3.4)
† United States	539 (4.9)	530 (5.2)	9 (7.2)
Singapore	612 (6.7)	603 (7.0)	9 (9.7)
Russian Federation	544 (4.9)	533 (3.7)	11 (6.2)
Ireland	544 (6.6)	532 (5.2)	12 (8.4)
Canada	537 (3.1)	525 (3.7)	12 (4.8)
Norway	534 (3.2)	520 (2.0)	14 (3.8)
[1] Lithuania	484 (3.8)	470 (4.0)	14 (5.5)
Sweden	543 (3.4)	528 (3.4)	15 (4.8)
[1] Latvia (LSS)	492 (3.3)	478 (3.2)	15 (4.6)
† Belgium (Fl)	558 (6.0)	543 (5.8)	15 (8.4)
[1] Switzerland	529 (3.2)	514 (3.0)	15 (4.4)
Slovak Republic	552 (3.5)	537 (3.9)	15 (5.2)
Iceland	501 (5.1)	486 (4.6)	16 (6.9)
France	506 (2.7)	490 (3.3)	16 (4.3)
Japan	579 (2.4)	562 (2.0)	17 (3.1)
Iran, Islamic Rep.	477 (3.8)	461 (3.2)	17 (4.9)
Spain	526 (2.1)	508 (2.3)	18 (3.1)
Hungary	563 (3.1)	545 (3.4)	18 (4.7)
†[2] England	562 (5.6)	542 (4.2)	20 (7.1)
Portugal	490 (2.8)	468 (2.7)	22 (3.9)
Czech Republic	586 (4.2)	562 (5.8)	24 (7.2)
Korea	576 (2.7)	551 (2.3)	24 (3.6)
New Zealand	538 (5.4)	512 (5.2)	25 (7.6)
Hong Kong	535 (5.5)	507 (5.1)	27 (7.5)
Countries Not Satisfying Guidelines for Sample Participation Rates (See Appendix A for Details):			
Australia	550 (5.2)	540 (4.1)	10 (6.6)
Austria	566 (4.0)	549 (4.6)	18 (6.1)
Belgium (Fr)	479 (4.8)	463 (2.9)	16 (5.6)
Netherlands	570 (6.4)	550 (4.9)	20 (8.1)
Scotland	527 (6.4)	507 (4.7)	20 (7.9)
Countries Not Meeting Age/Grade Specifications (High Percentage of Older Students; See Appendix A for Details):			
Colombia	418 (7.3)	405 (4.6)	13 (8.6)
†[1] Germany	542 (5.9)	524 (4.9)	18 (7.6)
Romania	492 (5.3)	480 (5.0)	12 (7.3)
Slovenia	573 (3.2)	548 (3.2)	25 (4.5)
Countries With Unapproved Sampling Procedures at Classroom Level (See Appendix A for Details):			
Denmark	494 (3.6)	463 (3.9)	31 (5.3)
Greece	505 (2.6)	489 (3.1)	16 (4.0)
Thailand	524 (3.9)	526 (4.3)	2 (5.8)
Unapproved Sampling Procedures at Classroom Level and Not Meeting Other Guidelines (See Appendix A for Details):			
[1] Israel	545 (6.4)	512 (6.1)	33 (8.9)
South Africa	337 (9.5)	315 (6.0)	21 (11.3)

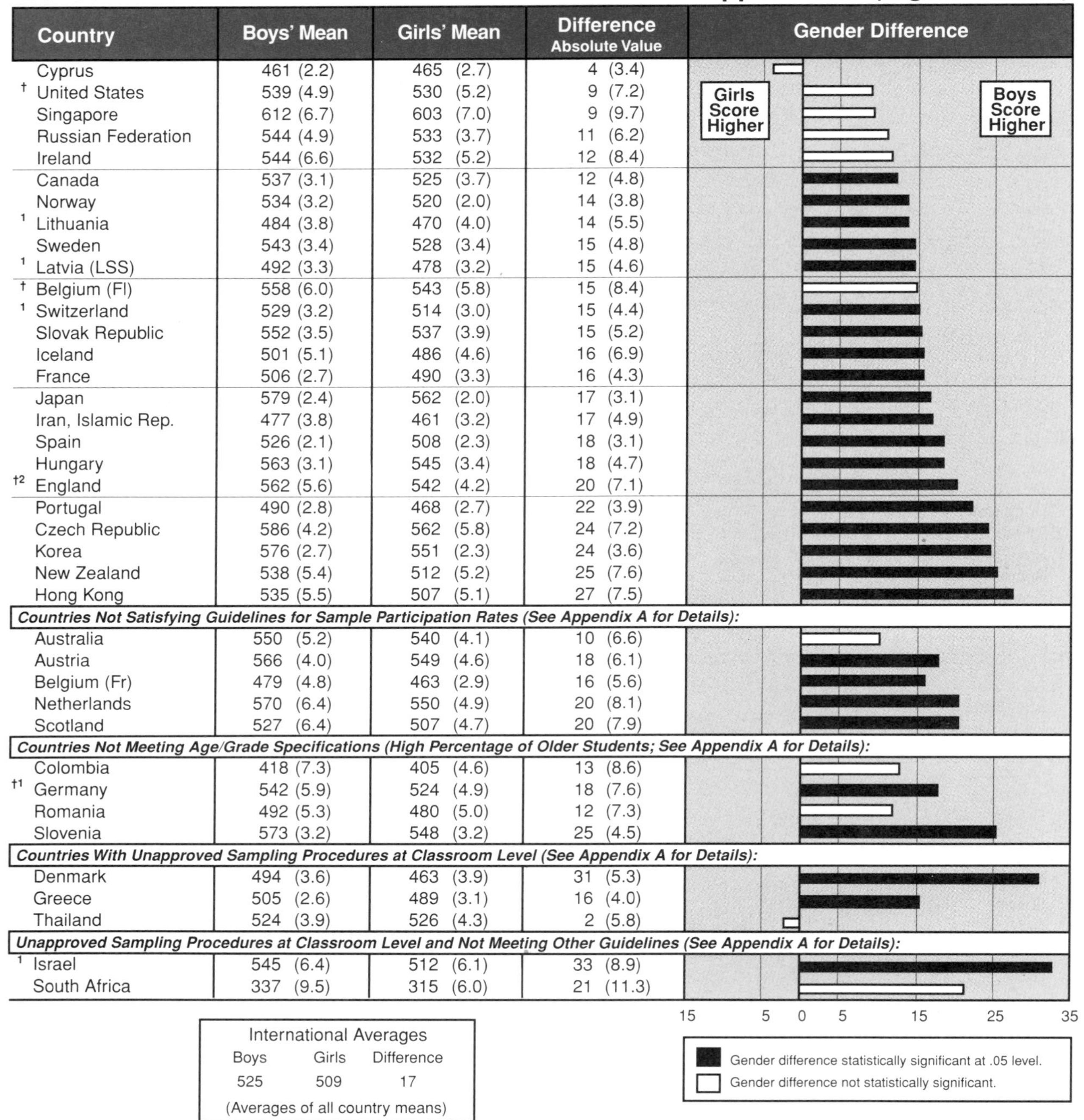

International Averages		
Boys	Girls	Difference
525	509	17

(Averages of all country means)

■ Gender difference statistically significant at .05 level.
□ Gender difference not statistically significant.

*Eighth grade in most countries; see Table 2 for information about the grades tested in each country.
†Met guidelines for sample participation rates only after replacement schools were included (see Appendix A for details).
[1]National Desired Population does not cover all of International Desired Population (see Table A.2). Because coverage falls below 65%, Latvia is annotated LSS for Latvian Speaking Schools only.
[2]National Defined Population covers less than 90 percent of National Desired Population (see Table A.2).
( ) Standard errors appear in parentheses. Because results are rounded to the nearest whole number, some totals may appear inconsistent.

SOURCE: IEA Third International Mathematics and Science Study (TIMSS), 1994-95.

Table 1.7

Gender Differences in Achievement in the Sciences - Lower Grade (Seventh Grade*)

Country	Boys' Mean	Girls' Mean	Difference (Absolute Value)	Gender Difference
Cyprus	420 (2.8)	420 (2.6)	0 (3.9)	
[1] Lithuania	405 (3.5)	401 (4.2)	5 (5.5)	
Singapore	548 (7.9)	541 (8.2)	7 (11.4)	
[1] Latvia (LSS)	440 (3.6)	430 (3.0)	9 (4.7)	
Sweden	493 (2.9)	484 (3.3)	10 (4.4)	
Japan	536 (2.6)	526 (1.9)	10 (3.2)	
Norway	489 (3.6)	477 (3.6)	12 (5.1)	
Iceland	468 (4.4)	456 (2.4)	12 (5.0)	
† United States	514 (6.3)	502 (5.8)	12 (8.6)	
Canada	505 (2.9)	493 (2.5)	12 (3.8)	
† Belgium (Fl)	536 (3.3)	521 (3.1)	14 (4.5)	
Hungary	525 (3.9)	510 (3.4)	15 (5.1)	
Iran, Islamic Rep.	443 (2.9)	428 (4.1)	15 (5.0)	
Portugal	436 (2.4)	420 (2.4)	16 (3.4)	
Ireland	504 (4.6)	487 (4.5)	17 (6.4)	
New Zealand	489 (4.3)	472 (3.7)	17 (5.7)	
Russian Federation	493 (5.3)	475 (3.8)	17 (6.5)	
[1] Switzerland	492 (2.9)	475 (2.9)	18 (4.1)	
† Scotland	477 (4.4)	459 (4.1)	18 (6.0)	
France	461 (3.1)	443 (3.0)	18 (4.3)	
Hong Kong	503 (6.6)	485 (5.8)	18 (8.7)	
Czech Republic	543 (3.2)	523 (4.1)	20 (5.2)	
† Belgium (Fr)	453 (3.6)	432 (3.5)	21 (5.0)	
Spain	487 (2.9)	467 (2.3)	21 (3.7)	
Slovak Republic	520 (4.0)	499 (3.1)	21 (5.1)	
†[2] England	522 (5.6)	500 (4.6)	22 (7.3)	
Korea	545 (2.8)	521 (3.2)	25 (4.2)	
Countries Not Satisfying Guidelines for Sample Participation Rates (See Appendix A for Details):				
Australia	507 (5.2)	502 (4.0)	4 (6.6)	
Austria	522 (4.3)	516 (4.1)	7 (6.0)	
Netherlands	523 (4.0)	512 (4.4)	11 (5.9)	
Countries Not Meeting Age/Grade Specifications (High Percentage of Older Students; See Appendix A for Details):				
Colombia	396 (3.8)	378 (4.4)	18 (5.8)	
†[1] Germany	505 (4.9)	495 (4.5)	10 (6.6)	
Romania	456 (4.7)	448 (4.9)	8 (6.7)	
Slovenia	539 (3.0)	521 (2.8)	18 (4.1)	
Countries With Unapproved Sampling Procedures at Classroom Level (See Appendix A for Details):				
Denmark	452 (3.0)	427 (2.8)	25 (4.1)	
Greece	452 (3.2)	446 (2.8)	6 (4.2)	
† South Africa	324 (6.4)	312 (5.2)	11 (8.3)	
Thailand	495 (3.3)	492 (3.5)	3 (4.8)	

Girls Score Higher — Boys Score Higher

15 5 0 5 15 25 35

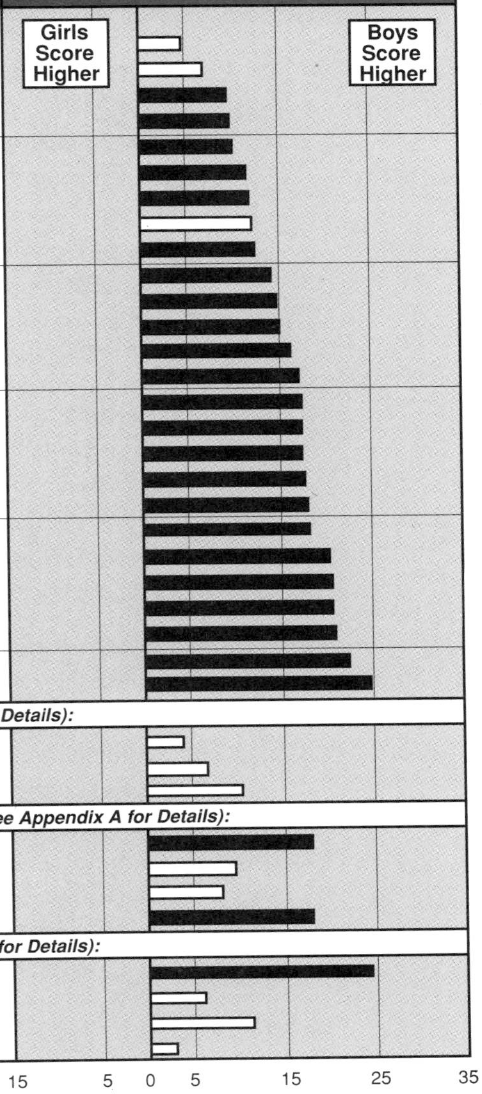

International Averages		
Boys	Girls	Difference
485	471	14

(Averages of all country means)

■ Gender difference statistically significant at .05 level.
□ Gender difference not statistically significant.

*Seventh grade in most countries; see Table 2 for information about the grades tested in each country.
†Met guidelines for sample participation rates only after replacement schools were included (see Appendix A for details).
[1]National Desired Population does not cover all of International Desired Population (see Table A.2). Because coverage falls below 65%, Latvia is annotated LSS for Latvian Speaking Schools only.
[2]National Defined Population covers less than 90 percent of National Desired Population (see Table A.2).
Standard errors appear in parentheses. Because results are rounded to the nearest whole number, some totals may appear inconsistent.

SOURCE: IEA Third International Mathematics and Science Study (TIMSS), 1994-95.

What Are the Differences in Median Performance at Age 13?

Testing the two adjacent grades with the most 13-year-olds provides the opportunity to compare achievement on the basis of age. For countries where the two grades tested contained at least 75% of the 13-year-olds, TIMSS estimated the median performance for this age group. Table 1.8 provides the estimated medians as well as the estimated distributions of 13-year-olds across grades.[12] For many countries, the two grades tested included practically all of their 13-year-olds (nine countries have at least 98%), whereas, for some others, there were substantial percentages outside these grades, mostly in the grade below.[13] For countries included in Table 1.8, Hong Kong, French-speaking Belgium, Hungary, France, Ireland, Latvia (LSS), Spain, Lithuania, Portugal, Austria, Romania, and Thailand had 10% or more of their 13-year-olds below the two grades tested.

The median is the point on the science scale that divides the higher-performing 50% of the students from the lower-performing 50%. Like the mean, the median provides a useful summary statistic on which to compare performance across countries. It is used instead of the mean in this table because it can be reliably estimated even when scores from some members of the population are not available[14] (that is, those 13-year-olds outside the tested grades).

Notwithstanding the additional difficulties in obtaining the achievement estimates for the age-based samples, the results for 13-year-olds appear quite consistent with those obtained for the two grade levels. The relative performance of countries in science achievement on the basis of median performance of 13-year-olds was quite similar to that based on average eighth-grade and/or seventh-grade performance, although there are a few exceptions. For example, the Czech Republic and Ireland did relatively less well among 13-year-olds compared to eighth-grade students. In general, however, the higher-performing countries in the eighth and seventh grades generally were those with higher-performing 13-year-olds.

[12] For information about the distribution of 13-year-olds in all countries, not just those with 75% coverage, see Table A.3 in Appendix A.

[13] The number of 13-year-olds below the lower grade and above the upper grade tested were extrapolated from the distribution of 13-year-olds in the tested grades.

[14] Because TIMSS sampled students in the two adjacent grades with the most 13-year-olds within a country, it was possible to estimate the median for the 13-year-old students when the two tested grades included at least an estimated 75% of the 13-year-olds in that country. To compute the median, TIMSS assumed that those 13-year-old students in the grades below the tested grades would score below the median and those in the grades above the tested grades would score above the median. The percentages assumed to be above and below the median were added to the tails of the distribution before calculating the median using the modified distribution.

Table 1.8

Median Achievement in the Sciences - 13-Year-Old Students

Includes Only Countries Where the Grades Tested Contained at Least 75% of the 13-Year-Olds

Country	Median	Lower Grade	Upper Grade	Estimated Distribution of 13-Year-Olds			
				Percent Below Lower Grade*	Percentage of 13-Year-Old Students Tested: Percent in Lower Grade	Percentage of 13-Year-Old Students Tested: Percent in Upper Grade	Percent Above Upper Grade*
Singapore	555 (6.8)	Secondary 1	Secondary 2	3.1%	82.2%	14.7%	0.0%
Korea	546 (2.3)	1st Grade Middle School	2nd Grade Middle School	1.5%	69.9%	28.2%	0.4%
† Belgium (Fl)	539 (2.4)	1A	2A & 2P	5.4%	45.6%	48.8%	0.2%
Japan	535 (3.0)	1st Grade Lower Secondary	2nd Grade Lower Secondary	0.3%	90.9%	8.8%	0.0%
Czech Republic	530 (3.4)	7	8	9.6%	73.3%	17.1%	0.0%
†[2] England	529 (4.2)	Year 8	Year 9	0.6%	57.2%	41.7%	0.5%
Hungary	521 (3.4)	7	8	10.5%	65.1%	24.2%	20.0%
Slovak Republic	513 (3.9)	7	8	4.7%	73.2%	22.1%	0.0%
Canada	511 (4.1)	7	8	8.1%	48.4%	42.9%	0.6%
Sweden	511 (2.8)	6	7	0.8%	44.9%	54.1%	0.1%
† United States	510 (5.1)	7	8	9.0%	57.8%	33.1%	0.2%
Norway	506 (2.9)	6	7	0.3%	42.5%	57.0%	0.2%
† Scotland	504 (4.2)	Secondary 1	Secondary 2	0.3%	24.0%	75.3%	0.5%
Russian Federation	503 (4.2)	7	8	4.5%	50.4%	44.3%	0.7%
Hong Kong	501 (4.9)	Secondary 1	Secondary 2	10.0%	44.2%	45.6%	0.2%
New Zealand	497 (4.6)	Form 2	Form 3	0.5%	51.7%	47.4%	0.4%
[1] Switzerland	495 (2.2)	6 or 7	7 or 8	8.3%	47.6%	43.9%	0.2%
Iceland	489 (3.4)	7	8	0.2%	16.5%	83.0%	0.4%
Ireland	486 (3.1)	1st Year	2nd Year	14.1%	69.0%	16.8%	0.2%
Spain	483 (3.1)	7 EGB	8 EGB	14.9%	45.8%	39.0%	0.3%
France	455 (3.7)	5ème	4ème (90%) or 4ème Technologique (10%)	20.5%	43.5%	34.7%	1.3%
† Belgium (Fr)	452 (3.9)	1A	2A & 2P	13.3%	40.6%	46.0%	0.2%
Cyprus	450 (2.9)	7	8	1.7%	27.7%	69.9%	0.7%
[1] Latvia (LSS)	436 (3.7)	7	8	14.3%	59.5%	26.0%	0.2%
Portugal	423 (3.4)	Grade 7	Grade 8	23.5%	44.1%	32.1%	0.3%
[1] Lithuania	413 (3.4)	7	8	10.1%	64.1%	25.6%	0.2%
Countries Not Satisfying Guidelines for Sample Participation Rates (See Appendix for Details):							
Australia	509 (3.9)	7 or 8	8 or 9	7.5%	63.6%	28.4%	0.5%
Austria	526 (3.4)	3. Klasse	4. Klasse	10.7%	62.4%	26.9%	0.0%
Bulgaria	543 (4.8)	7	8	3.2%	58.1%	36.9%	1.8%
Netherlands	522 (3.8)	Secondary 1	Secondary 2	9.8%	58.7%	31.2%	0.4%
Countries Not Meeting Age/Grade Specifications (High Percentage of Older Students; See Appendix for Details):							
Romania	414 (4.5)	7	8	23.9%	66.6%	9.3%	0.3%
Countries With Unapproved Sampling Procedures at Classroom Level (See Appendix for Details):							
Denmark	466 (2.8)	6	7	1.0%	34.6%	63.5%	0.9%
Greece	490 (2.9)	Secondary 1	Secondary 2	3.1%	11.2%	84.5%	1.2%
Thailand	485 (3.4)	Secondary 1	Secondary 2	18.0%	58.4%	19.6%	4.0%

*Data are extrapolated; students below the lower grade and above the upper grade were not included in the sample. Denmark, Sweden and Switzerland tested 3 grades.

†Met guidelines for sample participation rates only after replacement schools were included (see Appendix A for details).

[1] National Desired Population does not cover all of International Desired Population (see Table A.2). Because coverage falls below 65%, Latvia is annotated LSS for Latvian Speaking Schools only.

[2] National Defined Population covers less than 90 percent of National Desired Population (see Table A.2).

( ) Standard errors appear in parentheses. Because results are rounded, some totals may appear inconsistent.

SOURCE: IEA Third International Mathematics and Science Study (TIMSS), 1994-95.

Chapter 2

Average Achievement in the Science Content Areas

Recognizing that curricular differences exist between and within countries is an important aspect of IEA studies, and TIMSS attempted to measure achievement in different areas within the sciences that would be useful in relating achievement to curriculum. After much deliberation, the science test for the seventh and eighth grades was designed to enable reporting by five content areas in accordance with the TIMSS science framework.[1] These five content areas include:

- earth science
- life science
- physics
- chemistry
- environmental issues and the nature of science

Following the discussion in this chapter about differences in average achievement for the TIMSS countries across these content areas, Chapter 3 contains further information about the types of science items, including a range of four to six example items within each content area and the percent of correct responses on those items for each of the TIMSS countries.

How Does Achievement Differ Across Science Content Areas?

The results reported in Chapter 1 revealed substantial achievement differences among the participating countries on the TIMSS science test. This chapter examines the question of whether or not the participating countries achieved at the same level in each of the various content areas as they did on the science test as a whole.

Results in this chapter are based on the average percent of correct responses to items within each content area. Because of the additional resources and time that would have been required to use the more complex IRT scaling methodology that served as the basis for the overall achievement estimates in Chapter 1, TIMSS could not generate scale scores for the five content areas for this report.[2]

Tables 2.1 and 2.2 provide the average percent of correct responses to items in the different content areas for the eighth- and seventh-grade students, respectively. The countries are listed in order of their average percent correct across all items in the test. As indicated by the numbers of items overall and in each content area, the overall test contains the most items in life science and physics (both 30%) and the fewest

[1] Please see the test development section of Appendix A for more information about the process used to develop the TIMSS tests. Appendix B provides an analysis of the match between the test and curriculum in the different TIMSS countries and the effect of this match on the TIMSS results.

[2] TIMSS plans to generate IRT scale scores for the science content areas for future reports.

items in the category of environmental issues and the nature of science (10%). Thus, countries who performed very well in life science and physics were more likely to have higher scores overall.[3]

The results for the average percent correct across all science items are presented for each country primarily to provide a basis of comparison for performance in each of the content areas. For the purpose of comparing overall achievement between countries, it is preferable to use the results presented in Chapter 1.[4] It is interesting to note, however, that even though the relative standings of countries differ somewhat from Tables 1.1 and 1.2, the slight differences are well within the limits expected by sampling error and can be attributed to the differences in the methodologies used.

The data in each column show each country's average percent correct for items in that content area and the international average across all countries for the content area (shown as the last entry in the column). Looking down each of the columns, in turn, two findings become apparent. First, the countries that did well on the overall test generally did well in each of the various content areas, and those that did poorly overall also tended to do so in each of the content areas. There are differences between the relative standing of countries within each of the content areas and their overall standing, but these differences are small when sampling error is considered.

Second, the international averages show that the different content areas in the TIMSS test were not equally difficult for the students taking the test. The life science content area was the least difficult for both grades. On average, the items in this content area were answered correctly by 59% of the eighth-graders and 53% of the seventh-graders across countries. Internationally, the chemistry items (international averages of 51% at eighth grade, 43% at seventh grade) were the most difficult items for the students at both grades.

It is important to keep these differences in average difficulty in mind when reading across the rows of the table. These differences mean that for many countries, students will appear to have higher than average performance in life science and lower than average performance in chemistry. For example, even though the eighth-grade students in Japan performed above the international average in chemistry, they still performed less well in this area than they did on the test as a whole. That is, simply comparing performance across the rows gives an unclear picture of each country's relative performance across the content areas because the varying difficulty level of the items in each area has not been taken into account.

To facilitate more meaningful comparisons across rows, TIMSS has developed profiles of relative performance, which are shown for both grades in Table 2.3. These profiles are designed to show whether participating countries performed better or worse in some

[3] Table A.1 in Appendix A provides details about the distributions of items across the content areas, by format and score points (taking into account multi-part items and items scored for partial credit).

[4] The IRT scale scores provide better estimates of overall achievement, because they take the difficulty of items into account. This is important in a study such as TIMSS, where different students take overlapping but somewhat different sets of items.

Table 2.1

Average Percent Correct by Science Content Areas Upper Grade (Eighth Grade*)

	Country	Science Overall (135 items)	Earth Science (22 items)	Life Science (40 items)	Physics (40 items)	Chemistry (19 items)	Environmental Issues and the Nature of Science (14 items)
	Singapore	70 (1.0)	65 (1.1)	72 (1.0)	69 (0.8)	69 (1.2)	74 (1.1)
	Korea	66 (0.3)	63 (0.5)	70 (0.4)	65 (0.5)	63 (0.6)	64 (0.8)
	Japan	65 (0.3)	61 (0.4)	71 (0.4)	67 (0.3)	61 (0.5)	60 (0.7)
	Czech Republic	64 (0.8)	63 (1.2)	69 (0.8)	64 (0.7)	60 (1.2)	59 (1.1)
†2	England	61 (0.6)	59 (0.8)	64 (0.8)	62 (0.6)	55 (0.8)	65 (1.0)
	Hungary	61 (0.6)	60 (0.8)	65 (0.7)	60 (0.6)	60 (0.8)	53 (0.8)
†	Belgium (Fl)	60 (1.1)	62 (1.2)	64 (1.1)	61 (1.1)	51 (1.3)	58 (1.5)
	Slovak Republic	59 (0.6)	60 (0.7)	60 (0.6)	61 (0.6)	57 (0.8)	53 (0.9)
	Sweden	59 (0.6)	62 (0.7)	63 (0.7)	57 (0.5)	56 (0.7)	52 (0.8)
	Canada	59 (0.5)	58 (0.6)	62 (0.6)	59 (0.4)	52 (0.7)	61 (0.7)
	Ireland	58 (0.9)	61 (1.0)	60 (1.1)	56 (0.8)	54 (1.0)	60 (1.1)
†	United States	58 (1.0)	58 (1.0)	63 (1.1)	56 (0.8)	53 (1.2)	61 (1.0)
	Russian Federation	58 (0.8)	58 (0.8)	62 (0.7)	57 (0.9)	57 (1.3)	50 (0.8)
	New Zealand	58 (0.8)	56 (0.9)	60 (1.0)	58 (0.7)	53 (1.1)	59 (1.2)
	Norway	58 (0.4)	61 (0.6)	61 (0.5)	57 (0.4)	49 (0.6)	55 (0.8)
	Hong Kong	58 (1.0)	54 (1.0)	61 (1.0)	58 (0.9)	55 (1.0)	55 (1.3)
1	Switzerland	56 (0.5)	58 (0.6)	59 (0.6)	58 (0.5)	50 (0.7)	51 (0.8)
	Spain	56 (0.4)	57 (0.5)	58 (0.5)	55 (0.4)	51 (0.7)	53 (0.6)
	France	54 (0.6)	55 (0.8)	56 (0.8)	54 (0.5)	47 (0.9)	53 (0.9)
	Iceland	52 (0.9)	50 (1.2)	58 (1.0)	53 (0.9)	42 (0.8)	49 (1.0)
1	Latvia (LSS)	50 (0.6)	48 (0.8)	53 (0.7)	51 (0.7)	48 (0.8)	47 (1.0)
	Portugal	50 (0.6)	50 (0.7)	53 (0.6)	48 (0.5)	50 (0.9)	45 (0.8)
1	Lithuania	49 (0.7)	46 (0.9)	52 (0.9)	51 (0.7)	48 (0.9)	40 (1.0)
	Iran, Islamic Rep.	47 (0.6)	45 (0.6)	49 (0.6)	48 (0.7)	52 (0.8)	39 (1.1)
	Cyprus	47 (0.4)	46 (0.6)	49 (0.5)	46 (0.4)	45 (0.6)	46 (0.8)
	Countries Not Satisfying Guidelines for Sample Participation Rates (See Appendix A for Details):						
	Australia	60 (0.7)	57 (0.8)	63 (0.8)	60 (0.7)	54 (0.9)	62 (1.0)
	Austria	61 (0.7)	62 (0.8)	65 (0.7)	62 (0.7)	58 (1.1)	55 (0.9)
	Belgium (Fr)	50 (0.7)	50 (0.9)	55 (0.9)	51 (0.7)	41 (0.8)	46 (1.0)
	Bulgaria	62 (1.0)	58 (1.2)	64 (1.0)	60 (1.0)	65 (1.7)	59 (1.5)
	Netherlands	62 (1.0)	61 (1.4)	67 (1.4)	63 (0.9)	52 (0.9)	65 (1.6)
	Scotland	55 (1.0)	52 (1.0)	57 (1.1)	57 (0.8)	51 (1.3)	57 (1.4)
	Countries Not Meeting Age/Grade Specifications (High Percentage of Older Students; See Appendix A for Details):						
	Colombia	39 (0.8)	37 (0.8)	44 (0.9)	37 (0.8)	32 (1.0)	40 (1.1)
†1	Germany	58 (1.0)	57 (1.0)	63 (1.1)	57 (1.0)	54 (1.3)	51 (1.3)
	Romania	50 (0.8)	49 (1.0)	55 (1.0)	49 (0.8)	46 (1.0)	42 (1.0)
	Slovenia	62 (0.5)	64 (0.7)	65 (0.6)	61 (0.6)	56 (0.9)	59 (0.9)
	Countries With Unapproved Sampling Procedures at Classroom Level (See Appendix A for Details):						
	Denmark	51 (0.6)	49 (0.7)	56 (0.7)	53 (0.7)	41 (0.8)	47 (1.0)
	Greece	52 (0.5)	49 (0.6)	54 (0.6)	53 (0.5)	51 (0.5)	51 (1.0)
	Thailand	57 (0.9)	56 (1.0)	66 (0.9)	54 (0.7)	43 (1.2)	62 (1.1)
	Unapproved Sampling Procedures at Classroom Level and Not Meeting Other Guidelines (See Appendix A for Details):						
1	Israel	57 (1.1)	55 (1.1)	61 (1.1)	57 (1.1)	53 (1.5)	52 (1.6)
	Kuwait	43 (0.9)	43 (1.0)	45 (1.1)	43 (0.7)	40 (1.5)	39 (1.3)
	South Africa	27 (1.3)	26 (1.1)	27 (1.3)	27 (1.4)	26 (1.4)	26 (1.3)
	International Average Percent Correct	56 (0.1)	55 (0.1)	59 (0.1)	55 (0.1)	51 (0.2)	53 (0.2)

*Eighth grade in most countries; see Table 2 for information about the grades tested in each country.

†Met guidelines for sample participation rates only after replacement schools were included (see Appendix A for details).

[1]National Desired Population does not cover all of International Desired Population (see Table A.2). Because coverage falls below 65%, Latvia is annotated LSS for Latvian Speaking Schools only.

[2]National Defined Population covers less than 90 percent of National Desired Population (see Table A.2).

( ) Standard errors appear in parentheses. Because results are rounded to the nearest whole number, some totals may appear inconsistent.

SOURCE: IEA Third International Mathematics and Science Study (TIMSS), 1994-95.

Table 2.2

Average Percent Correct by Science Content Areas
Lower Grade (Seventh Grade*)

Country	Science Overall (135 items)	Earth Science (22 items)	Life Science (40 items)	Physics (40 items)	Chemistry (19 items)	Environmental Issues and the Nature of Science (14 items)
Singapore	61 (1.2)	60 (1.2)	62 (1.4)	63 (1.0)	57 (1.3)	62 (1.4)
Korea	61 (0.4)	59 (0.6)	65 (0.5)	63 (0.5)	54 (0.6)	61 (0.7)
Japan	59 (0.3)	56 (0.5)	64 (0.4)	63 (0.4)	49 (0.5)	53 (0.6)
Czech Republic	58 (0.8)	57 (0.9)	63 (0.7)	58 (0.7)	54 (1.1)	54 (1.1)
† Belgium (Fl)	57 (0.5)	60 (0.7)	61 (0.7)	58 (0.6)	46 (0.7)	54 (0.9)
†2 England	56 (0.6)	56 (0.8)	57 (0.7)	58 (0.7)	48 (1.0)	56 (0.9)
Hungary	56 (0.6)	54 (0.7)	61 (0.7)	54 (0.6)	54 (0.8)	48 (1.0)
Slovak Republic	54 (0.6)	55 (0.8)	56 (0.7)	55 (0.6)	50 (0.8)	50 (0.8)
† United States	54 (1.1)	54 (1.1)	59 (1.1)	51 (1.0)	48 (1.1)	56 (1.5)
Canada	54 (0.5)	53 (0.7)	57 (0.6)	54 (0.5)	46 (0.7)	56 (0.7)
Hong Kong	53 (1.2)	49 (1.1)	56 (1.2)	55 (1.1)	49 (1.3)	51 (1.6)
Ireland	52 (0.7)	56 (0.8)	52 (0.8)	51 (0.7)	47 (0.9)	54 (0.9)
Sweden	51 (0.5)	53 (0.6)	56 (0.7)	51 (0.6)	45 (0.7)	46 (0.8)
New Zealand	50 (0.7)	49 (0.7)	53 (0.8)	51 (0.7)	42 (0.8)	53 (1.1)
Norway	50 (0.6)	52 (0.8)	55 (0.7)	51 (0.7)	40 (0.8)	48 (0.9)
1 Switzerland	50 (0.4)	52 (0.6)	53 (0.5)	52 (0.5)	41 (0.5)	46 (0.7)
Russian Federation	50 (0.8)	54 (0.7)	54 (1.0)	50 (0.9)	42 (0.9)	43 (0.8)
Spain	49 (0.4)	52 (0.6)	53 (0.5)	48 (0.5)	43 (0.7)	47 (0.7)
† Scotland	48 (0.8)	46 (0.7)	49 (0.9)	51 (0.7)	41 (1.1)	50 (1.1)
Iceland	46 (0.6)	45 (0.7)	51 (0.6)	49 (0.8)	36 (1.0)	42 (1.1)
France	46 (0.6)	45 (0.7)	50 (0.7)	48 (0.6)	38 (0.7)	44 (1.0)
† Belgium (Fr)	45 (0.7)	46 (0.9)	49 (0.8)	46 (0.8)	37 (0.7)	40 (0.9)
Iran, Islamic Rep.	42 (0.6)	41 (0.8)	45 (0.8)	41 (0.7)	46 (0.9)	33 (1.0)
1 Latvia (LSS)	42 (0.5)	42 (0.7)	45 (0.6)	43 (0.6)	34 (0.8)	38 (0.9)
Portugal	41 (0.5)	46 (0.7)	46 (0.6)	39 (0.5)	34 (0.6)	37 (0.7)
Cyprus	40 (0.4)	39 (0.7)	42 (0.5)	39 (0.4)	38 (0.6)	40 (0.7)
1 Lithuania	38 (0.7)	39 (0.9)	40 (0.8)	40 (0.7)	28 (0.9)	32 (0.9)
Countries Not Satisfying Guidelines for Sample Participation Rates (See Appendix A for Details):						
Australia	54 (0.7)	52 (0.7)	56 (0.7)	55 (0.7)	46 (0.7)	56 (0.9)
Austria	55 (0.6)	55 (0.8)	60 (0.8)	55 (0.7)	51 (0.7)	49 (1.0)
Bulgaria	56 (1.0)	53 (1.0)	60 (1.1)	57 (1.2)	56 (1.3)	49 (1.3)
Netherlands	56 (0.7)	56 (0.9)	61 (0.8)	55 (0.8)	44 (0.8)	58 (1.3)
Countries Not Meeting Age/Grade Specifications (High Percentage of Older Students; See Appendix A for Details):						
Colombia	35 (0.7)	33 (0.8)	39 (0.8)	34 (0.8)	29 (0.7)	36 (0.8)
†1 Germany	53 (0.8)	52 (0.9)	58 (0.9)	53 (0.8)	47 (1.0)	46 (1.2)
Romania	45 (0.7)	44 (1.0)	51 (0.9)	44 (0.8)	41 (0.9)	37 (0.8)
Slovenia	57 (0.5)	59 (0.6)	60 (0.6)	55 (0.6)	55 (0.9)	55 (0.7)
Countries With Unapproved Sampling Procedures at Classroom Level (See Appendix A for Details):						
Denmark	44 (0.4)	42 (0.7)	49 (0.6)	47 (0.6)	34 (0.6)	39 (0.9)
Greece	45 (0.5)	43 (0.6)	48 (0.7)	44 (0.5)	41 (0.7)	43 (0.8)
† South Africa	26 (1.0)	26 (1.0)	26 (1.1)	26 (1.0)	23 (0.9)	25 (1.1)
Thailand	53 (0.8)	50 (0.8)	62 (0.9)	50 (0.7)	38 (0.8)	57 (1.1)
International Average Percent Correct	50 (0.1)	50 (0.1)	53 (0.1)	50 (0.1)	43 (0.1)	47 (0.2)

*Seventh grade in most countries; See Table 2 for information about the grades tested in each country.
†Met guidelines for sample participation rates only after replacement schools were included (see Appendix A for details).
[1]National Desired Population does not cover all of International Desired Population (see Table A.2). Because coverage falls below 65%, Latvia is annotated LSS for Latvian Speaking Schools only.
[2]National Defined Population covers less than 90 percent of National Desired Population (see Table A.2).
( ) Standard errors appear in parentheses. Because results are rounded to the nearest whole number, some totals may appear inconsistent.

SOURCE: IEA Third International Mathematics and Science Study (TIMSS), 1994-95.

content areas than they did on the test as a whole, after adjusting for the differing difficulty of the items in each of the content areas.[5] An up-arrow indicates that a country did significantly better in a content area than it did on the test as a whole, a down-arrow indicates significantly lower performance, and a circle indicates that the country's performance in a content area is not very different from its performance on the test as a whole.[6]

Table 2.3 reveals that many countries performed relatively better or worse in some content areas than they did overall. In fact, each country except Latvia, Israel, and Kuwait in the eighth grade and Belgium (French) in the seventh grade had at least one content area in which it did relatively better or worse than it did on the test as a whole. Although countries that did well in one content area tended to do well in others, there were still significant performance differences by content area among countries. For example, Japan, Hungary, Iceland, Germany, Romania, Denmark, and Thailand all performed relatively better in life science than they did on the test as a whole at both grades. Japan, Switzerland, Iceland, Lithuania, and Denmark performed relatively better in physics at both grades. A quite different set of countries – Hungary, the Slovak Republic, Hong Kong, Iran, Cyprus, and Greece – performed relatively better at both grades in chemistry. This is consistent with the existence of differing curricular patterns and approaches among countries as discussed in the curriculum analysis report, *Many Visions, Many Aims: A Cross-National Investigation of Curricular Intentions in School Science*.[7]

[5] Since the items in the different content areas varied in difficulty, the first step was to adjust the average percents to make all content areas equally difficult so that the comparisons would not reflect the various difficulties of the items in the content areas. The next step was to subtract these adjusted percentages for each content area from a country's average percentage over all five content areas. If the overall percentage of correct items by students in a country was the same as the adjusted average for that country for each of the content areas, then these differences would all be zero. The standard errors for these differences were computed, and then each difference was examined for statistical significance. This approach is similar to testing interaction terms in the analysis of variance. The jackknife method was used to compute the standard error of each interaction term. The significance level was adjusted using the Bonferroni method, assuming 5x41 (content areas by countries) comparisons at the eighth grade and 5x39 at the seventh grade.

[6] The statistics are not independent. That is, a country cannot do better (or worse) than its average on all scales, since a country's differences must add up to zero. However, it is possible for a country to have no statistically significant differences in performance.

[7] Schmidt, W.H., Raizen, S.A., Britton, E.D., Bianchi, L.J., and Wolfe, R.G. (in press). *Many Visions, Many Aims: A Cross-National Investigation of Curricular Intentions in School Science*. Dordrecht, The Netherlands: Kluwer Academic Publishers.

Table 2.3

Profiles of Relative Performance in Science Content Areas - Lower and Upper Grades (Seventh and Eighth Grades*) - Indicators of Statistically Significant Differences from Overall Percent Correct Adjusted for the Difficulty of the Content Areas

Seventh Grade						Eighth Grade					
Country	Earth Science	Life Science	Physics	Chemistry	Environmental Issues and the Nature of Science	Country	Earth Science	Life Science	Physics	Chemistry	Environmental Issues and the Nature of Science
Singapore	▼	▼	●	●	▲	Singapore	▼	▼	▼	▲	▲
Korea	▼	●	▲	●	▲	Korea	▼	●	●	▲	●
Japan	▼	▲	▲	▼	▼	Japan	▼	▲	▲	●	▼
Czech Republic	●	▲	●	▲	▼	Czech Republic	●	●	●	●	▼
† Belgium (Fl)	▲	●	●	▼	●	†[2] England	●	●	●	▼	▲
†[2] England	●	▼	●	●	▲	Hungary	●	▲	●	▲	▼
Hungary	●	▲	▼	▲	▼	† Belgium (Fl)	▲	●	●	▼	●
Slovak Republic	●	▼	●	▲	▼	Slovak Republic	●	▼	▲	▲	▼
† United States	●	●	▼	●	▲	Sweden	▲	●	▼	●	▼
Canada	●	●	●	▼	▲	Canada	●	●	●	▼	▲
Hong Kong	▼	●	▲	▲	●	Ireland	▲	▼	▼	●	▲
Ireland	▲	▼	▼	●	▲	† United States	●	●	▼	▼	▲
Sweden	▲	●	●	●	▼	Russian Federation	●	●	●	▲	▼
New Zealand	●	▼	●	▼	▲	New Zealand	▼	●	●	●	▲
Norway	▲	●	●	▼	●	Norway	▲	●	●	▼	●
[1] Switzerland	▲	●	▲	▼	●	Hong Kong	▼	●	●	▲	●
Russian Federation	▲	●	●	●	▼	[1] Switzerland	▲	●	▲	▼	▼
Spain	▲	●	▼	●	●	Spain	▲	●	●	●	●
† Scotland	▼	▼	▲	●	▲	France	▲	▼	●	▼	●
Iceland	●	▲	▲	▼	●	Iceland	●	▲	▲	▼	●
France	●	●	▲	●	●	[1] Latvia (LSS)	●	●	●	●	●
† Belgium (Fr)	●	●	●	●	●	Portugal	●	●	▼	▲	▼
Iran, Islamic Rep.	●	●	●	▲	▼	[1] Lithuania	●	●	▲	▲	▼
[1] Latvia (LSS)	●	●	▲	●	●	Iran, Islamic Rep.	▼	▼	●	▲	▼
Portugal	▲	●	▼	●	▼	Cyprus	●	▼	▼	▲	●
Cyprus	●	▼	▼	▲	●						
[1] Lithuania	▲	●	▲	▼	▼						
Countries Not Satisfying Guidelines for Sample Participation Rates (See Appendix A for Details):											
Australia	▼	▼	●	▼	▲	Australia	▼	●	●	▼	▲
Austria	●	●	●	▲	▼	Austria	●	●	●	●	▼
Bulgaria	▼	●	●	▲	▼	Belgium (Fr)	●	▲	▲	▼	●
Netherlands	●	▲	●	▼	▲	Bulgaria	▼	●	▼	▲	●
						Netherlands	●	●	●	▼	▲
						Scotland	▼	▼	●	●	▲
Countries Not Meeting Age/Grade Specifications (High Percentage of Older Students; See Appendix A for Details):											
Colombia	▼	●	●	●	▲	Colombia	●	▲	▼	▼	▲
†[1] Germany	●	▲	●	●	▼	†[1] Germany	●	▲	●	●	▼
Romania	●	▲	●	▲	▼	Romania	●	▲	●	●	▼
Slovenia	●	●	▼	▲	●	Slovenia	▲	●	●	●	●
Countries With Unapproved Sampling Procedures at Classroom Level (See Appendix A for Details):											
Denmark	●	▲	▲	▼	●	Denmark	●	▲	▲	▼	●
Greece	▼	●	▼	▲	●	Greece	▼	▼	●	▲	●
† South Africa	●	▼	●	▲	●	Thailand	●	▲	▼	▼	▲
Thailand	▼	▲	▼	▼	▲						
Unapproved Sampling Procedures at Classroom Level and Not Meeting Other Guidelines (See Appendix A for Details):											
						[1] Israel	●	●	●	●	●
						Kuwait	●	●	●	●	●
						South Africa	●	▼	●	▲	●

▲ = Significantly higher than overall average ● = No significant difference from overall average ▼ = Significantly lower than overall average

*Seventh and eighth grades in most countries; see Table 2 for information about the grades tested in each country.

†Met guidelines for sample participation rates only after replacement schools were included (see Appendix A for details).

[1]National Desired Population does not cover all of International Desired Population (see Table A.2). Because coverage falls below 65%, Latvia is annotated LSS for Latvian Speaking Schools only.

[2]National Defined Population covers less than 90 percent of National Desired Population (see Table A.2).

SOURCE: IEA Third International Mathematics and Science Study (TIMSS), 1994-95.

What Are the Increases in Achievement Between the Lower and Upper Grades?

Figure 2.1, which profiles the increases in average percent correct between the seventh and eighth grade for each country across content areas, also reflects these curricular differences. The countries are presented in descending order by the amount of overall increase between the grades, starting with Lithuania, Portugal, Latvia (LSS), and the Russian Federation, all of which had increases of 8% to 11% in overall percentage correct. As an aid in the comparison between the increase for the science test overall and each of the five content areas, a dashed line indicating the overall between-grade increase is shown in each country's profile.

These results show that for the majority of countries, the performance differences between grades vary across content areas, most likely reflecting a greater emphasis in the eighth-grade curriculum on some areas compared to others. There were several countries, however, with moderate between-grade increases that were more comparable across all content areas, including Cyprus, the Czech Republic, Hungary, Canada, the United States, and Denmark, for example. The chemistry content area has the largest increase from seventh to eighth grade for a large number of countries. This is particularly noticeable for Lithuania, Portugal, Latvia (LSS), and the Russian Federation, where large increases between 14% and 20% were observed for chemistry. For most countries, the increases in life science were similar to the overall between-grade increases in science as were the increases for the environmental issues and nature of science items. Several lower increases than overall were observed in earth science and physics, indicating that some countries may place less emphasis on these content areas in the eighth grade.

Figure 2.1

Difference in Average Percent Correct Between Lower and Upper Grades (Seventh and Eighth Grades*) Overall and in Science Content Areas

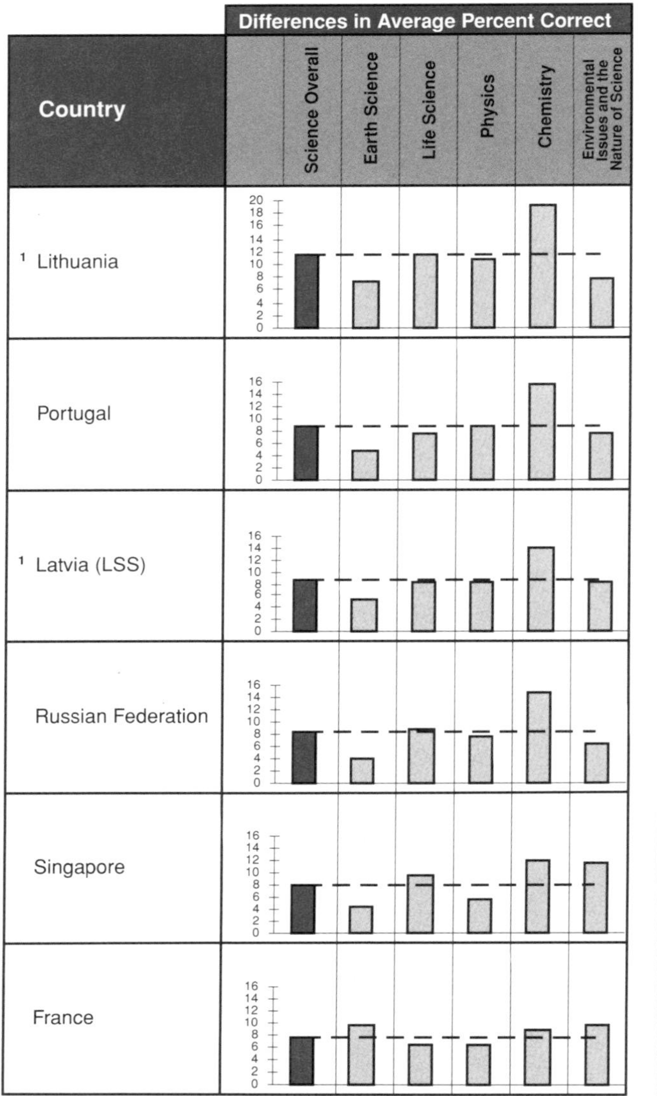

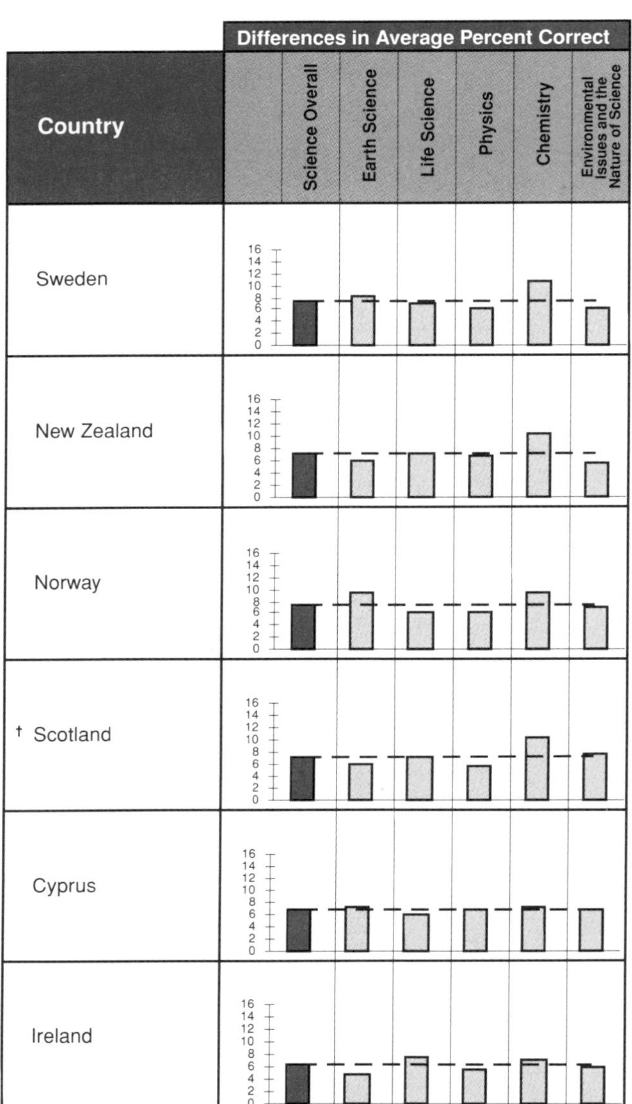

Legend:

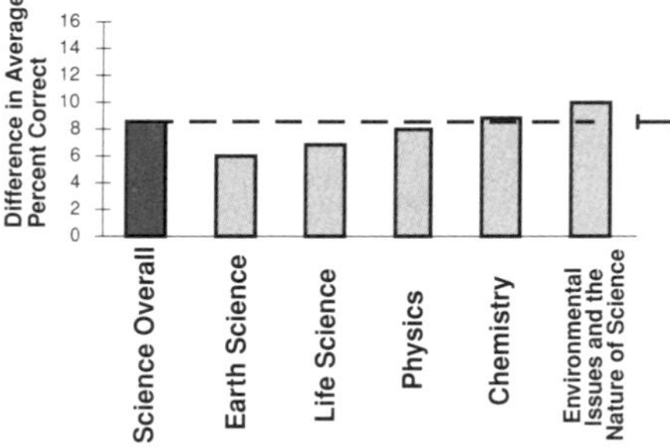

Dashed line indicates difference in science overall, in that country.

*Seventh and eighth grades in most countries; see Table 2 for information about the grades tested in each country.
†Met guidelines for sample participation rates only after replacement schools were included (see Appendix A for details).
[1]National Desired Population does not cover all of International Desired Population (see Table A.2). Because coverage falls below 65%, Latvia is annotated LSS for Latvian Speaking Schools only.
[2]National Defined Population covers less than 90 percent of National Desired Population (see Table A.2).
Because results are rounded to the nearest whole number, some totals may appear inconsistent.

SOURCE: IEA Third International Mathematics and Science Study (TIMSS), 1994-95.

Figure 2.1 (Continued-2)

Difference in Average Percent Correct Between Lower and Upper Grades (Seventh and Eighth Grades*) Overall and in Science Content Areas

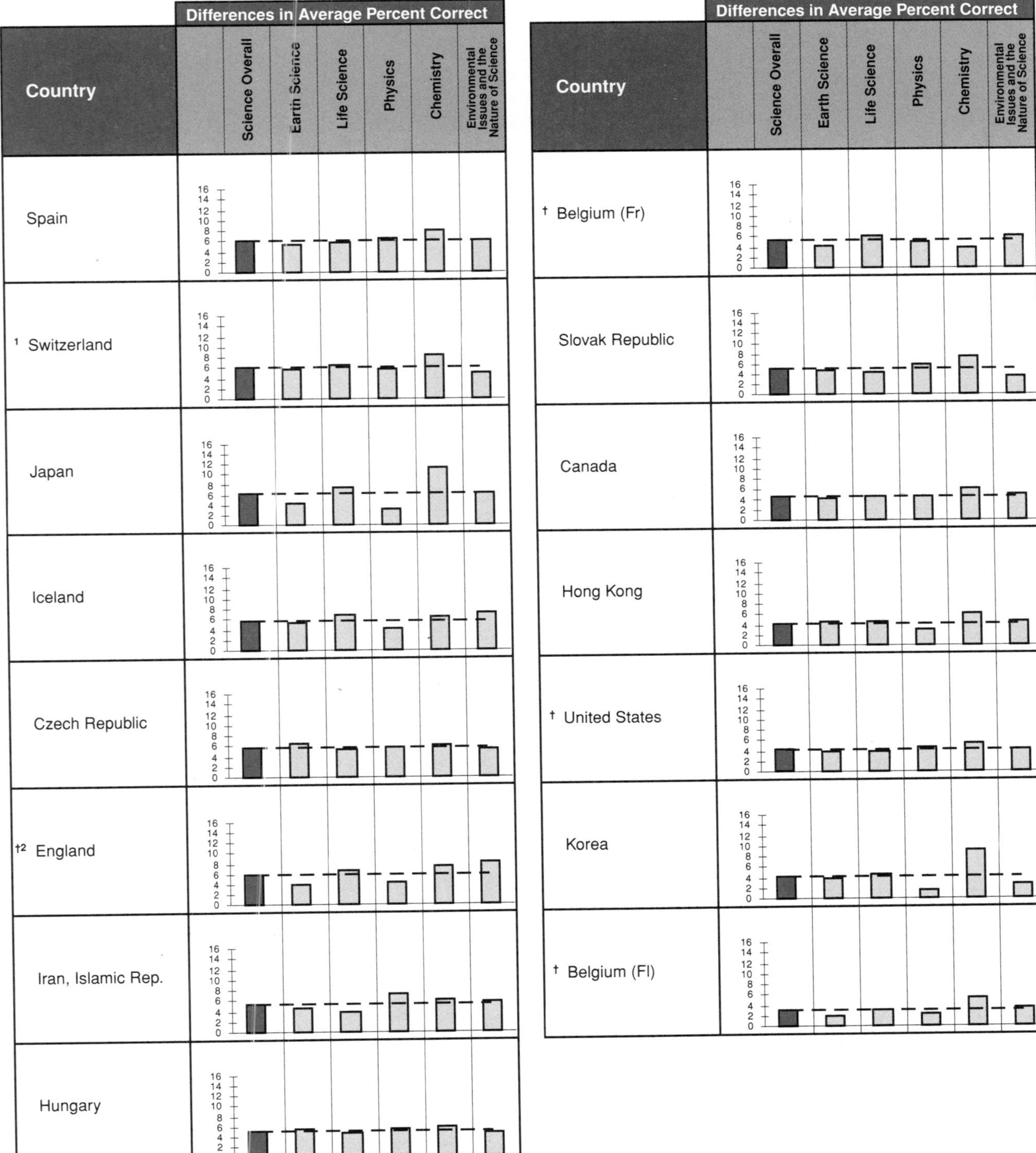

*Seventh and eighth grades in most countries; see Table 2 for information about the grades tested in each country.
†Met guidelines for sample participation rates only after replacement schools were included (see Appendix A for details).
1National Desired Population does not cover all of International Desired Population (see Table A.2). Because coverage falls below 65%, Latvia is annotated LSS for Latvian Speaking Schools only.
2National Defined Population covers less than 90 percent of National Desired Population (see Table A.2).
Because results are rounded to the nearest whole number, some totals may appear inconsistent.

SOURCE: IEA Third International Mathematics and Science Study (TIMSS), 1994-95.

Figure 2.1 (Continued-3)

Difference in Average Percent Correct Between Lower and Upper Grades (Seventh and Eighth Grades*) Overall and in Science Content Areas

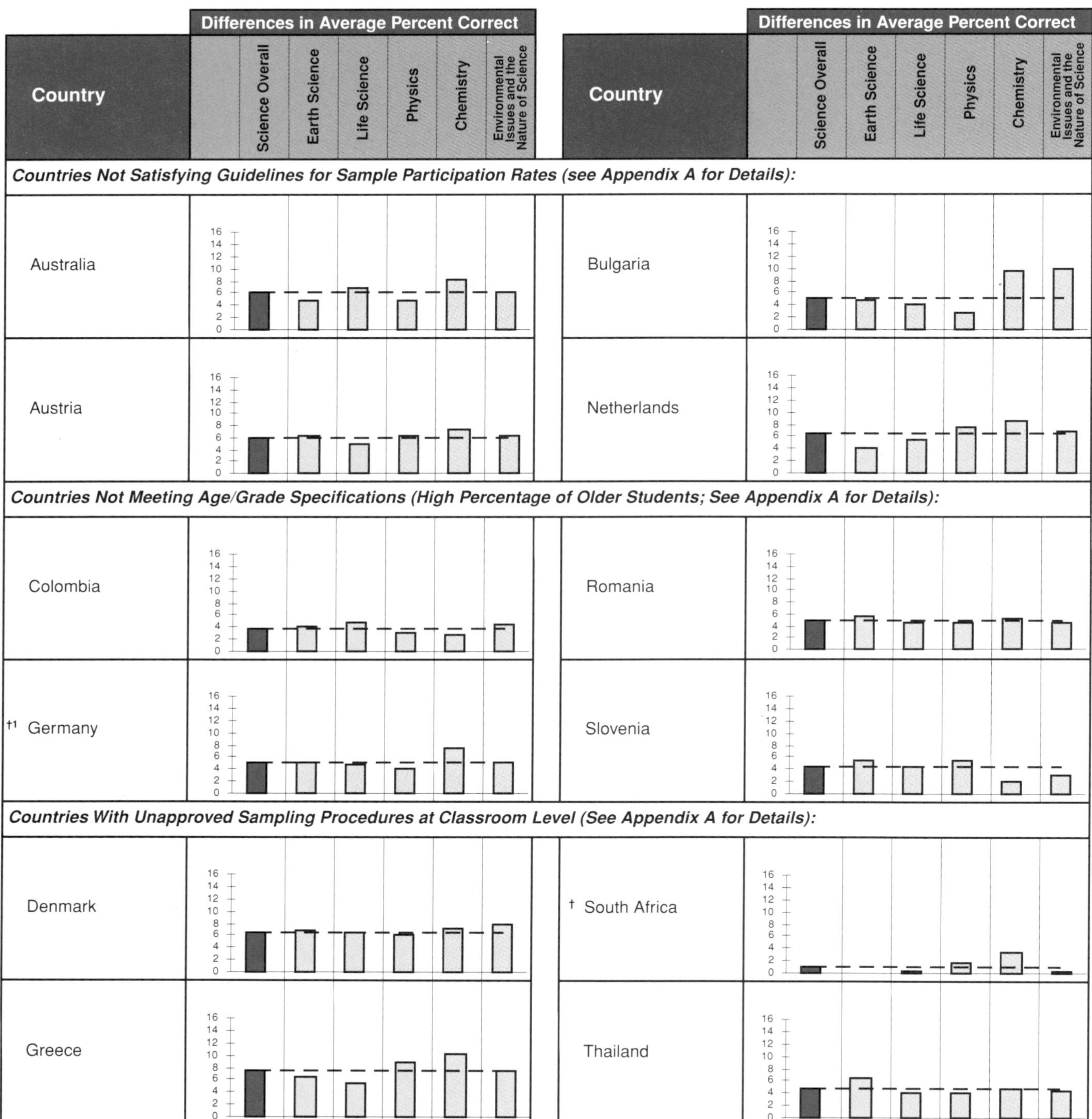

*Seventh and eighth grades in most countries; see Table 2 for information about the grades tested in each country.
†Met guidelines for sample participation rates only after replacement schools were included (see Appendix A for details).
[1]National Desired Population does not cover all of International Desired Population (see Table A.2). Because coverage falls below 65%, Latvia is annotated LSS for Latvian Speaking Schools only.
[2]National Defined Population covers less than 90 percent of National Desired Population (see Table A.2).
Because results are rounded to the nearest whole number, some totals may appear inconsistent.

SOURCE: IEA Third International Mathematics and Science Study (TIMSS), 1994-95.

What Are the Gender Differences in Achievement for the Content Areas?

Tables 2.4 and 2.5 present the gender differences for the science content areas for eighth-grade students and seventh grade-students, respectively. The countries are listed in descending order by overall percent correct. Although these overall differences are comparable to those for the TIMSS science scale discussed in Chapter 1, the reduced number of statistically significant differences reinforces the idea of less precision in the percent-correct metric.

The science content area data reveal that the gender differences vary depending on the science subject. In both the seventh and eighth grades, gender differences in earth science, physics, and chemistry reflected advantages for boys. In earth science, the boys had significantly higher averages than girls in 18 countries at the eighth grade and in 19 countries at the seventh grade. In physics, the corresponding results revealed advantages for boys in 25 and 23 countries. In chemistry, boys out-performed girls in 16 countries at the eighth grade and 20 countries at the seventh grade. For the remaining countries except Thailand, even though the differences were not statistically significant, the direction of the differences favored boys in all three content areas at both grades.

In life science and for the items covering environmental issues and the nature of science, girls and boys had similar performances at both grades. In life science, there were very few gender differences in average performance. In Spain, boys had significantly higher achievement than girls at both grades. Also, seventh-grade boys did better than girls in Korea. However, at the eighth grade, girls did better than boys in Cyprus. For the items in the area of environmental issues and the nature of science, eighth-grade boys had higher achievement than girls in two countries – the Czech Republic and Korea. At the seventh grade, there were no significant differences in average performance for this content area.

IEA's second science study conducted in 1983-84 found similar results for 14-year-olds in the content areas. There were negligible gender differences in biology, larger, but still small differences favoring boys in chemistry and earth science, and moderate to large advantages for boys in physics.[8]

[8] Keeves, J.P. and Kotte, D. (1992). "Disparities Between the Sexes in Science Education: 1970-84" in J.P. Keeves (ed.), *The IEA Study of Science (Vol.) III: Changes in Science Education and Achievement: 1970 to 1984.* New York, NY: Pergamon Press.

Table 2.4

Average Percent Correct for Boys and Girls by Science Content Areas Upper Grade (Eighth Grade*)

Country	Science Overall		Earth Science		Life Science	
	Boys	Girls	Boys	Girls	Boys	Girls
[†] Belgium (Fl)	62 (1.7)	59 (1.5)	64 (2.0)	60 (1.5)	64 (1.7)	64 (1.5)
Canada	60 (0.6)	58 (0.6)	59 (0.8)	56 (0.8)	62 (0.8)	63 (0.8)
Cyprus	46 (0.4)	47 (0.6)	47 (0.7)	46 (0.9)	47 (0.6)	▲ 51 (0.7)
Czech Republic	▲ 67 (0.8)	61 (1.1)	66 (1.1)	60 (1.6)	70 (0.9)	67 (1.2)
[†2] England	63 (1.0)	60 (0.7)	61 (1.2)	58 (0.9)	65 (1.2)	63 (1.1)
France	▲ 55 (0.7)	52 (0.7)	57 (0.9)	53 (1.0)	57 (0.8)	55 (0.9)
Hong Kong	▲ 60 (1.1)	55 (1.1)	▲ 57 (1.2)	51 (1.1)	63 (1.2)	59 (1.2)
Hungary	▲ 63 (0.7)	59 (0.7)	▲ 62 (1.0)	57 (0.9)	66 (0.8)	65 (0.8)
Iceland	53 (1.2)	51 (0.9)	52 (1.5)	48 (1.3)	58 (1.2)	58 (1.2)
Iran, Islamic Rep.	▲ 49 (0.8)	45 (0.8)	▲ 47 (0.8)	42 (0.9)	50 (0.9)	47 (0.9)
Ireland	60 (1.3)	57 (1.0)	64 (1.4)	59 (1.2)	60 (1.4)	60 (1.3)
Japan	▲ 67 (0.5)	64 (0.4)	▲ 64 (0.5)	58 (0.6)	71 (0.5)	70 (0.5)
Korea	▲ 67 (0.5)	64 (0.5)	▲ 65 (0.7)	60 (0.7)	71 (0.7)	69 (0.7)
[1] Latvia (LSS)	▲ 52 (0.8)	48 (0.6)	▲ 51 (1.1)	45 (1.0)	54 (0.9)	52 (0.8)
[1] Lithuania	▲ 51 (0.8)	47 (0.8)	▲ 49 (1.1)	44 (1.1)	52 (1.0)	52 (1.0)
New Zealand	60 (1.0)	56 (1.0)	▲ 59 (1.1)	52 (1.1)	61 (1.2)	60 (1.1)
Norway	59 (0.6)	56 (0.4)	▲ 64 (0.8)	59 (0.7)	60 (0.8)	62 (0.6)
Portugal	▲ 52 (0.7)	48 (0.6)	▲ 53 (1.0)	47 (0.8)	55 (0.8)	52 (0.8)
Russian Federation	60 (0.9)	57 (0.7)	61 (0.9)	57 (0.9)	62 (0.9)	63 (0.7)
Singapore	71 (1.2)	69 (1.1)	66 (1.4)	63 (1.3)	72 (1.2)	71 (1.2)
Slovak Republic	▲ 62 (0.6)	57 (0.7)	▲ 62 (0.9)	58 (0.9)	61 (0.7)	59 (0.8)
Spain	▲ 58 (0.5)	54 (0.5)	▲ 59 (0.7)	54 (0.7)	▲ 60 (0.7)	57 (0.6)
Sweden	▲ 60 (0.6)	57 (0.6)	63 (0.8)	60 (0.8)	63 (0.7)	63 (0.8)
[1] Switzerland	▲ 58 (0.6)	54 (0.5)	60 (0.9)	56 (0.7)	59 (0.8)	59 (0.7)
[†] United States	59 (1.0)	57 (1.0)	60 (1.0)	56 (1.1)	63 (1.2)	63 (1.1)
Countries Not Satisfying Guidelines for Sample Participation Rates (See Appendix A for Details):						
Australia	61 (1.0)	59 (0.8)	59 (1.0)	55 (0.9)	62 (1.0)	64 (0.8)
Austria	63 (0.8)	60 (0.8)	▲ 65 (0.9)	59 (1.0)	65 (0.8)	64 (0.9)
Belgium (Fr)	52 (1.0)	49 (0.7)	52 (1.3)	48 (0.9)	55 (1.1)	55 (1.0)
Netherlands	64 (1.2)	60 (1.1)	64 (1.6)	58 (1.4)	67 (1.4)	66 (1.6)
Scotland	57 (1.2)	53 (0.9)	▲ 56 (1.2)	48 (1.0)	58 (1.3)	55 (1.1)
Countries Not Meeting Age/Grade Specifications (High Percentage of Older Students; See Appendix A for Details):						
Colombia	40 (1.4)	37 (0.8)	39 (1.4)	35 (1.1)	45 (1.6)	42 (1.0)
[†1] Germany	59 (1.2)	57 (1.0)	58 (1.1)	56 (1.3)	63 (1.3)	63 (1.1)
Romania	51 (0.9)	49 (0.9)	50 (1.1)	48 (1.1)	55 (1.1)	55 (1.1)
Slovenia	▲ 64 (0.6)	59 (0.7)	▲ 67 (0.8)	62 (0.9)	66 (0.7)	63 (0.8)
Countries With Unapproved Sampling Procedures at Classroom Level (See Appendix A for Details):						
Denmark	▲ 54 (0.6)	48 (0.8)	▲ 53 (0.9)	44 (0.9)	57 (0.9)	55 (1.0)
Greece	▲ 54 (0.6)	50 (0.6)	▲ 51 (0.8)	46 (0.7)	55 (0.7)	53 (0.7)
Thailand	57 (0.9)	58 (1.0)	56 (1.2)	56 (1.1)	65 (1.0)	67 (1.1)
Unapproved Sampling Procedures at Classroom Level and Not Meeting Other Guidelines (See Appendix A for Details):						
[1] Israel	▲ 61 (1.2)	54 (1.1)	▲ 59 (1.4)	52 (1.3)	63 (1.5)	59 (1.4)
South Africa	28 (1.8)	25 (1.2)	28 (1.6)	24 (1.0)	29 (1.9)	25 (1.3)

▲ = Difference from other gender statistically significant at .05 level, adjusted for multiple comparisons

*Eighth grade in most countries; See Table 2 for information about the grades tested in each country.

[†]Met guidelines for sample participation rates only after replacement schools were included (see Appendix A for details).

[1]National Desired Population does not cover all of International Desired Population (see Table A.2). Because coverage falls below 65%, Latvia is annotated LSS for Latvian Speaking Schools only.

[2]National Defined Population covers less than 90 percent of National Desired Population (see Table A.2).

( ) Standard errors appear in parentheses. Because results are rounded to the nearest whole number, some totals may appear inconsistent.

SOURCE: IEA Third International Mathematics and Science Study (TIMSS), 1994-95.

Table 2.4 (Continued)

Average Percent Correct for Boys and Girls by Science Content Areas Upper Grade (Eighth Grade*)

Country	Physics		Chemistry		Environmental Issues and the Nature of Science	
	Boys	Girls	Boys	Girls	Boys	Girls
† Belgium (Fl)	63 (1.7)	58 (1.4)	53 (1.6)	50 (1.8)	59 (1.6)	57 (2.3)
Canada	▲ 61 (0.6)	57 (0.5)	53 (0.9)	50 (0.9)	62 (0.8)	60 (1.0)
Cyprus	47 (0.6)	45 (0.7)	45 (0.9)	44 (0.8)	45 (1.0)	47 (0.9)
Czech Republic	▲ 67 (0.8)	60 (0.9)	▲ 64 (1.2)	56 (1.7)	▲ 64 (1.2)	55 (1.6)
†2 England	63 (1.0)	60 (0.8)	57 (1.2)	53 (1.4)	65 (1.6)	64 (1.2)
France	▲ 57 (0.7)	52 (0.7)	49 (1.2)	45 (1.2)	54 (1.3)	53 (1.1)
Hong Kong	▲ 62 (0.9)	54 (1.1)	▲ 57 (1.3)	52 (1.2)	57 (1.6)	53 (1.5)
Hungary	▲ 63 (0.7)	56 (0.8)	▲ 62 (0.9)	58 (1.0)	55 (1.2)	52 (1.1)
Iceland	54 (1.6)	52 (0.9)	43 (1.1)	41 (1.4)	49 (1.8)	48 (1.2)
Iran, Islamic Rep.	▲ 51 (1.0)	44 (0.8)	53 (1.0)	51 (1.1)	40 (1.4)	37 (1.5)
Ireland	▲ 59 (1.3)	54 (1.0)	56 (1.5)	52 (1.2)	60 (1.6)	60 (1.3)
Japan	▲ 68 (0.5)	65 (0.4)	▲ 62 (0.7)	59 (0.6)	61 (0.9)	58 (0.8)
Korea	▲ 67 (0.7)	62 (0.6)	65 (0.8)	61 (0.9)	▲ 66 (1.0)	61 (1.1)
1 Latvia (LSS)	▲ 55 (1.0)	48 (0.7)	50 (1.2)	46 (1.1)	48 (1.3)	46 (1.2)
1 Lithuania	▲ 56 (0.9)	48 (0.7)	50 (1.1)	45 (1.1)	41 (1.4)	38 (1.2)
New Zealand	▲ 60 (0.8)	55 (0.8)	▲ 56 (1.3)	50 (1.4)	60 (1.5)	58 (1.3)
Norway	▲ 59 (0.6)	55 (0.5)	▲ 52 (0.9)	47 (0.8)	56 (1.0)	55 (1.1)
Portugal	▲ 52 (0.6)	45 (0.6)	▲ 54 (1.1)	46 (1.0)	45 (1.1)	45 (1.1)
Russian Federation	▲ 60 (1.0)	55 (0.9)	60 (1.6)	55 (1.2)	49 (1.1)	50 (1.0)
Singapore	71 (1.0)	67 (1.0)	70 (1.6)	68 (1.5)	74 (1.3)	74 (1.4)
Slovak Republic	▲ 65 (0.7)	58 (0.8)	▲ 61 (1.0)	54 (1.0)	55 (1.1)	52 (1.1)
Spain	▲ 58 (0.5)	52 (0.6)	▲ 54 (0.9)	49 (0.8)	53 (0.8)	53 (1.0)
Sweden	▲ 60 (0.6)	54 (0.7)	▲ 59 (1.0)	52 (0.7)	53 (1.0)	51 (0.9)
1 Switzerland	▲ 60 (0.7)	55 (0.6)	▲ 53 (0.9)	46 (0.9)	53 (1.0)	49 (1.0)
† United States	57 (0.9)	54 (0.9)	55 (1.3)	51 (1.2)	59 (1.2)	62 (1.2)
Countries Not Satisfying Guidelines for Sample Participation Rates (See Appendix A for Details):						
Australia	62 (0.9)	58 (0.8)	56 (1.2)	52 (1.0)	62 (1.3)	63 (1.1)
Austria	▲ 64 (0.8)	59 (0.9)	61 (1.3)	56 (1.5)	56 (1.1)	54 (1.3)
Belgium (Fr)	53 (1.1)	50 (0.6)	44 (1.1)	39 (1.1)	47 (1.6)	46 (1.1)
Netherlands	▲ 65 (1.2)	60 (1.0)	▲ 56 (1.0)	49 (1.1)	66 (2.1)	65 (1.9)
Scotland	59 (1.0)	55 (0.9)	▲ 55 (1.7)	47 (1.1)	58 (1.7)	56 (1.6)
Countries Not Meeting Age/Grade Specifications (High Percentage of Older Students; See Appendix A for Details):						
Colombia	39 (1.5)	35 (0.9)	34 (1.6)	30 (1.0)	41 (2.0)	40 (1.0)
†1 Germany	60 (1.1)	55 (1.0)	57 (1.6)	52 (1.6)	50 (1.6)	52 (1.3)
Romania	51 (0.9)	46 (1.0)	48 (1.2)	45 (1.1)	42 (1.2)	41 (1.3)
Slovenia	▲ 64 (0.7)	58 (0.8)	59 (1.1)	54 (1.1)	60 (1.1)	57 (1.1)
Countries With Unapproved Sampling Procedures at Classroom Level (See Appendix A for Details):						
Denmark	▲ 57 (0.7)	49 (0.9)	▲ 44 (1.1)	38 (1.1)	50 (1.4)	44 (1.3)
Greece	▲ 55 (0.6)	50 (0.6)	▲ 54 (0.7)	49 (0.7)	51 (1.1)	51 (1.1)
Thailand	54 (0.8)	54 (0.9)	42 (1.2)	44 (1.5)	62 (1.2)	62 (1.3)
Unapproved Sampling Procedures at Classroom Level and Not Meeting Other Guidelines (See Appendix A for Details):						
1 Israel	▲ 62 (1.1)	54 (1.1)	▲ 58 (1.7)	50 (1.6)	57 (2.1)	49 (1.9)
South Africa	29 (1.9)	25 (1.3)	28 (2.0)	25 (1.2)	27 (1.9)	24 (1.5)

▲ = Difference from other gender statistically significant at .05 level, adjusted for multiple comparisons

*Eighth grade in most countries; See Table 2 for information about the grades tested in each country.

†Met guidelines for sample participation rates only after replacement schools were included (see Appendix A for details).

[1]National Desired Population does not cover all of International Desired Population (see Table A.2). Because coverage falls below 65%, Latvia is annotated LSS for Latvian Speaking Schools only.

[2]National Defined Population covers less than 90 percent of National Desired Population (see Table A.2).

( ) Standard errors appear in parentheses. Because results are rounded to the nearest whole number, some totals may appear inconsistent.

SOURCE: IEA Third International Mathematics and Science Study (TIMSS), 1994-95.

Table 2.5

Average Percent Correct for Boys and Girls by Science Content Areas Lower Grade (Seventh Grade*)

Country	Science Overall		Earth Science		Life Science	
	Boys	Girls	Boys	Girls	Boys	Girls
† Belgium (Fl)	▲ 59 (0.7)	55 (0.7)	▲ 63 (0.9)	58 (0.9)	62 (0.9)	59 (0.8)
† Belgium (Fr)	▲ 47 (0.8)	43 (0.7)	▲ 49 (1.2)	43 (1.1)	49 (1.0)	48 (0.9)
Canada	55 (0.6)	53 (0.5)	55 (0.9)	52 (0.7)	57 (0.7)	58 (0.6)
Cyprus	40 (0.6)	40 (0.5)	40 (1.0)	38 (0.7)	42 (0.8)	43 (0.7)
Czech Republic	▲ 60 (0.7)	56 (0.9)	▲ 60 (1.0)	55 (1.1)	64 (0.7)	62 (0.9)
†2 England	57 (1.0)	54 (0.9)	58 (1.3)	53 (1.1)	58 (1.1)	56 (1.2)
France	▲ 48 (0.7)	44 (0.7)	▲ 48 (0.8)	42 (0.8)	51 (0.9)	49 (0.8)
Hong Kong	54 (1.5)	52 (1.2)	51 (1.4)	47 (1.2)	57 (1.5)	56 (1.3)
Hungary	57 (0.8)	54 (0.7)	▲ 56 (0.9)	52 (0.9)	61 (1.0)	61 (0.7)
Iceland	47 (0.9)	45 (0.6)	▲ 47 (0.9)	43 (0.8)	51 (0.9)	51 (0.8)
Iran, Islamic Rep.	43 (0.7)	40 (0.9)	▲ 43 (1.0)	38 (0.9)	46 (1.0)	43 (1.1)
Ireland	▲ 54 (1.0)	50 (0.8)	▲ 59 (1.2)	54 (0.9)	53 (1.1)	52 (1.1)
Japan	▲ 60 (0.4)	58 (0.3)	▲ 58 (0.7)	55 (0.5)	64 (0.6)	64 (0.4)
Korea	▲ 63 (0.5)	59 (0.6)	▲ 61 (0.6)	55 (0.9)	▲ 67 (0.7)	62 (0.8)
1 Latvia (LSS)	43 (0.7)	40 (0.6)	44 (1.0)	41 (0.8)	45 (0.8)	44 (0.8)
1 Lithuania	38 (0.7)	37 (0.8)	40 (0.9)	38 (1.1)	39 (0.9)	42 (1.0)
New Zealand	51 (0.8)	49 (0.7)	▲ 52 (1.0)	47 (0.9)	53 (1.0)	53 (1.0)
Norway	51 (0.7)	49 (0.8)	53 (1.0)	51 (1.0)	55 (0.9)	55 (0.8)
Portugal	▲ 43 (0.5)	39 (0.5)	47 (0.8)	44 (0.8)	47 (0.6)	44 (0.7)
Russian Federation	52 (1.0)	48 (0.7)	▲ 56 (1.0)	52 (0.7)	54 (1.2)	53 (0.9)
† Scotland	50 (0.9)	47 (0.8)	▲ 49 (1.0)	44 (0.9)	50 (1.0)	48 (1.0)
Singapore	62 (1.4)	61 (1.5)	62 (1.4)	58 (1.6)	62 (1.7)	63 (1.7)
Slovak Republic	▲ 57 (0.8)	52 (0.6)	▲ 58 (0.9)	53 (0.9)	58 (0.9)	54 (0.7)
Spain	▲ 51 (0.6)	47 (0.5)	▲ 54 (0.8)	49 (0.8)	▲ 54 (0.7)	51 (0.6)
Sweden	52 (0.6)	50 (0.7)	54 (0.8)	53 (0.9)	56 (0.8)	56 (0.8)
1 Switzerland	▲ 52 (0.5)	48 (0.5)	▲ 55 (0.7)	50 (0.7)	53 (0.6)	53 (0.6)
† United States	55 (1.3)	53 (1.1)	56 (1.3)	52 (1.3)	59 (1.2)	59 (1.2)
Countries Not Satisfying Guidelines for Sample Participation Rates (See Appendix A for Details):						
Australia	54 (1.0)	54 (0.7)	54 (1.2)	51 (0.8)	55 (1.1)	57 (0.8)
Austria	56 (0.9)	55 (0.7)	57 (1.0)	54 (1.0)	59 (1.1)	61 (0.9)
Netherlands	57 (0.9)	55 (0.8)	58 (1.1)	55 (1.1)	61 (1.1)	61 (0.9)
Countries Not Meeting Age/Grade Specifications (High Percentage of Older Students; See Appendix A for Details):						
Colombia	▲ 37 (0.9)	33 (0.8)	▲ 36 (1.0)	30 (1.0)	40 (1.0)	38 (0.9)
†1 Germany	55 (1.0)	51 (0.9)	53 (0.9)	50 (1.2)	58 (1.0)	58 (1.0)
Romania	46 (0.8)	44 (0.8)	45 (1.0)	43 (1.1)	51 (1.0)	51 (0.9)
Slovenia	59 (0.6)	56 (0.6)	▲ 61 (0.7)	57 (0.8)	60 (0.8)	60 (0.7)
Countries With Unapproved Sampling Procedures at Classroom Level (See Appendix A for Details):						
Denmark	▲ 46 (0.6)	42 (0.6)	▲ 44 (1.0)	39 (0.9)	50 (0.8)	49 (0.8)
Greece	45 (0.7)	44 (0.5)	44 (0.8)	42 (0.6)	48 (0.8)	49 (0.7)
† South Africa	27 (1.3)	25 (0.9)	27 (1.4)	26 (1.0)	27 (1.4)	26 (1.1)
Thailand	53 (0.8)	52 (0.9)	51 (0.9)	49 (1.0)	61 (0.9)	62 (1.0)

▲ = Difference from other gender statistically significant at .05 level, adjusted for multiple comparisons

*Seventh grade in most countries; See Table 2 for information about the grades tested in each country.

†Met guidelines for sample participation rates only after replacement schools were included (see Appendix A for details).

[1]National Desired Population does not cover all of International Desired Population (see Table A.2). Because coverage falls below 65%, Latvia is annotated LSS for Latvian Speaking Schools only.

[2]National Defined Population covers less than 90 percent of National Desired Population (see Table A.2).

( ) Standard errors appear in parentheses. Because results are rounded to the nearest whole number, some totals may appear inconsistent.

SOURCE: IEA Third International Mathematics and Science Study (TIMSS), 1994-95.

Table 2.5 (Continued)
Average Percent Correct for Boys and Girls by Science Content Areas Lower Grade (Seventh Grade*)

Country	Physics		Chemistry		Environmental Issues and the Nature of Science	
	Boys	Girls	Boys	Girls	Boys	Girls
† Belgium (Fl)	▲ 60 (0.8)	56 (0.7)	▲ 49 (0.8)	43 (0.9)	54 (1.4)	54 (1.2)
† Belgium (Fr)	▲ 49 (0.9)	44 (0.9)	▲ 41 (0.9)	34 (0.9)	40 (1.2)	40 (1.1)
Canada	▲ 56 (0.7)	52 (0.6)	▲ 48 (1.0)	43 (0.7)	56 (1.0)	56 (1.0)
Cyprus	40 (0.6)	38 (0.6)	38 (0.8)	37 (0.8)	38 (1.1)	41 (0.9)
Czech Republic	▲ 60 (0.7)	56 (0.9)	▲ 57 (1.1)	51 (1.4)	56 (1.2)	51 (1.3)
†2 England	59 (1.0)	55 (1.0)	▲ 51 (1.4)	44 (1.5)	57 (1.3)	56 (1.7)
France	▲ 50 (0.8)	46 (0.7)	▲ 41 (1.0)	36 (0.9)	43 (1.4)	44 (1.1)
Hong Kong	57 (1.5)	53 (1.1)	50 (1.5)	47 (1.5)	51 (2.0)	50 (1.9)
Hungary	▲ 57 (0.7)	51 (0.7)	56 (1.0)	52 (0.9)	48 (1.4)	49 (1.2)
Iceland	51 (1.2)	47 (0.8)	38 (1.5)	34 (1.0)	42 (1.3)	42 (1.5)
Iran, Islamic Rep.	▲ 43 (0.9)	38 (1.0)	46 (1.0)	46 (1.3)	34 (1.2)	33 (1.4)
Ireland	▲ 54 (1.0)	48 (0.8)	▲ 51 (1.1)	44 (1.1)	56 (1.3)	53 (1.1)
Japan	▲ 65 (0.4)	62 (0.5)	▲ 51 (0.7)	48 (0.6)	55 (0.8)	52 (0.8)
Korea	▲ 65 (0.6)	60 (0.7)	55 (0.6)	52 (0.8)	63 (1.0)	59 (0.9)
1 Latvia (LSS)	▲ 46 (0.9)	41 (0.7)	▲ 36 (0.9)	31 (1.0)	38 (1.4)	38 (1.1)
1 Lithuania	▲ 43 (0.8)	38 (0.9)	29 (1.0)	28 (1.1)	31 (1.2)	33 (1.1)
New Zealand	52 (0.9)	50 (0.7)	44 (0.9)	40 (1.1)	54 (1.2)	53 (1.2)
Norway	▲ 53 (0.9)	48 (1.0)	40 (1.1)	39 (1.1)	48 (1.3)	49 (1.3)
Portugal	▲ 43 (0.6)	37 (0.6)	▲ 38 (0.8)	31 (0.8)	37 (1.1)	37 (1.0)
Russian Federation	52 (1.1)	47 (0.9)	▲ 46 (1.2)	39 (1.0)	45 (1.3)	41 (0.8)
† Scotland	53 (0.9)	50 (0.8)	▲ 44 (1.3)	38 (1.1)	50 (1.2)	49 (1.3)
Singapore	65 (1.2)	62 (1.4)	57 (1.6)	56 (1.6)	61 (1.7)	64 (1.7)
Slovak Republic	▲ 58 (0.8)	53 (0.8)	▲ 54 (1.1)	46 (1.0)	51 (1.1)	49 (1.0)
Spain	▲ 51 (0.7)	46 (0.5)	▲ 46 (0.8)	41 (0.9)	47 (1.0)	47 (0.9)
Sweden	▲ 53 (0.7)	48 (0.8)	▲ 47 (0.8)	43 (1.0)	45 (1.1)	46 (0.9)
1 Switzerland	▲ 55 (0.6)	49 (0.5)	▲ 45 (0.8)	38 (0.7)	47 (1.0)	45 (0.8)
† United States	52 (1.3)	50 (1.0)	50 (1.6)	46 (1.1)	55 (1.9)	57 (1.5)
Countries Not Satisfying Guidelines for Sample Participation Rates (See Appendix A for Details):						
Australia	56 (1.0)	54 (0.8)	46 (1.1)	45 (1.0)	56 (1.3)	58 (1.1)
Austria	57 (0.9)	54 (0.9)	53 (1.3)	49 (1.0)	49 (1.4)	48 (1.1)
Netherlands	57 (0.9)	53 (1.0)	46 (1.2)	42 (1.1)	59 (1.7)	58 (1.6)
Countries Not Meeting Age/Grade Specifications (High Percentage of Older Students; See Appendix A for Details):						
Colombia	▲ 37 (1.0)	32 (0.9)	▲ 32 (1.0)	27 (0.8)	36 (1.1)	35 (1.0)
†1 Germany	▲ 56 (1.0)	51 (0.9)	▲ 51 (1.3)	43 (1.2)	47 (1.6)	45 (1.3)
Romania	46 (0.9)	42 (0.9)	43 (1.0)	40 (1.1)	37 (1.1)	37 (1.0)
Slovenia	▲ 57 (0.7)	53 (0.7)	▲ 57 (1.1)	52 (1.0)	55 (1.1)	56 (0.8)
Countries With Unapproved Sampling Procedures at Classroom Level (See Appendix A for Details):						
Denmark	▲ 50 (0.8)	43 (0.7)	▲ 37 (0.9)	31 (0.9)	39 (1.2)	39 (1.2)
Greece	▲ 46 (0.7)	42 (0.5)	42 (0.9)	40 (0.9)	43 (1.1)	44 (1.1)
† South Africa	28 (1.3)	24 (0.9)	23 (1.3)	23 (0.8)	25 (1.5)	25 (1.2)
Thailand	51 (0.8)	50 (0.8)	40 (1.1)	37 (1.0)	57 (1.3)	58 (1.2)

▲ = Difference from other gender statistically significant at .05 level, adjusted for multiple comparisons

*Seventh grade in most countries; See Table 2 for information about the grades tested in each country.

†Met guidelines for sample participation rates only after replacement schools were included (see Appendix A for details).

1National Desired Population does not cover all of International Desired Population (see Table A.2). Because coverage falls below 65%, Latvia is annotated LSS for Latvian Speaking Schools only.

2National Defined Population covers less than 90 percent of National Desired Population (see Table A.2).

( ) Standard errors appear in parentheses. Because results are rounded to the nearest whole number, some totals may appear inconsistent.

SOURCE: IEA Third International Mathematics and Science Study (TIMSS), 1994-95.

Chapter 3

Performance on Items Within Each Science Content Area

This chapter presents four to six example items within each of the science content areas, including the performance on these items for each of the TIMSS countries. The example items were selected to illustrate the different topics covered within each content area as well as the different performance expectations. The items also were chosen to show the range of item formats used within each area. To provide some sense of what types of items were answered correctly by higher-performing as compared to lower-performing students, the items show a range of difficulty within each content area. Finally, it should be noted that all these items and others have been released for use by the public.[1]

The presentation for each of the content areas begins with a brief description of the major topics included in the content area and a discussion of student performance in that content area. The discussion is followed by a table showing the percent correct on the example items for each of the TIMSS countries at both the seventh and eighth grades. After the table showing the country-by-country results, there is a figure relating achievement on each of the example items to performance on the TIMSS international science scale. This "difficulty map" provides a pictorial representation of achievement on the scale in relation to achievement on the items. Following the difficulty map, each item is presented in its entirety. The correct answer is circled for multiple-choice items and shown in the answer space for short-answer items. For extended-response questions, the answer shown exemplifies the type of student responses that were given full credit. All of the responses shown have been reproduced from students' actual test booklets.

What Have Students Learned About Earth Science?

Items in the earth science category measure students' knowledge of the scientific principles related to earth features, earth processes, and the earth in the universe. Table 3.1 shows the percent correct across the TIMSS countries for each of five example items (Example Items 1 - 5).

The international item difficulty map shown in Figure 3.1 presents a pictorial representation of the relationship between performance on the TIMSS international science scale and achievement on the five example items for earth science.[2] The international achievement on each example item is indicated both by the seventh- and eighth-grade international average percent correct and by the international

[1] The IEA retained about one-third of the TIMSS items as secure for possible future use in measuring international trends in mathematics and science achievement. All remaining items are available for general use.

[2] The three-digit item label shown in the lower right corner of the box locating each example item on the item difficulty map refers to the original item identification number used in the student test booklets.

Table 3.1

Percent Correct for Earth Science Example Items - Lower and Upper Grades (Seventh and Eighth Grades*)

Country	Example 1A River on the plain: Good place for farming.		Example 1B River on the plain: Bad place for farming.		Example 2 Fossil fuels.	
	Seventh Grade	Eighth Grade	Seventh Grade	Eighth Grade	Seventh Grade	Eighth Grade
† Belgium (Fl)	83 (1.4)	86 (1.8)	60 (2.3)	57 (3.2)	67 (2.8)	70 (3.5)
† Belgium (Fr)	53 (2.2)	62 (2.8)	30 (2.4)	34 (2.3)	39 (3.0)	47 (3.2)
Canada	83 (1.2)	88 (1.1)	44 (1.9)	47 (1.8)	67 (2.6)	69 (2.4)
Cyprus	76 (1.9)	77 (1.8)	21 (1.7)	23 (1.8)	42 (3.1)	33 (2.7)
Czech Republic	80 (2.1)	84 (1.9)	35 (2.0)	42 (2.5)	41 (3.3)	60 (3.1)
†2 England	91 (1.4)	92 (1.5)	68 (2.8)	74 (2.2)	76 (2.8)	85 (2.6)
France	67 (2.0)	76 (1.8)	30 (1.9)	37 (2.4)	36 (2.7)	61 (2.1)
Hong Kong	65 (2.1)	70 (2.0)	29 (2.0)	42 (2.4)	73 (3.1)	74 (2.6)
Hungary	73 (1.9)	77 (1.7)	39 (2.1)	45 (1.9)	42 (2.4)	55 (2.9)
Iceland	71 (2.5)	81 (2.2)	24 (2.5)	26 (2.9)	42 (3.9)	46 (6.4)
Iran, Islamic Rep.	81 (2.3)	82 (1.6)	19 (3.9)	25 (2.0)	68 (3.0)	75 (2.8)
Ireland	89 (1.5)	91 (1.2)	73 (2.0)	71 (1.8)	84 (2.4)	87 (2.3)
Japan	90 (1.0)	91 (0.7)	25 (1.3)	25 (1.3)	49 (2.1)	53 (2.3)
Korea	91 (1.0)	92 (1.2)	27 (2.0)	35 (2.1)	75 (2.4)	84 (2.2)
1 Latvia (LSS)	73 (1.9)	71 (2.2)	25 (1.9)	30 (2.1)	37 (3.0)	46 (3.6)
1 Lithuania	62 (2.7)	68 (1.9)	25 (1.9)	39 (2.4)	37 (3.3)	34 (3.4)
New Zealand	87 (1.2)	89 (1.3)	62 (1.7)	68 (1.8)	46 (2.9)	60 (2.1)
Norway	83 (2.0)	86 (1.3)	39 (2.6)	42 (1.8)	55 (3.1)	69 (2.6)
Portugal	67 (1.8)	79 (1.6)	14 (1.2)	24 (1.6)	76 (2.3)	78 (2.3)
Russian Federation	70 (1.9)	74 (1.6)	34 (2.0)	39 (2.3)	56 (3.3)	62 (3.3)
† Scotland	77 (1.8)	81 (1.7)	51 (2.2)	52 (2.0)	57 (2.8)	65 (2.8)
Singapore	91 (1.4)	94 (0.8)	52 (2.4)	62 (1.9)	83 (2.3)	85 (1.6)
Slovak Republic	79 (1.6)	83 (1.8)	39 (2.0)	40 (2.1)	34 (3.0)	55 (3.0)
Spain	81 (1.3)	87 (1.2)	33 (1.5)	35 (1.8)	60 (2.6)	73 (2.2)
Sweden	80 (1.7)	83 (1.4)	34 (2.3)	44 (2.0)	64 (2.8)	70 (2.0)
1 Switzerland	79 (1.7)	81 (1.5)	45 (1.8)	53 (1.6)	48 (2.7)	52 (2.5)
† United States	88 (1.4)	91 (0.8)	56 (1.7)	58 (1.7)	65 (3.1)	71 (2.0)
Countries Not Satisfying Guidelines for Sample Participation Rates (see Appendix A for Details):						
Australia	81 (1.5)	83 (1.4)	55 (1.7)	58 (1.8)	54 (2.3)	62 (2.2)
Austria	74 (2.3)	78 (2.0)	39 (2.2)	44 (2.3)	70 (2.9)	83 (2.2)
Bulgaria	70 (2.8)	65 (3.9)	28 (2.5)	36 (3.5)	65 (4.2)	68 (3.8)
Netherlands	73 (1.8)	78 (2.3)	55 (2.2)	54 (2.5)	61 (3.4)	71 (3.7)
Countries Not Meeting Age/Grade Specifications (High Percentage of Older Students; See Appendix A for Details):						
Colombia	54 (3.0)	62 (3.0)	22 (2.1)	26 (2.0)	46 (3.5)	51 (3.7)
†1 Germany	71 (2.2)	72 (2.1)	44 (1.9)	47 (3.0)	56 (2.8)	59 (3.1)
Romania	64 (2.2)	68 (2.3)	28 (2.2)	33 (2.5)	55 (2.8)	71 (2.7)
Slovenia	86 (1.4)	90 (1.2)	46 (2.2)	49 (2.1)	64 (2.7)	82 (2.4)
Countries With Unapproved Sampling Procedures at Classroom Level (See Appendix A for Details):						
Denmark	55 (2.7)	62 (2.2)	25 (2.4)	29 (2.3)	38 (3.2)	46 (3.2)
Greece	76 (1.8)	86 (1.2)	22 (1.3)	31 (1.8)	18 (1.7)	29 (2.6)
† South Africa	42 (2.7)	38 (2.5)	12 (1.8)	14 (2.0)	27 (2.3)	24 (2.4)
Thailand	94 (0.7)	95 (0.7)	72 (1.7)	75 (1.6)	44 (2.6)	58 (2.6)
Unapproved Sampling Procedures at Classroom Level and Not Meeting Other Guidelines (See Appendix A for Details):						
1 Israel	–	84 (2.4)	–	35 (3.8)	–	54 (4.1)
Kuwait	–	59 (4.3)	–	20 (2.6)	–	55 (3.8)

*Seventh and eighth grades in most countries; see Table 2 for information about the grades tested in each country.
†Met guidelines for sample participation rates only after replacement schools were included (see Appendix A for details).
¹National Desired Population does not cover all of International Desired Population (see Table A.2). Because coverage falls below 65%, Latvia is annotated LSS for Latvian Speaking Schools only.
²National Defined Population covers less than 90 percent of National Desired Population (see Table A.2).
( ) Standard errors appear in parentheses. Because results are rounded to the nearest whole number, some totals may appear inconsistent.
A dash (–) indicates data are not available. Israel and Kuwait did not test at the seventh grade.

SOURCE: IEA Third International Mathematics and Science Study (TIMSS), 1994-95.

Table 3.1 (Continued)

Percent Correct for Earth Science Example Items - Lower and Upper Grades (Seventh and Eighth Grades*)

Country	Example 3 Ozone layer.		Example 4 Diagram of Earth's water cycle.		Example 5 Gases in air.	
	Seventh Grade	Eighth Grade	Seventh Grade	Eighth Grade	Seventh Grade	Eighth Grade
† Belgium (Fl)	40 (2.7)	47 (3.1)	56 (2.2)	60 (3.4)	10 (1.9)	17 (2.1)
† Belgium (Fr)	38 (3.2)	48 (3.5)	24 (2.1)	32 (2.0)	22 (3.1)	20 (4.5)
Canada	53 (2.5)	63 (2.2)	36 (1.8)	39 (1.7)	9 (1.0)	21 (2.0)
Cyprus	25 (2.5)	42 (3.0)	17 (1.7)	24 (2.0)	23 (2.9)	33 (3.3)
Czech Republic	62 (3.7)	74 (2.7)	22 (2.3)	27 (2.9)	55 (3.1)	38 (3.8)
†2 England	35 (2.7)	38 (3.1)	44 (2.4)	53 (2.3)	21 (3.7)	17 (2.6)
France	29 (2.7)	42 (3.0)	25 (1.7)	32 (1.9)	11 (1.8)	13 (2.0)
Hong Kong	47 (3.3)	56 (3.2)	23 (1.9)	25 (1.7)	21 (2.3)	50 (3.3)
Hungary	52 (2.5)	63 (2.7)	24 (1.8)	22 (1.6)	42 (3.0)	43 (3.0)
Iceland	47 (3.6)	56 (4.2)	25 (2.8)	33 (3.3)	3 (1.1)	14 (2.3)
Iran, Islamic Rep.	16 (2.5)	20 (3.0)	15 (4.3)	11 (1.4)	7 (1.6)	4 (1.3)
Ireland	39 (2.4)	53 (3.1)	41 (2.1)	51 (2.2)	16 (2.3)	30 (3.0)
Japan	45 (2.2)	60 (2.0)	35 (1.5)	43 (1.6)	57 (2.2)	54 (2.2)
Korea	45 (2.9)	57 (2.5)	26 (1.6)	23 (1.7)	59 (3.2)	41 (3.2)
1 Latvia (LSS)	20 (2.5)	36 (3.4)	20 (1.9)	19 (2.0)	13 (2.5)	18 (2.6)
1 Lithuania	20 (2.7)	38 (3.6)	8 (1.2)	9 (1.4)	10 (1.9)	22 (2.7)
New Zealand	53 (2.9)	64 (2.7)	25 (1.9)	29 (1.9)	6 (1.1)	18 (2.2)
Norway	54 (4.6)	71 (2.5)	40 (3.3)	55 (2.0)	4 (1.1)	27 (2.7)
Portugal	40 (3.0)	50 (2.9)	17 (1.6)	24 (1.5)	17 (2.3)	8 (1.5)
Russian Federation	30 (3.1)	39 (3.3)	56 (1.8)	59 (2.0)	21 (2.4)	27 (3.4)
† Scotland	29 (2.3)	42 (2.7)	31 (2.4)	40 (2.2)	12 (2.3)	25 (2.9)
Singapore	71 (2.9)	78 (2.4)	45 (2.3)	57 (2.4)	72 (2.9)	58 (3.1)
Slovak Republic	67 (2.3)	71 (2.0)	24 (1.9)	25 (1.8)	51 (3.2)	32 (2.9)
Spain	63 (2.6)	68 (2.4)	24 (1.8)	34 (1.8)	9 (1.6)	9 (1.5)
Sweden	54 (2.9)	69 (2.0)	34 (2.0)	49 (2.0)	10 (1.9)	25 (2.5)
1 Switzerland	39 (2.9)	51 (2.6)	26 (1.6)	38 (1.9)	9 (1.4)	20 (2.5)
† United States	40 (3.7)	52 (2.7)	35 (2.4)	40 (2.3)	20 (2.6)	20 (1.8)
Countries Not Satisfying Guidelines for Sample Participation Rates (see Appendix A for Details):						
Australia	45 (2.8)	51 (1.8)	26 (1.7)	33 (1.7)	16 (2.3)	16 (1.6)
Austria	54 (2.7)	65 (3.1)	31 (2.0)	43 (2.3)	13 (1.8)	42 (3.6)
Bulgaria	64 (5.0)	67 (3.7)	21 (2.5)	19 (2.8)	31 (4.7)	45 (5.1)
Netherlands	47 (3.7)	57 (4.1)	47 (2.5)	57 (2.7)	15 (2.1)	31 (3.1)
Countries Not Meeting Age/Grade Specifications (High Percentage of Older Students; See Appendix A for Details):						
Colombia	51 (3.4)	55 (4.0)	12 (1.7)	15 (1.9)	–	–
†1 Germany	53 (3.2)	64 (2.9)	29 (1.9)	35 (2.5)	23 (2.6)	27 (3.2)
Romania	31 (2.4)	41 (3.0)	18 (1.8)	21 (2.0)	27 (3.0)	40 (2.9)
Slovenia	47 (3.2)	61 (2.8)	25 (2.0)	24 (1.9)	51 (3.6)	31 (3.2)
Countries With Unapproved Sampling Procedures at Classroom Level (See Appendix A for Details):						
Denmark	24 (3.4)	29 (3.1)	27 (2.5)	39 (2.3)	10 (2.8)	11 (1.8)
Greece	40 (2.3)	56 (2.5)	16 (1.5)	17 (1.4)	26 (2.2)	34 (2.7)
† South Africa	10 (2.3)	6 (1.8)	7 (1.3)	6 (1.2)	16 (1.6)	11 (1.5)
Thailand	32 (2.6)	45 (2.6)	13 (1.4)	16 (1.4)	19 (2.5)	18 (2.3)
Unapproved Sampling Procedures at Classroom Level and Not Meeting Other Guidelines (See Appendix A for Details):						
1 Israel	–	63 (4.9)	–	17 (2.3)	–	33 (4.6)
Kuwait	–	65 (4.5)	–	25 (2.7)	–	37 (3.9)

*Seventh and eighth grades in most countries; see Table 2 for information about the grades tested in each country.
†Met guidelines for sample participation rates only after replacement schools were included (see Appendix A for details).
[1]National Desired Population does not cover all of International Desired Population (see Table A.2). Because coverage falls below 65%, Latvia is annotated LSS for Latvian Speaking Schools only.
[2]National Defined Population covers less than 90 percent of National Desired Population (see Table A.2).
( ) Standard errors appear in parentheses. Because results are rounded to the nearest whole number, some totals may appear inconsistent.
A dash (–) indicates data are not available. Israel and Kuwait did not test at the seventh grade. Internationally comparable data are unavailable for Colombia on Example 5.

SOURCE: IEA Third International Mathematics and Science Study (TIMSS), 1994-95.

Figure 3.1

International Difficulty Map for Earth Science Example Items Lower and Upper Grades (Seventh and Eighth Grades*)

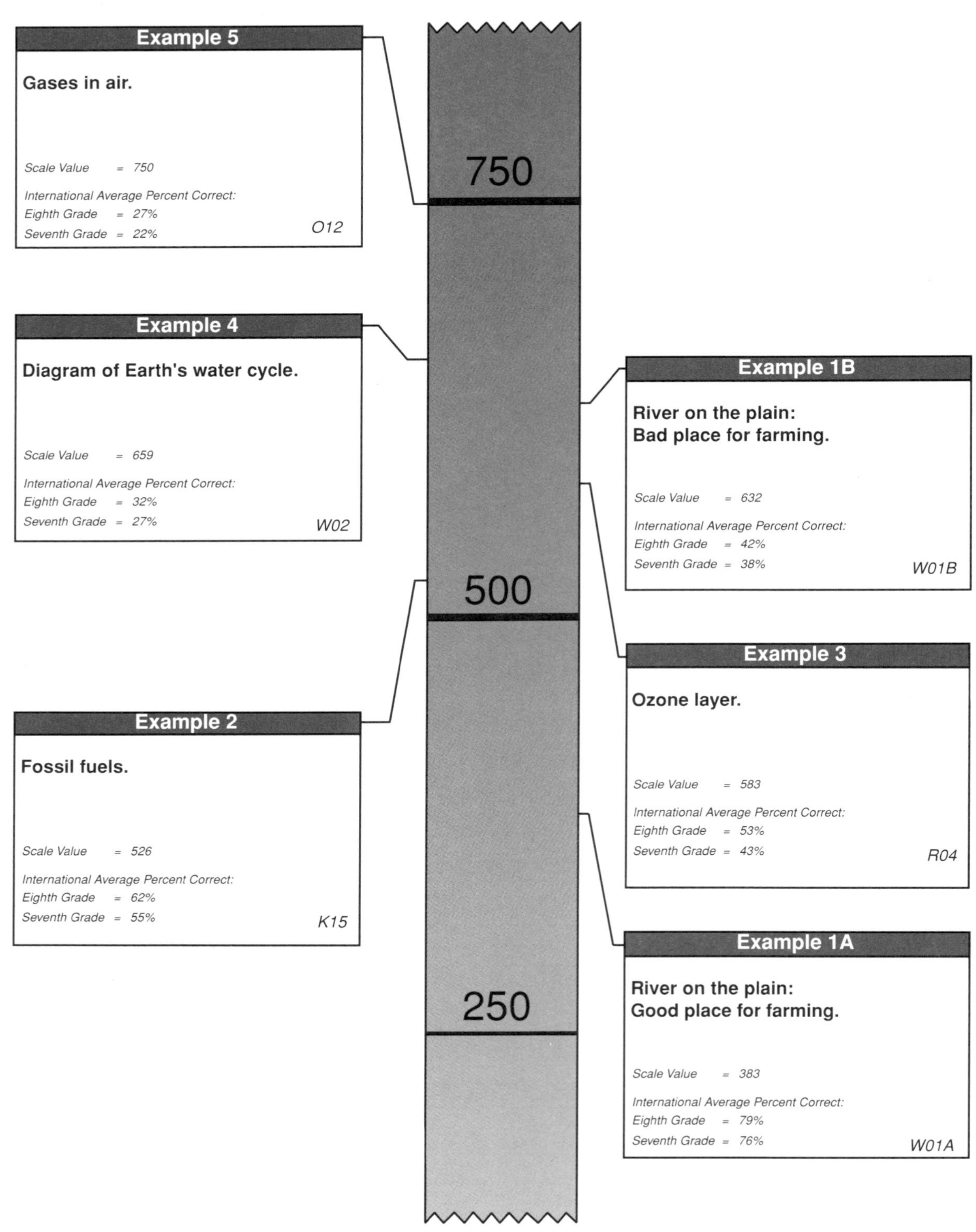

*Seventh and eighth grades in most countries; see Table 2 for information about the grades tested in each country.
NOTE: Each item was placed onto the TIMSS international science scale based on students' performance in both grades. Items are shown at the point on the scale where students with that level of proficiency had a 65 percent probability of providing a correct response.

science scale value, or item difficulty level, for each item. Since the scale was developed based on the performance of students at both grades in all countries, the international scale values apply to both grades and to all countries.

For the figure, the items results are placed on the scale at the point where students at the corresponding achievement level were more likely than not (65% probability) to answer the question correctly. Items at higher scale values are the more difficult items. For example, students scoring at or above 383 on the science scale were likely to correctly answer the question about advantages of farming by a river (Example Item 1A) but not the question about the source of fossil fuels (Example Item 2), while students scoring at or above 526 were also likely to answer this second item.

The international average on the science scale of 516 at the eighth grade indicates that students from many countries at this grade would be likely to correctly answer the lowest-difficulty items, such as Example Item 1A, but would not be likely to answer the more difficult items. These results, however, varied dramatically across countries. In Singapore, with an average scale value of 607, students were likely to respond correctly to more of the earth science example items than did students in other, lower-performing countries. This is reflected in Singapore's average percent correct at the eighth grade for the earth science items, which was 65% compared to 55% internationally.

The five earth science example items are presented in their entirety beginning on the next page. Example Item 1 asks students to apply scientific principles of water sources and physical cycles to explain why a plain containing a river might be both a good place (Part A) and a bad place (Part B) for farming. Most seventh- and eighth-graders were able to answer the first part of this open-ended item (international averages of 76% and 79%). Students were given credit for mentioning that the soil was fertile, good, or abundant; that the river would provide irrigation or water for animals; that there was plenty of space or flat areas for farmland; or any other acceptable reason related to facilitating farming. For the majority of countries, more than 70% of both seventh- and eighth-grade students provided a correct response, and several countries had more than 90% correct responses. Substantially fewer students were able to provide a correct response to the second part of this item. Reasons given credit for Part B included the possibility of flooding, wind or water erosion, or other acceptable problems related to farming. The international average percent correct levels were 38% and 42% for seventh and eighth grade. In addition, a much broader range of performance was observed across countries for this part of the item, with the percent of correct responses at the eighth grade ranging from 14% in South Africa to more than 70% in England, Ireland, and Thailand.

Example Item 2 is a multiple-choice item requiring knowledge of the source of fossil fuels. On average, 55% of seventh-graders and 62% of eighth-graders responded correctly to this item, but the across-country differences ranged widely. Eighth-grade students in several countries had 80% or more correct responses, with Ireland and England having two of the highest performances, together with Korea, Singapore,

Austria, and Slovenia. The across-grade differences for many countries were greater for Example Item 2 than Example Item 1, with fewer than half of seventh-grade students answering correctly in 17 countries.

Example Item 3 required students to write down a reason for the importance of the ozone layer. Internationally, about half of the students in both grades provided a correct response related to protection from the sun's ultraviolet radiation. Ultraviolet radiation did not need to be mentioned specifically; responses that included the idea of the ozone layer protecting humans from sunburn or skin cancer also were given credit. The between-grade increase in average percent correct, from 43% to 53%, represents one of the larger increases among the example items.

Example Item 4 is an extended-response item that required students to apply scientific principles and use a diagram to explain the earth's water cycle. A fully-correct response to this item needed to depict or otherwise indicate all three steps in the water cycle – evaporation, transportation, and precipitation. On average, students found this item to be rather difficult, with fewer than one-third in both the seventh (27%) and eighth grade (32%) providing a fully-correct drawing or diagram. For the majority of countries, performance at the eighth grade was not substantially better than at the seventh grade. The performance across countries ranged from less than 10% to 60%, with South Africa posting seventh- and eighth-grade percentages of 7% and 6% and Belgium (Flemish), percentages of 56% and 60%.

Example Item 5, requiring students to identify the most abundant gas found in air, was the most difficult earth science item. Only about one-quarter of students at either grade could identify the correct response of nitrogen gas (international averages of 22% and 27%). The most common misconception, chosen by more than 50% of students, was that oxygen is the most abundant gas in air. Performance patterns were very inconsistent for this item. The across-country performance varied dramatically at both grades, ranging from below 10% correct in several countries to 72% correct at the seventh grade and 58% at the eighth grade in Singapore. Across-grade comparisons revealed that in several countries, the seventh-grade students out-performed those in the eighth grade by a substantial margin.

EXAMPLE ITEM 1
EARTH SCIENCE

River on the plain

The diagram shows a river flowing through a wide plain. The plain is covered with several layers of soil and sediment.

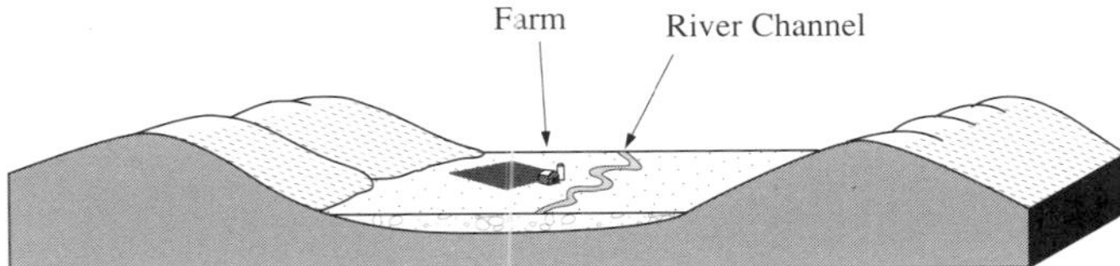

a. Write down one reason why this plain is a good place for farming.

This is a good place because the Soil is soft, and fertile.

b. Write down one reason why this plain is NOT a good place for farming.

This is not a good place because the river might flood.

Performance Category: Theorizing, Analyzing, and Solving Problems

EXAMPLE ITEM 2
EARTH SCIENCE

Fossil fuels

Fossil fuels were formed from

A. uranium

B. sea water

C. sand and gravel

(D.) dead plants and animals

Performance Category: Understanding Simple Information

EXAMPLE ITEM 3
EARTH SCIENCE

Ozone layer

Write down one reason why the ozone layer is important for all living things on Earth.

It protects a living thing from over-exposure to the sun's harmful rays.

Performance Category: Understanding Complex Information

EXAMPLE ITEM 4
EARTH SCIENCE

Diagram of Earth's water cycle

Draw a diagram to show how the water that falls as rain in one place may come from another place that is far away.

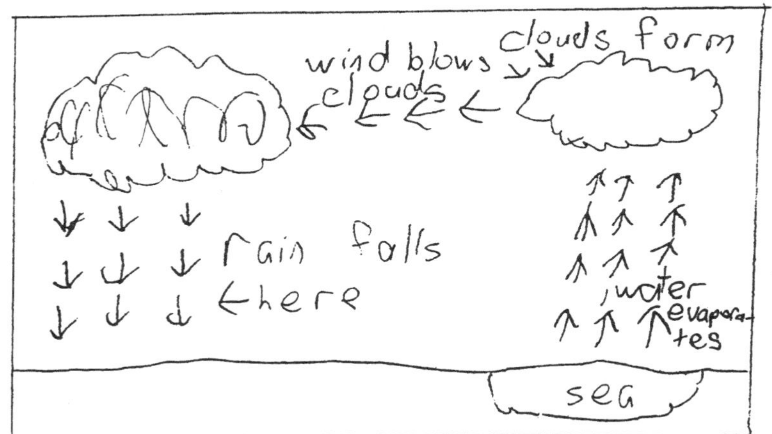

Performance Category: Theorizing, Analyzing, and Solving Problems

EXAMPLE ITEM 5
EARTH SCIENCE

Gases in air

Air is made up of many gases. Which gas is found in the greatest amount?

A. Nitrogen

B. Oxygen

C. Carbon dioxide

D. Hydrogen

Performance Category: Understanding Simple Information

WHAT HAVE STUDENTS LEARNED ABOUT LIFE SCIENCE?

Items in the life science category cover a broad range of content areas related to the structure, diversity, classification, processes, cycles, and interactions of plant and animal life. To answer these items, students were required to demonstrate and apply their knowledge of both simple and complex information. The percent correct values for five example items (Example Items 6 - 10) illustrating the life science content area are shown in Table 3.2, and Figure 3.2 presents the international difficulty map for these items.

Nearly three-quarters of both the seventh- and eighth-grade students correctly answered Example Item 6 about the growth and development of trees (international averages of 72% and 74% at the seventh and eighth grades). Belgium (Flemish), Korea, the Slovak Republic, Austria, the Netherlands, and all three Scandinavian countries had 90% or more correct responses at both grades.

Explaining the importance of plants and light in an aquarium ecosystem in Example Item 7 was more difficult for students. On average, Part A of this item, related to the importance of plants, was answered correctly by more than half of both seventh- and eighth-grade students (58% and 64%), with the majority identifying oxygen production. However, responses that mentioned that plants clean the water, provide food for fish, or provide a place to hide or to hide eggs, or other appropriate benefits also were counted as correct. One-third or fewer of the students, on average, provided a correct explanation for the importance of light (26% and 33% for Part B), with these students most frequently referring to photosynthesis or energy production. Other more general responses, such as "it helps to keep the plants alive," also were given credit.

Example Item 8 also measures students' knowledge of photosynthesis. On average, about half of the students at both grades (50% and 54%) correctly identified the function of chloroplasts in plant cells. Students in Hong Kong, Japan, Korea, and the Russian Federation did particularly well (75% or greater in both grades). In general, there was little increase in performance between seventh and eighth grades on this item.

Internationally, fewer than half of the students at both grades selected the correct response to Example Item 9 about insect features (45% at seventh grade and 43% at eighth grade, on average). Across countries, the percent correct for eighth-graders ranged from 20% in Colombia to 82% in Japan. In many countries, seventh- and eighth-grade students performed similarly. In fact, in a few countries, seventh-grade students performed somewhat better than did eighth-grade students, most notably Belgium (Flemish).

Example Item 10 required students to design and communicate a scientific investigation in the area of human biology. More specifically, students were asked to investigate how the heart rate changes with changes in activity. Fully-correct responses described a procedure in which the pulse is measured at rest using a timer or watch, the individual does an exercise or engages in some type of physical activity, and then the pulse is remeasured during or after the exercise. Across countries, students found this item to be quite difficult, with only 8% of seventh- and 14% of eighth-grade students, on average, providing a fully-correct extended response. A fully correct response required the student to include the use of a timer and describe the measurement of pulse rate both before and after exercise. In only seven countries did one-fourth or more of eighth-grade students receive full credit for their responses (Flemish-speaking Belgium, England, New Zealand, Scotland, Singapore, the Netherlands, and Israel).

Table 3.2

Percent Correct for Life Science Example Items - Lower and Upper Grades (Seventh and Eighth Grades*)

Country	Example 6 Tree rings.		Example 7A Aquarium: Importance of plant.		Example 7B Aquarium: Importance of light.	
	Seventh Grade	Eighth Grade	Seventh Grade	Eighth Grade	Seventh Grade	Eighth Grade
† Belgium (Fl)	95 (1.2)	92 (2.2)	62 (2.2)	75 (2.5)	26 (1.6)	43 (2.1)
† Belgium (Fr)	61 (3.5)	63 (3.5)	43 (2.8)	47 (2.4)	15 (1.6)	27 (2.2)
Canada	85 (1.5)	86 (1.7)	57 (1.7)	62 (1.6)	19 (1.7)	26 (1.5)
Cyprus	49 (2.7)	62 (3.1)	56 (1.9)	57 (1.7)	42 (2.2)	38 (2.4)
Czech Republic	89 (1.8)	88 (2.5)	69 (1.8)	74 (2.0)	34 (2.5)	42 (2.9)
†[2] England	78 (3.1)	79 (2.6)	64 (2.2)	69 (2.5)	14 (2.1)	22 (2.1)
France	60 (2.6)	66 (2.5)	51 (2.4)	63 (1.7)	22 (1.6)	27 (2.0)
Hong Kong	38 (2.5)	39 (2.5)	33 (1.8)	53 (2.6)	10 (1.3)	26 (2.0)
Hungary	84 (2.0)	81 (2.4)	66 (1.8)	65 (2.2)	39 (2.0)	40 (2.2)
Iceland	84 (2.7)	90 (2.4)	42 (3.1)	61 (3.9)	7 (1.6)	17 (2.2)
Iran, Islamic Rep.	77 (3.1)	81 (3.1)	37 (2.1)	44 (2.6)	23 (2.7)	32 (2.7)
Ireland	88 (1.5)	89 (1.8)	51 (2.2)	60 (2.3)	11 (1.2)	22 (2.0)
Japan	89 (1.3)	88 (1.5)	82 (1.2)	85 (1.0)	56 (1.6)	56 (1.8)
Korea	93 (1.7)	95 (1.2)	55 (2.2)	67 (1.9)	48 (2.4)	56 (1.7)
[1] Latvia (LSS)	80 (2.7)	87 (2.2)	48 (2.0)	53 (2.6)	8 (1.2)	13 (1.3)
[1] Lithuania	76 (3.1)	85 (2.5)	40 (2.9)	57 (2.9)	23 (2.6)	38 (2.6)
New Zealand	87 (1.9)	86 (2.0)	69 (2.1)	78 (1.4)	10 (1.5)	20 (1.9)
Norway	94 (1.3)	96 (1.0)	66 (2.5)	72 (1.6)	18 (1.9)	35 (1.9)
Portugal	46 (3.0)	45 (2.8)	55 (2.2)	56 (1.8)	27 (2.0)	27 (1.8)
Russian Federation	87 (1.3)	89 (1.6)	52 (2.5)	65 (2.4)	30 (2.4)	41 (2.6)
† Scotland	79 (2.2)	81 (2.1)	44 (1.8)	54 (2.3)	6 (1.0)	13 (1.9)
Singapore	45 (2.7)	59 (2.7)	91 (1.4)	96 (0.7)	65 (2.7)	78 (2.0)
Slovak Republic	94 (1.2)	96 (0.9)	61 (2.9)	67 (2.8)	22 (1.9)	34 (2.5)
Spain	66 (2.5)	73 (1.9)	52 (1.8)	57 (2.1)	26 (1.7)	35 (1.9)
Sweden	90 (1.7)	93 (1.1)	62 (1.9)	68 (1.6)	17 (1.5)	24 (1.4)
[1] Switzerland	87 (2.2)	86 (1.9)	66 (1.7)	73 (2.1)	16 (1.1)	33 (1.8)
† United States	76 (2.7)	81 (2.1)	61 (1.9)	63 (1.6)	21 (1.9)	26 (1.3)
Countries Not Satisfying Guidelines for Sample Participation Rates (see Appendix A for Details):						
Australia	60 (2.2)	67 (2.0)	55 (1.9)	63 (1.5)	12 (0.9)	24 (1.4)
Austria	91 (1.7)	92 (2.0)	80 (1.9)	85 (1.8)	45 (2.7)	45 (2.8)
Bulgaria	88 (2.4)	87 (2.7)	65 (3.0)	66 (4.5)	53 (3.7)	55 (4.7)
Netherlands	92 (1.5)	95 (1.3)	63 (4.0)	70 (2.3)	18 (2.0)	27 (3.0)
Countries Not Meeting Age/Grade Specifications (High Percentage of Older Students; See Appendix A for Details):						
Colombia	22 (3.3)	20 (3.0)	48 (3.2)	55 (3.4)	14 (2.2)	20 (2.3)
†[1] Germany	85 (2.4)	87 (2.1)	72 (2.1)	74 (2.3)	38 (2.3)	43 (2.2)
Romania	58 (3.0)	59 (2.9)	50 (2.5)	62 (2.1)	30 (2.2)	43 (2.4)
Slovenia	87 (1.8)	90 (1.6)	75 (2.0)	74 (2.0)	36 (2.5)	45 (2.2)
Countries With Unapproved Sampling Procedures at Classroom Level (See Appendix A for Details):						
Denmark	92 (1.7)	91 (1.8)	62 (2.6)	69 (2.4)	21 (1.9)	32 (2.1)
Greece	61 (2.4)	62 (2.5)	46 (1.9)	47 (1.6)	28 (2.0)	33 (1.8)
† South Africa	16 (2.7)	17 (2.9)	26 (2.1)	34 (2.8)	5 (0.8)	9 (1.7)
Thailand	40 (2.5)	48 (2.7)	77 (1.6)	79 (1.6)	45 (2.1)	49 (2.5)
Unapproved Sampling Procedures at Classroom Level and Not Meeting Other Guidelines (See Appendix A for Details):						
[1] Israel	–	63 (2.8)	–	59 (3.0)	–	29 (2.9)
Kuwait	–	31 (4.1)	–	48 (4.2)	–	22 (3.0)

*Seventh and eighth grades in most countries; see Table 2 for information about the grades tested in each country.

†Met guidelines for sample participation rates only after replacement schools were included (see Appendix A for details).

[1]National Desired Population does not cover all of International Desired Population (see Table A.2). Because coverage falls below 65%, Latvia is annotated LSS for Latvian Speaking Schools only.

[2]National Defined Population covers less than 90 percent of National Desired Population (see Table A.2).

( ) Standard errors appear in parentheses. Because results are rounded to the nearest whole number, some totals may appear inconsistent.

A dash (–) indicates data are not available. Israel and Kuwait did not test at the seventh grade.

SOURCE: IEA Third International Mathematics and Science Study (TIMSS), 1994-95.

Table 3.2 (Continued)

Percent Correct for Life Science Example Items - Lower and Upper Grades (Seventh and Eighth Grades*)

Country	Example 8 Chloroplasts in cells.		Example 9 Insect features.		Example 10 Heart rate changes.	
	Seventh Grade	Eighth Grade	Seventh Grade	Eighth Grade	Seventh Grade	Eighth Grade
† Belgium (Fl)	46 (3.1)	65 (4.9)	62 (2.8)	50 (3.5)	16 (1.8)	27 (1.7)
† Belgium (Fr)	38 (2.6)	49 (3.2)	39 (3.4)	53 (3.2)	8 (1.6)	13 (1.4)
Canada	44 (2.0)	50 (1.9)	47 (1.8)	49 (2.3)	12 (0.9)	21 (1.6)
Cyprus	51 (2.4)	52 (2.5)	42 (2.4)	36 (3.1)	2 (0.6)	6 (1.1)
Czech Republic	51 (2.5)	64 (2.6)	52 (2.7)	47 (3.0)	12 (1.6)	19 (1.6)
†2 England	55 (3.2)	58 (3.3)	47 (3.7)	50 (3.4)	17 (1.9)	26 (2.3)
France	46 (3.4)	48 (3.0)	42 (2.7)	35 (2.8)	5 (0.9)	10 (1.2)
Hong Kong	85 (1.9)	86 (1.8)	62 (2.5)	57 (2.7)	5 (0.8)	6 (0.9)
Hungary	25 (2.5)	26 (2.9)	50 (2.8)	53 (2.6)	5 (0.8)	8 (1.1)
Iceland	42 (3.6)	63 (3.2)	37 (3.6)	31 (3.4)	4 (0.9)	8 (1.5)
Iran, Islamic Rep.	43 (4.3)	38 (3.5)	29 (3.3)	28 (3.0)	4 (0.9)	4 (1.1)
Ireland	41 (3.0)	47 (2.6)	29 (2.3)	35 (2.7)	8 (1.1)	16 (1.5)
Japan	85 (1.3)	89 (1.3)	69 (1.9)	82 (1.6)	15 (1.1)	20 (1.4)
Korea	78 (2.3)	86 (2.0)	79 (2.2)	74 (2.4)	23 (2.0)	23 (1.9)
1 Latvia (LSS)	33 (3.2)	39 (3.4)	29 (2.6)	44 (2.8)	2 (0.6)	3 (0.6)
1 Lithuania	55 (3.4)	66 (2.8)	19 (2.5)	41 (3.3)	2 (1.0)	5 (0.9)
New Zealand	42 (3.0)	48 (2.3)	52 (3.0)	56 (2.6)	16 (1.8)	26 (1.9)
Norway	37 (3.0)	43 (2.6)	51 (3.5)	57 (2.3)	9 (1.2)	24 (1.8)
Portugal	36 (2.6)	39 (2.2)	20 (2.1)	27 (2.5)	1 (0.3)	3 (0.6)
Russian Federation	75 (2.1)	79 (1.3)	34 (2.5)	53 (2.2)	3 (0.7)	5 (1.2)
† Scotland	40 (2.9)	49 (2.7)	34 (3.2)	36 (3.0)	14 (1.4)	25 (2.4)
Singapore	56 (2.8)	57 (2.7)	61 (2.7)	68 (1.9)	19 (1.9)	32 (1.8)
Slovak Republic	43 (2.5)	55 (2.3)	40 (2.2)	47 (3.0)	9 (1.1)	12 (1.4)
Spain	46 (2.2)	54 (2.4)	29 (2.5)	30 (2.1)	5 (0.8)	10 (1.1)
Sweden	50 (3.1)	67 (2.2)	51 (2.9)	61 (2.1)	7 (1.0)	18 (1.6)
1 Switzerland	47 (2.8)	48 (2.7)	47 (2.7)	49 (2.2)	8 (0.8)	14 (1.2)
† United States	52 (3.0)	54 (2.3)	45 (3.6)	44 (2.1)	11 (1.4)	14 (1.2)
Countries Not Satisfying Guidelines for Sample Participation Rates (see Appendix A for Details):						
Australia	49 (2.7)	54 (1.9)	52 (2.7)	52 (2.3)	8 (0.8)	15 (1.2)
Austria	50 (3.2)	54 (3.2)	56 (2.9)	52 (3.1)	6 (1.0)	9 (1.3)
Bulgaria	57 (4.2)	58 (4.2)	34 (4.7)	42 (4.3)	8 (1.9)	7 (2.6)
Netherlands	68 (4.2)	72 (3.6)	55 (2.9)	53 (4.5)	13 (1.6)	25 (3.1)
Countries Not Meeting Age/Grade Specifications (High Percentage of Older Students; See Appendix A for Details):						
Colombia	38 (3.6)	31 (2.8)	18 (2.6)	20 (2.5)	3 (1.0)	6 (2.1)
†1 Germany	48 (3.1)	60 (3.4)	47 (3.1)	54 (3.1)	10 (1.6)	16 (2.0)
Romania	54 (2.9)	48 (3.0)	30 (2.3)	33 (2.7)	4 (0.7)	9 (1.6)
Slovenia	67 (2.4)	72 (3.1)	38 (2.7)	45 (3.2)	15 (1.6)	20 (1.9)
Countries With Unapproved Sampling Procedures at Classroom Level (See Appendix A for Details):						
Denmark	50 (3.4)	60 (3.3)	32 (2.7)	41 (3.4)	3 (0.9)	12 (1.8)
Greece	48 (2.7)	52 (2.8)	49 (2.8)	44 (2.6)	5 (0.7)	10 (1.0)
† South Africa	26 (2.0)	30 (2.4)	26 (2.7)	27 (2.5)	2 (0.6)	5 (1.4)
Thailand	48 (2.5)	47 (2.2)	44 (2.6)	43 (2.5)	4 (0.6)	18 (1.7)
Unapproved Sampling Procedures at Classroom Level and Not Meeting Other Guidelines (See Appendix A for Details):						
1 Israel	–	42 (4.4)	–	36 (4.0)	–	26 (3.0)
Kuwait	–	37 (3.6)	–	37 (3.8)	–	8 (1.1)

*Seventh and eighth grades in most countries; see Table 2 for information about the grades tested in each country.
†Met guidelines for sample participation rates only after replacement schools were included (see Appendix A for details).
1National Desired Population does not cover all of International Desired Population (see Table A.2). Because coverage falls below 65%, Latvia is annotated LSS for Latvian Speaking Schools only.
2National Defined Population covers less than 90 percent of National Desired Population (see Table A.2).
( ) Standard errors appear in parentheses. Because results are rounded to the nearest whole number, some totals may appear inconsistent.
A dash (–) indicates data are not available. Israel and Kuwait did not test at the seventh grade.

SOURCE: IEA Third International Mathematics and Science Study (TIMSS), 1994-95.

Figure 3.2

International Difficulty Map for Life Science Example Items Lower and Upper Grades (Seventh and Eighth Grades*)

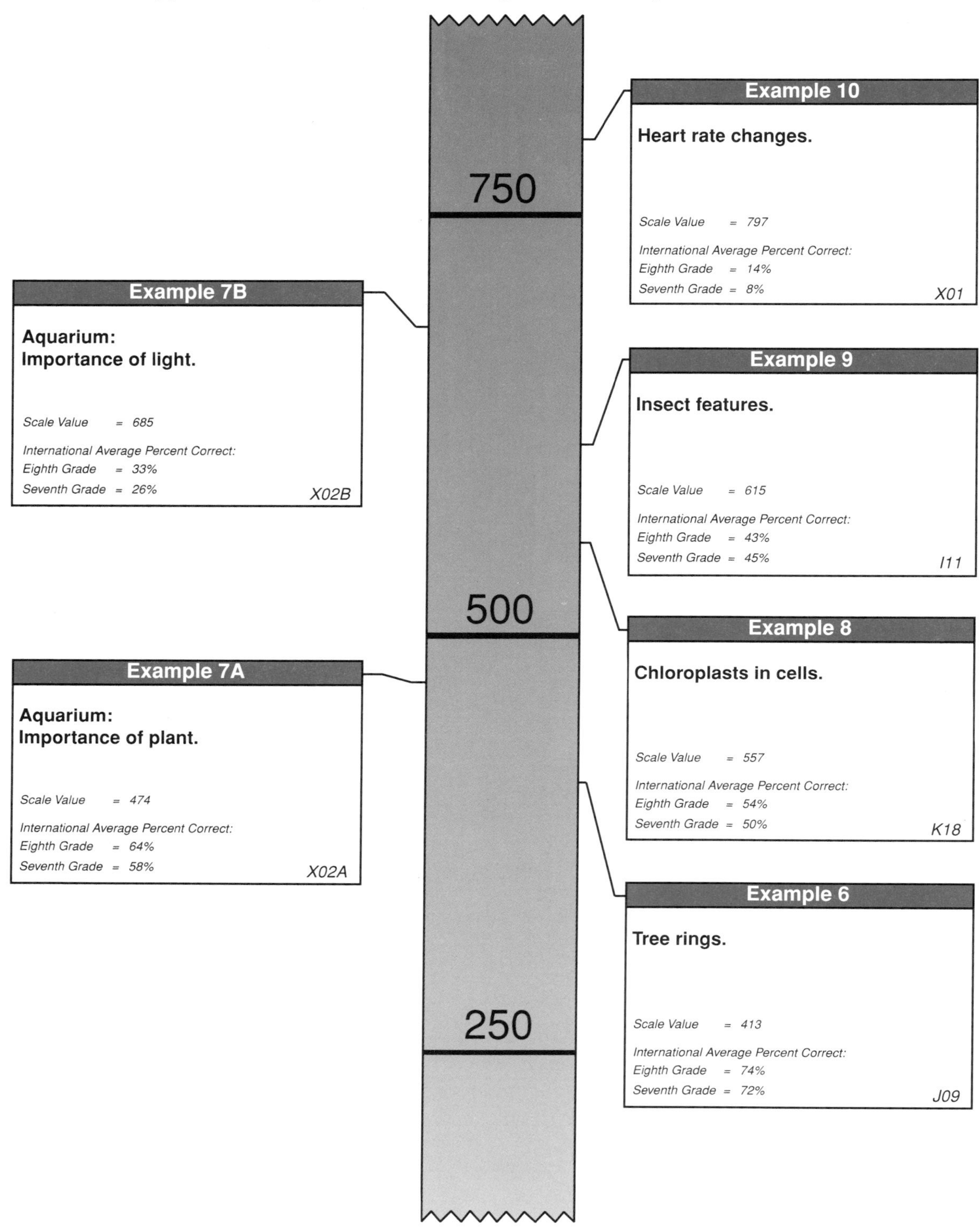

*Seventh and eighth grades in most countries; see Table 2 for information about the grades tested in each country.
NOTE: Each item was placed onto the TIMSS international science scale based on students' performance in both grades. Items are shown at the point on the scale where students with that level of proficiency had a 65 percent probability of providing a correct response.

EXAMPLE ITEM 6
LIFE SCIENCE

Tree rings

How could you find out how old a tree is after it is cut?

You could find out how old a tree was after it is cut by counting the rings. Every ring equals one year

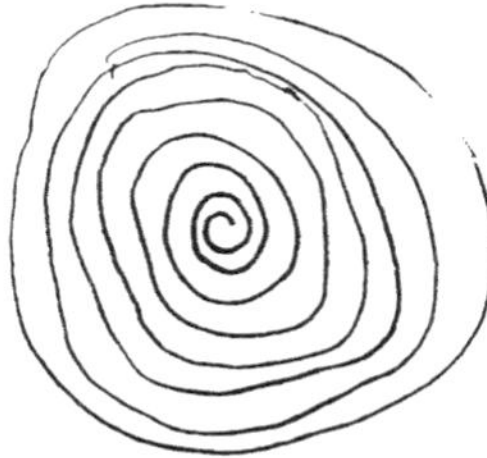

Performance Category: Understanding Complex Information

EXAMPLE ITEM 7
LIFE SCIENCE

Aquarium

In the picture of an aquarium, six items are labeled.

Explain why each of the following is important in maintaining the ecosystem in the aquarium.

(a) the plant

to give off oxegn and take in carlon dioxide which the animals breath out

(b) the light

to help the plant make photosynthesis and make its own food

Performance Category: Theorizing, Analyzing, and Solving Problems

EXAMPLE ITEM 8
LIFE SCIENCE

Chloroplasts in cells

What is the main function of chloroplasts in a plant cell?

(A.) To absorb light energy and manufacture food

B. To remove waste materials by active transport

C. To manufacture chemical energy from food

D. To control the shape of the cell

Performance Category: Understanding Simple Information

EXAMPLE ITEM 9
LIFE SCIENCE

Insect features

What features do all insects have?

	Number of LEGS	Number of BODY PARTS
A.	2	4
B.	4	2
(C.)	6	3
D.	8	3

Performance Category: Understanding Complex Information

EXAMPLE ITEM 10
LIFE SCIENCE

Heart rate changes

Suppose you want to investigate how the human heart rate changes with changes in activity. What materials would you use and what procedures would you follow?

materials: stopwatch

procedures: I would have a person sit and then take their pulse. I would have the person walk, then take their pulse again. Finally, I would ~~to~~ have the person run and take their pulse. Each tine I took their pulse I would time how many ~~beats~~ times per minute their heart was beating

Performance Category: Investigating the Natural World

What Have Students Learned About Physics?

Major topics covered by the physics items include different energy forms, physical transformations, forces and motion, and the properties of matter. Students were asked to solve problems and demonstrate their knowledge of scientific principles. Six example items (Example Items 11 - 16) are included to illustrate the range of item types and content areas as well as student performance in physics. The percent correct results for these items are shown in Table 3.3. The international difficulty map showing the physics example items is shown in Figure 3.3. The item positions and the international averages for correct responses indicate that for most countries, the majority of students had considerable difficulty on the more complex physics items.

Example Item 11 required extrapolating from a simple linear distance-versus-time graph, which proved to be an easy problem for most students. On average, more than three-fourths of the students across countries at both grades answered correctly (78% and 83%). Students' performance was quite high in most countries, with only three countries having performance below 50% at either grade – Kuwait (45%) at the eighth grade as well as Iran (47%) and Colombia (46%) at the seventh grade.

Students also did well on Example Item 12, which measured their knowledge of complete electronic circuits and conductive materials. The international average percent correct values of 69% and 78% at the seventh and eighth grades indicate a somewhat larger average between-grade difference than was generally observed. Several countries had a between-grade increase of 10% or more; the most notable was the increase from 48% to 74% for Portugal.

Student performance across countries on Example Item 13, measuring knowledge about the transmission of sound waves, averaged nearly 70% correct responses for both grades (67% and 70%). The variability across countries was moderately low on this item, with very few countries having percent correct levels below 60%. Korea and Japan had very high performances, with 88% to 90% correct at both grades.

Fewer students across countries demonstrated a knowledge of gravitational force as measured by Example Item 14. On average, only approximately half the students at either grade responded correctly (49% and 55%). The most commonly chosen incorrect option (B) reflected the misconception that the earth's gravitational force does not act upon a stationary object when it is on the ground. The top-performing country was the Czech Republic, where more than 80% of the students responded correctly at both grades.

Example Item 15 asked students to interpret data presented in a table to determine which of two machines would be more efficient. This is a relatively complex problem that required understanding the concepts of energy conversion and efficiency, recognizing and calculating the appropriate ratios, and explaining the results. In their explanations, students needed to choose machine A because it uses less gas per hectare, or to document this fact with the idea that 3/8 is less than 1/2, or a similar expression. On average, only 29% of seventh-grade and 36% of eighth-grade students answered correctly, and in only nine countries did half or more of the eighth-grade students give a fully-correct response.

Internationally, students also found Example Item 16 to be very difficult. This is a practical problem related to the nature of light requiring students to apply scientific principles to provide an explanation. Essentially, students needed to communicate that the same amount of light reaches the wall regardless of the distance the flashlight is from the wall. They may or may not have included the idea that the light becomes more or less spread out. On average, fewer than one-fourth of the students across countries correctly answered this item (18% and 23%). For most countries, performance at the eighth grade was not better than at the seventh grade. A common misconception identified in more than 30% of the student responses was that a larger area of illumination means there is more light.

Table 3.3

Percent Correct for Physics Example Items - Lower and Upper Grades (Seventh and Eighth Grades*)

Country	Example 11 Distance versus time graph.		Example 12 Light bulb in circuit.		Example 13 Sound in space.	
	Seventh Grade	Eighth Grade	Seventh Grade	Eighth Grade	Seventh Grade	Eighth Grade
† Belgium (Fl)	93 (1.5)	84 (5.2)	86 (2.0)	87 (2.8)	64 (3.4)	62 (3.3)
† Belgium (Fr)	86 (2.3)	86 (2.6)	54 (3.7)	62 (3.0)	66 (3.1)	74 (2.6)
Canada	88 (1.9)	92 (1.2)	76 (1.9)	79 (1.9)	71 (2.4)	72 (1.7)
Cyprus	53 (3.4)	64 (2.5)	64 (3.2)	73 (2.6)	57 (2.5)	62 (2.4)
Czech Republic	88 (2.0)	90 (1.7)	87 (1.6)	89 (1.4)	73 (1.9)	76 (2.8)
†2 England	87 (2.4)	88 (2.2)	89 (2.6)	90 (1.9)	76 (2.8)	76 (3.0)
France	90 (1.9)	97 (0.9)	67 (2.6)	79 (1.9)	70 (2.3)	72 (2.4)
Hong Kong	86 (2.2)	89 (1.7)	78 (2.7)	88 (1.7)	77 (2.1)	81 (2.2)
Hungary	81 (2.1)	83 (1.9)	74 (2.4)	85 (2.0)	73 (2.5)	82 (2.2)
Iceland	79 (3.6)	86 (3.1)	60 (4.3)	66 (4.2)	68 (4.3)	65 (4.8)
Iran, Islamic Rep.	47 (4.6)	65 (3.4)	59 (3.7)	59 (3.0)	62 (4.0)	65 (4.1)
Ireland	84 (2.1)	92 (1.4)	56 (2.4)	69 (2.6)	75 (2.4)	75 (2.3)
Japan	92 (1.0)	94 (0.9)	88 (1.6)	92 (1.1)	88 (1.4)	90 (1.2)
Korea	88 (1.7)	90 (1.7)	86 (1.9)	93 (1.3)	90 (1.7)	90 (1.5)
1 Latvia (LSS)	75 (2.6)	82 (2.6)	54 (3.3)	60 (3.5)	65 (3.2)	80 (2.9)
1 Lithuania	69 (3.1)	77 (2.9)	50 (3.4)	64 (3.0)	65 (3.3)	64 (2.9)
New Zealand	81 (2.2)	92 (1.6)	74 (2.5)	82 (1.7)	67 (2.8)	74 (2.0)
Norway	81 (2.9)	89 (1.8)	65 (3.6)	74 (2.4)	70 (2.7)	74 (2.6)
Portugal	72 (2.4)	89 (1.5)	48 (2.3)	74 (2.3)	57 (3.6)	71 (2.1)
Russian Federation	82 (2.2)	83 (2.4)	61 (2.5)	74 (2.3)	60 (3.3)	69 (2.4)
† Scotland	87 (1.7)	92 (1.5)	70 (2.4)	82 (2.6)	68 (2.6)	77 (2.2)
Singapore	94 (1.2)	96 (1.0)	95 (1.1)	97 (0.8)	66 (2.9)	86 (1.9)
Slovak Republic	78 (2.3)	86 (1.9)	83 (2.2)	91 (1.5)	71 (2.7)	73 (2.2)
Spain	78 (2.0)	85 (1.7)	77 (2.3)	82 (1.8)	63 (2.3)	69 (2.8)
Sweden	81 (2.4)	88 (1.6)	75 (2.7)	88 (1.8)	72 (2.3)	71 (2.3)
1 Switzerland	83 (2.2)	90 (1.5)	67 (2.4)	77 (2.1)	77 (2.2)	76 (2.3)
† United States	83 (1.6)	87 (1.8)	75 (2.3)	78 (2.0)	59 (3.0)	65 (2.6)
Countries Not Satisfying Guidelines for Sample Participation Rates (see Appendix A for Details):						
Australia	87 (1.5)	90 (1.2)	73 (2.2)	83 (1.4)	69 (2.3)	73 (2.0)
Austria	78 (2.4)	87 (2.0)	84 (2.4)	91 (1.7)	76 (2.6)	80 (2.5)
Bulgaria	75 (4.5)	78 (2.5)	72 (2.9)	75 (3.1)	85 (3.2)	74 (4.4)
Netherlands	94 (1.3)	95 (1.7)	74 (3.0)	81 (4.1)	49 (3.4)	58 (3.4)
Countries Not Meeting Age/Grade Specifications (High Percentage of Older Students; See Appendix A for Details):						
Colombia	46 (3.6)	59 (3.9)	47 (3.9)	63 (3.2)	51 (3.7)	52 (4.0)
†1 Germany	79 (2.6)	84 (2.3)	78 (2.5)	83 (2.7)	78 (2.1)	74 (2.4)
Romania	64 (2.3)	67 (2.6)	60 (3.0)	69 (2.6)	51 (2.7)	53 (2.8)
Slovenia	87 (2.0)	92 (1.4)	78 (2.2)	88 (1.7)	71 (2.5)	76 (2.5)
Countries With Unapproved Sampling Procedures at Classroom Level (See Appendix A for Details):						
Denmark	80 (2.6)	86 (2.0)	60 (3.1)	74 (2.9)	61 (3.4)	60 (3.0)
Greece	60 (2.3)	71 (2.3)	62 (2.5)	69 (2.4)	72 (2.1)	82 (1.8)
† South Africa	57 (2.8)	59 (2.8)	28 (2.1)	42 (3.2)	29 (1.9)	32 (2.6)
Thailand	81 (2.2)	83 (1.6)	73 (1.9)	78 (1.7)	65 (2.1)	70 (2.0)
Unapproved Sampling Procedures at Classroom Level and Not Meeting Other Guidelines (See Appendix A for Details):						
1 Israel	–	83 (3.6)	–	86 (1.9)	–	76 (3.4)
Kuwait	–	45 (4.1)	–	65 (3.3)	–	64 (3.2)

*Seventh and eighth grades in most countries; see Table 2 for information about the grades tested in each country.
†Met guidelines for sample participation rates only after replacement schools were included (see Appendix A for details).
[1]National Desired Population does not cover all of International Desired Population (see Table A.2). Because coverage falls below 65%, Latvia is annotated LSS for Latvian Speaking Schools only.
[2]National Defined Population covers less than 90 percent of National Desired Population (see Table A.2).
( ) Standard errors appear in parentheses. Because results are rounded to the nearest whole number, some totals may appear inconsistent.
A dash (–) indicates data are not available. Israel and Kuwait did not test at the seventh grade.

SOURCE: IEA Third International Mathematics and Science Study (TIMSS), 1994-95.

Table 3.3 (Continued)

Percent Correct for Physics Example Items - Lower and Upper Grades (Seventh and Eighth Grades*)

Country	Example 14 Falling apple.		Example 15 More efficient machine.		Example 16 Flashlight shining on wall.	
	Seventh Grade	Eighth Grade	Seventh Grade	Eighth Grade	Seventh Grade	Eighth Grade
† Belgium (Fl)	63 (2.6)	62 (2.3)	44 (2.8)	49 (2.3)	22 (2.1)	31 (3.1)
† Belgium (Fr)	48 (3.4)	52 (3.3)	37 (3.3)	42 (3.2)	14 (2.8)	15 (2.2)
Canada	59 (2.4)	63 (2.7)	42 (2.2)	49 (2.2)	23 (2.1)	29 (1.7)
Cyprus	25 (2.2)	36 (2.6)	22 (2.1)	36 (2.6)	7 (1.6)	6 (1.4)
Czech Republic	84 (2.0)	81 (2.6)	34 (3.0)	48 (3.2)	12 (1.9)	23 (2.7)
†2 England	51 (3.4)	51 (3.4)	42 (3.3)	51 (4.1)	23 (3.3)	35 (3.6)
France	36 (2.7)	51 (3.0)	21 (2.7)	29 (2.4)	11 (1.9)	19 (2.3)
Hong Kong	69 (2.8)	74 (2.2)	17 (2.2)	26 (2.5)	14 (1.7)	17 (2.2)
Hungary	69 (2.6)	72 (2.3)	22 (2.3)	36 (3.0)	38 (3.0)	40 (2.7)
Iceland	41 (3.0)	40 (5.0)	22 (2.7)	33 (4.4)	11 (2.1)	14 (2.6)
Iran, Islamic Rep.	51 (4.5)	51 (3.6)	28 (2.7)	25 (3.4)	40 (3.0)	37 (2.8)
Ireland	49 (3.1)	55 (2.7)	41 (3.0)	54 (2.7)	18 (1.9)	21 (2.1)
Japan	59 (2.0)	58 (2.2)	30 (2.0)	36 (2.0)	27 (1.9)	37 (2.0)
Korea	63 (2.6)	72 (2.6)	46 (2.8)	47 (2.6)	38 (3.1)	37 (2.5)
1 Latvia (LSS)	35 (2.8)	41 (3.3)	10 (1.8)	18 (2.5)	15 (2.3)	20 (2.4)
1 Lithuania	46 (3.4)	61 (3.1)	6 (1.4)	13 (2.1)	8 (1.8)	13 (2.5)
New Zealand	47 (3.0)	54 (2.7)	37 (2.5)	49 (2.6)	28 (2.4)	31 (2.5)
Norway	43 (3.8)	49 (2.9)	20 (2.4)	37 (2.4)	19 (2.6)	25 (2.4)
Portugal	43 (3.0)	53 (2.7)	20 (2.3)	21 (2.4)	9 (1.5)	17 (2.1)
Russian Federation	48 (3.3)	42 (2.4)	21 (2.1)	25 (2.8)	11 (2.3)	10 (1.6)
† Scotland	39 (3.2)	48 (2.6)	40 (3.0)	51 (2.7)	19 (2.2)	22 (2.6)
Singapore	50 (2.8)	59 (2.4)	41 (3.5)	48 (2.7)	20 (2.4)	28 (2.4)
Slovak Republic	77 (2.4)	72 (2.5)	34 (2.6)	48 (2.8)	29 (2.4)	28 (2.4)
Spain	48 (2.5)	55 (2.4)	17 (2.0)	24 (2.1)	19 (2.2)	20 (2.2)
Sweden	37 (2.7)	59 (2.6)	25 (2.2)	42 (2.8)	26 (2.9)	29 (1.8)
1 Switzerland	42 (2.8)	53 (2.9)	33 (2.2)	50 (2.5)	11 (1.3)	11 (1.2)
† United States	55 (3.2)	64 (2.2)	36 (3.2)	48 (2.6)	21 (2.0)	27 (2.5)
Countries Not Satisfying Guidelines for Sample Participation Rates (see Appendix A for Details):						
Australia	55 (2.9)	57 (2.0)	36 (2.5)	51 (2.1)	25 (2.1)	28 (1.6)
Austria	51 (3.3)	61 (2.9)	54 (3.1)	62 (3.2)	9 (1.9)	11 (2.3)
Bulgaria	37 (3.6)	41 (5.0)	25 (3.9)	19 (3.3)	38 (3.6)	29 (3.6)
Netherlands	41 (2.8)	58 (2.9)	50 (4.0)	58 (4.2)	22 (3.0)	30 (3.8)
Countries Not Meeting Age/Grade Specifications (High Percentage of Older Students; See Appendix A for Details):						
Colombia	43 (3.2)	48 (3.6)	10 (1.7)	10 (2.1)	4 (1.2)	6 (1.2)
†1 Germany	46 (3.1)	55 (3.2)	37 (2.9)	42 (3.2)	16 (2.1)	22 (2.9)
Romania	46 (2.7)	50 (2.6)	16 (1.9)	19 (2.4)	14 (2.0)	15 (2.3)
Slovenia	53 (3.4)	57 (2.9)	41 (2.7)	52 (2.7)	18 (2.1)	27 (2.7)
Countries With Unapproved Sampling Procedures at Classroom Level (See Appendix A for Details):						
Denmark	47 (3.8)	51 (3.3)	23 (2.6)	36 (3.3)	19 (2.3)	26 (2.7)
Greece	28 (2.1)	30 (2.2)	17 (1.8)	24 (2.2)	17 (1.7)	28 (2.7)
† South Africa	34 (2.4)	36 (2.5)	5 (1.5)	8 (1.8)	6 (1.1)	4 (1.2)
Thailand	59 (2.4)	57 (2.3)	3 (0.8)	5 (1.0)	4 (1.0)	5 (1.1)
Unapproved Sampling Procedures at Classroom Level and Not Meeting Other Guidelines (See Appendix A for Details):						
1 Israel	–	61 (2.9)	–	53 (3.9)	–	43 (5.2)
Kuwait	–	50 (4.1)	–	19 (4.0)	–	24 (3.0)

*Seventh and eighth grades in most countries; see Table 2 for information about the grades tested in each country.
†Met guidelines for sample participation rates only after replacement schools were included (see Appendix A for details).
1National Desired Population does not cover all of International Desired Population (see Table A.2). Because coverage falls below 65%, Latvia is annotated LSS for Latvian Speaking Schools only.
2National Defined Population covers less than 90 percent of National Desired Population (see Table A.2).
( ) Standard errors appear in parentheses. Because results are rounded to the nearest whole number, some totals may appear inconsistent.
A dash (–) indicates data are not available. Israel and Kuwait did not test at the seventh grade.

SOURCE: IEA Third International Mathematics and Science Study (TIMSS), 1994-95.

Figure 3.3

International Difficulty Map for Physics Example Items - Lower and Upper Grades (Seventh and Eighth Grades*)

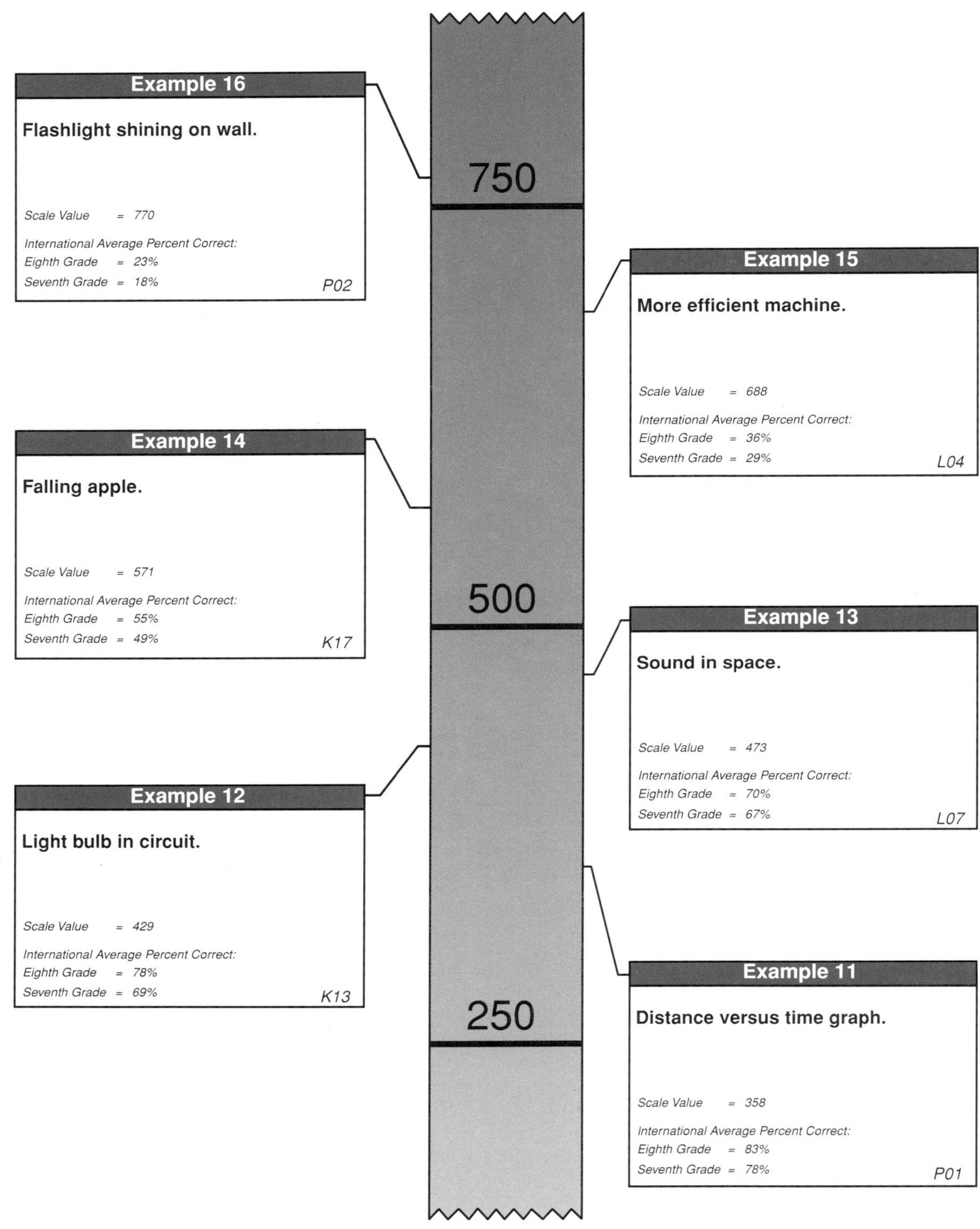

*Seventh and eighth grades in most countries; see Table 2 for information about the grades tested in each country.
NOTE: Each item was placed onto the TIMSS international science scale based on students' performance in both grades. Items are shown at the point on the scale where students with that level of proficiency had a 65 percent probability of providing a correct response.

EXAMPLE ITEM 11
PHYSICS

Distance versus time graph

The graph shows the progress made by an ant moving along a straight line.

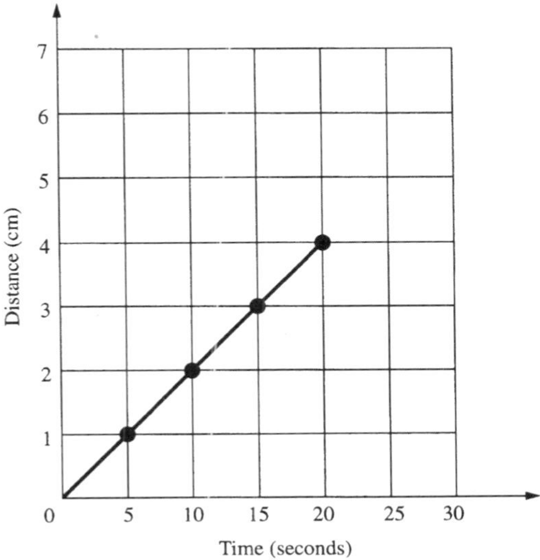

If the ant keeps moving at the same speed, how far will it have traveled at the end of 30 seconds?

A. 5 cm

B. 6 cm

C. 20 cm

D. 30 cm

Performance Category: Using Tools, Routine Procedures, and Science Processes

EXAMPLE ITEM 12
PHYSICS

Light bulb in circuit

The following diagrams show a flashlight battery and a bulb connected by wires to various substances.

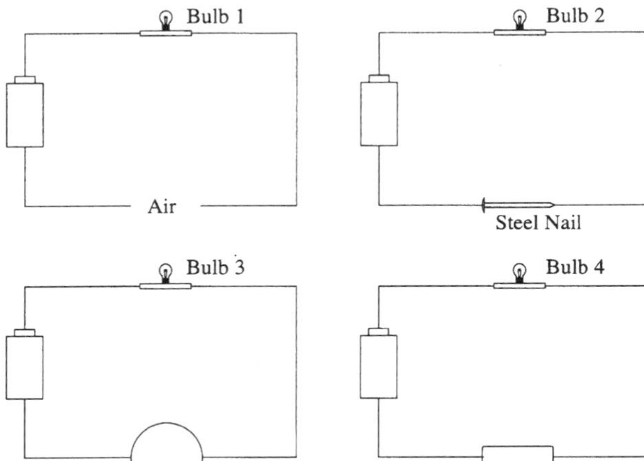

Which of the bulbs will light?

A. 1 and 2 only

B. 2 and 3 only

C. 3 and 4 only

D. 1, 2, and 3 only

E. 2, 3, and 4 only

Performance Category: Understanding Complex Information

EXAMPLE ITEM 13
PHYSICS

Sound in space

The crews of two boats at sea can communicate with each other by shouting. Why is it impossible for the crews of two spaceships a similar distance apart in space to do this?

A. The sound is reflected more in space.

B. The pressure is too high inside the spaceships.

C. The spaceships are traveling faster than sound.

D. There is no air in space for the sound to travel through.

Performance Category: Understanding Complex Information

Example Item 14 Physics

Falling apple

The drawing shows an apple falling to the ground. In which of the three positions does gravity act on the apple?

A. 2 only

B. 1 and 2 only

C. 1 and 3 only

(D.) 1, 2, and 3

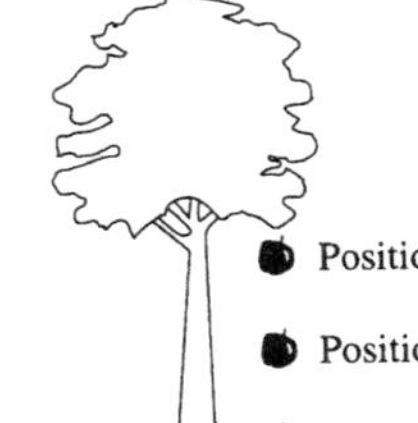

Performance Category: Understanding Simple Information

Example Item 15 Physics

More efficient machine

Machine A and Machine B are each used to clear a field. The table shows how large an area each cleared in 1 hour and how much gasoline each used.

	Area of field cleared in 1 hour	Gasoline used in 1 hour
Machine A	2 hectares	3/4 liter
Machine B	1 hectare	1/2 liter

Which machine is more efficient in converting the energy in gasoline to work? Explain your answer.

Machine A because it did double the amount of work but didn't use ~~dob~~ dauble the amount of gasoline.

Performance Category: Theorizing, Analyzing, and Solving Problems

EXAMPLE ITEM 16
PHYSICS

Flashlight shining on wall

A flashlight close to a wall produces a small circle of light compared to the circle it makes when the flashlight is far from the wall. Does more light reach the wall when the flashlight is further away?

___ Yes

✓ No (Check one)

Explain your answer.

The same amount of light reaches the wall except when it is close it is all on a smaller area.

Performance Category: Theorizing, Analyzing, and Solving Problems

What Have Students Learned About Chemistry?

The chemistry items measured students' knowledge of topics related to chemical transformations as well as the chemical properties and classification of matter. The country-by-country results for the five example items (Examples 17 - 21) are shown in Table 3.4. The item difficulty map for the chemistry example items is portrayed in Figure 3.4. As discussed in Chapter 2, the items covering chemistry were the most difficult for students compared to the other science content areas (international averages correct across all chemistry items of 51% for eighth grade and 43% for seventh grade).

Both Example Items 17 and 18 required students to supply explanations that demonstrated knowledge of the necessity of oxygen for combustion, but performance was very different on the two items. On average, nearly 90% of both seventh- and eighth-grade students (86% and 89%) explained the loss of oxygen or air (using either scientific or non-scientific language) in Example Item 17, which directly indicates the isolation of the flame from the air in the provided diagram. In most countries, seventh- and eighth-grade students performed comparably, with all except Colombia and South Africa having more than 70% correct responses at both grades.

Compared to Example Item 17, Example Item 18 was more complicated, requiring students to explain that carbon dioxide in fire extinguishers displaces oxygen and prevents it from reaching the fire. As might be expected, this item was much more difficult for students, which is reflected in the international averages of 42% and 50%

correct responses for seventh and eighth grades. Across countries, correct responses on 70% or more of the items were achieved on average by eighth-grade students in England (71%), Singapore (70%), Sweden (70%), and Austria (74%). In general, the eighth-grade students performed better than the seventh-grade students, with the most notable increase observed in Scotland (40% to 59%).

Across countries, especially at the seventh-grade, students found Example Item 19 to be rather difficult. On average, 43% of the eighth-grade students across countries, but only 28% of the seventh-grade students, identified ion formation as the correct response. At both grades, about one-third of the students, on average, incorrectly identified the formation of molecules as the result of electron loss. Dramatic across-country variations in performance point to differences in the stage at which atomic structure is first introduced into the curriculum.[3] Many countries had relatively low performance in both seventh and eighth grades, indicating that this topic had not been taught by the eighth grade (Iceland, Norway, and Denmark, for example). For other countries, such as Lithuania and Greece, the substantial increases between seventh and eighth grades indicate curriculum coverage of this topic in the eighth grade. Topic coverage by the seventh grade is indicated by relatively high performances in both grades for several countries, including the eastern European countries of the Czech Republic, Hungary, the Slovak Republic, Bulgaria, Romania, and Slovenia.

In Example Item 20, students were required to use knowledge of the difference between chemical and physical transformations. International averages were low (26% and 31%), and only three countries had more than 50% correct responses at the eighth grade (Iran, Japan, and Singapore). The largest between-grade increase was seen for Japan, from 19% to 54%. As was observed with Example Item 19, Lithuania also had a substantial increase for Example Item 20, from 10% to 37%. Large between-grade differences for Lithuania are also reflected in their achievement on the overall science scale (Table 1.3) and on chemistry, in particular (Table 2.3).

Example Item 21 measured knowledge about the chemical make-up of cells. Internationally, students found this short-answer-format item to be quite difficult, with about one-third (32%) of the eighth-grade and only 21% of seventh-grade students providing the correct response, on average. The highest performance on this item was achieved in Bulgaria, with 50% of seventh- and 68% of eighth-grade students responding correctly. In a few countries, there were large increases in performance between the seventh and eighth grades. This was most pronounced for Singapore, with an increase from 21% to 66%.

3 These results are supported, in most cases, by review of the reports provided by NRCs for the Test-Curriculum Matching Analysis (Appendix B), identifying whether the topic covered by this item was in the intended curriculum at the seventh or eighth grade.

Table 3.4

Percent Correct for Chemistry Example Items - Lower and Upper Grades (Seventh and Eighth Grades*)

Country	Example 17 Glass over candle flame.		Example 18 Carbon dioxide fire extinguisher.		Example 19 Atom loses electron.	
	Seventh Grade	Eighth Grade	Seventh Grade	Eighth Grade	Seventh Grade	Eighth Grade
† Belgium (Fl)	92 (1.7)	97 (1.3)	44 (2.8)	58 (4.1)	23 (2.2)	20 (2.7)
† Belgium (Fr)	87 (2.2)	84 (2.5)	30 (3.3)	33 (3.5)	19 (2.8)	25 (4.6)
Canada	91 (1.4)	93 (1.2)	52 (2.9)	61 (2.0)	19 (1.6)	25 (2.1)
Cyprus	78 (1.8)	82 (1.8)	29 (2.4)	41 (3.3)	19 (3.0)	22 (2.8)
Czech Republic	97 (0.9)	98 (1.0)	47 (3.3)	57 (2.8)	72 (2.4)	73 (3.0)
†2 England	92 (1.7)	97 (1.1)	59 (3.3)	71 (3.1)	14 (2.1)	28 (2.9)
France	85 (1.9)	86 (2.0)	34 (2.7)	50 (3.6)	18 (2.1)	40 (3.6)
Hong Kong	90 (1.7)	91 (1.9)	32 (2.6)	37 (2.6)	56 (2.6)	58 (2.2)
Hungary	94 (1.4)	98 (0.6)	60 (3.1)	62 (2.4)	67 (2.5)	73 (2.7)
Iceland	94 (1.7)	91 (2.6)	45 (4.0)	57 (4.5)	8 (2.0)	9 (2.5)
Iran, Islamic Rep.	93 (1.6)	94 (1.2)	63 (3.9)	63 (2.7)	19 (2.9)	40 (3.8)
Ireland	89 (1.8)	93 (1.5)	54 (2.7)	66 (3.2)	20 (2.4)	46 (2.9)
Japan	86 (1.6)	90 (1.2)	36 (1.9)	45 (2.0)	27 (2.0)	33 (2.0)
Korea	90 (1.8)	93 (1.3)	52 (2.4)	54 (2.5)	20 (2.1)	45 (3.0)
1 Latvia (LSS)	81 (2.4)	86 (2.8)	28 (3.0)	42 (3.0)	15 (2.1)	39 (3.0)
1 Lithuania	85 (2.2)	95 (1.7)	17 (2.7)	29 (3.2)	8 (1.9)	65 (3.4)
New Zealand	89 (1.9)	93 (1.3)	48 (3.1)	65 (2.4)	12 (1.9)	18 (2.2)
Norway	93 (1.8)	95 (1.1)	52 (4.3)	63 (2.2)	9 (1.7)	19 (1.9)
Portugal	77 (2.0)	89 (1.5)	24 (2.4)	35 (2.7)	19 (2.2)	68 (2.5)
Russian Federation	92 (1.4)	93 (1.5)	43 (2.5)	54 (3.2)	36 (3.0)	75 (2.4)
† Scotland	79 (2.1)	93 (1.4)	40 (2.6)	59 (3.5)	15 (1.9)	21 (2.1)
Singapore	92 (1.6)	96 (0.7)	56 (3.3)	70 (2.3)	23 (2.5)	51 (2.9)
Slovak Republic	96 (1.0)	95 (1.4)	48 (2.6)	46 (2.8)	69 (2.6)	77 (2.6)
Spain	85 (1.9)	89 (1.7)	36 (2.6)	43 (2.9)	51 (3.5)	70 (2.3)
Sweden	94 (1.2)	97 (0.9)	70 (2.7)	70 (2.3)	10 (1.8)	44 (3.1)
1 Switzerland	95 (1.0)	96 (1.0)	48 (2.6)	57 (2.5)	15 (1.7)	22 (2.2)
† United States	86 (2.0)	90 (1.3)	53 (3.0)	62 (2.7)	30 (2.8)	47 (2.7)
Countries Not Satisfying Guidelines for Sample Participation Rates (see Appendix A for Details):						
Australia	89 (1.8)	91 (1.2)	57 (2.4)	61 (1.9)	13 (1.4)	31 (2.2)
Austria	95 (1.3)	95 (1.5)	63 (3.1)	74 (2.9)	64 (3.2)	64 (3.1)
Bulgaria	92 (2.7)	92 (2.5)	44 (4.5)	46 (4.0)	64 (3.5)	70 (4.4)
Netherlands	93 (1.7)	96 (1.3)	41 (3.4)	56 (3.3)	12 (2.1)	21 (3.2)
Countries Not Meeting Age/Grade Specifications (High Percentage of Older Students; See Appendix A for Details):						
Colombia	54 (3.1)	58 (3.1)	13 (2.4)	23 (4.1)	31 (3.6)	40 (4.1)
†1 Germany	92 (1.6)	92 (2.0)	62 (3.3)	69 (3.0)	24 (3.0)	38 (4.0)
Romania	84 (1.9)	87 (1.7)	34 (2.9)	33 (2.5)	60 (3.0)	74 (2.6)
Slovenia	97 (1.0)	99 (0.4)	49 (3.2)	52 (3.2)	81 (2.5)	80 (2.1)
Countries With Unapproved Sampling Procedures at Classroom Level (See Appendix A for Details):						
Denmark	90 (2.0)	97 (1.0)	21 (2.4)	33 (3.0)	8 (2.4)	17 (2.2)
Greece	79 (2.0)	86 (1.8)	31 (2.3)	37 (2.3)	15 (1.8)	53 (2.6)
† South Africa	35 (3.5)	35 (3.3)	12 (2.2)	15 (2.9)	14 (1.4)	13 (1.7)
Thailand	78 (2.0)	81 (1.8)	27 (2.7)	34 (2.4)	10 (1.2)	15 (1.6)
Unapproved Sampling Procedures at Classroom Level and Not Meeting Other Guidelines (See Appendix A for Details):						
1 Israel	–	82 (2.9)	–	63 (4.5)	–	72 (4.9)
Kuwait	–	71 (4.8)	–	49 (4.6)	–	31 (3.0)

*Seventh and eighth grades in most countries; see Table 2 for information about the grades tested in each country.
†Met guidelines for sample participation rates only after replacement schools were included (see Appendix A for details).
[1]National Desired Population does not cover all of International Desired Population (see Table A.2). Because coverage falls below 65%, Latvia is annotated LSS for Latvian Speaking Schools only.
[2]National Defined Population covers less than 90 percent of National Desired Population (see Table A.2).
( ) Standard errors appear in parentheses. Because results are rounded to the nearest whole number, some totals may appear inconsistent.
A dash (–) indicates data are not available. Israel and Kuwait did not test at the seventh grade.

SOURCE: IEA Third International Mathematics and Science Study (TIMSS), 1994-95.

Table 3.4 (Continued)

Percent Correct for Chemistry Example Items - Lower and Upper Grades (Seventh and Eighth Grades*)

Country	Example 20 Chemical change.		Example 21 Molecules, atoms, and cells.	
	Seventh Grade	Eighth Grade	Seventh Grade	Eighth Grade
† Belgium (Fl)	25 (2.4)	31 (3.0)	17 (1.8)	19 (2.3)
† Belgium (Fr)	11 (2.2)	13 (1.9)	9 (1.7)	20 (2.8)
Canada	37 (2.1)	38 (2.6)	23 (2.3)	24 (1.6)
Cyprus	–	–	11 (1.6)	35 (2.9)
Czech Republic	31 (3.2)	34 (4.0)	32 (3.0)	43 (3.9)
†2 England	37 (3.4)	41 (3.5)	25 (2.9)	34 (3.0)
France	21 (2.1)	19 (2.8)	17 (2.0)	25 (2.6)
Hong Kong	24 (2.6)	30 (2.5)	26 (2.5)	32 (2.5)
Hungary	17 (2.1)	18 (2.2)	32 (2.2)	42 (3.1)
Iceland	21 (2.6)	20 (2.9)	9 (1.8)	12 (2.8)
Iran, Islamic Rep.	46 (2.8)	52 (2.5)	14 (2.2)	23 (2.4)
Ireland	35 (2.3)	39 (2.9)	25 (2.3)	25 (2.4)
Japan	19 (1.8)	54 (1.9)	32 (2.0)	47 (2.2)
Korea	24 (2.8)	48 (3.0)	17 (1.9)	30 (2.3)
1 Latvia (LSS)	15 (2.4)	26 (3.0)	12 (1.8)	38 (2.9)
1 Lithuania	10 (2.1)	37 (3.4)	14 (2.1)	39 (2.9)
New Zealand	33 (2.6)	42 (2.4)	16 (2.0)	27 (2.5)
Norway	6 (1.5)	12 (1.7)	12 (1.8)	29 (1.9)
Portugal	20 (2.1)	40 (2.7)	18 (1.7)	37 (2.4)
Russian Federation	15 (1.8)	31 (4.6)	41 (3.4)	53 (3.6)
† Scotland	24 (2.3)	33 (2.9)	21 (2.1)	27 (2.8)
Singapore	62 (3.0)	62 (2.1)	21 (2.2)	66 (2.6)
Slovak Republic	31 (2.1)	31 (2.4)	28 (2.3)	42 (2.6)
Spain	13 (1.9)	17 (2.2)	30 (2.4)	41 (2.2)
Sweden	16 (2.0)	22 (1.9)	21 (2.7)	39 (2.6)
1 Switzerland	19 (1.8)	25 (2.4)	9 (1.3)	20 (1.6)
† United States	40 (2.7)	43 (2.7)	27 (2.7)	29 (1.9)
Countries Not Satisfying Guidelines for Sample Participation Rates (see Appendix A for Details):				
Australia	37 (2.4)	47 (2.3)	18 (1.4)	27 (2.0)
Austria	28 (2.4)	34 (3.5)	17 (2.2)	28 (3.6)
Bulgaria	33 (3.2)	33 (4.1)	50 (4.9)	68 (4.7)
Netherlands	31 (4.1)	35 (3.7)	15 (2.8)	24 (3.1)
Countries Not Meeting Age/Grade Specifications (High Percentage of Older Students; See Appendix A for Details):				
Colombia	17 (2.0)	18 (3.9)	17 (2.6)	21 (2.5)
†1 Germany	21 (2.4)	25 (2.7)	16 (2.1)	21 (2.5)
Romania	25 (2.2)	21 (2.4)	29 (2.5)	31 (3.2)
Slovenia	28 (2.6)	22 (2.6)	24 (2.1)	28 (2.9)
Countries With Unapproved Sampling Procedures at Classroom Level (See Appendix A for Details):				
Denmark	31 (3.2)	32 (3.1)	14 (2.3)	29 (2.8)
Greece	21 (2.0)	27 (2.0)	32 (2.2)	44 (2.5)
† South Africa	21 (1.5)	26 (2.1)	7 (1.3)	7 (1.6)
Thailand	23 (1.6)	16 (1.9)	21 (2.0)	31 (2.8)
Unapproved Sampling Procedures at Classroom Level and Not Meeting Other Guidelines (See Appendix A for Details):				
1 Israel	–	23 (3.5)	–	26 (3.6)
Kuwait	–	31 (3.3)	–	20 (3.3)

*Seventh and eighth grades in most countries; see Table 2 for information about the grades tested in each country.
†Met guidelines for sample participation rates only after replacement schools were included (see Appendix A for details).
1National Desired Population does not cover all of International Desired Population (see Table A.2). Because coverage falls below 65%, Latvia is annotated LSS for Latvian Speaking Schools only.
2National Defined Population covers less than 90 percent of National Desired Population (see Table A.2).
( ) Standard errors appear in parentheses. Because results are rounded to the nearest whole number, some totals may appear inconsistent.
Israel and Kuwait did not test at the seventh grade. Internationally comparable data are unavailable for Cyprus on Example 20.

SOURCE: IEA Third International Mathematics and Science Study (TIMSS), 1994-95.

Figure 3.4

International Difficulty Map for Chemistry Example Items - Lower and Upper Grades (Seventh and Eighth Grades*)

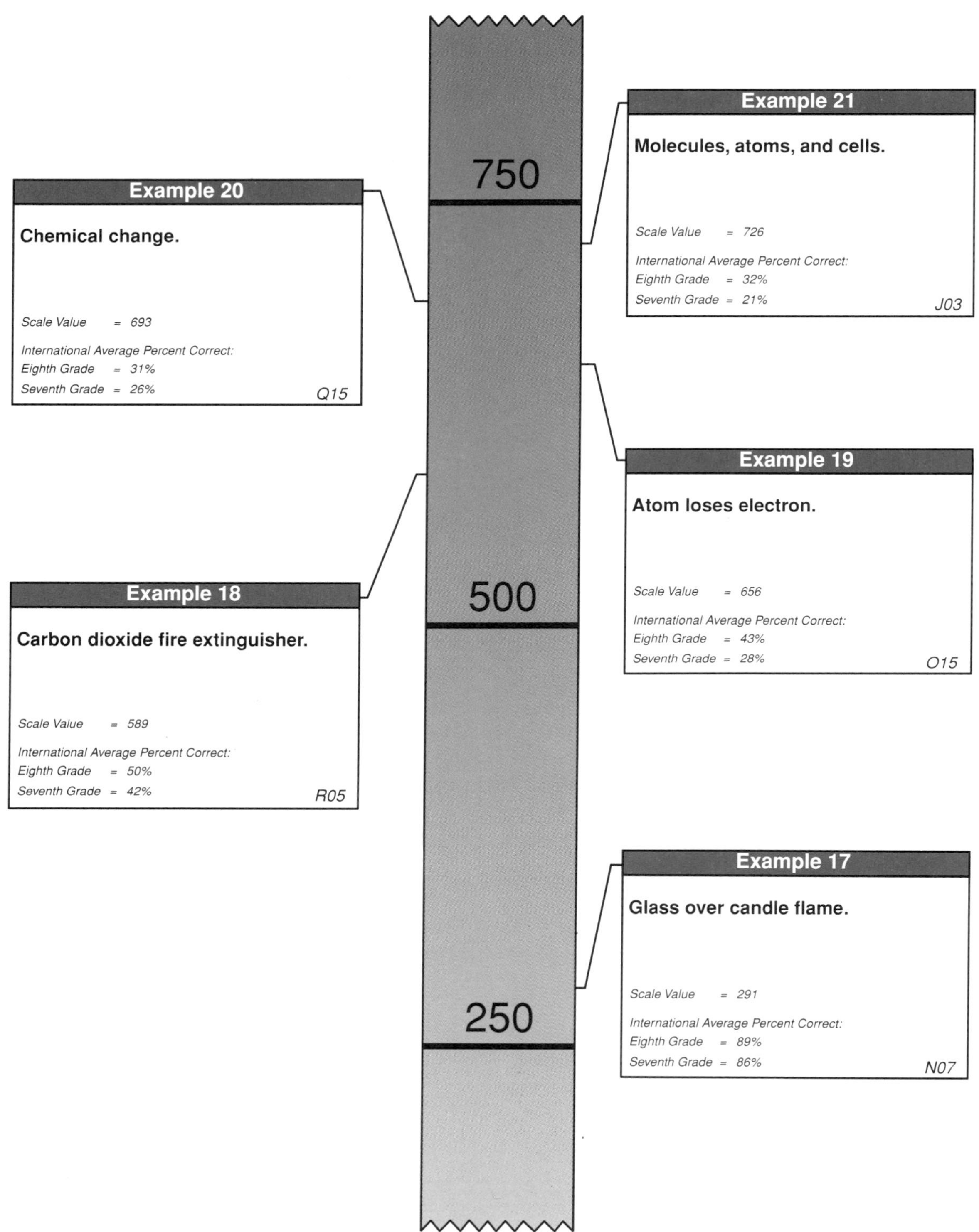

*Seventh and eighth grades in most countries; see Table 2 for information about the grades tested in each country.
NOTE: Each item was placed onto the TIMSS international science scale based on students' performance in both grades. Items are shown at the point on the scale where students with that level of proficiency had a 65 percent probability of providing a correct response.

EXAMPLE ITEM 17
CHEMISTRY

Glass over candle flame

When a glass jar is placed over a lighted candle, the flame goes out.

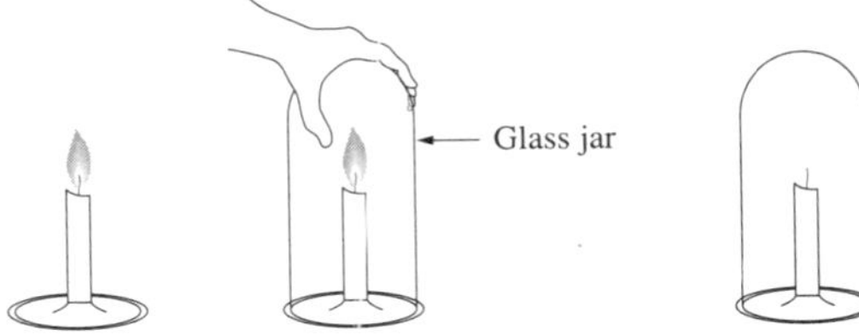

Why does this happen? The flame needs a supply of oxygen to stay alive. The jar cuts off the supply and when it is all burnt by the candle the candle cannot burn anymore so it goes out.

Performance Category: Theorizing, Analyzing, and Solving Problems

EXAMPLE ITEM 18
CHEMISTRY

Carbon dioxide fire extinguisher

Carbon dioxide is the active material in some fire extinguishers. How does carbon dioxide extinguish a fire?

A fire needs oxygen to burn so a fire extinguisher sprays out the carbon dioxide to replace the presence of oxygen. without oxygen, a fire can't burn.

Performance Category: Theorizing, Analyzing, and Solving Problems

EXAMPLE ITEM 19
CHEMISTRY

Atom loses electron

If a neutral atom loses an electron, what is formed?

A. A gas

(B.) An ion

C. An acid

D. A molecule

Performance Category: Understanding Simple Information

EXAMPLE ITEM 20
CHEMISTRY

Chemical change

Which is NOT an example of a chemical change?

A. Boiling water

B. Rusting iron

C. Burning wood

D. Baking bread

Performance Category: Understanding simple Information

EXAMPLE ITEM 21
CHEMISTRY

Molecules, atoms, and cells

The words *cloth, thread,* and *fiber* can be used in the following sentence: *cloth* consists of *threads* which are made of *fiber.*

Use the words *molecules, atoms,* and *cells* to complete the following sentence:

__cells__ consist of __molecules__ which are made of __atoms__.

Performance Category: Understanding Simple Information

What Have Students Learned About Environmental Issues and the Nature of Science?

The fifth science category includes six items about environmental and resource issues, six items covering the nature of scientific knowledge, and two items involving the interaction of science and technology. Table 3.5 shows the percent correct and Figure 3.5 the international difficulty map for four example items (Example Items 22 - 25), illustrating the types of items and student performance expectations covered in these science areas.

Example Items 22, 23, and 24 are all related to the nature of scientific knowledge. Item 22, requiring deductive reasoning to draw conclusions based on experimental observations, was the easiest of the three internationally. On average, nearly two-thirds of the eighth-grade and more than half of the seventh-grade students answered this item correctly (62% and 55%). Performances for individual countries ranged from a low of 23% to 30% correct at both grades in Japan, South Africa, and Kuwait, to more than 75% correct at both grades in Bulgaria. In comparison to Example Item 22, Example Item 23, requiring knowledge of the precision of replicated scientific measurements, was slightly more difficult. On average, it was answered correctly by about half of the students at both the seventh and eighth grades (49% and 53%). Even a little more difficult for students was Example Item 24, which involved the design of experiments and required choosing the experimental procedure required to test a hypothesis. Internationally, at both grades, fewer than half of the students, on average, chose the correct response (40% at seventh grade and 45% at eighth grade). There was little between-grade improvement in most of the individual countries.

Example Item 25, measuring knowledge of the principal cause of acid rain, was related to environmental issues. Across countries, about one-third or fewer students in both grades selected the correct response related to the burning of fossil fuels (on average, 31% at seventh grade and 35% at eighth grade). There was little variation across countries, and in only two countries (Slovenia and Thailand) did 50% or more of the students respond correctly at both grades.

Table 3.5

Percent Correct for Environmental Issues and the Nature of Science Example Items - Lower and Upper Grade (Seventh and Eighth Grades*)

Country	Example 22 Liquid evaporation experiment.		Example 23 Replication of measurements.	
	Seventh Grade	Eighth Grade	Seventh Grade	Eighth Grade
† Belgium (Fl)	71 (2.5)	76 (3.4)	47 (2.5)	42 (3.4)
† Belgium (Fr)	68 (2.6)	77 (3.2)	42 (3.1)	45 (2.9)
Canada	70 (2.1)	78 (1.8)	61 (2.4)	58 (2.0)
Cyprus	49 (2.6)	65 (2.5)	46 (2.8)	51 (3.3)
Czech Republic	46 (3.2)	59 (2.9)	61 (2.9)	64 (2.7)
†2 England	59 (3.3)	72 (3.4)	62 (2.7)	64 (3.5)
France	65 (2.6)	75 (2.3)	42 (2.6)	51 (2.6)
Hong Kong	63 (2.7)	68 (2.6)	70 (3.5)	70 (2.5)
Hungary	68 (2.5)	68 (2.7)	29 (2.4)	39 (2.9)
Iceland	48 (4.2)	56 (2.8)	52 (3.6)	59 (3.5)
Iran, Islamic Rep.	63 (4.8)	67 (2.7)	32 (3.9)	39 (3.0)
Ireland	62 (2.2)	74 (2.3)	55 (2.3)	54 (2.7)
Japan	27 (1.7)	30 (2.1)	30 (2.1)	39 (2.0)
Korea	76 (2.6)	79 (2.4)	78 (2.7)	85 (1.8)
1 Latvia (LSS)	54 (2.8)	69 (3.0)	45 (3.0)	49 (3.4)
1 Lithuania	39 (3.1)	58 (3.4)	48 (3.1)	50 (3.1)
New Zealand	63 (2.7)	68 (2.5)	49 (2.9)	63 (2.8)
Norway	53 (3.3)	57 (2.8)	54 (3.6)	53 (2.7)
Portugal	34 (2.6)	54 (2.9)	35 (2.7)	35 (1.9)
Russian Federation	48 (2.3)	59 (2.7)	60 (3.0)	61 (2.0)
† Scotland	67 (3.0)	72 (2.8)	53 (2.6)	63 (2.8)
Singapore	68 (2.4)	80 (1.8)	58 (2.9)	65 (2.2)
Slovak Republic	33 (2.6)	50 (3.3)	65 (2.5)	70 (2.6)
Spain	53 (2.7)	60 (2.8)	24 (2.1)	28 (2.3)
Sweden	51 (2.9)	61 (2.3)	62 (2.7)	68 (2.1)
1 Switzerland	43 (2.7)	52 (2.7)	26 (2.2)	25 (1.9)
† United States	69 (2.4)	75 (2.0)	58 (3.0)	61 (1.9)
Countries Not Satisfying Guidelines for Sample Participation Rates (see Appendix A for Details):				
Australia	66 (2.3)	70 (2.5)	62 (2.5)	63 (1.9)
Austria	57 (2.9)	58 (2.8)	29 (2.5)	36 (2.7)
Bulgaria	77 (3.2)	84 (2.8)	50 (4.1)	56 (4.4)
Netherlands	72 (3.7)	77 (3.0)	55 (3.3)	58 (4.2)
Countries Not Meeting Age/Grade Specifications (High Percentage of Older Students; See Appendix A for Details):				
Colombia	44 (4.2)	42 (3.7)	32 (3.1)	39 (4.0)
†1 Germany	42 (3.0)	60 (3.1)	32 (2.9)	33 (2.9)
Romania	48 (2.6)	53 (2.9)	46 (2.8)	54 (2.7)
Slovenia	73 (2.4)	77 (2.7)	77 (2.2)	73 (2.7)
Countries With Unapproved Sampling Procedures at Classroom Level (See Appendix A for Details):				
Denmark	48 (2.9)	61 (3.4)	48 (3.7)	58 (3.1)
Greece	44 (2.4)	57 (2.5)	56 (2.0)	63 (3.3)
† South Africa	23 (2.8)	25 (3.1)	26 (2.0)	23 (2.1)
Thailand	47 (2.4)	45 (2.1)	70 (2.5)	77 (2.1)
Unapproved Sampling Procedures at Classroom Level and Not Meeting Other Guidelines (See Appendix A for Details):				
1 Israel	–	64 (3.9)	–	28 (3.8)
Kuwait	–	28 (3.0)	–	60 (3.5)

*Seventh and eighth grades in most countries; see Table 2 for information about the grades tested in each country.
†Met guidelines for sample participation rates only after replacement schools were included (see Appendix A for details).
[1]National Desired Population does not cover all of International Desired Population (see Table A.2). Because coverage falls below 65%, Latvia is annotated LSS for Latvian Speaking Schools only.
[2]National Defined Population covers less than 90 percent of National Desired Population (see Table A.2).
( ) Standard errors appear in parentheses. Because results are rounded to the nearest whole number, some totals may appear inconsistent.
Israel and Kuwait did not test at the seventh grade.

SOURCE: IEA Third International Mathematics and Science Study (TIMSS), 1994-95.

Table 3.5 (Continued)

Percent Correct for Environmental Issues and the Nature of Science Example Items - Lower and Upper Grade (Seventh and Eighth Grades*)

Country	Example 24 Plant/mineral experiment.		Example 25 Acid rain.	
	Seventh Grade	Eighth Grade	Seventh Grade	Eighth Grade
† Belgium (Fl)	42 (2.7)	47 (4.1)	30 (2.6)	30 (3.1)
† Belgium (Fr)	40 (3.2)	40 (2.9)	–	–
Canada	46 (2.5)	50 (2.1)	27 (2.3)	31 (2.3)
Cyprus	30 (2.7)	31 (2.9)	25 (2.5)	23 (2.2)
Czech Republic	39 (3.1)	42 (2.5)	38 (3.3)	45 (3.0)
†[2] England	40 (2.7)	44 (3.2)	29 (3.3)	44 (3.5)
France	43 (2.4)	43 (2.6)	–	–
Hong Kong	52 (2.4)	57 (2.7)	34 (2.3)	38 (2.6)
Hungary	25 (2.4)	30 (2.6)	40 (2.6)	41 (2.7)
Iceland	33 (4.0)	47 (4.1)	36 (2.9)	35 (4.5)
Iran, Islamic Rep.	22 (2.3)	31 (3.5)	24 (5.3)	23 (2.7)
Ireland	38 (2.3)	36 (2.4)	36 (2.6)	43 (2.6)
Japan	58 (2.2)	57 (1.9)	37 (1.8)	46 (2.0)
Korea	30 (2.5)	36 (2.8)	48 (2.9)	50 (3.0)
[1] Latvia (LSS)	37 (2.9)	45 (3.3)	21 (2.5)	25 (2.8)
[1] Lithuania	29 (2.8)	26 (3.1)	23 (2.7)	24 (2.8)
New Zealand	44 (2.7)	47 (2.6)	26 (2.4)	31 (2.0)
Norway	47 (3.0)	50 (2.7)	24 (2.4)	31 (2.3)
Portugal	36 (2.4)	49 (2.2)	25 (2.3)	32 (2.2)
Russian Federation	26 (2.3)	35 (4.0)	19 (2.1)	21 (2.5)
† Scotland	39 (2.4)	40 (2.8)	28 (2.2)	32 (3.0)
Singapore	64 (2.6)	71 (1.8)	31 (2.2)	31 (2.3)
Slovak Republic	44 (2.8)	43 (3.0)	21 (2.7)	14 (1.9)
Spain	45 (2.5)	49 (2.7)	37 (2.4)	34 (2.5)
Sweden	59 (2.8)	63 (2.1)	26 (2.5)	31 (1.9)
[1] Switzerland	46 (2.8)	51 (3.0)	35 (2.4)	39 (2.6)
† United States	41 (2.6)	47 (2.5)	32 (2.5)	32 (1.7)
Countries Not Satisfying Guidelines for Sample Participation Rates (see Appendix A for Details):				
Australia	42 (2.1)	48 (1.5)	32 (2.0)	42 (2.0)
Austria	43 (2.8)	52 (3.1)	40 (2.2)	55 (3.1)
Bulgaria	42 (4.2)	71 (3.7)	20 (2.8)	47 (4.5)
Netherlands	62 (3.4)	71 (2.9)	38 (3.6)	44 (3.0)
Countries Not Meeting Age/Grade Specifications (High Percentage of Older Students; See Appendix A for Details):				
Colombia	44 (3.5)	44 (4.4)	25 (2.6)	31 (3.9)
†[1] Germany	40 (3.1)	42 (2.8)	38 (2.8)	40 (2.8)
Romania	30 (2.7)	35 (2.7)	25 (2.5)	26 (2.4)
Slovenia	35 (2.8)	41 (2.9)	59 (2.6)	55 (3.4)
Countries With Unapproved Sampling Procedures at Classroom Level (See Appendix A for Details):				
Denmark	39 (2.8)	36 (3.6)	22 (2.5)	27 (2.6)
Greece	42 (2.1)	44 (2.3)	21 (1.8)	21 (1.9)
† South Africa	35 (2.2)	33 (2.2)	23 (1.9)	22 (2.1)
Thailand	28 (2.3)	29 (2.6)	51 (2.5)	62 (2.2)
Unapproved Sampling Procedures at Classroom Level and Not Meeting Other Guidelines (See Appendix A for Details):				
[1] Israel	–	52 (4.6)	–	30 (3.4)
Kuwait	–	36 (3.7)	–	46 (4.0)

*Seventh and eighth grades in most countries; see Table 2 for information about the grades tested in each country.

†Met guidelines for sample participation rates only after replacement schools were included (see Appendix A for details).

[1] National Desired Population does not cover all of International Desired Population (see Table A.2). Because coverage falls below 65%, Latvia is annotated LSS for Latvian Speaking Schools only.

[2] National Defined Population covers less than 90 percent of National Desired Population (see Table A.2).

( ) Standard errors appear in parentheses. Because results are rounded to the nearest whole number, some totals may appear inconsistent.

Israel and Kuwait did not test at the seventh grade. Internationally comparable data are unavailable for Belgium (Fr), France, and Japan on Example 25.

SOURCE: IEA Third International Mathematics and Science Study (TIMSS), 1994-95.

Figure 3.5

International Difficulty Map for Environmental Issues and the Nature of Science Example Items - Lower and Upper Grades (Seventh and Eighth Grades*)

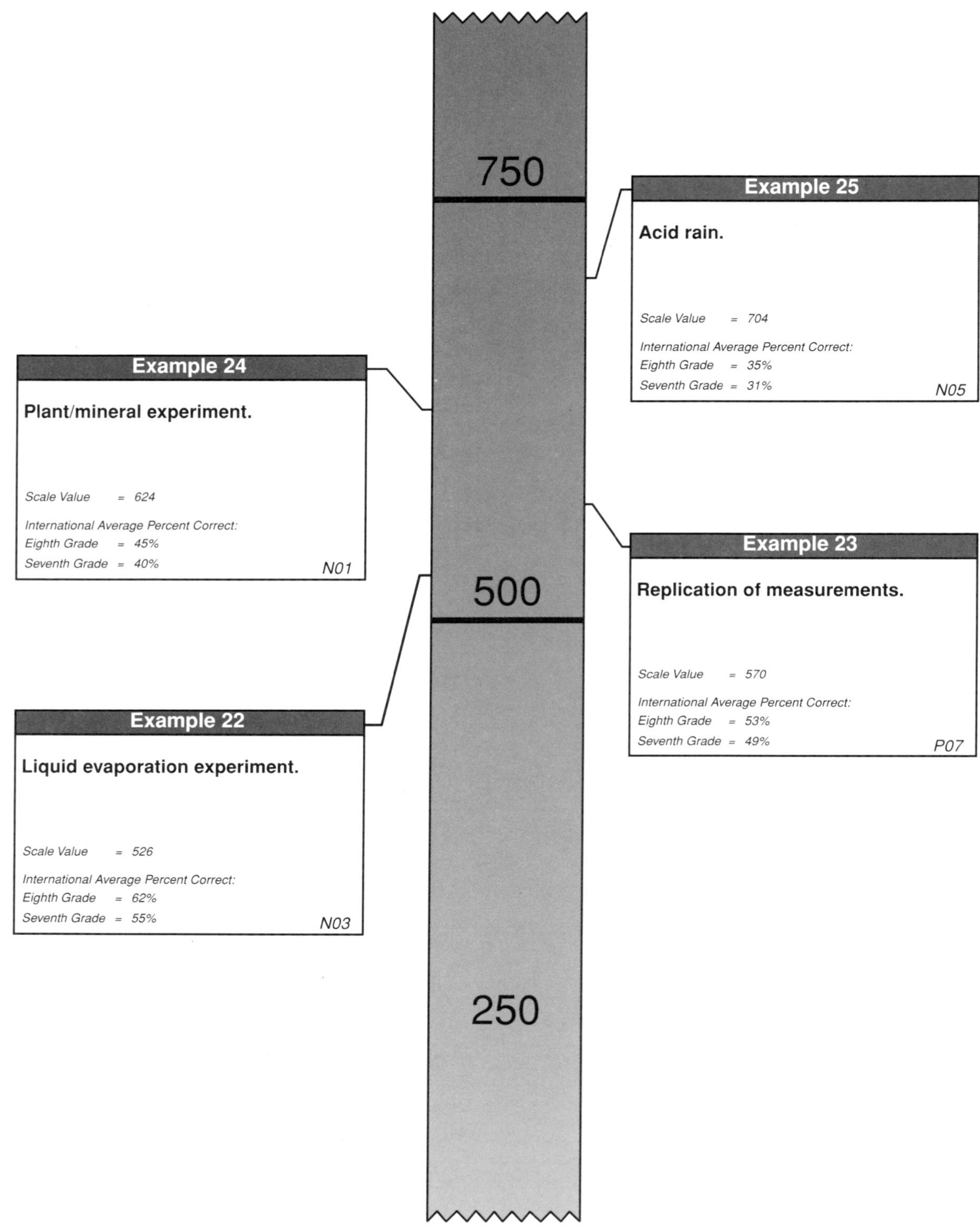

*Seventh and eighth grades in most countries; see Table 2 for information about the grades tested in each country.
NOTE: Each item was placed onto the TIMSS international science scale based on students' performance in both grades. Items are shown at the point on the scale where students with that level of proficiency had a 65 percent probability of providing a correct response.

Example Item 22
Environmental Issues and the Nature of Science

Liquid evaporation experiment

A cupful of water and a similar cupful of gasoline were placed on a table near a window on a hot sunny day. A few hours later it was observed that both the cups had less liquid in them but that there was less gasoline left than water. What does this experiment show?

A. All liquids evaporate.

B. Gasoline gets hotter than water.

C. Some liquids evaporate faster than others.

D. Liquids will only evaporate in sunshine.

E. Water gets hotter than gasoline

Performance Category: Theorizing, Analyzing, and Solving Problems

Example Item 23
Environmental Issues and the Nature of Science

Replication of measurements

Whenever scientists carefully measure any quantity many times, they expect that

A. all of the measurements will be exactly the same

B. only two of the measurements will be exactly the same

C. all but one of the measurements will be exactly the same

D. most of the measurements will be close but not exactly the same

Performance Category: Understanding Simple Information

EXAMPLE ITEM 24
ENVIRONMENTAL ISSUES AND THE NATURE OF SCIENCE

Plant/mineral experiment

A girl had an idea that plants needed minerals from the soil for healthy growth. She placed a plant in the Sun, as shown in the diagram below.

In order to check her idea she also needed to use another plant. Which of the following should she use?

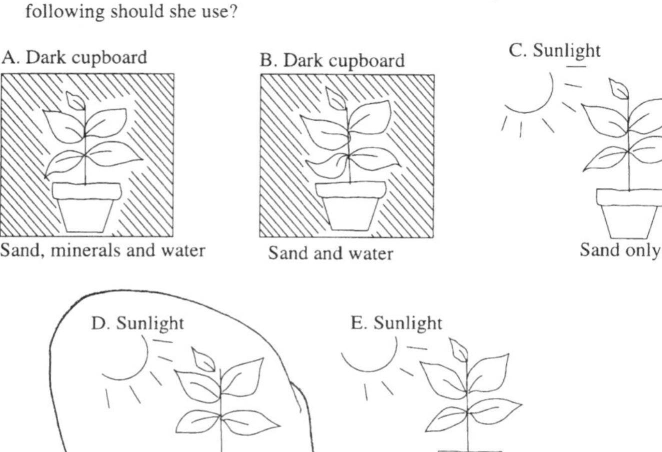

D. Sunlight

Sand and water

E. Sunlight

Sand and minerals

Performance Category: Investigating the Natural World

EXAMPLE ITEM 25
ENVIRONMENTAL ISSUES AND THE NATURE OF SCIENCE

Acid rain

One of the principal causes of acid rain is

A. waste acid from chemical factories being pumped into rivers

B. acid from chemical laboratories evaporating into the air

C. gases from burning coal and oil dissolving in water in the atmosphere

D. gases from air conditioners and refrigerators escaping into the atmosphere

Performance Category: Understanding Simple Information

Chapter 4

Students' Backgrounds and Attitudes Toward the Sciences

To provide an educational context for interpreting the science achievement results, TIMSS collected a full range of descriptive information from students about their backgrounds as well as their activities in and out of school. This chapter presents eighth-grade students' responses to a selected subset of these questions. In an effort to explore the degree to which the students' home and social environment fostered academic development, some of the questions presented herein address the availability of educational resources in the home. Another group of questions is provided to help examine whether or not students typically spend their out-of-school time in ways that support their in-school academic performance. Because students' attitudes and opinions about science reflect what happens in school and their perceptions of the value of science in broader social contexts, results also are described for several questions from the affective domain. More specifically, these questions asked students to express their opinions about the abilities necessary for success in science, provide information about what motivates them to do well in science, and indicate their attitudes towards science.

Student and teacher questionnaire data for two countries are unavailable for this report and thus do not appear in this chapter – Bulgaria and South Africa. Bulgaria had complications with data entry, and South Africa joined the study later than the other countries.

What Educational Resources Do Students Have in Their Homes?

Students specifically were asked about the availability at home of three types of educational resources – a dictionary, a study desk or table for their own use, and a computer. Table 4.1 reveals that in most countries, eighth-grade students with all three of these educational study aids had higher science achievement than students who did not have ready access to these study aids. In almost all the countries, nearly all students reported having a dictionary in their homes. There was more variation among countries in the percentages of students reporting their own study desk or table. Of the three study aids, the most variation was in the number of eighth-grade students reporting having a home computer. In several countries, more than 70% of students reported having a computer in the home, including the more than 85% who so reported in England, the Netherlands, and Scotland. For these three countries, it is likely that these high percentages include computers used for entertainment purposes, such as computer games.

The number of books in the home can be an indicator of a home environment that values literacy, the acquisition of knowledge, and general academic support. Table 4.2 presents eighth-grade students' reports about the number of books in their homes in relation to their achievement on the TIMSS science test. In most countries, the

Table 4.1

Students' Reports on Educational Aids in the Home: Dictionary, Study Desk/Table and Computer - Science - Upper Grade (Eighth Grade*)

Country	Have All Three Educational Aids		Do Not Have All Three Educational Aids		Have Dictionary	Have Study Desk/Table for Own Use	Have Computer
	Percent of Students	Mean Achievement	Percent of Students	Mean Achievement	Percent of Students	Percent of Students	Percent of Students
Australia	66 (1.2)	557 (4.3)	34 (1.2)	524 (4.2)	88 (0.7)	97 (0.4)	73 (1.2)
Austria	56 (1.5)	566 (4.1)	44 (1.5)	547 (4.5)	98 (0.3)	93 (0.8)	59 (1.5)
Belgium (Fl)	64 (1.3)	559 (3.9)	36 (1.3)	536 (5.2)	99 (0.5)	96 (0.5)	67 (1.3)
Belgium (Fr)	58 (1.4)	483 (3.1)	42 (1.4)	456 (3.6)	97 (0.5)	96 (0.5)	60 (1.4)
Canada	57 (1.4)	545 (2.5)	43 (1.4)	514 (3.0)	97 (0.4)	89 (0.6)	61 (1.3)
Colombia	10 (1.2)	431 (10.3)	90 (1.2)	410 (3.9)	96 (0.5)	84 (1.0)	11 (1.2)
Cyprus	37 (0.9)	475 (3.0)	63 (0.9)	458 (2.5)	97 (0.3)	96 (0.5)	39 (0.9)
Czech Republic	33 (1.3)	596 (6.6)	67 (1.3)	563 (3.3)	94 (0.6)	90 (0.6)	36 (1.2)
Denmark	66 (1.5)	487 (3.2)	34 (1.5)	465 (4.4)	85 (1.1)	98 (0.3)	76 (1.2)
England	80 (1.0)	558 (3.8)	20 (1.0)	534 (5.3)	98 (0.4)	90 (0.8)	89 (0.8)
France	49 (1.3)	505 (2.9)	51 (1.3)	492 (3.1)	99 (0.2)	96 (0.4)	50 (1.3)
Germany	66 (1.1)	542 (4.3)	34 (1.1)	514 (6.5)	98 (0.4)	93 (0.6)	71 (1.0)
Greece	28 (1.0)	513 (4.3)	72 (1.0)	493 (2.2)	97 (0.3)	93 (0.5)	29 (1.0)
Hong Kong	33 (1.8)	540 (5.2)	67 (1.8)	516 (4.8)	99 (0.1)	80 (1.1)	39 (1.9)
Hungary	32 (1.2)	586 (3.3)	68 (1.2)	540 (3.1)	77 (1.2)	92 (0.7)	37 (1.2)
Iceland	72 (1.6)	495 (5.1)	28 (1.6)	488 (2.9)	95 (0.5)	96 (0.6)	77 (1.4)
Iran, Islamic Rep.	1 (0.3)	~ ~	99 (0.3)	472 (2.3)	54 (1.5)	40 (2.0)	4 (0.4)
Ireland	67 (1.2)	548 (4.4)	33 (1.2)	522 (6.1)	99 (0.3)	86 (0.9)	78 (1.1)
Israel	75 (2.1)	540 (5.9)	25 (2.1)	495 (4.7)	100 (0.2)	98 (0.4)	76 (2.1)
Japan	- -	- -	- -	- -	- -	- -	- -
Korea	38 (1.2)	585 (2.7)	62 (1.2)	553 (2.2)	98 (0.2)	95 (0.4)	39 (1.2)
Kuwait	38 (2.0)	434 (6.9)	62 (2.0)	429 (3.4)	84 (1.1)	73 (2.0)	53 (2.1)
Latvia (LSS)	13 (0.8)	487 (5.4)	87 (0.8)	486 (2.6)	94 (0.6)	98 (0.3)	13 (0.9)
Lithuania	35 (1.3)	481 (4.3)	65 (1.3)	474 (3.9)	88 (1.0)	95 (0.6)	42 (1.4)
Netherlands	83 (1.3)	563 (6.4)	17 (1.3)	548 (6.1)	100 (0.1)	99 (0.2)	85 (1.2)
New Zealand	56 (1.4)	541 (4.9)	44 (1.4)	509 (4.9)	99 (0.2)	91 (0.6)	60 (1.3)
Norway	63 (1.1)	535 (2.3)	37 (1.1)	516 (3.0)	97 (0.3)	98 (0.2)	64 (1.1)
Portugal	35 (1.8)	496 (3.1)	65 (1.8)	471 (2.1)	98 (0.4)	84 (0.9)	39 (1.8)
Romania	8 (1.0)	534 (9.5)	92 (1.0)	483 (4.7)	60 (1.6)	69 (1.3)	19 (1.2)
Russian Federation	30 (1.4)	545 (4.9)	70 (1.4)	536 (4.3)	88 (1.1)	95 (0.7)	35 (1.5)
Scotland	74 (1.2)	527 (5.4)	26 (1.2)	494 (6.5)	96 (0.5)	84 (1.2)	90 (0.6)
Singapore	47 (1.5)	627 (6.1)	53 (1.5)	591 (5.5)	99 (0.1)	92 (0.5)	49 (1.5)
Slovak Republic	27 (1.2)	567 (4.0)	73 (1.2)	536 (3.5)	96 (0.5)	86 (0.9)	31 (1.2)
Slovenia	43 (1.4)	581 (3.2)	57 (1.4)	544 (2.8)	94 (0.5)	93 (0.6)	47 (1.3)
Spain	40 (1.3)	529 (2.7)	60 (1.3)	509 (2.0)	99 (0.1)	93 (0.5)	42 (1.2)
Sweden	58 (1.3)	549 (2.9)	42 (1.3)	518 (3.7)	94 (0.4)	100 (0.1)	60 (1.3)
Switzerland	63 (1.2)	532 (2.8)	37 (1.2)	507 (3.1)	97 (0.4)	95 (0.4)	66 (1.2)
Thailand	4 (0.8)	545 (11.0)	96 (0.8)	525 (3.7)	68 (2.1)	66 (2.1)	4 (0.9)
United States	56 (1.7)	559 (4.1)	44 (1.7)	505 (5.2)	97 (0.4)	90 (0.7)	59 (1.7)

*Eighth grade in most countries; see Table 2 for more information about the grades tested in each country.
( ) Standard errors appear in parentheses. Because results are rounded to the nearest whole number, some totals may appear inconsistent.
Countries shown in italics did not satisfy one or more guidelines for sample participation rates, age/grade specifications, or classroom sampling procedures (see Figure A.3). Background data for Bulgaria and South Africa are unavailable.
Because population coverage falls below 65%, Latvia is annotated LSS for Latvian Speaking Schools only.
A dash (-) indicates data are not available. A tilde (~) indicates insufficient data to report achievement.

SOURCE: IEA Third International Mathematics and Science Study (TIMSS), 1994-95.

Table 4.2

Students' Reports on the Number of Books in the Home
Science - Upper Grade (Eighth Grade*)

Country	None or Very Few (0-10 Books)		About One Shelf (11–25 Books)		About One Bookcase (26-100 Books)		About Two Bookcases (101-200 Books)		Three or More Bookcases (More than 200 Books)	
	Percent of Students	Mean Achieve-ment	Percent of Students	Mean Achieve-ment	Percent of Students	Mean Achieve-ment	Percent of Students	Mean Achieve-ment	Percent of Students	Mean Achieve-ment
Australia	3 (0.3)	460 (7.8)	7 (0.6)	492 (7.5)	24 (0.8)	524 (4.3)	25 (0.6)	549 (3.8)	42 (1.4)	573 (4.2)
Austria	11 (1.0)	509 (6.5)	17 (1.1)	528 (7.5)	31 (1.2)	554 (5.1)	17 (0.9)	582 (4.9)	24 (1.4)	590 (4.7)
Belgium (Fl)	11 (1.2)	515 (6.5)	18 (0.8)	537 (6.0)	33 (1.0)	552 (5.2)	18 (1.0)	566 (4.9)	21 (0.9)	563 (5.0)
Belgium (Fr)	7 (0.7)	408 (11.0)	10 (0.7)	433 (4.5)	28 (1.1)	462 (4.7)	21 (0.9)	482 (4.0)	34 (1.5)	497 (3.3)
Canada	4 (0.3)	482 (8.0)	10 (0.7)	493 (4.0)	28 (1.0)	522 (3.5)	25 (0.8)	542 (3.5)	33 (1.4)	550 (3.6)
Colombia	26 (1.5)	397 (4.5)	31 (1.1)	404 (5.3)	27 (1.3)	424 (4.4)	9 (0.7)	426 (8.4)	7 (1.0)	434 (9.9)
Cyprus	6 (0.6)	425 (6.5)	18 (0.8)	438 (3.7)	34 (0.8)	465 (3.4)	23 (0.8)	486 (3.6)	20 (0.8)	480 (4.5)
Czech Republic	1 (0.2)	~ ~	4 (0.5)	520 (7.1)	30 (1.5)	552 (3.9)	32 (0.9)	577 (4.3)	34 (1.8)	597 (6.6)
Denmark	3 (0.6)	425 (12.6)	9 (0.8)	446 (8.6)	30 (1.2)	467 (4.1)	21 (0.9)	484 (3.9)	37 (1.5)	499 (4.0)
England	6 (0.6)	472 (8.9)	13 (1.0)	502 (4.4)	27 (1.3)	536 (5.3)	22 (0.8)	564 (6.2)	32 (1.5)	596 (4.6)
France	5 (0.5)	460 (8.6)	17 (1.0)	477 (4.0)	36 (1.1)	497 (3.8)	21 (1.0)	514 (3.9)	20 (1.2)	511 (4.5)
Germany	8 (0.8)	456 (7.4)	14 (1.1)	483 (6.9)	26 (1.0)	519 (4.4)	19 (0.9)	555 (6.8)	33 (1.7)	569 (5.1)
Greece	5 (0.4)	467 (6.1)	22 (0.9)	475 (2.9)	43 (0.9)	499 (2.5)	18 (0.7)	515 (4.8)	12 (0.7)	525 (4.8)
Hong Kong	21 (1.2)	500 (6.7)	29 (1.0)	525 (4.5)	29 (0.9)	529 (5.2)	10 (0.7)	542 (6.8)	10 (0.9)	536 (7.0)
Hungary	4 (0.6)	487 (12.8)	8 (0.7)	510 (5.8)	25 (1.0)	534 (3.8)	21 (1.0)	559 (4.2)	42 (1.4)	579 (3.0)
Iceland	1 (0.2)	~ ~	5 (0.8)	463 (10.9)	29 (1.4)	482 (4.8)	28 (1.2)	491 (5.1)	37 (1.7)	510 (6.7)
Iran, Islamic Rep.	37 (1.8)	457 (3.5)	32 (0.9)	475 (3.3)	17 (0.9)	478 (5.9)	6 (0.5)	481 (10.1)	7 (0.7)	487 (6.7)
Ireland	7 (0.6)	471 (7.4)	16 (0.8)	504 (5.2)	34 (1.0)	538 (4.5)	21 (0.7)	560 (4.5)	22 (1.2)	568 (5.9)
Israel	4 (0.6)	487 (12.5)	13 (1.6)	495 (8.3)	31 (1.9)	517 (7.2)	26 (1.4)	541 (6.4)	25 (2.0)	555 (7.7)
Japan	- -	- -	- -	- -	- -	- -	- -	- -	- -	- -
Korea	10 (0.6)	510 (5.2)	12 (0.8)	531 (3.9)	33 (0.9)	562 (2.9)	23 (0.8)	581 (2.8)	21 (0.9)	597 (4.1)
Kuwait	22 (1.4)	424 (5.3)	27 (1.5)	428 (4.8)	28 (1.6)	443 (4.3)	10 (1.0)	443 (6.9)	13 (0.9)	428 (6.0)
Latvia (LSS)	1 (0.3)	~ ~	4 (0.6)	434 (7.3)	17 (1.0)	474 (4.1)	21 (1.1)	477 (4.7)	57 (1.4)	496 (3.0)
Lithuania	3 (0.4)	429 (9.9)	17 (0.9)	451 (5.6)	35 (1.2)	469 (4.0)	21 (0.9)	491 (4.5)	24 (1.1)	501 (4.4)
Netherlands	8 (1.0)	523 (8.5)	16 (1.3)	533 (8.9)	34 (1.3)	553 (5.8)	19 (0.9)	580 (5.9)	22 (1.7)	591 (5.9)
New Zealand	3 (0.4)	441 (9.8)	7 (0.6)	466 (6.4)	24 (0.8)	506 (4.9)	25 (0.7)	533 (4.7)	41 (1.4)	551 (4.6)
Norway	2 (0.3)	~ ~	6 (0.4)	490 (7.7)	25 (0.9)	511 (2.9)	22 (0.7)	524 (3.4)	45 (1.2)	547 (2.4)
Portugal	10 (0.8)	456 (3.8)	26 (1.3)	464 (2.9)	32 (1.0)	479 (2.7)	15 (0.8)	493 (4.0)	17 (1.4)	508 (3.9)
Romania	24 (1.3)	467 (8.3)	22 (1.3)	476 (7.1)	19 (1.0)	483 (5.5)	11 (0.7)	503 (7.9)	24 (1.7)	518 (5.9)
Russian Federation	2 (0.3)	~ ~	11 (0.8)	508 (10.1)	36 (1.3)	527 (4.5)	24 (0.8)	550 (4.1)	26 (1.3)	561 (5.0)
Scotland	11 (1.2)	453 (5.5)	17 (1.1)	483 (4.2)	28 (1.0)	507 (4.2)	19 (1.0)	546 (4.7)	25 (2.0)	567 (7.8)
Singapore	11 (0.8)	567 (5.3)	22 (0.9)	583 (5.3)	41 (0.8)	610 (5.5)	14 (0.7)	640 (6.5)	12 (1.0)	648 (7.0)
Slovak Republic	2 (0.3)	~ ~	11 (0.6)	506 (5.3)	45 (1.1)	536 (3.5)	23 (0.9)	562 (3.9)	18 (1.0)	573 (5.1)
Slovenia	2 (0.4)	~ ~	15 (0.9)	522 (4.3)	38 (1.2)	555 (2.9)	22 (0.9)	574 (4.3)	22 (1.1)	587 (4.4)
Spain	4 (0.4)	487 (8.1)	18 (1.1)	490 (2.5)	33 (1.0)	511 (2.1)	20 (0.8)	528 (3.3)	26 (1.2)	540 (2.8)
Sweden	3 (0.3)	473 (9.9)	8 (0.7)	482 (5.6)	24 (1.0)	517 (4.3)	24 (0.8)	540 (3.6)	41 (1.5)	560 (3.5)
Switzerland	8 (1.0)	456 (8.1)	16 (0.9)	485 (6.1)	30 (1.0)	516 (3.4)	20 (0.9)	546 (3.7)	26 (1.2)	557 (4.2)
Thailand	19 (1.2)	514 (3.3)	30 (1.0)	519 (3.4)	33 (1.2)	529 (4.0)	9 (0.6)	538 (6.8)	9 (1.0)	546 (7.2)
United States	8 (0.8)	459 (6.2)	13 (0.8)	489 (5.0)	28 (0.9)	527 (4.2)	21 (0.6)	554 (4.3)	31 (1.5)	570 (5.2)

*Eighth grade in most countries; see Table 2 for more information about the grades tested in each
( ) Standard errors appear in parentheses. Because results are rounded to the nearest whole number, some totals may appear
Countries shown in italics did not satisfy one or more guidelines for sample participation rates, age/grade specifications, or sampling procedures (see Figure A.3). Background data for Bulgaria and South Africa are unavailable.
Because population coverage falls below 65%, Latvia is annotated LSS for Latvian Speaking Schools only.
A dash (-) indicates data are not available. A tilde (~) indicates insufficient data to report achievement.

SOURCE: IEA Third International Mathematics and Science Study (TIMSS), 1994-95.

more books students reported in the home, the higher their science achievement. Although the main purpose of the question was to gain some information about the relative importance of academic pursuits in the students' home environments rather than to determine the actual number of books in students' homes, there was a substantial amount of variation from country to country in eighth-grade students' reports about the number of books in their homes. In Colombia, Hong Kong, Iran, Kuwait, Romania, and Thailand, 40% or more of the students reported 25 or fewer books in the home. Conversely, 40% or more of the students in Australia, Hungary, Latvia (LSS), New Zealand, Norway, and Sweden reported more than 200 books in their homes.

Information about their parents' educational levels was gathered by asking students to indicate the highest level of education completed by their fathers and mothers. Table 4.3 presents the relationship between eighth-grade students' science achievement and their reports of the highest level of education of either parent. Results are presented at three educational levels: finished university, finished upper secondary school but not university, and finished primary school but not upper secondary school. These three educational levels are based on internationally-defined categories, which may not be strictly comparable across countries due to differences in national education systems. Although the majority of countries translated and defined the educational categories used in their questionnaires to be comparable to the internationally-defined levels, some countries used modified response options to conform to their national education systems. Also, for a few countries, the percentages of students responding to this question fell below 85%. When this happened, the percentages shown in the table are annotated with an "r" for a response rate of 70% to 84% or an "s" if the response rate was from 50% to 69%.

Despite the different educational approaches, structures, and organizations across the TIMSS countries, it is clear from the data in Table 4.3 that parents' education is positively related to students' science achievement. In every country, the pattern was for those eighth-grade students whose parents had more education to also be those who have higher achievement in science. Once again, the purpose of this question was not to ascertain precisely the educational levels of students' parents, but to gain further understanding about the relative importance of schooling in their home environments. As indicated by the results, there was variation among countries in the percentages of students reporting that they did not know their parents' educational levels, as well as in the percentages of students reporting that their parents had completed successively higher educational levels. For example, in Canada, Israel, Lithuania, the Russian Federation, and the United States, more than 30% of the students reported that at least one of their parents had finished university, and only relatively small percentages (fewer than 12%) reported that they did not know the educational levels of their parents. In contrast, almost all students (90% or more) in Hong Kong, Iran, Kuwait, Portugal, and Thailand also reported knowing their parents' educational levels, but for these countries fewer than 10% of students reported that either parent had finished university.

Figure 4.1 shows the definitions of the educational categories used by TIMSS and the modifications made to them by some countries. In several countries, the finished primary school but not upper secondary school category included only a single level

Table 4.3

Students' Reports on the Highest Level of Education of Either Parent[1] Science - Upper Grade (Eighth Grade*)

Country	Finished University[2]		Finished Upper Secondary School But Not University[3]		Finished Primary School But Not Upper Secondary School[4]		Do Not Know	
	Percent of Students	Mean Achievement	Percent of Students	Mean Achievement	Percent of Students	Mean Achievement	Percent of Students	Mean Achievement
Australia	28 (1.4)	587 (4.5)	37 (0.9)	544 (4.1)	24 (0.9)	527 (4.4)	11 (0.6)	499 (5.3)
Austria	10 (0.7)	588 (7.7)	70 (1.1)	566 (4.1)	8 (0.9)	508 (8.3)	12 (0.9)	530 (6.0)
Belgium (Fl)	20 (1.6)	574 (4.5)	34 (1.3)	554 (5.0)	21 (2.4)	532 (9.1)	25 (1.4)	535 (3.7)
Belgium (Fr)	27 (1.6)	497 (4.3)	34 (1.3)	481 (4.1)	11 (1.3)	434 (5.3)	27 (1.6)	450 (5.8)
Canada	37 (1.3)	549 (3.9)	39 (1.2)	532 (3.0)	13 (0.9)	501 (4.4)	10 (0.5)	517 (4.0)
Colombia	15 (1.6)	441 (7.9)	28 (1.6)	425 (4.2)	47 (2.3)	402 (3.7)	10 (0.9)	393 (6.3)
Cyprus	r 15 (0.9)	504 (6.3)	29 (1.1)	486 (3.6)	52 (1.4)	448 (2.7)	4 (0.5)	438 (10.5)
Czech Republic	21 (1.7)	606 (7.2)	47 (1.5)	579 (4.1)	25 (1.5)	550 (3.9)	7 (0.8)	536 (7.3)
Denmark	13 (1.0)	509 (6.0)	46 (1.5)	489 (3.8)	8 (0.7)	458 (8.6)	33 (1.7)	470 (4.6)
England	- -	- -	- -	- -	- -	- -	- -	- -
France	r 13 (1.2)	524 (6.6)	36 (1.3)	505 (3.5)	19 (1.2)	493 (3.3)	31 (1.3)	488 (3.5)
Germany	11 (1.0)	573 (8.6)	32 (1.3)	550 (4.7)	38 (1.6)	529 (4.2)	19 (1.3)	502 (7.7)
Greece	18 (1.1)	536 (4.8)	39 (1.3)	506 (3.1)	40 (1.8)	479 (2.3)	3 (0.3)	463 (7.8)
Hong Kong	7 (1.0)	547 (8.6)	30 (1.2)	537 (5.1)	55 (1.8)	519 (4.7)	7 (0.7)	498 (8.5)
Hungary	r 24 (1.8)	603 (4.1)	66 (1.7)	554 (3.0)	11 (0.9)	505 (6.0)	- -	- -
Iceland	25 (2.8)	513 (8.4)	44 (2.0)	499 (3.9)	15 (1.4)	477 (8.1)	15 (1.0)	475 (8.1)
Iran, Islamic Rep.	r 3 (0.6)	505 (8.4)	21 (1.8)	488 (4.4)	68 (2.2)	469 (3.0)	7 (1.0)	453 (6.7)
Ireland	17 (1.3)	573 (6.3)	46 (1.0)	546 (4.4)	26 (1.2)	522 (5.2)	10 (0.7)	506 (6.1)
Israel	37 (2.5)	560 (7.9)	45 (2.2)	523 (5.5)	10 (1.3)	485 (7.4)	8 (0.9)	508 (8.4)
Japan	- -	- -	- -	- -	- -	- -	- -	- -
Korea	22 (1.3)	593 (3.9)	47 (1.3)	566 (2.4)	26 (1.1)	546 (3.4)	5 (0.5)	529 (7.1)
Kuwait	s 3 (1.2)	459 (11.1)	3 (0.9)	425 (13.9)	92 (2.1)	427 (4.8)	1 (0.7)	~ ~
Latvia (LSS)	r 27 (1.5)	515 (5.0)	49 (1.4)	488 (3.0)	13 (1.0)	466 (5.7)	11 (1.0)	463 (6.8)
Lithuania	s 37 (1.6)	500 (4.7)	44 (1.6)	474 (4.4)	7 (1.0)	449 (8.6)	12 (1.2)	475 (6.5)
Netherlands	12 (1.4)	586 (8.2)	55 (1.8)	567 (6.4)	10 (0.7)	547 (8.0)	23 (1.4)	542 (5.6)
New Zealand	25 (1.3)	560 (5.5)	38 (1.1)	530 (4.4)	15 (0.8)	503 (6.0)	21 (1.1)	505 (5.8)
Norway	25 (1.2)	544 (4.2)	38 (1.1)	532 (2.4)	9 (0.6)	505 (4.5)	27 (1.2)	520 (3.3)
Portugal	9 (1.2)	525 (4.6)	13 (1.0)	498 (4.1)	73 (2.0)	472 (2.1)	5 (0.4)	469 (5.6)
Romania	10 (1.3)	522 (9.7)	47 (1.5)	498 (5.0)	33 (1.9)	477 (7.7)	10 (0.9)	463 (10.0)
Russian Federation	34 (1.8)	567 (3.7)	54 (1.6)	528 (4.9)	5 (0.5)	493 (8.7)	6 (0.8)	522 (11.3)
Scotland	14 (1.4)	579 (7.1)	33 (1.4)	521 (5.4)	14 (0.8)	501 (5.1)	39 (1.3)	507 (6.2)
Singapore	8 (1.0)	661 (8.4)	69 (1.0)	612 (5.5)	23 (1.2)	578 (5.1)	- -	- -
Slovak Republic	20 (1.4)	580 (4.9)	50 (1.1)	549 (3.2)	23 (1.2)	519 (4.8)	6 (0.5)	513 (7.5)
Slovenia	19 (1.1)	600 (4.2)	59 (1.4)	558 (2.6)	18 (1.3)	533 (3.7)	4 (0.4)	545 (8.9)
Spain	15 (1.2)	547 (3.9)	21 (0.9)	531 (2.9)	54 (1.8)	509 (2.1)	10 (0.8)	504 (3.9)
Sweden	22 (1.2)	561 (4.2)	34 (1.1)	541 (3.3)	9 (0.6)	517 (5.0)	35 (1.1)	527 (3.4)
Switzerland	11 (0.8)	559 (6.4)	61 (1.3)	531 (2.7)	13 (0.9)	493 (3.9)	15 (1.0)	506 (4.5)
Thailand	9 (1.4)	557 (6.7)	14 (1.4)	540 (5.9)	73 (2.6)	519 (2.9)	3 (0.5)	522 (10.2)
United States	33 (1.4)	562 (5.9)	54 (1.3)	530 (4.1)	7 (0.8)	483 (5.7)	5 (0.4)	512 (8.1)

*Eighth grade in most countries; see Table 2 for more information about the grades tested in each country.

[1]The response categories were defined by each country to conform to their own educational system and may not be strictly comparable across countries. See Figure 4.1 for country modifications to the definitions of educational levels. Also, no response category was provided for students whose parents had no formal education or did not finish primary school, except in France where a small percentage of students in this category are included in the missing responses.

[2]In most countries, defined as completion of at least a 4-year degree program at a university or an equivalent institute of higher education.

[3]Finished upper secondary school with or without some tertiary education not equivalent to a university degree. In most countries, finished secondary corresponds to completion of an upper-secondary track terminating after 11 to 13 years of schooling.

[4]Finished primary school or some secondary school not equivalent to completion of upper secondary.

( ) Standard errors appear in parentheses. Because results are rounded to the nearest whole number, some totals may appear inconsistent.

Countries shown in italics did not satisfy one or more guidelines for sample participation rates, age/grade specifications, or classroom sampling procedures (see Figure A.3). Background data for Bulgaria and South Africa are unavailable.

Because population coverage falls below 65%, Latvia is annotated LSS for Latvian Speaking Schools only.

A dash (-) indicates data are not available. A tilde (~) indicates insufficient data to report achievement.

An "r" indicates a 70-84% student response rate. An "s" indicates a 50-69% student response rate.

Data for Singapore not obtained from students; entered at ministry level.

SOURCE: IEA Third International Mathematics and Science Study (TIMSS), 1994-95.

Figure 4.1 Country Modifications to the Definitions of Educational Levels for Parents' Highest Level of Education[1]

Finished Primary School But Not Upper Secondary School

Internationally-Defined Levels: *Finished Primary School or Finished Some Secondary School*

Countries with Modified Nationally-Defined Levels:

Austria:	*Compulsory (Pflichtschulabschluß; 9 grades)*
Denmark:	*Basic school (Folkeskolen, Realeksamen; 9 or 10 grades)*
France:	*Lower Secondary (Collége, CAP)*
Germany:	*Lower secondary (Hauptschulabschluß; 9 or 10 grades) or Medium secondary (Fachoberschulreife, Realschulabschluß or Polytechnische Oberschule; 10 grades)*
Hungary:	*Some or all of general school (8 grades)*
Norway:	*Compulsory (9 grades) or some upper secondary*
Scotland:	*Some secondary school*
Singapore:	*Primary school*
Sweden:	*Compulsory (9 grades) or started upper secondary*
Switzerland:	*Compulsory (9 grades)*

Finished Upper Secondary School[2] But Not University

Internationally-Defined Levels: *Finished Secondary School or Some Vocational/Technical Education After Secondary School or Some University*

Countries with Modified Nationally-Defined Levels:

Austria:	*Upper-secondary tracks: apprenticeship (Berufsschul-/Lehrabschluß), medium vocational (Handelsschule, Fachschule), higher vocational (HAK, HTL, etc.), or higher academic (Gymnasium, Realgymnasium)*
Cyprus:	*Upper-secondary tracks: academic or vocational/technical or* *Post-Secondary: Finished college*
Denmark:	*Upper-secondary tracks: academic or general/vocational (gymnasium, hf, htx, hhx) vocational training (erhvervsfaglig uddannelse)* *Post-Secondary: Medium-cycle higher education (mellemlang uddannselse)*
France:	*Upper-secondary tracks: BEP (11 grades) or baccalauréat (général, technologique or professionnel; 12 or 13 grades)* *Post-Secondary: 2 or 3 years study after baccalauréat (BTS, DUT, Licence)*
Germany:	*Upper-secondary tracks: general/academic or apprenticeship/vocational training (Lehrabschluß, Berufsfachschule)* *Post-Secondary: Higher vocational schools (Fachhochschulabschluß)*
Hungary:	*Upper-secondary tracks: apprenticeship (general + 3 years) or final exam in secondary (general + 4 years)*
Sweden:	*Upper-secondary tracks: academic or vocational (gymnasieutbildning or yrkesinriktad utbildning)* *Post-Secondary: Less than 3 years of university studies*
Switzerland:	*Upper-secondary tracks: occupational (apprentissage, école professionnelle), academic (gymnase, baccalauréat, maturité cantonale), or teacher training (école normale, formation d'enseignant)* *Post-Secondary: Applied science university (haute école professionnelle ou commerciale)*

Finished University

Internationally-Defined Level: *Finished University*

Countries with Modified Nationally-Defined Levels:

Austria:	*University (master's degree)*
Canada:	*University or college*
Cyprus:	*University degree or post-graduate studies*
France:	*4 years of study after baccalauréat*
Germany:	*University, Technical University or Pedagogical Institute*
Hungary:	*University or college diploma*
New Zealand:	*University or Teachers' College*
Norway:	*University or college*
Portugal:	*University or polytechnic*
Sweden:	*3 years university studies or more*
Switzerland:	*University or insitute of technology*
United States:	*Bachelor's degree at college or university*

[1]Educational levels were translated and defined in most countries to be comparable to the internationally-defined levels. Countries that used modified response options to conform to their national education systems are indicated to aid in the interpretation of the reporting categories presented in Table 4.3.

[2]Upper-secondary corresponds to ISCED level 3 tracks terminating after 11 to 13 years in most countries. (Education at a Glance, OECD, 1995)

SOURCE: IEA Third International Mathematics and Science Study (TIMSS), 1994-95.

corresponding to finishing compulsory education (8 to 10 grades) and did not include finishing only primary school. In addition, in Germany, the completion of medium secondary education was considered part of this category, while in Austria, which has an educational system similar to Germany's, the medium-level vocational education was included in the second category reporting upper-secondary education.

The second reporting category (finished upper secondary school but not university) was complicated because, in many countries, particularly in Europe, there are several upper-secondary tracks leading to university or other tertiary institutions as well as vocational/apprenticeship programs. In most countries, finishing upper secondary means completion of 11 to 13 years of education. In some systems, however, the general secondary education may be completed after 9 or 10 years, followed by 2 to 4 years of full- or part-time vocational/apprenticeship training that may be either included as part of the secondary educational system or considered as post-secondary. All of the upper-secondary tracks and any upper-secondary or post-secondary vocational education programs included as response options are combined in the second reporting category.

Several countries also differed in their interpretation of what is included in the category of finished university. For example, degrees obtained from technical institutes and other non-university institutions of higher education are considered equivalent to a university degree in some countries but not in others. Therefore, completion of a degree at one of these institutions may have been included in either the finished university or the finished upper secondary school but not university categories. In countries such as Canada, New Zealand, Portugal, and the United States, the finished university category includes the completion of the equivalent of a bachelor's degree at either a university, college or polytechnic, while in Austria and France, this category corresponds to the equivalent of a master's degree received at a university.

What Are the Academic Expectations of Students, Their Families, and Their Friends?

Tables 4.4, 4.5, and 4.6 present eighth-grade students' reports about how they themselves, their mothers, and their friends feel about the importance of doing well in various academic and non-academic activities. The first three questions asked about the degree of agreement with the importance of doing well in the academic subjects of science, mathematics, and language, respectively. For most of the countries, from 80% to 95% of the students agreed or strongly agreed that it was important to do well in science. Countries with very high percentages of students agreeing that it was important to do well included Colombia (99%), England (96%), Iran (98%), Kuwait (96%), Portugal (97%), Singapore (99%), Spain (99%), and the United States (96%). Countries with fewer than 80% of the students agreeing that it was important to do well in science included Germany (72%), Lithuania (78%), and Switzerland (68%). Compared to science, somewhat more students agreed or strongly agreed that it was important to do well in mathematics and language. In part, however, the lower percentages in science may be because students in many countries, including most of the European countries, take separate science subjects in the middle school years. Therefore, the general term of "science" may not be clearly or uniformly interpreted by students across all countries.

For the most part, eighth-grade students indicated that their mothers' opinions about the importance of these academic activities corresponded very closely to their own feelings. In contrast, however, students reported that their friends were not in as much agreement about the importance of academic success, particularly in science.

Students' reports of their friends opinions about the importance of doing well in science varied substantially across countries, ranging from as low as 35% in Germany to as high as 96% in Singapore. Countries where fewer than two-thirds of eighth-graders reported that their friends agreed or strongly agreed it was important to do well in science included Australia (64%), Austria (45%), the Czech Republic (61%), France (53%), Germany (35%), Hungary (66%), Iceland (65%), Ireland (59%), Israel (56%), Latvia (LSS) (53%), Lithuania (55%), New Zealand (66%), the Slovak Republic (60%), Slovenia (56%), Sweden (61%), and Switzerland (40%).

Although students' friends reportedly were in general agreement about the importance of doing well in mathematics, the percentages were generally in the 80s, rather than the 90s as for the students themselves. According to students, their friends were in the lowest degree of agreement about doing well in mathematics in Germany and Sweden (70% for both countries).

As with the students' reports about their own feelings and those of their mothers, students indicated a close alignment in their friends' degree of agreement about the importance of academic success in mathematics and that in language. Apparently, even though the relative importance varies from group to group, students, their mothers, and their friends find it very nearly equally important to do well in mathematics and language. According to students in some countries, however, their friends do not have nearly the same positive feeling about the importance of doing well in science.

For purposes of comparison, eighth-grade students also were asked about the importance of two non-academic activities – having time to have fun and being good at sports. In most countries, very high percentages of the students (more than 95%) felt it was important to have time to have fun. The percentages in agreement were similar to those agreeing that it was important to do well in mathematics and language. Generally, there was less agreement about the importance of being good at sports, which was rather similar to the level of agreement about the importance of doing well in science. It needs to be emphasized, however, that the relative rankings given to the five activities by students varied from country to country.

In nearly all countries, 80% or more of the eighth-grade students reported that their mothers agreed that it was important to have time to have fun. The exceptions were Hong Kong (74%), Iran (79%), Korea (58%), Kuwait (63%), and Singapore (79%), where students reported from 8% to 29% lower agreement for their mothers than for themselves. According to students, their mothers give a moderate to high degree of support to the importance of being good at sports. In nearly all countries the percentages of students' reporting such agreement were in the 70s, 80s, and 90s, except in Austria (56%), Germany (48%), Kuwait (69%), the Netherlands (63%), and Switzerland (59%).

As might be anticipated, students reported that most of their friends agreed that it was important to have fun -- more than 90% in all countries except Iran (87%), Korea (88%), Kuwait (77%), and Romania (86%). Internationally, eighth-graders reported that their friends generally were in moderate agreement that it was important to do well in sports. The percentages of their friends' agreement as reported by students ranged from a low of 64% in Germany to a high of 96% in Colombia.

Table 4.4

Students' Reports on Whether They Agree or Strongly Agree That It Is Important to Do Various Activities - Science - Upper Grade (Eighth Grade*)

Country	Percent of Students				
	Do Well in Science	Do Well in Mathematics	Do Well in Language	Have Time to Have Fun	Be Good at Sports
Australia	89 (0.6)	96 (0.4)	95 (0.4)	98 (0.2)	85 (0.6)
Austria	82 (1.2)	94 (0.5)	93 (0.6)	98 (0.3)	82 (0.9)
Belgium (Fl)	93 (0.6)	98 (0.3)	98 (0.4)	98 (0.3)	80 (1.0)
Belgium (Fr)	94 (0.7)	98 (0.3)	98 (0.3)	98 (0.4)	87 (0.8)
Canada	94 (0.7)	98 (0.2)	97 (0.3)	99 (0.2)	86 (0.6)
Colombia	99 (0.2)	99 (0.2)	99 (0.2)	98 (0.3)	97 (0.3)
Cyprus	86 (1.0)	94 (0.5)	94 (0.6)	94 (0.5)	85 (1.0)
Czech Republic	88 (1.0)	98 (0.5)	98 (0.3)	98 (0.3)	84 (0.9)
Denmark	87 (1.0)	97 (0.4)	97 (0.4)	99 (0.3)	83 (0.8)
England	96 (0.5)	99 (0.2)	99 (0.3)	99 (0.3)	80 (1.1)
France	83 (1.2)	97 (0.4)	97 (0.5)	97 (0.4)	80 (0.8)
Germany	72 (1.0)	93 (0.6)	91 (0.6)	97 (0.4)	72 (1.1)
Greece	93 (0.5)	96 (0.4)	96 (0.4)	96 (0.4)	91 (0.6)
Hong Kong	90 (0.9)	96 (0.5)	96 (0.5)	94 (0.5)	83 (0.9)
Hungary	86 (0.8)	95 (0.5)	95 (0.5)	96 (0.5)	78 (0.9)
Iceland	90 (1.2)	97 (1.0)	97 (1.0)	98 (0.4)	90 (1.6)
Iran, Islamic Rep.	98 (0.4)	97 (0.4)	96 (0.6)	87 (1.1)	95 (0.7)
Ireland	86 (1.1)	97 (0.3)	96 (0.4)	99 (0.2)	85 (0.8)
Israel	85 (1.0)	98 (0.5)	89 (1.5)	98 (0.5)	84 (1.3)
Japan	87 (0.6)	92 (0.4)	91 (0.5)	99 (0.1)	83 (0.7)
Korea	91 (0.6)	94 (0.5)	93 (0.6)	87 (0.8)	86 (0.8)
Kuwait	96 (0.6)	96 (0.6)	96 (0.5)	85 (2.0)	81 (1.2)
Latvia (LSS)	84 (1.0)	97 (0.4)	97 (0.3)	97 (0.4)	87 (0.8)
Lithuania	78 (1.1)	93 (0.6)	96 (0.4)	94 (0.6)	93 (0.5)
Netherlands	95 (0.7)	97 (0.6)	99 (0.3)	98 (0.6)	78 (1.2)
New Zealand	92 (0.6)	97 (0.3)	96 (0.5)	99 (0.3)	86 (0.7)
Norway	92 (0.6)	96 (0.5)	96 (0.5)	99 (0.1)	79 (0.9)
Portugal	97 (0.3)	97 (0.3)	99 (0.2)	93 (0.5)	94 (0.5)
Romania	86 (0.8)	88 (0.8)	88 (0.8)	86 (1.0)	80 (1.1)
Russian Federation	95 (0.6)	97 (0.4)	97 (0.5)	98 (0.4)	88 (0.9)
Scotland	92 (0.7)	98 (0.4)	98 (0.3)	98 (0.3)	82 (0.9)
Singapore	99 (0.2)	99 (0.2)	100 (0.1)	96 (0.3)	89 (0.6)
Slovak Republic	86 (0.8)	96 (0.4)	96 (0.4)	98 (0.2)	91 (0.5)
Slovenia	86 (0.9)	96 (0.5)	96 (0.4)	95 (0.5)	87 (0.7)
Spain	99 (0.2)	99 (0.2)	99 (0.2)	99 (0.1)	95 (0.3)
Sweden	84 (0.8)	92 (0.6)	90 (0.6)	99 (0.2)	84 (0.7)
Switzerland	68 (1.1)	96 (0.4)	94 (0.4)	95 (0.6)	78 (0.9)
Thailand	94 (0.5)	93 (0.5)	96 (0.4)	95 (0.3)	91 (0.5)
United States	96 (0.5)	97 (0.3)	96 (0.3)	99 (0.2)	88 (0.6)

*Eighth grade in most countries; see Table 2 for more information about the grades tested in each country.
( ) Standard errors appear in parentheses. Because results are rounded to the nearest whole number, some totals may appear inconsistent.
Countries shown in italics did not satisfy one or more guidelines for sample participation rates, age/grade specifications, or classroom sampling procedures (see Figure A.3). Background data for Bulgaria and South Africa are unavailable.
Because population coverage falls below 65%, Latvia is annotated LSS for Latvian Speaking Schools only.

SOURCE: IEA Third International Mathematics and Science Study (TIMSS), 1994-95.

Table 4.5

Students' Reports on Whether Their Mothers Agree or Strongly Agree That It Is Important to Do Various Activities - Science - Upper Grade (Eighth Grade*)

Country	Percent of Students				
	Do Well in Science	Do Well in Mathematics	Do Well in Language	Have Time to Have Fun	Be Good at Sports
Australia	94 (0.4)	98 (0.2)	98 (0.2)	94 (0.4)	83 (0.7)
Austria	81 (1.0)	96 (0.4)	95 (0.5)	90 (0.7)	56 (1.1)
Belgium (Fl)	93 (0.8)	97 (0.4)	98 (0.4)	94 (0.5)	73 (1.2)
Belgium (Fr)	98 (0.3)	99 (0.3)	99 (0.3)	95 (0.6)	85 (0.7)
Canada	98 (0.3)	99 (0.1)	99 (0.1)	96 (0.4)	83 (0.7)
Colombia	99 (0.3)	99 (0.4)	99 (0.2)	93 (0.6)	94 (1.0)
Cyprus	89 (0.8)	95 (0.4)	95 (0.5)	91 (0.6)	80 (0.8)
Czech Republic	93 (0.8)	99 (0.2)	98 (0.3)	90 (0.7)	74 (1.1)
Denmark	95 (0.6)	99 (0.3)	99 (0.3)	98 (0.3)	81 (1.0)
England	96 (0.5)	99 (0.3)	99 (0.3)	94 (0.6)	74 (1.2)
France	88 (0.9)	98 (0.3)	99 (0.3)	91 (0.7)	74 (1.0)
Germany	71 (1.4)	94 (0.8)	93 (0.7)	88 (0.7)	48 (1.2)
Greece	94 (0.5)	96 (0.3)	96 (0.4)	89 (0.6)	83 (0.7)
Hong Kong	86 (0.7)	93 (0.6)	93 (0.6)	74 (0.9)	71 (1.3)
Hungary	85 (0.8)	96 (0.4)	96 (0.4)	96 (0.4)	73 (1.1)
Iceland	95 (1.3)	97 (0.8)	98 (0.5)	95 (0.7)	87 (1.6)
Iran, Islamic Rep.	96 (0.5)	96 (0.5)	95 (0.5)	79 (1.8)	90 (1.5)
Ireland	89 (1.0)	98 (0.3)	98 (0.2)	94 (0.5)	83 (0.8)
Israel	89 (0.9)	99 (0.4)	93 (0.6)	95 (0.7)	79 (1.4)
Japan	- -	- -	- -	- -	- -
Korea	92 (0.5)	96 (0.4)	94 (0.5)	58 (1.1)	72 (0.9)
Kuwait	r 91 (0.9)	91 (1.0)	r 91 (0.8)	r 63 (2.2)	r 69 (2.0)
Latvia (LSS)	85 (1.1)	97 (0.4)	97 (0.5)	90 (0.8)	82 (0.9)
Lithuania	77 (1.1)	91 (0.6)	95 (0.5)	86 (0.8)	87 (0.9)
Netherlands	94 (0.7)	96 (0.5)	97 (0.4)	96 (0.4)	63 (1.4)
New Zealand	95 (0.4)	98 (0.3)	97 (0.3)	95 (0.5)	86 (0.8)
Norway	95 (0.5)	97 (0.4)	97 (0.4)	97 (0.3)	71 (1.1)
Portugal	98 (0.3)	96 (0.4)	98 (0.3)	87 (0.7)	91 (0.6)
Romania	94 (0.6)	93 (0.5)	90 (0.7)	83 (1.0)	76 (1.0)
Russian Federation	95 (0.4)	96 (0.3)	97 (0.4)	92 (0.6)	84 (0.7)
Scotland	93 (0.6)	98 (0.3)	99 (0.2)	94 (0.5)	77 (1.0)
Singapore	99 (0.2)	99 (0.2)	99 (0.1)	79 (0.8)	84 (0.8)
Slovak Republic	94 (0.5)	99 (0.2)	99 (0.2)	95 (0.4)	88 (0.6)
Slovenia	85 (0.7)	91 (0.7)	92 (0.6)	88 (0.7)	81 (0.9)
Spain	99 (0.2)	99 (0.2)	99 (0.2)	96 (0.4)	93 (0.5)
Sweden	92 (0.5)	96 (0.4)	95 (0.4)	97 (0.3)	83 (0.7)
Switzerland	69 (1.0)	96 (0.3)	95 (0.4)	83 (0.9)	59 (1.1)
Thailand	95 (0.4)	94 (0.5)	96 (0.4)	84 (0.9)	90 (0.5)
United States	97 (0.2)	98 (0.2)	98 (0.2)	93 (0.4)	81 (0.8)

*Eighth grade in most countries; see Table 2 for more information about the grades tested in each country.
Data are reported as percent of students.
( ) Standard errors appear in parentheses. Because results are rounded to the nearest whole number, some totals may appear inconsistent.
Countries shown in italics did not satisfy one or more guidelines for sample participation rates, age/grade specifications, or classroom sampling procedures (see Figure A.3). Background data for Bulgaria and South Africa are unavailable.
Because population coverage falls below 65%, Latvia is annotated LSS for Latvian Speaking Schools only.
A dash (–) indicates data are not available.
An "r" indicates a 70-84% student response rate.

SOURCE: IEA Third International Mathematics and Science Study (TIMSS), 1994-95.

Table 4.6

Students' Reports on Whether Their Friends Agree or Strongly Agree That It Is Important to Do Various Activities - Science - Upper Grade (Eighth Grade*)

Country	Percent of Students				
	Do Well in Science	Do Well in Mathematics	Do Well in Language	Have Time to Have Fun	Be Good at Sports
Australia	64 (1.0)	78 (0.8)	76 (0.8)	98 (0.2)	83 (0.8)
Austria	45 (1.8)	77 (1.2)	74 (1.1)	97 (0.4)	79 (1.2)
Belgium (Fl)	70 (1.6)	84 (1.7)	83 (1.8)	98 (0.4)	76 (1.5)
Belgium (Fr)	78 (1.3)	86 (1.1)	87 (0.9)	97 (0.4)	84 (1.2)
Canada	68 (1.3)	80 (0.8)	78 (0.8)	99 (0.2)	87 (0.6)
Colombia	93 (0.6)	95 (0.5)	95 (0.5)	97 (0.4)	96 (0.4)
Cyprus	71 (1.1)	85 (0.8)	85 (0.9)	91 (0.6)	82 (1.0)
Czech Republic	61 (1.5)	84 (1.3)	84 (1.2)	98 (0.3)	82 (1.1)
Denmark	82 (1.0)	94 (0.6)	95 (0.6)	99 (0.2)	92 (0.7)
England	80 (1.1)	88 (0.9)	88 (0.9)	99 (0.3)	79 (1.2)
France	53 (1.5)	85 (1.3)	88 (1.1)	97 (0.4)	80 (1.0)
Germany	35 (1.4)	70 (1.3)	68 (1.3)	94 (0.5)	64 (1.3)
Greece	82 (0.8)	87 (0.7)	89 (0.6)	96 (0.3)	85 (0.8)
Hong Kong	74 (1.3)	86 (0.9)	87 (0.9)	93 (0.5)	76 (1.0)
Hungary	66 (1.2)	81 (0.9)	83 (0.8)	94 (0.5)	74 (1.1)
Iceland	65 (2.0)	85 (1.4)	85 (1.1)	98 (0.4)	89 (1.2)
Iran, Islamic Rep.	95 (0.9)	95 (0.5)	93 (0.6)	87 (1.3)	93 (0.9)
Ireland	59 (1.4)	80 (0.9)	78 (0.8)	99 (0.2)	85 (0.7)
Israel	56 (2.5)	93 (1.1)	75 (2.0)	98 (0.5)	79 (1.9)
Japan	83 (0.7)	90 (0.5)	88 (0.6)	99 (0.2)	81 (0.7)
Korea	79 (0.9)	86 (0.8)	81 (0.8)	88 (0.7)	78 (1.0)
Kuwait	90 (0.6)	90 (0.8)	86 (0.9)	77 (2.4)	78 (1.5)
Latvia (LSS)	53 (1.3)	86 (0.9)	87 (1.0)	97 (0.4)	87 (0.8)
Lithuania	55 (1.3)	83 (0.9)	88 (0.9)	95 (0.5)	90 (0.7)
Netherlands	82 (1.2)	87 (0.9)	90 (0.7)	97 (0.6)	66 (1.2)
New Zealand	66 (1.2)	77 (1.0)	76 (1.0)	98 (0.3)	87 (0.8)
Norway	72 (1.2)	84 (0.8)	83 (0.9)	99 (0.2)	83 (1.0)
Portugal	88 (0.8)	89 (0.7)	93 (0.4)	92 (0.6)	94 (0.5)
Romania	80 (1.0)	87 (0.8)	88 (0.8)	86 (1.0)	81 (1.0)
Russian Federation	81 (0.8)	88 (0.8)	88 (0.8)	97 (0.4)	84 (0.8)
Scotland	70 (1.3)	81 (1.2)	82 (1.0)	98 (0.3)	84 (0.8)
Singapore	96 (0.5)	97 (0.4)	98 (0.2)	96 (0.3)	86 (0.8)
Slovak Republic	60 (1.3)	83 (0.7)	84 (0.7)	98 (0.2)	92 (0.5)
Slovenia	56 (1.6)	77 (1.2)	78 (1.1)	95 (0.5)	81 (0.9)
Spain	89 (0.7)	91 (0.6)	91 (0.5)	99 (0.2)	94 (0.4)
Sweden	61 (1.4)	70 (1.2)	68 (1.2)	97 (0.3)	75 (0.8)
Switzerland	40 (1.4)	85 (0.8)	82 (1.0)	93 (0.8)	75 (1.1)
Thailand	94 (0.5)	93 (0.6)	95 (0.4)	95 (0.4)	91 (0.4)
United States	69 (1.2)	75 (1.0)	73 (0.9)	98 (0.2)	90 (0.7)

*Eighth grade in most countries; see Table 2 for more information about the grades tested in each country.
Data are reported as percent of students.
( ) Standard errors appear in parentheses. Because results are rounded to the nearest whole number, some totals may appear inconsistent.
Countries shown in italics did not satisfy one or more guidelines for sample participation rates, age/grade specifications, or classroom sampling procedures (see Figure A.3). Background data for Bulgaria and South Africa are unavailable.
Because population coverage falls below 65%, Latvia is annotated LSS for Latvian Speaking Schools only.

SOURCE: IEA Third International Mathematics and Science Study (TIMSS), 1994-95.

How Do Students Spend Their Out-of-School Time During the School Week?

Even though education may be thought to be the dominant activity of school-aged children, young people actually spend much more of their time outside of school. Some of this out-of-school time is spent at furthering academic development – for example, in studying or doing homework in school subjects. Table 4.7 presents eighth-grade students' reports about the average number of hours per day they spend studying or doing homework in science, mathematics, and other subjects. Students in most countries reported spending between half an hour and an hour per day studying science. Eighth-graders in Australia, Denmark, and Scotland were at the lower end of the range, reporting an average of about one-half hour or less per day (.3 to .5 of an hour). Those in Colombia, Greece, Hungary, Iran, Kuwait, Romania, and Singapore reported more than one hour of science homework per day, on average, with Iran at nearly two hours (1.9). On average, students in nearly all countries reported spending somewhat more time studying mathematics, roughly an hour per day in many countries.

Participating countries showed some variation in the amount of time students spent doing homework each day across all school subjects. The most common response about the amount of homework done, reported by eighth-graders in about half the countries, was an average of two to three hours per day, but there was a range. Students in Iran and Kuwait reported spending the most time on homework, more than five hours per day. Students in the Czech Republic, Denmark, and Scotland reported spending the least amount of time per day on homework, less than two hours.

The students also were asked about a variety of other ways they could spend their time out of school. Eighth-graders were asked about watching television, playing computer games, playing or talking with friends, doing jobs at home, playing sports, and reading books for enjoyment. Their reports about the amount of time spent daily in each of these activities are shown in Table 4.8. Granted, some television programming and some computer games are targeted at developing children's academic abilities, and leisure reading also can be related to higher academic achievement. Still, much fare on television is not educationally related, and eighth-grade students in many countries reported spending nearly as much time each day watching television – an average of two to three hours per day – as they did doing homework. Eighth-graders in many countries also appear to spend several hours per day playing or talking with friends, and nearly two hours playing sports. The time spent on leisure activities is not additive, because students often do these activities simultaneously (e.g., talk with friends and watch television). Nevertheless, it does appear that in most countries at least as much time is spent in these largely non-academic activities as in studying and doing homework, and probably more time.

Table 4.9 shows the relationship between time spent doing homework in all subjects and students' average science achievement. The relationship was curvilinear in many countries, with the highest achievement being associated with a moderate amount of homework per day (one to three hours). This pattern suggests that, compared

Table 4.7

Students' Reports on How They Spend Their Daily Out-of School Study Time[1]
Science - Upper Grade (Eighth Grade*)

Country	Average Hours Each Day Studying Science or Doing Science Homework After School	Average Hours Each Day Studying Mathematics or Doing Mathematics Homework After School	Average Hours Each Day Studying or Doing Homework in Other School Subjects	Total Hours Each Day on Average
Australia	0.5 (0.01)	0.7 (0.02)	0.9 (0.02)	2.0 (0.04)
Austria	0.7 (0.03)	0.8 (0.02)	0.8 (0.02)	2.4 (0.07)
Belgium (Fl)	0.8 (0.02)	1.1 (0.03)	1.5 (0.03)	3.4 (0.07)
Belgium (Fr)	0.8 (0.02)	1.0 (0.02)	1.2 (0.03)	3.0 (0.07)
Canada	0.6 (0.02)	0.7 (0.02)	0.9 (0.03)	2.2 (0.07)
Colombia	1.2 (0.06)	1.3 (0.06)	2.0 (0.07)	4.6 (0.15)
Cyprus	0.9 (0.02)	1.2 (0.02)	1.5 (0.03)	3.6 (0.06)
Czech Republic	0.6 (0.02)	0.6 (0.02)	0.6 (0.02)	1.8 (0.05)
Denmark	0.3 (0.02)	0.5 (0.02)	0.5 (0.02)	1.4 (0.05)
England	- -	- -	- -	- -
France	0.6 (0.01)	0.9 (0.02)	1.2 (0.03)	2.7 (0.05)
Germany	0.6 (0.02)	0.6 (0.02)	0.8 (0.02)	2.0 (0.05)
Greece	1.2 (0.03)	1.2 (0.03)	2.0 (0.05)	4.4 (0.08)
Hong Kong	0.6 (0.02)	0.9 (0.02)	1.1 (0.03)	2.5 (0.06)
Hungary	1.1 (0.02)	0.8 (0.02)	1.2 (0.03)	3.1 (0.06)
Iceland	0.6 (0.03)	0.9 (0.03)	0.9 (0.03)	2.4 (0.07)
Iran, Islamic Rep.	1.9 (0.05)	2.0 (0.05)	2.5 (0.05)	6.4 (0.13)
Ireland	0.6 (0.01)	0.7 (0.02)	1.4 (0.03)	2.7 (0.05)
Israel	0.6 (0.03)	1.0 (0.04)	1.2 (0.05)	2.8 (0.10)
Japan	0.6 (0.01)	0.8 (0.01)	1.0 (0.02)	2.3 (0.04)
Korea	0.6 (0.02)	0.8 (0.02)	1.1 (0.02)	2.5 (0.05)
Kuwait	1.5 (0.05)	1.6 (0.04)	2.3 (0.07)	5.3 (0.12)
Latvia (LSS)	0.6 (0.02)	0.9 (0.02)	1.2 (0.03)	2.7 (0.05)
Lithuania	0.7 (0.02)	0.8 (0.02)	1.2 (0.04)	2.7 (0.06)
Netherlands	0.6 (0.01)	0.6 (0.01)	1.0 (0.03)	2.2 (0.04)
New Zealand	0.6 (0.01)	0.7 (0.02)	0.9 (0.02)	2.1 (0.05)
Norway	0.6 (0.01)	0.7 (0.02)	1.0 (0.02)	2.3 (0.04)
Portugal	0.9 (0.02)	1.0 (0.02)	1.1 (0.02)	3.0 (0.05)
Romania	1.6 (0.06)	1.8 (0.07)	1.6 (0.06)	5.0 (0.18)
Russian Federation	1.0 (0.02)	0.9 (0.02)	1.0 (0.02)	2.9 (0.05)
Scotland	0.5 (0.01)	0.6 (0.02)	0.7 (0.02)	1.8 (0.04)
Singapore	1.3 (0.02)	1.4 (0.02)	1.9 (0.03)	4.6 (0.04)
Slovak Republic	0.8 (0.02)	0.7 (0.01)	0.9 (0.02)	2.4 (0.04)
Slovenia	1.0 (0.02)	0.9 (0.02)	0.9 (0.02)	2.9 (0.05)
Spain	1.0 (0.02)	1.2 (0.02)	1.4 (0.03)	3.6 (0.06)
Sweden	0.7 (0.01)	0.7 (0.01)	0.9 (0.02)	2.3 (0.04)
Switzerland	0.7 (0.01)	0.9 (0.02)	1.0 (0.02)	2.7 (0.04)
Thailand	1.0 (0.02)	1.2 (0.03)	1.3 (0.02)	3.5 (0.06)
United States	0.6 (0.01)	0.8 (0.02)	0.9 (0.02)	2.3 (0.04)

[1]Average hours based on: No Time = 0; Less Than 1 Hour = .5; 1-2 Hours =1.5; 3-5 Hours = 4; More Than 5 Hours = 7.
*Eighth grade in most countries; see Table 2 for more information about the grades tested in each country.
( ) Standard errors appear in parentheses. Because results are rounded to the nearest whole number, some totals may appear inconsistent.
Countries shown in italics did not satisfy one or more guidelines for sample participation rates, age/grade specifications, or classroom sampling procedures (see Figure A.3). Background data for Bulgaria and South Africa are unavailable.
Because population coverage falls below 65%, Latvia is annotated LSS for Latvian Speaking Schools only.
A dash (-) indicates data are not available.

SOURCE: IEA Third International Mathematics and Science Study (TIMSS), 1994-95.

Table 4.8

Students' Reports on How They Spend Their Daily Leisure Time [1]
Science - Upper Grade (Eighth Grade*)

Country	Average Hours Each Day Watching Television or Videos	Average Hours Each Day Playing Computer Games	Average Hours Each Day Playing or Talking with Friends	Average Hours Each Day Doing Jobs at Home	Average Hours Each Day Playing Sports	Average Hours Each Day Reading a Book for Enjoyment
Australia	2.4 (0.05)	0.6 (0.02)	1.4 (0.03)	0.9 (0.02)	1.6 (0.03)	0.6 (0.02)
Austria	1.9 (0.06)	0.6 (0.03)	2.9 (0.08)	0.8 (0.03)	1.9 (0.07)	0.8 (0.03)
Belgium (Fl)	2.0 (0.05)	0.5 (0.06)	1.6 (0.05)	1.1 (0.03)	1.8 (0.07)	0.7 (0.03)
Belgium (Fr)	1.9 (0.08)	0.7 (0.03)	1.7 (0.10)	0.8 (0.03)	1.8 (0.04)	0.8 (0.03)
Canada	2.3 (0.04)	0.5 (0.02)	2.2 (0.05)	1.0 (0.02)	1.9 (0.03)	0.8 (0.02)
Colombia	2.2 (0.07)	r 0.4 (0.06)	1.9 (0.06)	2.3 (0.07)	1.9 (0.06)	0.9 (0.05)
Cyprus	2.3 (0.04)	0.8 (0.03)	1.7 (0.04)	1.0 (0.03)	1.4 (0.04)	0.8 (0.02)
Czech Republic	2.6 (0.05)	0.6 (0.03)	2.9 (0.09)	1.3 (0.04)	1.9 (0.06)	1.0 (0.03)
Denmark	2.2 (0.06)	0.7 (0.03)	2.8 (0.07)	1.1 (0.04)	1.7 (0.06)	0.7 (0.03)
England	2.7 (0.07)	0.9 (0.05)	2.5 (0.06)	0.8 (0.03)	1.5 (0.05)	0.7 (0.03)
France	1.5 (0.04)	0.5 (0.02)	1.5 (0.05)	0.9 (0.03)	1.7 (0.04)	0.8 (0.03)
Germany	1.9 (0.04)	0.8 (0.04)	3.5 (0.07)	0.9 (0.02)	1.7 (0.04)	0.7 (0.02)
Greece	2.1 (0.04)	0.7 (0.03)	1.5 (0.04)	0.9 (0.03)	1.8 (0.04)	1.0 (0.03)
Hong Kong	2.6 (0.05)	0.8 (0.03)	1.2 (0.04)	0.7 (0.02)	0.9 (0.03)	0.9 (0.02)
Hungary	3.0 (0.06)	0.7 (0.03)	2.3 (0.05)	2.0 (0.04)	1.7 (0.04)	1.2 (0.04)
Iceland	2.2 (0.05)	0.7 (0.06)	3.1 (0.06)	0.8 (0.03)	1.8 (0.06)	0.9 (0.06)
Iran, Islamic Rep.	1.8 (0.06)	r 0.2 (0.02)	1.2 (0.04)	1.8 (0.06)	1.2 (0.09)	1.1 (0.04)
Ireland	2.1 (0.03)	0.5 (0.03)	1.5 (0.06)	0.9 (0.03)	1.4 (0.05)	0.6 (0.02)
Israel	3.3 (0.10)	0.9 (0.04)	2.4 (0.08)	1.2 (0.05)	1.9 (0.09)	1.0 (0.04)
Japan	2.6 (0.04)	0.6 (0.02)	1.9 (0.04)	0.6 (0.01)	1.3 (0.03)	0.9 (0.02)
Korea	2.0 (0.04)	0.3 (0.02)	0.9 (0.03)	0.5 (0.02)	0.5 (0.02)	0.8 (0.03)
Kuwait	1.9 (0.07)	0.7 (0.05)	1.5 (0.11)	1.2 (0.08)	1.5 (0.10)	1.0 (0.04)
Latvia (LSS)	2.6 (0.05)	0.7 (0.04)	2.1 (0.06)	1.5 (0.04)	1.2 (0.04)	1.1 (0.03)
Lithuania	2.8 (0.05)	0.9 (0.04)	2.7 (0.06)	1.2 (0.03)	1.2 (0.04)	1.0 (0.03)
Netherlands	2.5 (0.09)	0.7 (0.04)	2.8 (0.08)	0.9 (0.04)	1.8 (0.06)	0.6 (0.03)
New Zealand	2.5 (0.05)	0.7 (0.03)	1.5 (0.04)	0.9 (0.02)	1.5 (0.04)	0.8 (0.02)
Norway	2.5 (0.04)	0.8 (0.03)	3.2 (0.06)	1.1 (0.03)	1.9 (0.05)	0.7 (0.02)
Portugal	2.0 (0.04)	0.7 (0.03)	1.7 (0.05)	1.0 (0.04)	1.7 (0.04)	0.7 (0.02)
Romania	1.9 (0.06)	0.6 (0.05)	1.5 (0.06)	1.9 (0.08)	1.3 (0.05)	1.3 (0.07)
Russian Federation	2.9 (0.05)	1.0 (0.04)	2.9 (0.05)	1.5 (0.03)	1.0 (0.03)	1.3 (0.04)
Scotland	2.7 (0.05)	1.0 (0.04)	2.8 (0.08)	0.7 (0.02)	1.9 (0.05)	0.7 (0.02)
Singapore	2.7 (0.05)	0.6 (0.03)	1.5 (0.04)	1.0 (0.03)	0.7 (0.03)	1.1 (0.02)
Slovak Republic	2.7 (0.05)	0.6 (0.03)	2.9 (0.07)	1.5 (0.05)	1.8 (0.04)	1.0 (0.03)
Slovenia	2.0 (0.04)	0.6 (0.02)	1.7 (0.05)	1.6 (0.05)	1.6 (0.03)	0.9 (0.02)
Spain	1.8 (0.05)	0.3 (0.02)	1.8 (0.06)	1.1 (0.03)	1.7 (0.04)	0.6 (0.02)
Sweden	2.3 (0.04)	0.6 (0.02)	2.3 (0.05)	0.9 (0.02)	1.6 (0.04)	0.7 (0.02)
Switzerland	1.3 (0.03)	0.4 (0.02)	2.4 (0.05)	1.0 (0.03)	1.8 (0.03)	0.8 (0.02)
Thailand	2.1 (0.07)	0.3 (0.02)	1.2 (0.03)	1.6 (0.03)	1.1 (0.02)	1.0 (0.02)
United States	2.6 (0.07)	0.7 (0.03)	2.5 (0.06)	1.2 (0.04)	2.2 (0.05)	0.7 (0.02)

[1] Average hours based on: No Time = 0; Less Than 1 Hour = .5; 1-2 Hours = 1.5; 3-5 Hours = 4; More Than 5 Hours = 7.

*Eighth grade in most countries; see Table 2 for more information about the grades tested in each country.

( ) Standard errors appear in parentheses. Because results are rounded to the nearest whole number, some totals may appear inconsistent.

Countries shown in italics did not satisfy one or more guidelines for sample participation rates, age/grade specifications, or classroom sampling procedures (see Figure A.3). Background data for Bulgaria and South Africa are unavailable.

Because population coverage falls below 65%, Latvia is annotated LSS for Latvian Speaking Schools only.

An "r" indicates a 70 - 84% student response rate.

SOURCE: IEA Third International Mathematics and Science Study (TIMSS), 1994-95.

Table 4.9

Students' Reports on Total Amount of Daily Out-of-School Study Time[1] Science - Upper Grade (Eighth Grade*)

Country	Less than 1 Hour		1 to < 2 Hours		2 to 3 Hours		More than 3 Hours	
	Percent of Students	Mean Achievement	Percent of Students	Mean Achievement	Percent of Students	Mean Achievement	Percent of Students	Mean Achievement
Australia	15 (0.9)	505 (6.9)	46 (1.0)	556 (4.1)	22 (0.6)	557 (4.9)	17 (0.7)	546 (5.0)
Austria	9 (0.8)	551 (9.9)	46 (1.3)	563 (4.8)	21 (0.9)	561 (5.0)	24 (1.2)	553 (4.8)
Belgium (Fl)	2 (0.4)	~ ~	25 (1.3)	545 (5.0)	28 (1.1)	562 (5.9)	45 (1.6)	547 (3.6)
Belgium (Fr)	7 (0.8)	428 (6.9)	32 (1.0)	481 (4.7)	21 (1.3)	481 (4.5)	40 (1.5)	467 (4.0)
Canada	14 (1.2)	524 (6.1)	47 (1.1)	541 (2.8)	18 (0.7)	531 (3.9)	21 (1.1)	517 (3.6)
Colombia	2 (0.4)	~ ~	17 (1.1)	421 (5.3)	20 (1.2)	422 (4.9)	61 (1.9)	413 (5.8)
Cyprus	9 (0.5)	430 (7.0)	19 (0.7)	468 (4.4)	26 (0.8)	475 (3.4)	46 (0.9)	466 (2.9)
Czech Republic	13 (1.1)	558 (9.0)	57 (1.1)	579 (3.9)	17 (0.9)	582 (7.2)	13 (0.8)	560 (6.4)
Denmark	39 (1.6)	494 (4.4)	39 (1.4)	479 (4.1)	13 (0.8)	459 (5.5)	9 (0.7)	457 (6.8)
England	- -	- -	- -	- -	- -	- -	- -	- -
France	8 (0.7)	481 (6.8)	33 (1.2)	497 (3.3)	28 (1.0)	506 (4.0)	31 (1.2)	499 (3.4)
Germany	14 (1.1)	505 (8.2)	51 (1.2)	541 (4.6)	18 (1.0)	544 (7.0)	17 (0.9)	525 (6.5)
Greece	6 (0.6)	473 (4.8)	14 (0.7)	497 (5.0)	21 (0.7)	500 (3.1)	59 (1.2)	502 (2.5)
Hong Kong	13 (1.0)	489 (7.3)	32 (0.9)	519 (4.7)	25 (0.9)	534 (4.8)	30 (1.1)	534 (5.2)
Hungary	4 (0.4)	519 (10.0)	33 (1.1)	553 (4.4)	22 (0.9)	557 (5.6)	41 (1.3)	557 (3.0)
Iceland	5 (1.0)	470 (8.7)	46 (1.7)	505 (5.6)	25 (1.3)	493 (4.5)	23 (1.4)	488 (7.5)
Iran, Islamic Rep.	1 (0.2)	~ ~	5 (0.5)	476 (6.0)	12 (1.0)	479 (5.2)	82 (1.3)	471 (2.7)
Ireland	5 (0.6)	475 (9.0)	29 (1.0)	529 (5.4)	40 (1.1)	550 (4.7)	26 (1.2)	550 (4.9)
Israel	5 (0.6)	532 (13.5)	36 (2.2)	555 (7.7)	26 (1.5)	523 (6.9)	33 (2.1)	505 (5.2)
Japan	13 (0.8)	551 (4.4)	39 (0.8)	573 (2.2)	20 (0.6)	572 (3.0)	28 (1.0)	577 (2.4)
Korea	15 (0.9)	544 (5.0)	32 (1.1)	564 (2.9)	25 (0.8)	562 (3.1)	29 (1.2)	581 (3.7)
Kuwait	3 (0.6)	400 (10.4)	13 (1.5)	436 (7.8)	19 (1.3)	432 (7.1)	65 (1.8)	431 (3.4)
Latvia (LSS)	4 (0.5)	468 (8.5)	35 (1.1)	492 (4.1)	32 (1.2)	490 (4.1)	29 (1.2)	481 (3.0)
Lithuania	5 (0.6)	457 (9.1)	39 (1.4)	484 (4.5)	28 (1.0)	483 (3.8)	28 (1.4)	472 (4.7)
Netherlands	3 (0.9)	519 (17.1)	54 (1.7)	559 (6.1)	27 (1.7)	578 (5.4)	16 (0.8)	545 (5.7)
New Zealand	12 (0.9)	488 (7.6)	51 (1.2)	536 (4.6)	21 (1.0)	537 (5.7)	17 (0.9)	516 (5.7)
Norway	6 (0.5)	501 (7.3)	50 (1.2)	533 (2.5)	24 (0.9)	536 (3.4)	21 (0.9)	516 (3.7)
Portugal	3 (0.3)	465 (8.8)	41 (1.1)	488 (2.9)	18 (0.7)	478 (4.1)	38 (1.2)	474 (2.8)
Romania	9 (0.7)	460 (11.7)	16 (1.0)	468 (7.0)	15 (0.7)	487 (5.7)	60 (1.6)	499 (5.2)
Russian Federation	4 (0.5)	511 (10.1)	33 (1.1)	542 (4.4)	25 (1.0)	538 (4.4)	38 (1.4)	543 (4.6)
Scotland	17 (1.4)	470 (5.3)	54 (1.2)	526 (5.1)	17 (1.0)	537 (8.5)	12 (0.8)	532 (6.5)
Singapore	2 (0.3)	~ ~	7 (0.4)	604 (8.4)	13 (0.6)	617 (7.3)	78 (0.9)	607 (5.4)
Slovak Republic	6 (0.5)	551 (7.1)	46 (0.9)	552 (3.7)	25 (0.7)	541 (3.8)	23 (1.0)	536 (4.7)
Slovenia	5 (0.5)	559 (9.2)	36 (1.0)	580 (3.5)	21 (0.8)	557 (3.2)	37 (1.1)	544 (3.3)
Spain	3 (0.4)	482 (7.9)	26 (1.0)	522 (2.8)	18 (0.9)	522 (3.5)	53 (1.3)	516 (2.2)
Sweden	7 (0.6)	520 (6.0)	55 (1.2)	544 (3.2)	17 (0.8)	539 (4.9)	21 (0.9)	523 (4.9)
Switzerland	4 (0.3)	500 (8.3)	44 (1.2)	530 (3.1)	19 (0.8)	526 (6.2)	33 (1.1)	514 (3.5)
Thailand	3 (0.3)	510 (8.8)	26 (1.0)	520 (4.0)	18 (0.7)	519 (4.3)	54 (1.5)	532 (4.1)
United States	17 (1.1)	507 (9.5)	42 (0.9)	548 (4.1)	17 (0.7)	541 (5.2)	24 (0.8)	533 (5.7)

[1]Sum of time reported spent studying or doing homework in science, mathematics, and other subjects.
*Eighth grade in most countries; see Table 2 for more information about the grades tested in each country.
( ) Standard errors appear in parentheses. Because results are rounded to the nearest whole number, some totals may appear inconsistent.
Countries shown in italics did not satisfy one or more guidelines for sample participation rates, age/grade specifications, or classroom sampling procedures (see Figure A.3). Background data for Bulgaria and South Africa are unavailable.
Because population coverage falls below 65%, Latvia is annotated LSS for Latvian Speaking Schools only.
A dash (-) indicates data are not available. A tilde (~) indicates insufficient data to report achievement.

SOURCE: IEA Third International Mathematics and Science Study (TIMSS), 1994-95.

to their higher-achieving counterparts, the lower-performing students may do less homework, either because they do not do it or because their teachers do not assign it, or more homework, perhaps because they need to spend the extra time to keep up academically. In some countries, students doing one hour a day of homework or more had higher average science achievement than students doing less than one hour a day (e.g., Greece, Hungary, Japan, Kuwait, and the Russian Federation), although in these countries there was little difference in achievement as the time spent increased from at least one hour to more than three hours. A more direct positive relationship between time spent doing homework and science achievement was found in other countries, such as Hong Kong, Korea, and Romania. The only inverse relationship was noted for Denmark. Clearly, different countries have different policies and practices about assigning homework.

The relationship between science achievement and amount of time spent watching television each day was more consistent across countries than that spent doing homework (see Table 4.10). In about half the TIMSS countries, the highest science achievement was associated with watching from one to two hours of television per day. This was the most common response, reflecting from 33% to 54% of the students for all countries. That watching less than one hour of television per day generally was associated with lower average science achievement than watching one to two hours in many countries most likely has little to do with the influence of television viewing on science achievement. For these students, low television viewing may be a surrogate socio-economic indicator, suggesting something about children's access to television sets across countries. Because students with fewer socio-economic advantages generally perform less well than their counterparts academically, it may be that students' who reported less than one hour watching television each day simply do not have television sets in their homes, or come from homes with only one television set where they have less opportunity to spend a lot of time watching their choice of programming.

In general, beyond one to two hours of television viewing per day, the more television eighth-graders reported watching, the lower their science achievement, although there were several countries where students watching three to five hours of television did not have lower achievement than those watching one to two hours. In all countries, however, students watching more than five hours of television per day had the lowest average science achievement. Countries where 10% or more of the students reported watching more than five hours of television each day included Colombia, England, Hong Kong, Hungary, Israel, Latvia (LSS), Lithuania, New Zealand, the Russian Federation, Scotland, the Slovak Republic, and the United States.

Table 4.10

Students' Reports on the Hours Spent Each Day Watching Television and Videos Science - Upper Grade (Eighth Grade*)

Country	Less than 1 Hour		1 to 2 Hours		3 to 5 Hours		More than 5 Hours	
	Percent of Students	Mean Achievement	Percent of Students	Mean Achievement	Percent of Students	Mean Achievement	Percent of Students	Mean Achievement
Australia	24 (0.9)	556 (5.3)	41 (0.8)	554 (3.7)	27 (0.8)	541 (4.5)	9 (0.6)	502 (5.7)
Austria	25 (1.4)	562 (5.7)	53 (1.1)	561 (4.8)	17 (1.0)	558 (4.7)	5 (0.6)	522 (9.7)
Belgium (Fl)	24 (1.2)	563 (4.5)	52 (1.2)	556 (4.8)	19 (1.0)	526 (6.3)	5 (0.5)	517 (8.8)
Belgium (Fr)	33 (1.3)	480 (3.6)	44 (1.8)	476 (4.3)	17 (1.3)	467 (5.2)	6 (1.0)	413 (8.7)
Canada	22 (0.7)	528 (3.5)	46 (0.8)	536 (3.2)	25 (0.7)	535 (3.2)	7 (0.6)	508 (6.1)
Colombia	31 (1.5)	411 (4.3)	39 (1.2)	419 (4.5)	20 (1.2)	417 (7.3)	11 (1.0)	412 (6.2)
Cyprus	25 (1.1)	453 (3.6)	45 (1.1)	474 (2.4)	21 (0.8)	469 (4.0)	9 (0.7)	440 (5.1)
Czech Republic	15 (0.8)	578 (6.2)	45 (1.2)	581 (4.7)	31 (1.2)	571 (4.8)	9 (0.8)	546 (8.7)
Denmark	28 (1.1)	476 (3.9)	42 (1.2)	484 (4.3)	22 (1.0)	484 (4.9)	8 (0.7)	464 (7.8)
England	20 (1.3)	545 (9.8)	37 (1.2)	565 (4.9)	31 (1.2)	558 (4.2)	11 (0.9)	530 (7.5)
France	42 (1.3)	503 (3.6)	45 (1.1)	498 (2.9)	9 (0.7)	493 (4.9)	4 (0.5)	467 (7.3)
Germany	31 (1.0)	533 (6.0)	47 (1.1)	542 (4.9)	16 (0.8)	530 (6.5)	6 (0.6)	477 (9.2)
Greece	32 (0.9)	499 (2.7)	42 (0.7)	502 (3.1)	17 (0.7)	496 (3.6)	9 (0.5)	488 (4.9)
Hong Kong	22 (0.9)	520 (5.3)	39 (0.9)	529 (5.5)	28 (1.0)	526 (4.7)	11 (0.8)	506 (7.0)
Hungary	11 (0.7)	569 (5.9)	41 (1.1)	564 (3.6)	33 (0.9)	552 (3.7)	15 (1.0)	522 (5.0)
Iceland	24 (1.3)	485 (8.9)	47 (1.3)	496 (3.5)	22 (1.2)	504 (5.0)	7 (0.8)	492 (8.4)
Iran, Islamic Rep.	32 (1.3)	463 (3.4)	46 (0.9)	473 (2.9)	17 (0.9)	485 (6.1)	5 (0.6)	474 (6.7)
Ireland	20 (0.8)	530 (5.6)	51 (1.1)	546 (4.3)	23 (0.8)	546 (5.2)	5 (0.5)	501 (9.0)
Israel	9 (1.4)	507 (19.9)	33 (2.1)	538 (6.8)	44 (1.7)	532 (5.0)	14 (1.2)	513 (9.4)
Japan	9 (0.5)	579 (4.9)	53 (0.9)	578 (2.3)	30 (0.8)	564 (2.3)	9 (0.5)	547 (4.8)
Korea	32 (1.0)	574 (3.2)	40 (1.0)	569 (2.6)	20 (0.8)	555 (4.5)	7 (0.6)	534 (6.1)
Kuwait	39 (1.7)	425 (4.3)	38 (1.3)	435 (4.5)	14 (1.2)	441 (7.2)	9 (0.8)	420 (8.1)
Latvia (LSS)	16 (1.0)	473 (5.0)	44 (1.1)	487 (3.4)	29 (1.2)	497 (3.9)	10 (0.7)	477 (5.0)
Lithuania	12 (0.7)	469 (7.2)	44 (1.3)	485 (3.8)	32 (1.2)	476 (4.1)	12 (0.9)	467 (5.8)
Netherlands	17 (1.8)	562 (11.5)	47 (1.7)	572 (4.7)	27 (1.5)	550 (6.2)	9 (0.9)	527 (6.1)
New Zealand	24 (1.0)	530 (5.8)	38 (0.9)	538 (4.8)	26 (0.9)	525 (5.1)	12 (0.8)	489 (5.5)
Norway	15 (0.7)	536 (4.7)	48 (1.0)	534 (2.2)	30 (1.0)	523 (3.5)	7 (0.4)	496 (6.1)
Portugal	27 (1.0)	474 (3.6)	48 (0.9)	481 (2.8)	20 (0.8)	488 (3.0)	5 (0.5)	471 (5.8)
Romania	38 (1.4)	479 (7.2)	39 (1.2)	493 (5.6)	16 (0.9)	503 (6.0)	8 (0.7)	475 (7.3)
Russian Federation	12 (1.0)	526 (6.7)	42 (1.4)	540 (4.4)	32 (1.0)	544 (4.2)	14 (0.9)	538 (6.2)
Scotland	15 (0.7)	509 (8.1)	43 (1.0)	525 (6.4)	31 (1.0)	525 (5.4)	11 (0.7)	491 (5.4)
Singapore	7 (0.6)	633 (8.5)	50 (1.1)	615 (6.2)	37 (1.2)	597 (5.4)	6 (0.5)	582 (6.5)
Slovak Republic	14 (0.7)	558 (6.4)	47 (1.0)	548 (3.5)	28 (0.9)	545 (4.5)	11 (0.8)	521 (5.5)
Slovenia	23 (1.1)	568 (3.9)	54 (1.1)	559 (2.9)	19 (0.9)	558 (3.5)	4 (0.4)	547 (8.7)
Spain	33 (1.2)	514 (2.8)	46 (1.0)	522 (2.2)	17 (0.8)	517 (3.6)	4 (0.5)	496 (6.0)
Sweden	16 (0.7)	540 (5.2)	51 (0.9)	543 (3.1)	27 (0.8)	531 (4.1)	6 (0.5)	490 (5.5)
Switzerland	45 (1.5)	534 (3.9)	44 (1.3)	518 (3.2)	9 (0.7)	502 (5.2)	2 (0.2)	~ ~
Thailand	28 (1.4)	518 (3.8)	46 (1.0)	527 (4.0)	19 (1.1)	534 (4.7)	8 (0.7)	524 (5.9)
United States	22 (0.8)	542 (6.0)	40 (0.9)	548 (4.3)	25 (0.6)	533 (5.4)	13 (1.0)	493 (5.9)

*Eighth grade in most countries; see Table 2 for more information about the grades tested in each country.
( ) Standard errors appear in parentheses. Because results are rounded to the nearest whole number, some totals may appear inconsistent.
Countries shown in italics did not satisfy one or more guidelines for sample participation rates, age/grade specifications, or classroom sampling procedures (see Figure A.3). Background data for Bulgaria and South Africa are unavailable.
Because population coverage falls below 65%, Latvia is annotated LSS for Latvian Speaking Schools only.
A tilde (~) indicates insufficient data to report achievement.

SOURCE: IEA Third International Mathematics and Science Study (TIMSS), 1994-95.

How Do Students Perceive Success in the Sciences?

Table 4.11 presents eighth-grade students' perceptions about doing well in the sciences. The results for each country are reported for either integrated science or separately for the science subject areas of biological science, earth science and physical science, depending on the form of the student questionnaire used. In all but three countries (Hong Kong, Japan, and Korea), the majority of students agreed or strongly agreed that they did well in either integrated science or in all of the science subject areas. Interestingly, two of these three countries where fewer than half of students thought they did well in science, Japan (45%) and Korea (35%), were among the highest performing countries on the TIMSS science test.

In several countries, more than 85% of students reported doing well in integrated science, including Colombia (91%), England (88%), Iran (95%), Kuwait (89%), and the United States (86%). Corresponding student reports for the separate sciences included Lithuania (85% in biological science), Slovak Republic (89% in biological science and 91% in earth science), and Slovenia (86% in biological science). For most separate-subject countries, more students reported doing well in biological science than in physical science.

Figure 4.2 indicates that for most countries, both boys and girls tended to agree that they did well in the sciences – a perception that did not always coincide with their achievement on the TIMSS science test. Among the countries that administered the integrated science form of the questionnaire, eighth-grade girls in England, Hong Kong, Japan, New Zealand, Norway, Scotland, Singapore, and Switzerland reported significantly lower self-perceptions than boys about doing well in science.

Among countries that asked about the separate science subject areas, fewer differences between girls' and boys' self-perceptions about doing well in the sciences were reported, but the differences that did exist indicated higher self-perceptions for boys. More than half of the countries had no or very small gender differences in self-perception about doing well in any of the subject areas, while in seven countries, boys had higher self-perceptions than girls in at least one of the subject areas (Austria, Flemish-speaking Belgium, Denmark, France, Germany, the Netherlands, and Sweden). Only in the Netherlands did boys have higher self-perceptions about doing well in all three subject areas.

The gender differences in self-perceptions differed across subject areas, with the physical sciences having the largest number of countries where boys reported higher self-perceptions than girls. In the biological sciences, there was very little difference across all countries between boys and girls in their self-perceptions about doing well. These differences in the self-perceptions of boys and girls across science subject areas correspond to the higher performance of boys on the physics and chemistry content areas of the TIMSS science test (Table 2.4).

Students were asked about the necessity of various attributes or activities to do well in science (see Table 4.12). There was enormous variation from country to country in the percentage of eighth-grade students agreeing that natural talent or ability were

Table 4.11

Students' Reports on Their Self-Perceptions About Usually Doing Well in the Sciences[1] - Upper Grade (Eighth Grade*)

Country	Percent of Students Responding Agree or Strongly Agree			
	Science (Integrated)	Science Subject Areas		
		Biological Science	Earth Science	Physical Science
Australia	77 (1.0)	. .	. .	. .
Austria	. .	84 (1.2)	76 (1.4)	70 (1.5)
Belgium (Fl)	. .	71 (2.4)	65 (2.7)	s 56 (3.8)
Belgium (Fr)	s 85 (1.9)	. .	. .	. .
Canada	82 (1.2)	. .	. .	. .
Colombia	91 (0.8)	. .	. .	. .
Cyprus	76 (1.2)	. .	. .	. .
Czech Republic	. .	82 (2.0)	84 (1.1)	69 (2.0)
Denmark	. .	79 (1.0)	78 (1.3)	72 (1.3)
England	88 (1.0)	. .	. .	. .
[2] **France**	. .	71 (1.5)	. .	74 (1.7)
Germany	. .	79 (1.1)	70 (1.3)	63 (1.6)
Greece	. .	. .	. .	81 (0.9)
Hong Kong	43 (1.6)	. .	. .	. .
Hungary	. .	82 (1.2)	76 (1.3)	63 (1.5)
Iceland	. .	81 (1.6)	s 60 (1.8)	72 (1.5)
Iran, Islamic Rep.	95 (0.5)	. .	. .	. .
Ireland	74 (1.6)	. .	. .	. .
Israel	84 (1.3)	. .	. .	. .
Japan	45 (0.9)	. .	. .	. .
Korea	35 (1.1)	. .	. .	. .
Kuwait	89 (1.0)	. .	. .	. .
Latvia (LSS)	. .	74 (1.2)	. .	72 (1.4)
Lithuania	. .	85 (1.0)	61 (1.7)	60 (1.8)
Netherlands	. .	r 83 (1.4)	81 (1.7)	83 (1.6)
New Zealand	80 (0.9)	. .	. .	. .
Norway	80 (1.1)	. .	. .	. .
[3] **Portugal**	. .	72 (1.3)	. .	68 (1.5)
Romania	. .	77 (1.1)	77 (1.3)	69 (1.3)
Russian Federation	. .	84 (1.4)	74 (1.6)	70 (1.3)
Scotland	84 (0.9)	. .	. .	. .
Singapore	73 (1.2)	. .	. .	. .
Slovak Republic	. .	89 (0.8)	91 (0.7)	78 (1.2)
Slovenia	. .	86 (1.2)	. .	82 (1.1)
Spain	80 (1.2)	. .	. .	. .
Sweden	. .	82 (0.9)	83 (0.8)	77 (1.1)
Switzerland	76 (1.2)	. .	. .	. .
Thailand	67 (1.4)	. .	. .	. .
United States	86 (0.7)	. .	. .	. .

[1]Countries administered either an integrated science or separate subject area form of the questionnaire. A dot (.) denotes questions not administered by design. Percentages for separate science subject areas are based only on those students taking each subject.

[2]Biological science data for France are for students taking biology/geology classes.

[3]Biological science data for Portugal are for students taking natural science classes.

*Eighth grade in most countries; see Table 2 for more information about the grades tested in each country.

Countries shown in italics did not satisfy one or more guidelines for sample participation rates, age/grade specifications, or classroom sampling procedures (see Figure A.3). Background data for Bulgaria and South Africa are unavailable.

Because population coverage falls below 65%, Latvia is annotated LSS for Latvian Speaking Schools only.

( ) Standard errors appear in parentheses. Because results are rounded to the nearest whole number, some totals may appear inconsistent.

An "r" indicates a 70-84% student response rate. An "s" indicates a 50-69% student response rate.

SOURCE: IEA Third International Mathematics and Science Study (TIMSS), 1994-95.

Figure 4.2

Gender Differences in Students' Self-Perceptions About Usually Doing Well in the Sciences[1] - Upper Grade (Eighth Grade*)

Science (Integrated)

Country | Strongly Disagree | Disagree | Agree | Strongly Agree

Australia
Belgium (Fr)
Canada
Colombia
Cyprus
England
Hong Kong
Iran, Islamic Rep.
Ireland
Israel
Japan
Korea
New Zealand
Norway
Scotland
Singapore
Spain
Switzerland
Thailand
United States

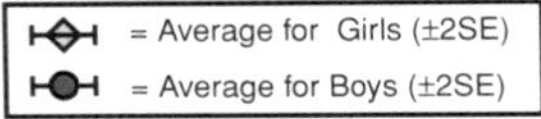

[1]Countries administered either an integrated science or separate subject area form of the questionnaire. Percentages for separate science subject areas are based only on those students taking each subject.
*Eighth grade in most countries; see Table 2 for more information about the grades tested in each country.
Countries shown in italics did not satisfy one or more guidelines for sample participation rates, age/grade specifications, or classroom sampling procedures (see Figure A.3). Background data for Bulgaria and South Africa are unavailable.
Because population coverage falls below 65%, Latvia is annotated LSS for Latvian Speaking Schools only.

SOURCE: IEA Third International Mathematics and Science Study (TIMSS), 1994-95.

Figure 4.2 (Continued)

Gender Differences in Students' Self-Perceptions About Usually Doing Well in the Sciences[1] - Upper Grade (Eighth Grade*)

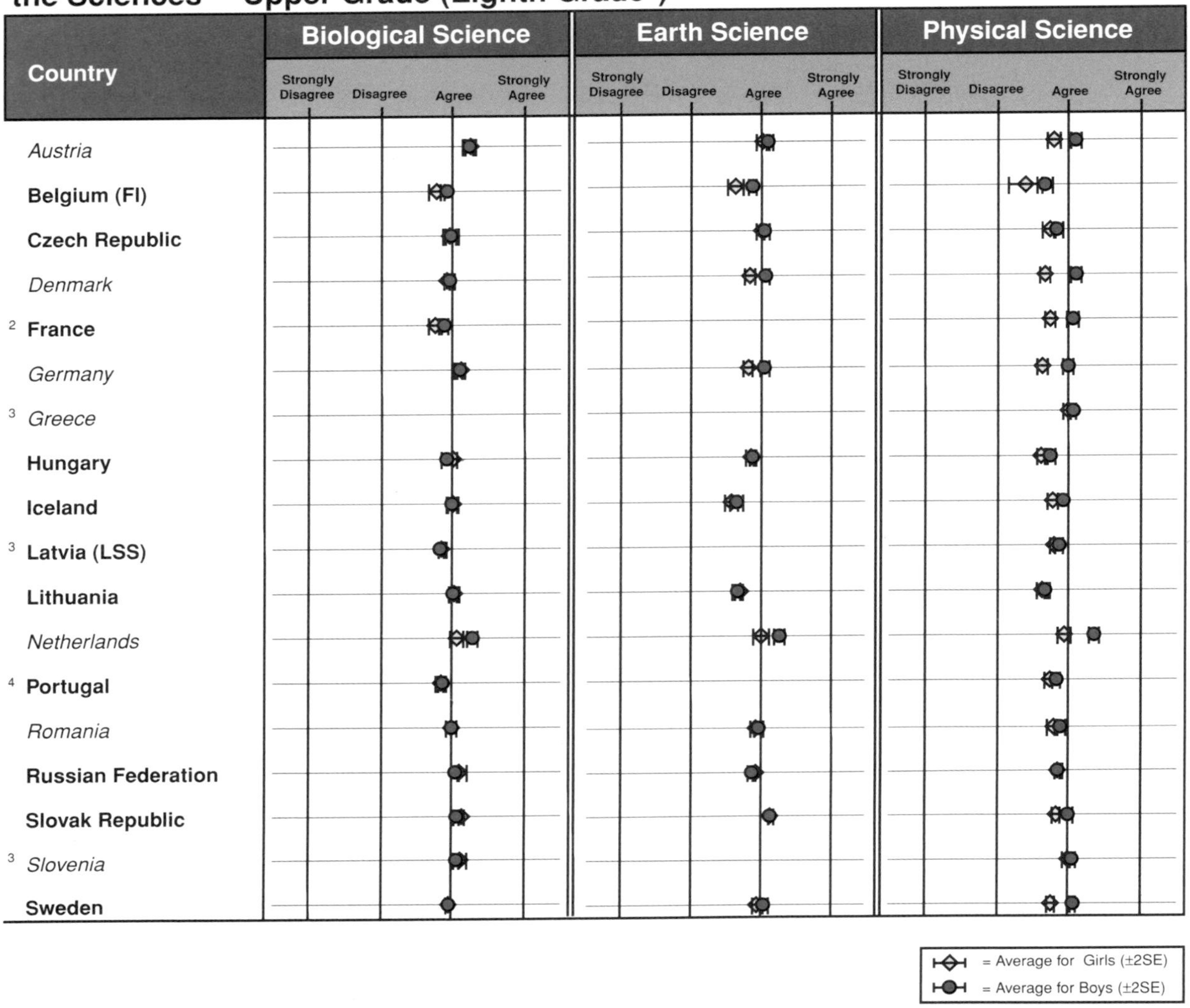

Country	Biological Science	Earth Science	Physical Science
Austria			
Belgium (Fl)			
Czech Republic			
Denmark			
[2] **France**			
Germany			
[3] *Greece*			
Hungary			
Iceland			
[3] **Latvia (LSS)**			
Lithuania			
Netherlands			
[4] **Portugal**			
Romania			
Russian Federation			
Slovak Republic			
[3] *Slovenia*			
Sweden			

Scale for each subject: Strongly Disagree, Disagree, Agree, Strongly Agree

= Average for Girls (±2SE)
= Average for Boys (±2SE)

[1]Countries administered either an integrated science or separate subject area form of the questionnaire. Percentages for separate science subject areas are based only on those students taking each subject.
[2]Biological science data for France are for students taking biology/geology classes.
[3]Greece, Latvia, and Slovenia did not ask about all three science subjects.
[4]Biological science data for Portugal are for students taking natural science classes.
*Eighth grade in most countries; see Table 2 for more information about the grades tested in each country.
Countries shown in italics did not satisfy one or more guidelines for sample participation rates, age/grade specifications, or classroom sampling procedures (see Figure A.3). Background data for Bulgaria and South Africa are unavailable.
Because population coverage falls below 65%, Latvia is annotated LSS for Latvian Speaking Schools only.

SOURCE: IEA Third International Mathematics and Science Study (TIMSS), 1994-95.

important to do well in science. Fewer than 50% of the students agreed in the Czech Republic, England, France, Iceland, the Netherlands, and Sweden compared to 90% or more in Colombia, Iran, and Kuwait. Internationally, relatively few students agreed that good luck was important to do well. The countries where more than 50% of the eighth-graders agreed that good luck was needed to do well in science included Colombia, the Czech Republic, Hungary, Iran, Japan, Korea, Kuwait, Latvia (LSS), Lithuania, Romania, the Russian Federation, and the Slovak Republic.

Internationally, there was a high degree of agreement among students that lots of hard work studying at home was necessary in order to do well in science. Percentages of agreement were in the 80s and 90s for most countries and in the 70s for Austria, Hungary, Lithuania, and Switzerland. The variation was substantial from country to country regarding students' agreement with the necessity of memorizing the textbook or notes. In Belgium (French), France, Iceland, Iran, Japan, Korea, Kuwait, and Thailand, 90% or more of the eighth-grade students agreed or strongly agreed that memorization was important to doing well in science. In contrast, fewer than 50% agreed in Latvia (LSS), Lithuania, and Sweden.

Students also were asked about why they need to do well in the sciences. Depending on which questionnaire each country used, the results are reported for either integrated science or the separate science subject areas of biology, chemistry, earth science, and physics. Students could agree with any or all of three areas of possible motivation presented in Table 4.13 (to get their desired job), in Table 4.14 (to get into their preferred university or secondary school) and in Table 4.15 (to please their parents). There were substantial differences from country to country in students' responses for the three motivational factors.

As indicated in Table 4.13, the majority of eighth-grade students in many countries asked about integrated science either agreed or strongly agreed that getting their desired job was a motivating factor, although there were several countries where only slightly more than half of the students agreed. Eighty-five percent or more of students agreed in Iran (90%), Kuwait (85%), and Thailand (94%), compared to fewer than half of the students in Austria (38%), Japan (40%), Korea (44%), Norway (47%), and Switzerland (33%).

Compared to the integrated-science students, in general, fewer students in the countries asking about separate science subject areas agreed with the need to do well to get their desired job. Fewer than 60% of students in nearly all of these countries (primarily in Europe) agreed for any of the science subject areas that this was a reason to do well. In particular, fewer than 30% of students in Belgium (Flemish) and Hungary agreed for any subject, and only in Greece, Latvia (LSS), Lithuania, and Romania, did 50% or more of students agree for all subject areas. At the eighth grade, it appears that many students in these countries do not make a connection between getting a job they want and their performance in specific science subject areas. While this may be due to fewer students in these countries desiring jobs that use a particular science, it is also very likely that many students in this age group do not yet have a clear conception of either the type of job they want to pursue or the specific science education requirements for different jobs.

In the majority of countries, pleasing their parents and getting into their preferred university or secondary school were both stronger motivators than getting their desired job for eighth-grade students in either integrated science or separate science subject areas. However, 40% or fewer students in Denmark, Iceland, Japan, Lithuania (biology and chemistry), and Slovenia agreed that doing well was important in order to please their parents.

Table 4.12

Students' Reports on Things Necessary to Do Well in the Sciences
Upper Grade (Eighth Grade*)

Country	Percent of Students Responding Agree or Strongly Agree			
	Natural Talent/Ability	Good Luck	Lots of Hard Work Studying at Home	Memorize the Textbook or Notes
Australia	66 (0.8)	33 (0.8)	91 (0.5)	71 (0.9)
Austria	61 (1.5)	31 (1.3)	78 (1.4)	65 (1.2)
Belgium (Fl)	53 (1.5)	24 (1.8)	85 (0.9)	63 (1.9)
Belgium (Fr)	67 (1.2)	25 (1.1)	94 (0.7)	94 (0.6)
Canada	61 (1.0)	30 (1.0)	89 (0.7)	52 (1.0)
Colombia	91 (0.7)	64 (1.5)	97 (0.4)	79 (1.2)
Cyprus	51 (1.0)	34 (0.9)	93 (0.6)	76 (0.9)
Czech Republic	45 (1.0)	55 (1.2)	82 (1.2)	59 (1.4)
Denmark	89 (0.6)	35 (1.3)	82 (1.2)	65 (1.4)
England	47 (1.4)	25 (1.0)	93 (0.6)	56 (1.0)
France	38 (1.3)	23 (1.1)	88 (0.8)	95 (0.8)
Germany	57 (1.5)	28 (1.2)	82 (1.1)	70 (1.0)
Greece	58 (1.0)	27 (0.9)	96 (0.4)	87 (0.6)
Hong Kong	74 (0.9)	38 (1.0)	96 (0.5)	84 (0.7)
Hungary	88 (0.7)	56 (1.1)	79 (0.9)	57 (1.3)
Iceland	36 (1.4)	26 (1.6)	90 (0.9)	95 (0.8)
Iran, Islamic Rep.	95 (0.7)	51 (2.3)	97 (0.4)	91 (0.7)
Ireland	70 (1.0)	32 (1.1)	95 (0.6)	78 (0.9)
Israel	53 (1.9)	19 (1.8)	95 (0.9)	54 (2.1)
Japan	82 (0.6)	60 (1.0)	97 (0.3)	97 (0.3)
Korea	85 (0.7)	62 (1.0)	98 (0.2)	94 (0.4)
Kuwait	90 (1.4)	78 (1.7)	83 (1.3)	92 (0.7)
Latvia (LSS)	50 (1.2)	61 (1.2)	87 (0.8)	42 (1.3)
Lithuania	76 (1.0)	68 (1.1)	76 (1.1)	31 (1.2)
Netherlands	46 (1.4)	25 (1.6)	93 (0.8)	67 (1.2)
New Zealand	63 (1.1)	29 (1.2)	92 (0.5)	75 (1.0)
Norway	84 (0.7)	22 (0.9)	92 (0.6)	81 (0.9)
Portugal	72 (1.1)	39 (1.3)	98 (0.2)	66 (1.3)
Romania	64 (1.1)	59 (1.3)	86 (0.9)	78 (1.1)
Russian Federation	77 (0.7)	53 (1.7)	87 (0.9)	66 (1.8)
Scotland	- -	- -	- -	- -
Singapore	86 (0.7)	40 (0.9)	98 (0.3)	87 (0.8)
Slovak Republic	61 (1.1)	52 (1.1)	92 (0.6)	55 (1.2)
Slovenia	75 (1.0)	41 (1.4)	90 (0.6)	- -
Spain	66 (1.1)	35 (1.0)	96 (0.4)	79 (1.0)
Sweden	45 (1.0)	26 (1.1)	87 (0.6)	42 (1.0)
Switzerland	56 (1.2)	25 (0.7)	75 (1.1)	58 (1.5)
Thailand	69 (1.1)	35 (1.3)	80 (0.8)	97 (0.3)
United States	51 (0.8)	34 (1.3)	90 (0.6)	66 (1.0)

*Eighth grade in most countries; see Table 2 for more information about the grades tested in each country.
( ) Standard errors appear in parentheses. Because results are rounded to the nearest whole number, some totals may appear inconsistent.
Countries shown in italics did not satisfy one or more guidelines for sample participation rates, age/grade specifications, or classroom sampling procedures (see Figure A.3). Background data for Bulgaria and South Africa are unavailable.
Because population coverage falls below 65%, Latvia is annotated LSS for Latvian Speaking Schools only.
A dash (-) indicates data are not available.

SOURCE: IEA Third International Mathematics and Science Study (TIMSS), 1994-95.

Table 4.13

Students' Perceptions About the Need to Do Well in the Sciences to Get Their Desired Job[1] - Upper Grade (Eighth Grade*)

Country	Percent of Students Responding Agree or Strongly Agree				
	Science (Integrated)	Science Subject Areas			
		Biology	Chemistry	Earth Science	Physics
Australia	52 (1.0)	. .	. .	. .	. .
Austria	38 (1.4)	. .	. .	. .	. .
Belgium (Fl)	. .	28 (1.4)	. .	18 (0.8)	x x
[2] *Belgium (Fr)*	s 53 (2.3)	x x	. .	. .	x x
Canada	63 (1.2)	. .	. .	. .	. .
Colombia	74 (1.3)	. .	. .	. .	. .
Cyprus	57 (1.3)	. .	. .	. .	. .
Czech Republic	. .	36 (1.0)	40 (1.3)	42 (1.2)	48 (1.5)
[3] *Denmark*	. .	31 (1.3)	. .	r 32 (1.4)	37 (1.1)
England	62 (1.5)	. .	. .	. .	. .
[4] **France**	. .	36 (1.1)	. .	. .	39 (1.3)
Germany	. .	33 (1.1)	s 32 (1.8)	. .	34 (1.2)
Greece	. .	. .	60 (0.8)	54 (0.9)	70 (0.8)
Hong Kong	55 (1.0)	. .	. .	. .	. .
Hungary	. .	26 (1.1)	20 (0.9)	19 (0.9)	25 (0.9)
Iceland	. .	44 (1.6)	x x	x x	s 46 (1.7)
Iran, Islamic Rep.	90 (1.0)	. .	. .	. .	. .
Ireland	50 (1.2)	. .	. .	. .	. .
Israel	51 (1.9)	. .	. .	. .	. .
Japan	40 (0.7)	. .	. .	. .	. .
Korea	44 (1.0)	. .	. .	. .	. .
Kuwait	85 (1.3)	. .	. .	. .	. .
Latvia (LSS)	. .	50 (1.3)	54 (1.2)	. .	61 (1.3)
Lithuania	. .	52 (1.5)	53 (1.3)	55 (1.3)	59 (1.2)
[5] *Netherlands*	. .	r 39 (1.9)	. .	22 (1.4)	36 (1.7)
New Zealand	55 (1.1)	. .	. .	. .	. .
Norway	47 (1.1)	. .	. .	. .	. .
[6] **Portugal**	. .	55 (1.2)	. .	. .	49 (1.1)
Romania	. .	59 (1.3)	55 (1.4)	57 (1.4)	57 (1.2)
Russian Federation	. .	45 (1.1)	46 (0.9)	44 (1.2)	55 (0.9)
Scotland	65 (1.1)	. .	. .	. .	. .
Singapore	71 (1.4)	. .	. .	. .	. .
Slovak Republic	. .	36 (1.2)	31 (1.0)	34 (1.0)	42 (1.2)
Slovenia	. .	37 (1.4)	38 (1.4)	. .	45 (1.4)
Spain	65 (1.0)	. .	. .	. .	. .
Sweden	. .	36 (1.2)	s 38 (1.5)	r 47 (1.1)	r 45 (1.1)
Switzerland	33 (0.9)	. .	. .	. .	. .
Thailand	94 (0.5)	. .	. .	. .	. .
United States	65 (0.9)	. .	. .	. .	. .

[1]Countries administered either an integrated science or separate subject area form of the questionnaire. A dot (.) denotes questions not administered by design. Percentages for separate science subject areas are based only on those students taking each subject.
[2]Data for Belgium (Fr) are reported for students in both integrated science classes and separate biology and physics classes.
[3]Physics data for Denmark are for students taking physics/chemistry classes.
[4]Biology data for France are for students taking biology/geology classes; physics data are for students taking physics/chemistry classes.
[5]Physics data for the Netherlands include students in both physics classes and physics/chemistry classes.
[6]Biology data for Portugal are for students taking natural science classes; physics data are for students taking physical science classes.
*Eighth grade in most countries; see Table 2 for more information about the grades tested in each country.
( ) Standard errors appear in parentheses. Because results are rounded to the nearest whole number, some totals may appear inconsistent.
Countries shown in italics did not satisfy one or more guidelines for sample participation rates, age/grade specifications, or classroom sampling procedures (see Figure A.3). Background data for Bulgaria and South Africa are unavailable.
Because population coverage falls below 65%, Latvia is annotated LSS for Latvian Speaking Schools only.
An "r" indicates a 70-84% student response rate. An "s" indicates a 50-69% student response rate. An "x" indicates a <50% student response rate.

SOURCE: IEA Third International Mathematics and Science Study (TIMSS), 1994-95.

Table 4.14

Students' Perceptions About the Need to Do Well in the Sciences to Get Into Their Preferred University or Secondary School[1] - Upper Grade (Eighth Grade*)

Country	Percent of Students Responding Agree or Strongly Agree				
	Science (Integrated)	Science Subject Areas			
		Biology	Chemistry	Earth Science	Physics
Australia	59 (1.0)	. .	. .	. .	. .
Austria	48 (1.5)	. .	. .	. .	. .
Belgium (Fl)	. .	38 (1.5)	. .	28 (1.2)	x x
[2] *Belgium (Fr)*	s 59 (2.6)	x x	. .	. .	x x
Canada	81 (0.9)	. .	. .	. .	. .
Colombia	87 (0.8)	. .	. .	. .	. .
Cyprus	68 (1.1)	. .	. .	. .	. .
Czech Republic	. .	57 (1.1)	57 (1.3)	55 (1.2)	61 (1.5)
[3] *Denmark*	. .	49 (1.4)	. .	r 55 (1.5)	59 (1.5)
England	75 (1.2)	. .	. .	. .	. .
[4] **France**	. .	57 (1.1)	. .	. .	59 (1.1)
Germany	. .	36 (1.4)	s 35 (1.8)	. .	35 (1.3)
Greece	. .	. .	77 (1.1)	67 (0.9)	77 (0.6)
Hong Kong	74 (0.9)	. .	. .	. .	. .
Hungary	. .	63 (1.2)	61 (1.3)	61 (1.2)	63 (1.4)
Iceland	. .	76 (1.6)	x x	x x	s 70 (1.7)
Iran, Islamic Rep.	93 (0.5)	. .	. .	. .	. .
Ireland	66 (1.3)	. .	. .	. .	. .
Israel	83 (1.2)	. .	. .	. .	. .
Japan	86 (0.8)	. .	. .	. .	. .
Korea	80 (0.8)	. .	. .	. .	. .
Kuwait	86 (1.1)	. .	. .	. .	. .
Latvia (LSS)	. .	69 (1.2)	70 (1.2)	. .	71 (1.1)
Lithuania	. .	57 (1.2)	57 (1.3)	59 (1.0)	61 (1.3)
[5] *Netherlands*	. .	r 47 (1.5)	. .	29 (1.4)	42 (1.9)
New Zealand	60 (1.0)	. .	. .	. .	. .
Norway	64 (1.0)	. .	. .	. .	. .
[6] **Portugal**	. .	71 (1.0)	. .	. .	65 (1.2)
Romania	. .	64 (1.2)	61 (1.2)	61 (1.3)	60 (1.2)
Russian Federation	. .	62 (1.1)	64 (1.0)	59 (1.1)	67 (0.9)
Scotland	71 (1.2)	. .	. .	. .	. .
Singapore	93 (0.5)	. .	. .	. .	. .
Slovak Republic	. .	49 (1.2)	44 (1.2)	43 (1.1)	52 (1.0)
Slovenia	. .	55 (1.3)	54 (1.5)	. .	58 (1.3)
Spain	78 (0.8)	. .	. .	. .	. .
Sweden	. .	54 (1.1)	s 53 (1.1)	r 58 (0.9)	r 56 (0.9)
Switzerland	43 (0.9)	. .	. .	. .	. .
Thailand	97 (0.4)	. .	. .	. .	. .
United States	89 (0.6)	. .	. .	. .	. .

[1]Countries administered either an integrated science or separate subject area form of the questionnaire. A dot (.) denotes questions not administered by design. Percentages for separate science subject areas are based only on those students taking each subject.
[2]Data for Belgium (Fr) are reported for students in both integrated science classes and separate biology and physics classes.
[3]Physics data for Denmark are for students taking physics/chemistry classes.
[4]Biology data for France are for students taking biology/geology classes; physics data are for students taking physics/chemistry classes.
[5]Physics data for the Netherlands include students in both physics classes and physics/chemistry classes.
[6]Biology data for Portugal are for students taking natural science classes; physics data are for students taking physical science classes.
*Eighth grade in most countries; see Table 2 for more information about the grades tested in each country.
( ) Standard errors appear in parentheses. Because results are rounded to the nearest whole number, some totals may appear inconsistent.
Countries shown in italics did not satisfy one or more guidelines for sample participation rates, age/grade specifications, or classroom sampling procedures (see Figure A.3). Background data for Bulgaria and South Africa are unavailable.
Because population coverage falls below 65%, Latvia is annotated LSS for Latvian Speaking Schools only.
An "r" indicates a 70-84% student response rate. An "s" indicates a 50-69% student response rate. An "x" indicates a <50% student response rate.

SOURCE: IEA Third International Mathematics and Science Study (TIMSS), 1994-95.

Table 4.15

Students' Perceptions About the Need to Do Well in the Sciences to Please Their Parents[1] - Upper Grade (Eighth Grade*)

Country	Percent of Students Responding Agree or Strongly Agree				
	Science (Integrated)	Science Subject Areas			
		Biology	Chemistry	Earth Science	Physics
Australia	66 (0.8)	. .	. .	. .	. .
Austria	48 (1.3)	. .	. .	. .	. .
Belgium (Fl)	. .	66 (1.0)	. .	67 (1.1)	x x
[2] *Belgium (Fr)*	s 73 (2.1)	x x	. .	. .	x x
Canada	63 (1.3)	. .	. .	. .	. .
Colombia	75 (1.4)	. .	. .	. .	. .
Cyprus	65 (1.1)	. .	. .	. .	. .
Czech Republic	. .	80 (1.1)	81 (1.1)	82 (1.1)	83 (1.0)
[3] *Denmark*	. .	27 (1.4)	. .	30 (1.5)	30 (1.4)
England	63 (1.4)	. .	. .	. .	. .
[4] **France**	. .	48 (1.3)	. .	. .	52 (1.3)
Germany	. .	41 (1.3)	s 48 (1.5)	. .	46 (1.2)
Greece	. .	. .	73 (0.9)	74 (0.9)	76 (0.8)
Hong Kong	56 (1.0)	. .	. .	. .	. .
Hungary	. .	41 (1.1)	41 (1.1)	43 (1.2)	46 (1.2)
Iceland	. .	37 (1.7)	x x	x x	s 38 (1.9)
Iran, Islamic Rep.	95 (0.6)	. .	. .	. .	. .
Ireland	56 (1.0)	. .	. .	. .	. .
Israel	47 (2.1)	. .	. .	. .	. .
Japan	33 (0.8)	. .	. .	. .	. .
Korea	53 (1.2)	. .	. .	. .	. .
Kuwait	93 (0.9)	. .	. .	. .	. .
Latvia (LSS)	. .	71 (1.3)	77 (1.1)	. .	77 (1.2)
Lithuania	. .	36 (1.4)	39 (1.3)	41 (1.2)	45 (1.4)
[5] *Netherlands*	. .	r 49 (2.0)	. .	50 (1.7)	52 (1.8)
New Zealand	61 (0.9)	. .	. .	. .	. .
Norway	48 (1.1)	. .	. .	. .	. .
[6] **Portugal**	. .	64 (1.2)	. .	. .	63 (1.2)
Romania	. .	61 (1.4)	62 (1.4)	62 (1.3)	63 (1.2)
Russian Federation	. .	62 (1.1)	63 (1.3)	64 (1.3)	67 (1.4)
Scotland	60 (1.2)	. .	. .	. .	. .
Singapore	68 (1.0)	. .	. .	. .	. .
Slovak Republic	. .	64 (1.2)	64 (1.1)	68 (1.2)	68 (1.2)
Slovenia	. .	33 (1.3)	33 (1.4)	. .	37 (1.3)
Spain	83 (0.9)	. .	. .	. .	. .
Sweden	. .	40 (1.2)	s 42 (1.4)	r 46 (1.3)	r 44 (1.2)
Switzerland	42 (1.1)	. .	. .	. .	. .
Thailand	98 (0.2)	. .	. .	. .	. .
United States	79 (0.7)	. .	. .	. .	. .

[1]Countries administered either an integrated science or separate subject area form of the questionnaire. A dot (.) denotes questions not administered by design. Percentages for separate science subject areas are based only on those students taking each subject.
[2]Data for Belgium (Fr) are reported for students in both integrated science classes and separate biology and physics classes.
[3]Physics data for Denmark are for students taking physics/chemistry classes.
[4]Biology data for France are for students taking biology/geology classes; physics data are for students taking physics/chemistry classes.
[5]Physics data for the Netherlands include students in both physics classes and physics/chemistry classes.
[6]Biology data for Portugal are for students taking natural science classes; physics data are for students taking physical science classes.
*Eighth grade in most countries; see Table 2 for more information about the grades tested in each country.
( ) Standard errors appear in parentheses. Because results are rounded to the nearest whole number, some totals may appear inconsistent.
Countries shown in italics did not satisfy one or more guidelines for sample participation rates, age/grade specifications, or classroom sampling procedures (see Figure A.3). Background data for Bulgaria and South Africa are unavailable.
Because population coverage falls below 65%, Latvia is annotated LSS for Latvian Speaking Schools only.
An "r" indicates a 70-84% student response rate. An "s" indicates a 50-69% student response rate. An "x" indicates a <50% student response rate.

SOURCE: IEA Third International Mathematics and Science Study (TIMSS), 1994-95.

What Are Students' Attitudes Towards the Sciences?

To collect information on eighth-grade students' perceptions of the sciences, TIMSS asked them a series of questions about the utility, importance, and enjoyability of science and science subject areas. Students' perceptions about the value of learning the sciences may be considered as both an input and outcome variable, because their attitudes towards science subjects can be related to educational achievement in ways that reinforce higher or lower performance. That is, students who do well in the sciences generally have more positive attitudes towards the science subjects, and those who have more positive attitudes tend to perform better.

Table 4.16 summarizes students' responses to the questions about how much they like or dislike science or the separate science subject areas of biological science, earth science, and physical science. Even though the majority of eighth-graders in nearly every country indicated they liked science or liked science a lot, clearly not all students feel equally positive about these subject areas. For example, 60% or fewer of students reported that they liked integrated science in Australia (60%), Israel (59%), Japan (56%), and Korea (59%). For biology, this was the case only in Denmark (52%). Fewer than 60% of the students reported liking earth science in 7 out of 13 countries. For physics, the figures fell below 60% in 10 out of 18 countries. More than 80% of students reported liking science (integrated) in several countries, including Colombia, Iran, Kuwait, Singapore, and Thailand. Similarly, more than 80% of the students in Latvia (LSS), Portugal, and the Russian Federation reported liking biology. More eighth-grade students internationally reported liking biological science than either earth science or physical science. For example, the percent of students agreeing or strongly agreeing that they liked biological science ranged from 52% in Denmark to 90% in Portugal, whereas the range in physical science was from 44% in the Czech Republic to 81% in Portugal. In Denmark, fewer than 60% of students reported liking any of the three science subject areas.

The data in Figure 4.3 reveal that, on average, in the majority of countries eighth-graders of both genders were relatively neutral about liking the sciences. There was, however, more variation in the average response across countries asking about integrated science than across those asking about the separate science subject areas. Boys reported liking science (integrated) more than did girls in England, Hong Kong, Japan, New Zealand, Norway, and Singapore.

Across the separate science subject areas, the greatest number of statistically significant gender differences were found in physical science, with boys liking physical science more than girls did. In contrast, in all countries, girls reported liking biological science at least as much as did boys. In fact, the only statistically significant gender differences in liking biological science favored girls in Austria, Hungary, and Slovenia. These differences in students' reports of liking science subjects correspond with the relative performance of boys and girls on the life science and physical science content areas on the TIMSS test, with the majority of statistically significant gender differences in performance favoring boys on the physics and chemistry items (Table 2.4).

Table 4.16

Students' Reports About Liking the Sciences[1] Upper Grade (Eighth Grade*)

Country	Percent of Students Responding Like or Like a Lot			
	Science (Integrated)	Science Subject Areas		
		Biological Science	Earth Science	Physical Science
Australia	60 (1.2)	. .	. .	. .
Austria	. .	70 (1.7)	55 (2.0)	49 (2.0)
Belgium (Fl)	. .	68 (2.0)	53 (2.2)	s 54 (2.3)
Belgium (Fr)	s 71 (2.2)	. .	. .	. .
Canada	68 (1.3)	. .	. .	. .
Colombia	87 (0.9)	. .	. .	. .
Cyprus	70 (1.3)	. .	. .	. .
Czech Republic	. .	65 (2.4)	65 (2.3)	44 (1.6)
Denmark	. .	52 (2.1)	51 (1.9)	56 (1.7)
England	78 (1.1)	. .	. .	. .
[2] **France**	. .	67 (1.7)	. .	65 (2.1)
Germany	. .	65 (1.5)	55 (1.5)	49 (1.5)
Greece	. .	. .	. .	76 (1.0)
Hong Kong	69 (1.5)	. .	. .	. .
Hungary	. .	73 (1.4)	63 (1.5)	49 (1.3)
Iceland	. .	72 (2.8)	r 53 (2.2)	59 (2.3)
Iran, Islamic Rep.	93 (0.8)	. .	. .	. .
Ireland	67 (1.6)	. .	. .	. .
Israel	59 (2.0)	. .	. .	. .
Japan	56 (1.1)	. .	. .	. .
Korea	59 (1.5)	. .	. .	. .
Kuwait	89 (1.2)	. .	. .	. .
Latvia (LSS)	. .	81 (1.3)	. .	74 (1.3)
Lithuania	. .	77 (1.2)	56 (1.4)	55 (1.6)
Netherlands	. .	r 72 (1.9)	55 (2.6)	57 (2.2)
New Zealand	68 (1.2)	. .	. .	. .
Norway	67 (1.6)	. .	. .	. .
[3] **Portugal**	. .	90 (0.8)	. .	81 (1.3)
Romania	. .	76 (1.2)	75 (1.1)	65 (1.4)
Russian Federation	. .	85 (1.0)	70 (1.3)	71 (1.4)
Scotland	78 (1.3)	. .	. .	. .
Singapore	92 (0.6)	. .	. .	. .
Slovak Republic	. .	69 (1.4)	72 (1.4)	51 (1.7)
Slovenia	. .	74 (1.7)	. .	66 (1.4)
Spain	73 (1.3)	. .	. .	. .
Sweden	. .	61 (1.4)	66 (1.3)	63 (1.3)
Switzerland	67 (1.5)	. .	. .	. .
Thailand	90 (0.7)	. .	. .	. .
United States	71 (1.1)	. .	. .	. .

[1]Countries administered either an integrated science or separate subject area form of the questionnaire. A dot (.) denotes questions not administered by design. Percentages for separate science subject areas are based only on those students taking each subject.
[2]Biological science data for France are for students taking biology/geology classes.
[3]Biological science data for Portugal are for students taking natural science classes.
*Eighth grade in most countries; see Table 2 for more information about the grades tested in each country.
( ) Standard errors appear in parentheses. Because results are rounded to the nearest whole number, some totals may appear inconsistent.
Countries shown in italics did not satisfy one or more guidelines for sample participation rates, age/grade specifications, or classroom sampling procedures (see Figure A.3). Background data for Bulgaria and South Africa are unavailable.
Because population coverage falls below 65%, Latvia is annotated LSS for Latvian Speaking Schools only.
An "r" indicates a 70-84% student response rate. An "s" indicates a 50-69% student response rate.

SOURCE: IEA Third International Mathematics and Science Study (TIMSS), 1994-95.

Figure 4.3

Gender Differences in Liking the Sciences[1]
Upper Grade (Eighth Grade*)

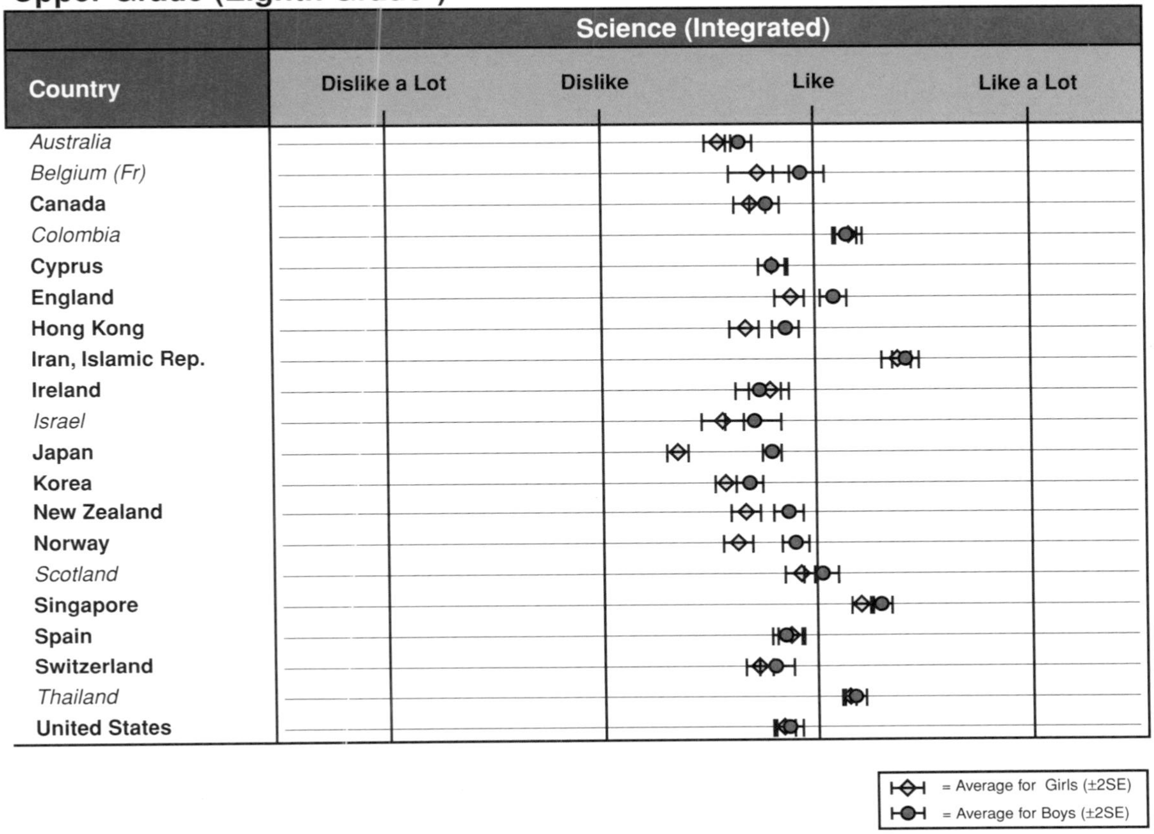

Science (Integrated)

Country | Dislike a Lot | Dislike | Like | Like a Lot

Australia
Belgium (Fr)
Canada
Colombia
Cyprus
England
Hong Kong
Iran, Islamic Rep.
Ireland
Israel
Japan
Korea
New Zealand
Norway
Scotland
Singapore
Spain
Switzerland
Thailand
United States

= Average for Girls (±2SE)
= Average for Boys (±2SE)

[1]Countries administered either an integrated science or separate subject area form of the questionnaire. Percentages for separate science subject areas are based only on those students taking each subject.
*Eighth grade in most countries; see Table 2 for more information about the grades tested in each country.
Countries shown in italics did not satisfy one or more guidelines for sample participation rates, age/grade specifications, or classroom sampling procedures (see Figure A.3). Background data for Bulgaria and South Africa are unavailable.
Because population coverage falls below 65%, Latvia is annotated LSS for Latvian Speaking Schools only.

SOURCE: IEA Third International Mathematics and Science Study (TIMSS), 1994-95.

Figure 4.3 (Continued)

Gender Differences in Liking the Sciences[1]
Upper Grade (Eighth Grade*)

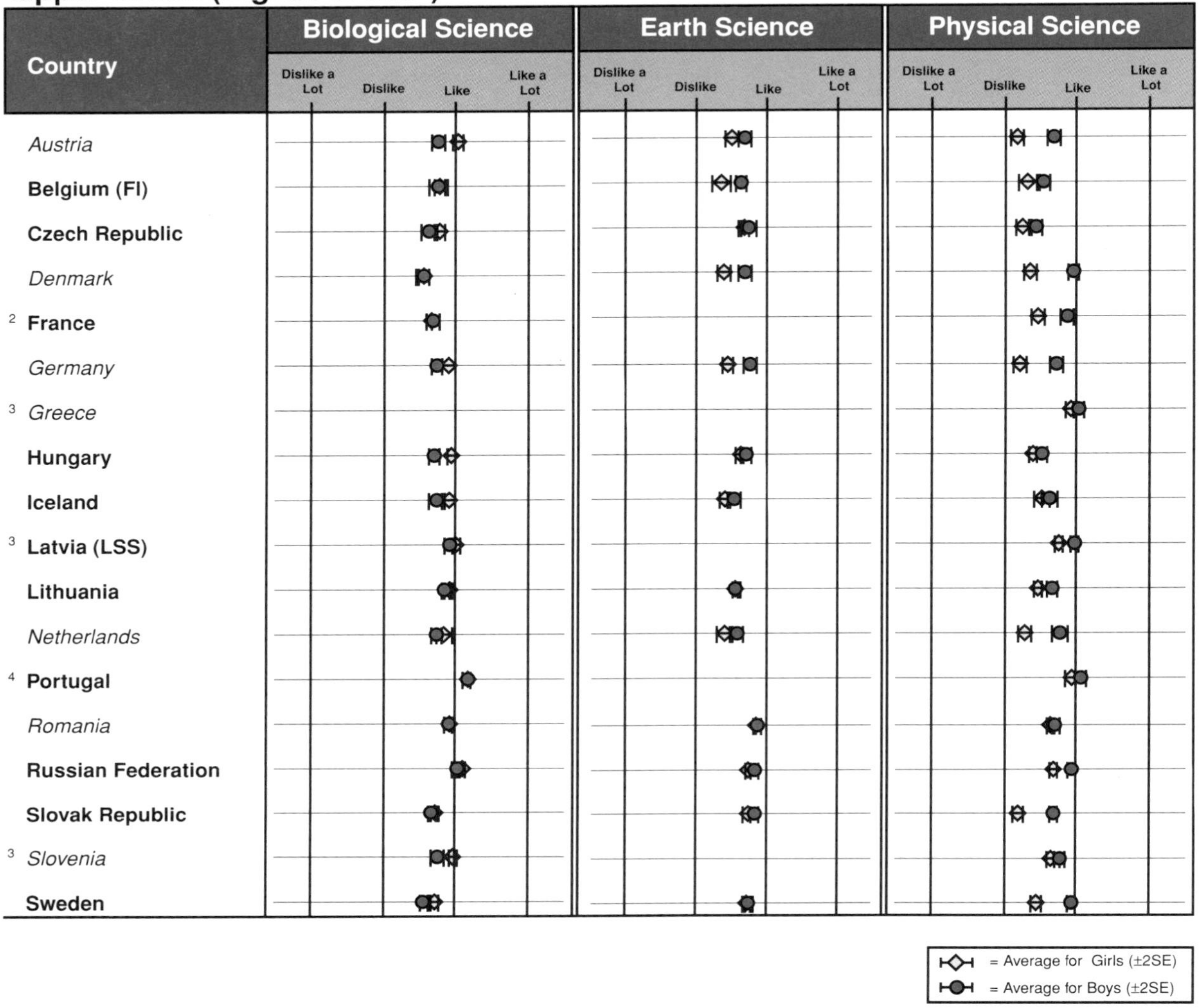

Country	Biological Science	Earth Science	Physical Science
	Dislike a Lot · Dislike · Like · Like a Lot	Dislike a Lot · Dislike · Like · Like a Lot	Dislike a Lot · Dislike · Like · Like a Lot
Austria			
Belgium (Fl)			
Czech Republic			
Denmark			
[2] France			
Germany			
[3] *Greece*			
Hungary			
Iceland			
[3] Latvia (LSS)			
Lithuania			
Netherlands			
[4] Portugal			
Romania			
Russian Federation			
Slovak Republic			
[3] *Slovenia*			
Sweden			

= Average for Girls (±2SE)
= Average for Boys (±2SE)

[1]Countries administered either an integrated science or separate subject area form of the questionnaire. Percentages for separate science subject areas are based only on those students taking each subject.
[2]Biological science data for France are for students taking biology/geology classes.
[3]Greece, Latvia, and Slovenia did not ask about all three science subjects.
[4]Biological science data for Portugal are for students taking natural science classes.
*Eighth grade in most countries; see Table 2 for more information about the grades tested in each country.
Countries shown in italics did not satisfy one or more guidelines for sample participation rates, age/grade specifications, or classroom sampling procedures (see Figure A.3). Background data for Bulgaria and South Africa are unavailable.
Because population coverage falls below 65%, Latvia is annotated LSS for Latvian Speaking Schools only.

SOURCE: IEA Third International Mathematics and Science Study (TIMSS), 1994-95.

Chapter 5

Teachers and Instruction

Teachers and the instructional approaches they use are fundamental in building students' understanding of science. Primary among their many duties and responsibilities, teachers structure and guide the pace of individual, small-group, and whole-class work to present new material, engage students in scientific tasks, and help deepen students' grasp of the science being studied. Teachers may help students use technology and laboratory equipment to investigate scientific ideas, develop their understanding of scientific approaches to problem solving, and promote positive attitudes towards science. They also may assign homework and conduct informal as well as formal assessments to monitor progress in student learning, make ongoing instructional decisions, and evaluate achievement outcomes.

Effective science teaching is a complex endeavor requiring knowledge of the subject matter of science, understanding of student learning, and appreciation of the pedagogy of science. It can be fostered through institutional support and adequate resources. Teachers also can support each other in planning instructional strategies, devising real-world applications of scientific concepts, and developing sequences that move students from concrete tasks to the ability to think for themselves and explore scientific theories.

TIMSS administered a background questionnaire to teachers to gather information about their backgrounds, training, and how they think about science. The questionnaire also asked about how they spend their time related to their teaching tasks and the instructional approaches they use in their classrooms. Information was collected about the materials used in instruction, the activities students do in class, the use of calculators and computers in science lessons, the role of homework, and the reliance on different types of assessment approaches.

This chapter presents the results of teacher's responses to some of these questions. Because the sampling for the teacher questionnaires was based on participating students, the responses to the science teacher questionnaire do not necessarily represent all of the eighth-grade science teachers in each of the TIMSS countries. Rather, they represent teachers of the representative samples of students assessed. It is important to note that in this report, the student is always the unit of analysis, even when information from the teachers' questionnaires is being reported. Using the student as the unit of analysis makes it possible to describe the instruction received by representative samples of students. Although this approach may provide a different perspective from that obtained by simply collecting information from teachers, it is consistent with the TIMSS goals of providing information about the educational contexts and performance of students.

The tables in this chapter contain special notation regarding response rates. For a country where teacher responses were available for 70% to 84% of the students, an "r" is included next to the data for that country. When teacher responses were available for 50% to 69% of the students, an "s" is included next to the data for that country. When teacher responses were available for less than 50% of the students, an "x" replaces the data.[1]

Who Delivers Science Instruction?

This section provides information about the science teaching force in each of the participating countries, in terms of certification, degrees, age, gender, and years of teaching experience.

Table 5.1 summarizes information gathered from each country about the requirements for certification held by the majority of the seventh- and eighth-grade teachers. In many countries, the type of education required for qualification includes a university degree. In other countries, study at a teacher training institution is required, or even both a university degree and study at a teacher training institution. The number of years of post-secondary education required for a teaching qualification ranged from two years in Iran to as much as six years in Canada, although many countries reported four years. All of the countries except Colombia, Cyprus, Greece, and Lithuania reported that teaching practice was required. A large number of countries reported that an evaluation or examination was required for certification. Those countries not having such a requirement included Canada, Colombia, Cyprus, Greece, Iran, Israel, Korea, Portugal, Sweden, and the United States.

Table 5.2 contains teachers' reports on their age and gender. If a constant supply of teachers were entering the teaching force, devoting their careers to the classroom, and then retiring, one might expect approximately equivalent percentages of students taught by teachers in their 20s, 30s, 40s, and 50s, and this does appear to hold for some countries. In most countries, however, the majority of the eighth-grade students were taught science by teachers in their 30s or 40s. Very few countries seemed to have a comparatively younger teaching force, with only Iran having 40% or more of the students with science teachers in their 20s or younger, and just five countries (Hong Kong, Iran, Korea, Kuwait, and Portugal) having 70% or more students with teachers in their 30s or younger. Countries with a comparatively older teaching force included Cyprus, the Czech Republic, and Germany, where 70% or more of the eighth-grade students had science teachers in their 40s or older.

In a number of countries, approximately equivalent percentages of eighth-grade students were taught science by male teachers and female teachers. However, at least 70% of the eighth-grade students had female science teachers in the Czech Republic, Hungary, Israel, Latvia (LSS), Lithuania, Portugal, Romania, the Russian Federation, and Slovenia. In contrast, at least 70% of the students had male teachers in Denmark, Japan, the Netherlands, and Switzerland.

As might be expected from the differences in teachers' ages from country to country, the TIMSS data indicate differences in teacher experience across countries (see Table 5.3). Those countries with younger teaching forces tended to have more students

[1] Similar to Chapter 4, background data are not available for Bulgaria and South Africa.

taught by less experienced teachers. At least half the eighth-grade students had science teachers with 10 years or less of experience in Hong Kong, Iceland, Iran, Israel, Korea, Kuwait, Portugal, and Thailand. Fewer countries had relatively experienced teaching forces. Only in the Czech Republic, France, and Romania did more than half the students have science teachers with more than 20 years of experience.

The relationship between years of teaching experience and science achievement is not clear in many countries. In about one-fourth of the countries, the eighth-grade students with the most experienced teachers (more than 20 years) had higher science achievement than did those with less experienced teachers (5 years or fewer). This may reflect the practice of giving teachers with more seniority the more advanced classes. However, there were also several countries where the students with less experienced teachers had higher achievement than did those with the most experienced teachers.

Table 5.1

Requirements for Certification Held by the Majority of Lower- and Upper-Grade (Seventh and Eighth Grade*) Teachers[1]

Country	Type of Education Required for Qualification	Number of Years of Post-Secondary Education Required	Teaching or Practice Experience Required	Evaluation or Examination Required
Australia	University or Teacher Training Institution	4	yes	yes
Austria	Teacher Training Institution: Teachers in the general secondary schools (70%) are required to have an education from a teacher training institution. Teachers in the academic secondary schools (30%) are required to have a university education.	3–5	yes	yes
Belgium (Fl)	Teacher Training Institution	3	yes	yes
Belgium (Fr)	Teacher Training Institution	3	yes	yes
Bulgaria	University	5	yes	yes
Canada	University	5–6	yes	no
Colombia	University	4	no	no
Cyprus	University	4	no	no
Czech Republic	University	4–5	yes	yes
Denmark	Teacher Training Institution	4	yes	yes
England	University or Higher Education Institution: Teachers of lower- and upper-grade students normally study their specialist subject area for their degree for 3 or 4 years. This is followed by a one-year post graduate course. However, some teachers study education and specialty concurrently. All teachers who qualified since 1975 are graduates. Some teachers who qualified before this date hold teacher certificates but are not graduates.	3–5	yes	yes
France	University and Teacher Training: As of 1991, teachers of lower- and upper-grade students are required to have a 3-year university diploma, followed by a competitive examination and professional training. The majority of teachers (more than 50%) meet the requirements (more in the public schools than in the private sector). Yet, there are still many teachers recruited before 1991 who do not have the same level of qualification.	4 or 5	yes	yes
Germany	University and Post-University Teacher Training Institution	3–5 +2 years	yes	yes
Greece	University	4	no	no
Hong Kong	University and one year Post-Graduate training	4	yes	yes
Hungary	Teacher Training Institution	4	yes	yes
Iceland	University	3	yes	yes
Iran	Teacher Training Institution	2	yes	no
Ireland	University with Post Graduate University Training	4–5	yes	yes
Israel	University	4	yes	no
Japan	University	4	yes	yes

*Seventh and eighth grades in most countries; see Table 2 for more information about the grades tested in each country.
[1]Certification pertains to the majority (more than 50%) of teachers of lower- and upper-grade students in each country.

SOURCE: IEA Third International Mathematics and Science Study (TIMSS), 1994-95. Information provided by TIMSS National Research Coordinators.

Table 5.1 (Continued)

Requirements for Certification Held by the Majority of Lower- and Upper-Grade (Seventh and Eighth Grade*) Teachers [1]

Country	Type of Education Required for Qualification	Number of Years of Post-Secondary Education Required	Teaching or Practice Experience Required	Evaluation or Examination Required
Korea	University	4	yes	no
Kuwait	University	4	yes	yes
Latvia	Pedagogical Institution	4	yes	yes
Lithuania	University or Teacher Training Institution	5	no	yes
Netherlands	Teacher Training Institution	4	yes	yes
New Zealand	Teacher Training Institution or University with Teacher Training Institution: Teachers of students in the lower grade are required to attend a teacher training institution. Teachers in the upper grade are required to have a university and teacher training institution education.	3 (lower gr.) 4 (upper gr.)	yes	yes
Norway	Teacher Training Institution or University: Most teachers of students in the lower grade have a certificate from a teacher training institution. For teachers of students in the upper grade there is about an equal distribution between those who attended a teacher training institution and those who attended university.	3–4[2]	yes	yes
Philippines	Teacher Training Institution or University	4	yes	yes
Portugal	University	3–5	yes	no
Romania	University	4–5	yes	yes
Russian Federation	University or Teacher Training Institution or Post-Graduate University Training	4–5	yes	yes
Scotland	University or Teacher Training Institution	4	yes	yes
Singapore	Post-Graduate University Training	4–5	yes	yes
Slovak Republic	Teacher Training Institution or University	4–5[3]	yes	yes
Slovenia	University	4–5	yes	yes
South Africa	Teacher Training Institution	3	yes	yes
Spain	Teacher Training Institution or University	3	yes	yes
Sweden	Teacher Training Institution (lower grade) University (upper grade)	3-3.5 (lower gr.)[4] 4-4.5 (upper gr.)[4]	yes	yes
Switzerland	University or Teacher Training Institution	2–4	yes	yes
Thailand	Teacher Training Institution or University	4	yes	yes
United States	University	4	yes	no

*Seventh and eighth grades in most countries; see Table 2 for more information about the grades tested in each country.
[1]Certification pertains to the majority (more than 50%) of teachers of lower- and upper-grade students in each country.
[2]Norway: Until 1965 2 years of post-secondary education were required. Between 1965 and 1995 3 years were required. As of 1996, new certified teachers are required to have completed 4 years of post-secondary education.
[3]Slovak Republic: In the past, 4 years of study at a teacher training institution were required. Currently, the requirement is 5 years at a teacher training institution or university.
[4]Sweden: Until 1988 3 years of post-secondary education were required for lower-grade teachers and 4 years for upper-grade teachers. Since 1988 3.5 years of post-secondary education are required for lower-grade teachers and 4-4.5 years are required for upper-grade teachers.

SOURCE: IEA Third International Mathematics and Science Study (TIMSS), 1994-95. Information provided by TIMSS National Research Coordinators.

Table 5.2

Teachers' Reports on Their Age and Gender Science - Upper Grade (Eighth Grade*)

Country		Percent of Students Taught by Teachers					Percent of Students Taught by Teachers	
		29 Years or Under	30 - 39 Years	40 - 49 Years	50 Years or Older		Female	Male
Australia	r	17 (2.2)	31 (3.2)	37 (3.3)	16 (2.2)	r	39 (3.5)	61 (3.5)
Austria	r	6 (1.8)	41 (4.0)	43 (3.6)	10 (2.0)	r	52 (3.4)	48 (3.4)
Belgium (Fl)		13 (2.5)	30 (3.9)	32 (4.3)	25 (3.4)		55 (4.2)	45 (4.2)
Belgium (Fr)	s	15 (3.5)	33 (5.8)	31 (4.7)	21 (3.8)	s	56 (5.8)	44 (5.8)
Canada		21 (3.5)	27 (2.9)	33 (4.0)	19 (3.1)		37 (3.6)	63 (3.6)
Colombia		18 (4.6)	31 (4.2)	36 (4.5)	14 (3.6)		39 (5.0)	61 (5.0)
Cyprus	r	0 (0.0)	28 (3.1)	53 (3.7)	19 (3.3)	r	52 (4.0)	48 (4.0)
Czech Republic		8 (2.1)	18 (2.9)	32 (2.8)	42 (3.0)		76 (2.5)	24 (2.5)
Denmark	s	8 (3.5)	23 (5.7)	39 (6.1)	30 (5.8)	s	23 (4.4)	77 (4.4)
England	s	15 (2.0)	25 (2.5)	41 (2.9)	19 (2.6)	s	39 (3.2)	61 (3.2)
France		13 (1.9)	19 (2.7)	41 (3.5)	27 (3.3)		51 (3.9)	49 (3.9)
Germany	s	0 (0.0)	15 (3.7)	37 (4.0)	47 (3.9)	s	39 (4.8)	61 (4.8)
Greece		2 (0.4)	43 (3.4)	43 (3.4)	12 (2.1)		43 (3.9)	57 (3.9)
Hong Kong		34 (5.8)	38 (6.1)	20 (4.3)	8 (3.1)		32 (5.4)	68 (5.4)
Hungary		14 (1.7)	27 (2.3)	39 (2.2)	20 (2.1)		74 (2.2)	26 (2.2)
Iceland	r	22 (4.2)	46 (4.9)	24 (3.4)	8 (2.9)	r	44 (7.4)	56 (7.4)
Iran, Islamic Rep.		45 (5.5)	39 (5.7)	15 (3.9)	1 (0.9)		40 (4.7)	60 (4.7)
Ireland	r	18 (2.6)	40 (3.7)	29 (4.0)	13 (2.7)	r	54 (4.6)	46 (4.6)
Israel	s	26 (7.8)	49 (8.8)	11 (5.4)	14 (6.8)	s	91 (5.4)	9 (5.4)
Japan		19 (3.6)	48 (4.4)	20 (3.8)	13 (3.2)		20 (3.6)	80 (3.6)
Korea		24 (3.2)	46 (4.1)	21 (3.4)	10 (2.2)		48 (4.0)	52 (4.0)
Kuwait	r	33 (8.1)	48 (8.1)	19 (4.9)	1 (0.6)	r	50 (8.0)	50 (8.0)
Latvia (LSS)	r	13 (1.5)	34 (2.8)	25 (2.2)	28 (2.4)	r	75 (2.1)	25 (2.1)
Lithuania		17 (2.0)	32 (2.3)	26 (2.2)	24 (2.2)		78 (1.8)	22 (1.8)
Netherlands		11 (2.3)	27 (3.4)	35 (3.7)	27 (3.4)		20 (3.1)	80 (3.1)
New Zealand		11 (2.6)	28 (3.8)	39 (4.2)	22 (3.3)		40 (4.3)	60 (4.3)
Norway		12 (2.9)	19 (3.6)	41 (3.9)	28 (3.8)		31 (3.9)	69 (3.9)
Portugal		37 (3.0)	44 (3.2)	13 (2.4)	6 (1.5)		78 (3.0)	22 (3.0)
Romania		11 (1.6)	21 (2.0)	38 (2.2)	30 (2.3)		74 (1.9)	26 (1.9)
Russian Federation		18 (3.7)	26 (3.0)	31 (2.5)	25 (2.4)		86 (2.0)	14 (2.0)
Scotland	s	9 (1.7)	26 (4.3)	43 (4.8)	22 (3.9)	s	37 (3.8)	63 (3.8)
Singapore		30 (4.3)	23 (4.0)	28 (4.9)	19 (3.6)		69 (4.6)	31 (4.6)
Slovak Republic		13 (2.7)	25 (3.9)	40 (4.4)	21 (3.5)		63 (4.2)	37 (4.2)
Slovenia	r	13 (2.4)	45 (3.2)	24 (2.8)	18 (2.9)	r	77 (2.6)	23 (2.6)
Spain		3 (1.5)	31 (3.8)	50 (4.1)	16 (3.1)		44 (4.2)	56 (4.2)
Sweden		11 (1.9)	23 (2.6)	28 (2.7)	39 (3.0)		37 (2.9)	63 (2.9)
Switzerland	r	15 (4.1)	26 (4.1)	39 (4.6)	19 (3.3)	r	14 (2.5)	86 (2.5)
Thailand	r	22 (5.0)	43 (5.7)	33 (6.2)	2 (2.2)	r	64 (5.7)	36 (5.7)
United States	r	17 (2.9)	27 (2.5)	34 (3.5)	23 (3.4)	r	54 (4.1)	46 (4.1)

*Eighth grade in most countries; see Table 2 for more information about the grades tested in each country.
Countries shown in italics did not satisfy one or more guidelines for sample participation rates, age/grade specifications, or classroom sampling procedures (see Figure A.3). Background data for Bulgaria and South Africa are unavailable.
Because population coverage falls below 65%, Latvia is annotated LSS for Latvian Speaking Schools only.
( ) Standard errors appear in parentheses. Because results are rounded to the nearest whole number, some totals may appear inconsistent.
An "r" indicates teacher response data available for 70-84% of students. An "s" indicates teacher response data available for 50-69% of students.

SOURCE: IEA Third International Mathematics and Science Study (TIMSS), 1994-95.

Table 5.3

Teachers' Reports on Their Years of Teaching Experience
Science - Upper Grade (Eighth Grade*)

Country		0 - 5 Years		6-10 Years		11-20 Years		More than 20 Years	
		Percent of Students	Mean Achievement	Percent of Students	Mean Achievement	Percent of Students	Mean Achievement	Percent of Students	Mean Achievement
Australia	r	19 (2.3)	537 (8.4)	20 (2.9)	539 (10.4)	38 (3.5)	555 (7.9)	23 (2.7)	548 (7.9)
Austria	r	5 (1.1)	553 (11.5)	17 (2.3)	567 (5.0)	49 (3.5)	560 (4.9)	30 (3.3)	562 (4.7)
Belgium (Fl)		11 (2.3)	548 (8.0)	11 (2.8)	574 (6.2)	38 (5.3)	549 (8.8)	40 (4.8)	549 (7.7)
Belgium (Fr)	s	13 (3.6)	482 (8.7)	8 (2.7)	492 (8.1)	44 (5.7)	485 (4.8)	35 (5.0)	478 (5.8)
Canada		25 (3.3)	535 (7.2)	18 (2.5)	542 (6.7)	23 (3.0)	521 (4.4)	33 (3.6)	529 (5.6)
Colombia	r	18 (3.4)	404 (9.5)	10 (2.8)	410 (9.7)	36 (3.7)	415 (5.5)	36 (4.6)	421 (4.5)
Cyprus	s	34 (5.1)	457 (5.0)	10 (2.9)	461 (11.7)	24 (3.1)	454 (4.8)	32 (4.1)	463 (3.4)
Czech Republic		11 (1.8)	566 (8.1)	12 (1.9)	589 (14.2)	13 (2.0)	573 (5.9)	64 (2.5)	572 (4.1)
Denmark	s	14 (4.2)	482 (8.0)	15 (4.6)	461 (7.2)	32 (5.9)	478 (4.6)	40 (6.3)	484 (6.2)
England	s	21 (2.2)	559 (11.5)	14 (2.2)	559 (10.7)	33 (3.2)	566 (8.3)	32 (3.0)	569 (8.3)
France		16 (2.2)	498 (4.3)	9 (2.2)	489 (7.1)	19 (2.5)	492 (4.3)	55 (4.0)	501 (3.8)
Germany	s	5 (2.0)	557 (30.0)	13 (3.2)	529 (14.0)	39 (4.3)	546 (7.4)	43 (4.4)	526 (10.2)
Greece		19 (3.0)	485 (4.4)	26 (4.2)	481 (3.3)	42 (4.0)	508 (3.6)	14 (2.3)	512 (4.5)
Hong Kong		38 (6.3)	532 (7.6)	23 (4.8)	516 (11.3)	25 (5.4)	504 (10.4)	14 (4.1)	536 (13.5)
Hungary		15 (1.9)	545 (5.6)	12 (1.8)	552 (4.9)	32 (2.7)	556 (4.6)	41 (2.7)	552 (3.9)
Iceland	r	34 (4.6)	489 (8.9)	21 (5.6)	492 (6.1)	31 (6.5)	485 (5.1)	14 (3.5)	483 (5.3)
Iran, Islamic Rep.		37 (4.7)	456 (4.2)	20 (5.7)	473 (5.6)	34 (4.7)	478 (4.8)	9 (3.2)	487 (6.2)
Ireland	r	18 (3.1)	563 (11.3)	17 (2.9)	533 (12.0)	38 (4.1)	547 (7.0)	27 (3.9)	527 (10.2)
Israel	r	28 (7.8)	501 (15.7)	27 (7.6)	512 (12.8)	31 (7.4)	553 (13.4)	14 (6.2)	552 (23.0)
Japan		19 (3.4)	563 (4.1)	21 (3.4)	573 (3.4)	36 (4.2)	574 (3.9)	23 (3.5)	573 (3.2)
Korea		23 (3.5)	562 (4.9)	31 (3.3)	568 (4.0)	32 (3.7)	562 (3.8)	13 (2.7)	567 (5.9)
Kuwait	s	37 (7.0)	433 (5.0)	25 (7.3)	445 (8.4)	33 (8.5)	413 (10.8)	5 (4.2)	421 (41.2)
Latvia (LSS)	r	13 (1.8)	485 (3.6)	20 (2.3)	482 (3.9)	28 (2.7)	486 (4.2)	39 (2.6)	485 (3.6)
Lithuania	r	19 (2.2)	483 (4.7)	14 (1.7)	479 (5.4)	28 (2.0)	474 (5.1)	39 (2.8)	474 (5.0)
Netherlands		20 (2.9)	556 (9.2)	11 (2.4)	558 (7.0)	32 (2.8)	562 (7.5)	37 (3.6)	567 (11.6)
New Zealand		16 (3.1)	525 (9.1)	21 (3.6)	531 (10.7)	38 (3.7)	528 (7.0)	25 (3.3)	523 (9.5)
Norway		16 (3.4)	533 (5.1)	8 (2.4)	528 (5.6)	36 (4.2)	527 (3.1)	40 (4.5)	528 (3.9)
Portugal		46 (3.4)	473 (3.0)	25 (2.7)	482 (3.2)	21 (2.6)	484 (4.3)	7 (1.7)	502 (6.3)
Romania		12 (1.6)	465 (9.4)	11 (1.4)	484 (8.7)	22 (2.0)	488 (6.5)	55 (2.5)	492 (6.1)
Russian Federation		17 (3.9)	541 (8.7)	13 (1.8)	531 (7.2)	28 (3.4)	536 (6.1)	43 (3.4)	538 (5.6)
Scotland	s	19 (3.0)	499 (7.3)	15 (3.1)	510 (11.6)	36 (4.7)	533 (10.1)	31 (4.5)	523 (7.6)
Singapore		30 (4.4)	615 (11.4)	13 (3.0)	591 (18.0)	21 (4.0)	599 (9.8)	36 (4.4)	610 (9.7)
Slovak Republic		15 (2.8)	546 (7.4)	18 (3.5)	548 (6.7)	18 (3.2)	540 (8.7)	49 (4.7)	545 (4.4)
Slovenia	r	11 (2.3)	569 (5.6)	17 (2.2)	560 (4.9)	38 (3.5)	553 (3.5)	33 (3.3)	560 (3.6)
Spain		9 (2.1)	527 (9.4)	13 (2.9)	516 (5.1)	40 (4.2)	516 (3.7)	39 (4.3)	514 (3.2)
Sweden		19 (2.3)	538 (4.1)	12 (2.0)	539 (6.9)	27 (2.3)	534 (5.0)	42 (3.0)	538 (3.4)
Switzerland	r	17 (3.7)	516 (9.4)	10 (2.5)	540 (11.6)	37 (4.4)	520 (6.9)	35 (4.1)	521 (6.7)
Thailand	r	41 (7.0)	522 (6.1)	20 (5.1)	537 (10.2)	36 (6.8)	535 (7.7)	3 (1.8)	529 (47.6)
United States	r	30 (3.8)	538 (8.0)	15 (3.0)	549 (10.5)	26 (3.7)	534 (7.0)	29 (3.8)	542 (7.4)

*Eighth grade in most countries; see Table 2 for more information about the grades tested in each country.
Countries shown in italics did not satisfy one or more guidelines for sample participation rates, age/grade specifications, or classroom sampling procedures (see Figure A.3). Background data for Bulgaria and South Africa are unavailable.
Because population coverage falls below 65%, Latvia is annotated LSS for Latvian Speaking Schools only.
( ) Standard errors appear in parentheses. Because results are rounded to the nearest whole number, some totals may appear inconsistent.
An "r" indicates teacher response data available for 70-84% of students. An "s" indicates teacher response data available for 50-69% of students.

SOURCE: IEA Third International Mathematics and Science Study (TIMSS), 1994-95.

What Are Teachers' Perceptions About Science?

Figure 5.1 depicts the percentages of eighth-grade students whose science teachers reported certain beliefs about science and the way science should be taught. Teacher views about the nature of science varied considerably across countries. In many countries, most notably Thailand, Iran, Cyprus, Canada, and Singapore, teachers agreed that science is primarily a formal way of representing the real world, while in the Slovak Republic, Slovenia, the Czech Republic, Hungary, the Russian Federation, and Sweden, less than 40% of students had teachers holding this view. However, teachers in most countries indicated a fairly practical view of science, agreeing that it is primarily a practical and structured guide for addressing real situations. In most countries also, the majority of eighth-grade students had teachers who agreed that some students have a natural talent for science.

Regarding perceptions about how to teach science, there seemed to be widespread agreement that it is important to give students prescriptive and sequential directions for doing science experiments. Only in the Slovak Republic, New Zealand, Iceland, Denmark, and Korea did fewer than 60% of the eighth-grade students have teachers who agreed with this approach.

TIMSS also queried teachers about the cognitive demands of science, asking them to rate the importance of various skills for success in the discipline. Figure 5.2 shows the percentages of students whose teachers rated each of four different skills as very important. Internationally, most science teachers felt it was very important for students to be able to think in a sequential and procedural manner, to be able to think creatively, to understand how science is used in the real world, and to be able to provide reasons to support their conclusions. However, there was some variation across countries. In every country except Slovenia and Israel, the majority of students were taught by teachers who considered it very important that students be able to think in a sequential and procedural manner. Fewer than half of the eighth-grade students in Austria, Singapore, the Netherlands, Switzerland, Israel, Belgium (Flemish), Ireland, and France had teachers who felt it was very important to think creatively, and fewer than half in Switzerland, France, Austria and Belgium (Flemish) had teachers who felt it was very important to understand how science is used in the real world. With the current calls from business and industry on helping students improve their ability to apply scientific and solve practical problems in job-related situations, it might be rather surprising that teachers in these countries do not place more importance on these two aspects of science. In all countries except Korea, Switzerland, the Slovak Republic, Kuwait, and Austria, the majority of students had teachers who felt it was very important to be able to provide reasons to support their conclusions.

Figure 5.1

Percent of Students Whose Science Teachers Agree or Strongly Agree with Statements About the Nature of Science and Science Teaching Upper Grade (Eighth Grade*)

*Eighth grade in most countries; see Table 2 for more information about the grades tested in each country.
Countries shown in italics did not satisfy one or more guidelines for sample participation rates, age/grade specifications, or classroom sampling procedures (see Figure A.3). Background data for Bulgaria and South Africa are unavailable.
Because population coverage falls below 65%, Latvia is annotated LSS for Latvian Speaking Schools only.
An "r" indicates teacher response data available for 70-84% of students. An "s" indicates teacher response data available for 50-69% of students.
Countries where data were not available or where teacher response data were available for <50% of students are omitted from the figure (England).
Scotland did not ask these questions.

SOURCE: IEA Third International Mathematics and Science Study (TIMSS), 1994-95.

Figure 5.1 (Continued)

Percent of Students Whose Science Teachers Agree or Strongly Agree with Statements About the Nature of Science and Science Teaching Upper Grade (Eighth Grade*)

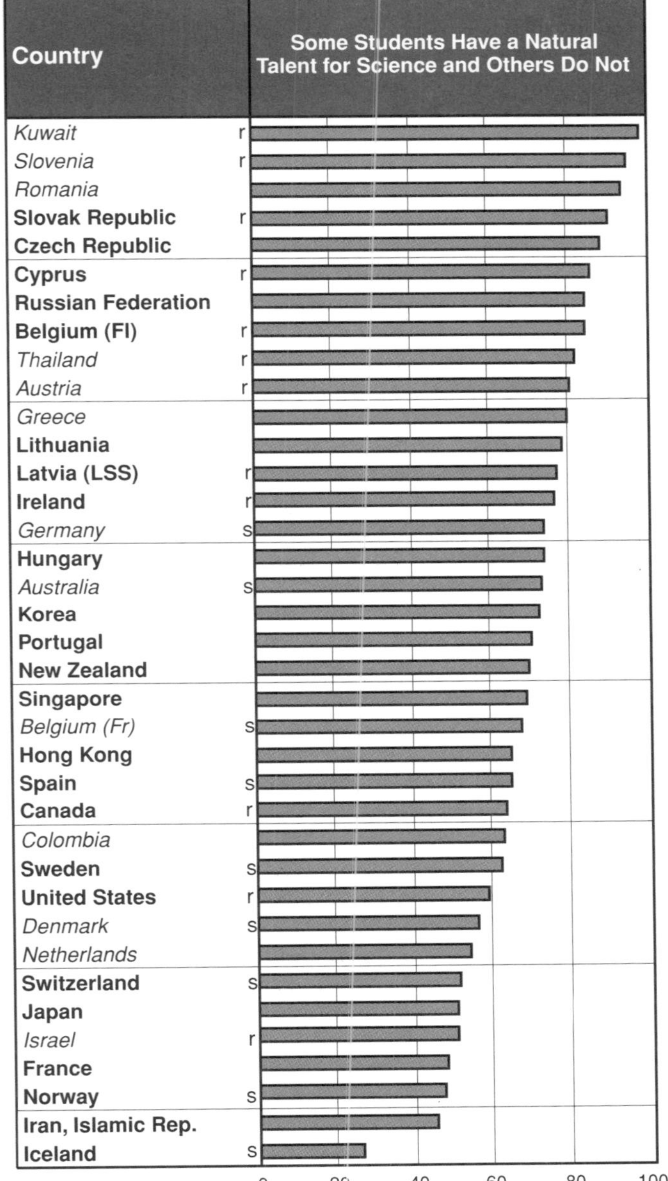

*Eighth grade in most countries; see Table 2 for more information about the grades tested in each country.
Countries shown in italics did not satisfy one or more guidelines for sample participation rates, age/grade specifications, or classroom sampling procedures (see Figure A.3). Background data for Bulgaria and South Africa are unavailable.
Because population coverage falls below 65%, Latvia is annotated LSS for Latvian Speaking Schools only.
An "r" indicates teacher response data available for 70-84% of students. An "s" indicates teacher response data available for 50-69% of students.
Countries where data were not available or where teacher response data were available for <50% of students are omitted from the figure (England).
Scotland did not ask these questions.

SOURCE: IEA Third International Mathematics and Science Study (TIMSS), 1994-95.

Figure 5.2

Percent of Students Whose Science Teachers Think Particular Abilities Are Very Important for Students' Success in the Sciences in School - Upper Grade (Eighth Grade*)

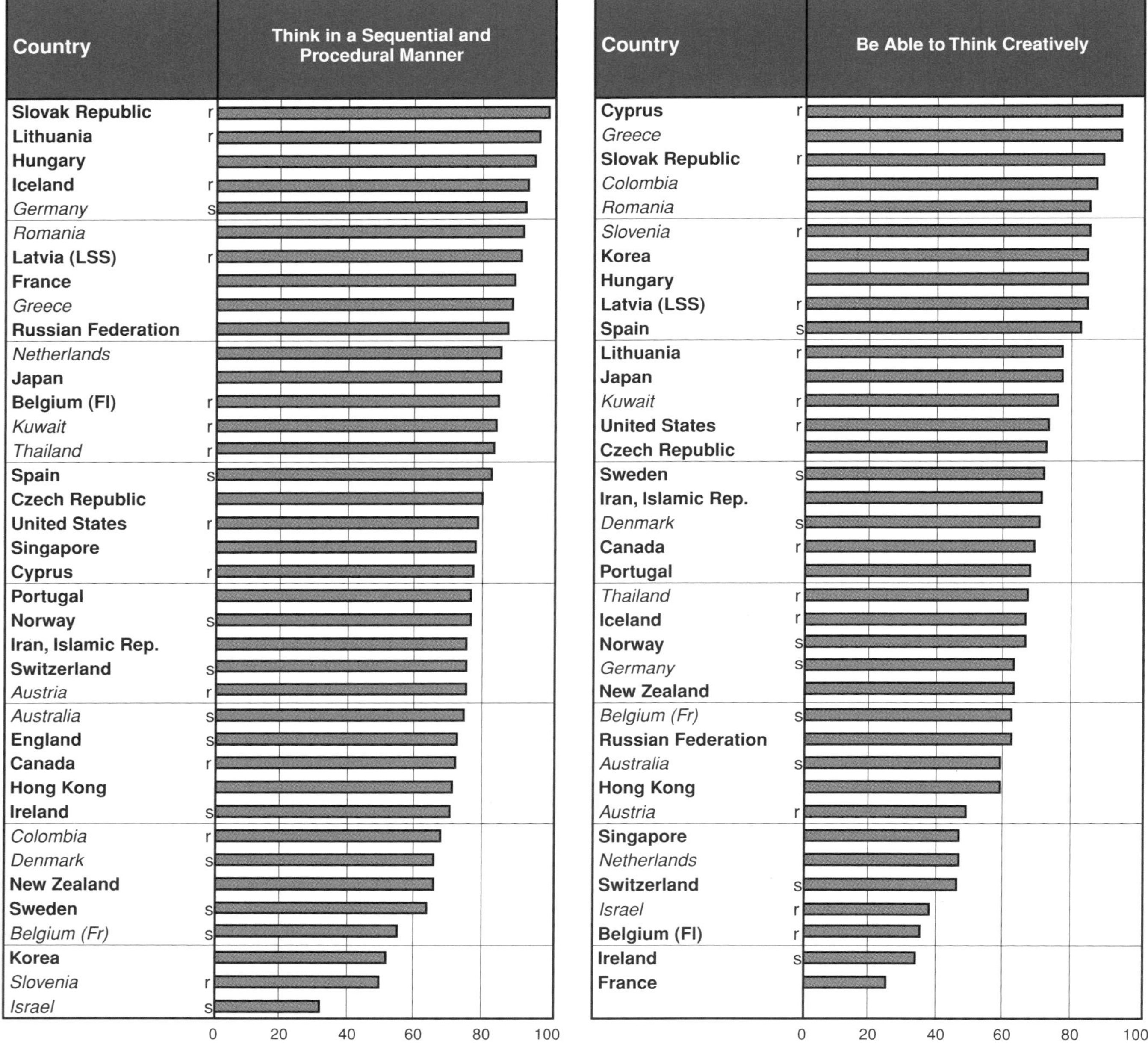

*Eighth grade in most countries; see Table 2 for more information about the grades tested in each country.
Countries shown in italics did not satisfy one or more guidelines for sample participation rates, age/grade specifications, or classroom sampling procedures (see Figure A.3). Background data for Bulgaria and South Africa are unavailable.
Because population coverage falls below 65%, Latvia is annotated LSS for Latvian Speaking Schools only.
An "r" indicates teacher response data available for 70-84% of students. An "s" indicates teacher response data available for 50-69% of students.
Countries where data were not available or where teacher response data were available for <50% of students are omitted from the figure (England).
Scotland did not ask these questions.

SOURCE: IEA Third International Mathematics and Science Study (TIMSS), 1994-95.

Figure 5.2 (Continued)

Percent of Students Whose Science Teachers Think Particular Abilities Are Very Important for Students' Success in the Sciences in School - Upper Grade (Eighth Grade*)

*Eighth grade in most countries; see Table 2 for more information about the grades tested in each country.
Countries shown in italics did not satisfy one or more guidelines for sample participation rates, age/grade specifications, or classroom sampling procedures (see Figure A.3). Background data for Bulgaria and South Africa are unavailable.
Because population coverage falls below 65%, Latvia is annotated LSS for Latvian Speaking Schools only.
An "r" indicates teacher response data available for 70-84% of students. An "s" indicates teacher response data available for 50-69% of students.
Countries where data were not available or where teacher response data were available for <50% of students are omitted from the figure (England in the second, third, and fourth panels).
Scotland did not ask these questions.

SOURCE: IEA Third International Mathematics and Science Study (TIMSS), 1994-95.

How Do Science Teachers Spend Their School-Related Time?

The data in Table 5.4 reveal that in a number of countries, eighth-grade science teachers are specialists. In Belgium (Flemish), Cyprus, France, Kuwait, Latvia (LSS), Lithuania, the Netherlands, New Zealand, Portugal, the Russian Federation, and Scotland, the majority of eighth-grade students had teachers who spent at least 75% of their formally scheduled school time teaching science. For most participating countries, there was little difference in students' achievement according to whether they were taught by specialists.

As shown in Table 5.5, teachers in most countries where science is taught as an integrated subject reported that science classes typically meet for less than 3.5 hours per week, although 3.5 to nearly 5 hours was reported for more than three-quarters of the eighth-grade students in Singapore and almost half of those in New Zealand. The data reveal no clear pattern between the number of in-class instructional hours and achievement either across or between countries. Common sense and research both support the idea that increased time on task can yield commensurate increases in achievement, yet this time also can be spent outside of school on homework or in special tutoring. The ability to use straightforward analyses such as these to disentangle complicated relationships also is made difficult by the practice of providing additional in-school instruction for lower-performing students.

In addition to their formally scheduled duties, teachers were asked about the number of hours per week spent on selected school-related activities outside the regular school day. Table 5.6 presents the results. For example, on average, eighth-grade students in Australia had science teachers who spent 2.1 hours per week preparing or grading tests, and another 2.3 hours per week reading and grading student work. Their teachers spent 2.8 hours per week on lesson planning and 1.6 hours combined on meeting students and parents. They spent 1.2 hours on professional reading and development, and 3.2 hours on record-keeping and administrative tasks combined. Across countries, teachers reported that grading tests, grading student work, and lesson planning were the most time-consuming activities, averaging as much as 10 hours per week in Singapore. In general, teachers also reported several hours per week spent on keeping students' records and other administrative tasks.

Opportunities to meet with colleagues to plan curriculum or teaching approaches enable teachers to expand their views of science, their resources for teaching, and their repertoire of teaching and learning skills. Table 5.7 contains teachers' reports on how often they meet with other teachers in their subject area to discuss and plan curriculum or teaching approaches. Teachers of the majority of the students reported weekly or even daily planning meetings in Cyprus, the Czech Republic, England, Hungary, Korea, Kuwait, Norway, Scotland, the Slovak Republic, and Sweden. In the remaining countries, however, most students had science teachers who reported only limited opportunities to plan curriculum or teaching approaches with other teachers (monthly or even yearly meetings).

Table 5.4

Teachers' Reports on the Proportion of Their Formally Scheduled School Time Spent Teaching the Sciences[1] - Upper Grade (Eighth Grade*)

Country		Less Than 50 Percent		50-74 Percent		75-100 Percent	
		Percent of Students	Mean Achievement	Percent of Students	Mean Achievement	Percent of Students	Mean Achievement
Australia	r	34 (2.7)	539 (6.3)	25 (3.1)	551 (7.0)	42 (3.2)	554 (8.4)
Austria	r	67 (2.8)	550 (4.1)	16 (2.5)	566 (6.1)	17 (1.9)	602 (4.3)
Belgium (Fl)		20 (3.2)	548 (6.7)	18 (3.1)	569 (4.5)	61 (4.0)	548 (6.2)
Belgium (Fr)	s	24 (4.5)	477 (6.1)	33 (4.6)	487 (5.4)	43 (5.2)	484 (4.3)
Canada		55 (3.5)	523 (3.0)	24 (3.5)	549 (6.2)	22 (2.7)	534 (5.8)
Colombia		27 (4.2)	399 (11.1)	39 (4.8)	415 (4.5)	34 (4.0)	419 (4.8)
Cyprus	r	12 (2.0)	448 (4.9)	22 (3.8)	455 (4.6)	66 (4.0)	463 (2.6)
Czech Republic		69 (2.9)	569 (3.7)	18 (2.7)	574 (6.7)	13 (2.5)	597 (8.2)
Denmark	s	66 (5.2)	481 (4.0)	20 (3.8)	481 (8.3)	15 (4.1)	463 (8.6)
England		x x	x x	x x	x x	x x	x x
France		15 (2.1)	489 (4.3)	8 (1.7)	495 (10.1)	77 (2.5)	501 (2.6)
Germany	s	47 (3.8)	524 (10.0)	22 (3.4)	534 (8.8)	31 (3.7)	556 (7.0)
Greece		- -	- -	- -	- -	- -	- -
Hong Kong		32 (6.1)	506 (11.0)	26 (5.2)	530 (8.7)	42 (5.3)	530 (7.5)
Hungary		- -	- -	- -	- -	- -	- -
Iceland	r	64 (6.5)	488 (5.0)	14 (6.1)	490 (5.5)	21 (7.1)	486 (8.3)
Iran, Islamic Rep.		- -	- -	- -	- -	- -	- -
Ireland	r	25 (3.7)	541 (10.2)	36 (4.6)	546 (7.5)	39 (4.2)	538 (8.7)
Israel	s	32 (9.3)	549 (17.0)	22 (6.4)	548 (10.6)	46 (9.5)	507 (10.1)
Japan		28 (3.8)	571 (3.5)	38 (3.9)	574 (3.6)	34 (4.4)	568 (3.2)
Korea		51 (3.4)	565 (3.0)	41 (3.4)	563 (3.2)	8 (1.9)	576 (6.7)
Kuwait	r	23 (6.1)	422 (10.2)	26 (4.6)	432 (4.2)	51 (7.4)	425 (6.0)
Latvia (LSS)	r	25 (2.5)	484 (5.0)	18 (2.0)	484 (3.6)	57 (3.0)	484 (3.0)
Lithuania		20 (2.0)	481 (6.9)	15 (1.8)	472 (5.9)	65 (2.3)	476 (4.0)
Netherlands		16 (2.5)	539 (12.3)	15 (2.5)	556 (12.3)	68 (3.7)	569 (5.8)
New Zealand		19 (3.0)	514 (9.9)	24 (2.9)	527 (7.4)	57 (4.0)	532 (5.9)
Norway		81 (3.5)	532 (2.2)	7 (2.2)	513 (6.2)	12 (3.0)	512 (5.7)
Portugal		15 (2.3)	477 (3.5)	22 (2.5)	478 (3.6)	63 (2.9)	481 (3.0)
Romania		81 (2.3)	489 (5.0)	14 (2.1)	472 (9.3)	4 (1.0)	489 (13.1)
Russian Federation		5 (1.2)	537 (12.6)	5 (1.3)	529 (10.8)	90 (2.0)	538 (4.1)
Scotland	s	0 (0.0)	~ ~	3 (1.5)	499 (16.9)	97 (1.5)	521 (5.6)
Singapore		10 (2.3)	577 (12.6)	56 (5.3)	608 (7.8)	34 (4.9)	613 (10.4)
Slovak Republic		83 (2.9)	543 (3.7)	14 (2.6)	549 (6.7)	3 (1.6)	572 (17.2)
Slovenia	r	29 (2.5)	558 (3.8)	30 (3.6)	554 (4.5)	41 (3.4)	561 (3.2)
Spain		85 (3.3)	515 (1.9)	14 (3.2)	524 (7.0)	1 (0.9)	~ ~
Sweden		62 (2.6)	538 (3.1)	28 (2.5)	533 (5.0)	9 (1.7)	540 (5.8)
Switzerland	r	70 (3.4)	520 (4.1)	14 (3.1)	507 (9.6)	16 (2.2)	544 (7.3)
Thailand	r	27 (5.6)	526 (9.5)	28 (5.3)	528 (7.7)	45 (6.2)	532 (6.2)
United States	r	40 (3.5)	546 (4.5)	36 (3.9)	541 (7.1)	25 (3.5)	526 (9.8)

*Eighth grade in most countries; see Table 2 for more information about the grades tested in each country.

[1]Formally scheduled school time included time scheduled for teaching all subjects, as well as student supervision, student counseling/appraisal, administrative duties, individual curriculum planning, cooperative curriculum planning, and other non-student contact time.

Countries shown in italics did not satisfy one or more guidelines for sample participation rates, age/grade specifications, or classroom sampling procedures (see Figure A.3). Background data for Bulgaria and South Africa are unavailable.

Because population coverage falls below 65%, Latvia is annotated LSS for Latvian Speaking Schools only.

( ) Standard errors appear in parentheses. Because results are rounded to the nearest whole number, some totals may appear inconsistent.

A dash (-) indicates data are not available. A tilde (~) indicates insufficient data to report achievement.

An "r" indicates teacher response data available for 70-84% of students. An "s" indicates teacher response data available for 50-69% of students.

An "x" indicates teacher response data available for <50% of students.

SOURCE: IEA Third International Mathematics and Science Study (TIMSS), 1994-95.

Table 5.5

Teachers' Reports[1] on Average Number of Hours Integrated Science Is Taught Weekly to Their Science Classes - Upper Grade (Eighth Grade*)

Country		Less Than 2 Hours		2 Hours to < 3.5		3.5 hours to < 5		5 Hours or More	
		Percent of Students	Mean Achievement	Percent of Students	Mean Achievement	Percent of Students	Mean Achievement	Percent of Students	Mean Achievement
Australia		x x	x x	x x	x x	x x	x x	x x	x x
Canada	r	11 (2.1)	512 (8.9)	69 (3.9)	540 (3.8)	11 (2.5)	528 (5.5)	8 (2.1)	517 (10.3)
Colombia	r	6 (2.3)	416 (4.5)	75 (4.2)	415 (5.6)	13 (3.2)	404 (5.5)	6 (2.4)	403 (18.6)
Cyprus		x x	x x	x x	x x	x x	x x	x x	x x
England		- -	- -	- -	- -	- -	- -	- -	- -
Hong Kong		7 (2.3)	492 (29.9)	82 (3.9)	526 (5.3)	9 (3.3)	518 (8.6)	2 (1.6)	~ ~
Iran, Islamic Rep.		- -	- -	- -	- -	- -	- -	- -	- -
Ireland	s	4 (1.9)	578 (16.5)	94 (2.1)	540 (6.2)	2 (0.8)	~ ~	0 (0.0)	~ ~
Israel	s	19 (7.9)	547 (19.6)	77 (7.2)	520 (9.1)	4 (3.5)	529 (0.0)	0 (0.0)	~ ~
Japan		5 (1.6)	618 (15.2)	94 (1.7)	569 (1.5)	0 (0.0)	~ ~	1 (0.6)	~ ~
Korea		43 (2.9)	569 (3.3)	51 (3.2)	561 (3.1)	1 (0.8)	~ ~	5 (2.3)	568 (12.7)
Kuwait	r	3 (2.6)	409 (1.9)	97 (2.6)	426 (4.4)	1 (0.5)	~ ~	0 (0.0)	~ ~
New Zealand		1 (0.9)	~ ~	52 (4.1)	527 (6.3)	47 (4.2)	525 (6.6)	0 (0.0)	~ ~
Norway	s	27 (4.9)	526 (3.0)	73 (4.9)	524 (2.6)	1 (0.6)	~ ~	0 (0.0)	~ ~
Scotland	s	14 (3.1)	538 (23.4)	83 (3.6)	519 (4.8)	3 (1.7)	488 (22.5)	0 (0.0)	~ ~
Singapore		0 (0.0)	~ ~	24 (4.4)	618 (14.6)	76 (4.4)	603 (6.0)	0 (0.0)	~ ~
Spain	r	5 (2.6)	532 (2.5)	84 (3.9)	518 (2.1)	11 (3.0)	502 (9.4)	1 (0.7)	~ ~
Switzerland	s	41 (4.7)	532 (6.6)	37 (4.4)	524 (8.4)	9 (3.1)	486 (13.7)	13 (3.5)	519 (15.6)
Thailand		x x	x x	x x	x x	x x	x x	x x	x x
United States		x x	x x	x x	x x	x x	x x	x x	x x

*Eighth grade in most countries; see Table 2 for more information about the grades tested in each country.

[1]Reported for countries using integrated science form of student questionnaire.

Countries shown in italics did not satisfy one or more guidelines for sample participation rates, age/grade specifications, or classroom sampling procedures (see Figure A.3). Background data for Bulgaria and South Africa are unavailable.

Because population coverage falls below 65%, Latvia is annotated LSS for Latvian Speaking Schools only.

( ) Standard errors appear in parentheses. Because results are rounded to the nearest whole number, some totals may appear inconsistent.

A dash (-) indicates data are not available. A tilde (~) indicates insufficient data to report achievement.

An "r" indicates teacher response data available for 70-84% of students. An "s" indicates teacher response data available for 50-69% of students.

An "x" indicates teacher response data available for <50% of students.

SOURCE: IEA Third International Mathematics and Science Study (TIMSS), 1994-95.

Table 5.6

Average Number of Hours[1] Students' Teachers Spend on Various School-Related Activities Outside the Formal School Day During the School Week
Science - Upper Grade (Eighth Grade*)

Country	Preparing or Grading Tests	Reading and Grading Student Work	Planning Lessons by Self	Meeting with Students Outside Classroom Time	Meeting with Parents	Professional Reading and Development	Keeping Students' Records	Adminis-trative Tasks
Australia	r 2.1 (0.1)	s 2.3 (0.1)	r 2.8 (0.1)	s 1.1 (0.1)	s 0.5 (0.0)	r 1.2 (0.1)	s 1.1 (0.1)	r 2.1 (0.1)
Austria	r 1.7 (0.1)	r 2.6 (0.1)	r 3.6 (0.1)	r 0.5 (0.0)	r 0.6 (0.0)	r 1.9 (0.1)	r 0.9 (0.1)	r 1.1 (0.1)
Belgium (Fl)	3.5 (0.1)	1.5 (0.1)	3.6 (0.1)	0.7 (0.1)	r 0.6 (0.1)	1.2 (0.1)	r 0.5 (0.1)	1.4 (0.1)
Belgium (Fr)	s 3.2 (0.2)	s 1.7 (0.1)	s 3.5 (0.2)	s 0.7 (0.1)	s 0.5 (0.1)	s 1.4 (0.1)	s 0.8 (0.1)	s 1.1 (0.1)
Canada	2.2 (0.1)	2.5 (0.1)	2.6 (0.1)	1.4 (0.1)	0.5 (0.0)	r 0.8 (0.1)	1.1 (0.0)	1.7 (0.1)
Colombia	2.9 (0.1)	r 2.5 (0.2)	3.1 (0.1)	r 1.5 (0.2)	r 0.9 (0.1)	r 2.4 (0.2)	r 0.8 (0.1)	r 1.4 (0.2)
Cyprus	r 3.4 (0.1)	r 1.6 (0.1)	r 3.5 (0.1)	s 0.3 (0.0)	r 1.0 (0.1)	r 1.0 (0.1)	s 0.5 (0.1)	r 1.3 (0.1)
Czech Republic	2.5 (0.1)	1.2 (0.1)	4.0 (0.1)	1.1 (0.1)	0.5 (0.0)	1.0 (0.1)	0.9 (0.0)	1.3 (0.1)
Denmark	- -	- -	- -	- -	- -	- -	- -	- -
England	x x	x x	x x	x x	x x	x x	x x	x x
France	3.8 (0.1)	r 1.0 (0.1)	3.6 (0.1)	0.6 (0.0)	0.5 (0.0)	1.4 (0.1)	0.9 (0.0)	1.3 (0.1)
Germany	s 2.7 (0.1)	s 2.3 (0.1)	s 4.1 (0.1)	s 0.7 (0.1)	s 0.7 (0.1)	s 1.9 (0.1)	s 1.0 (0.1)	s 1.7 (0.1)
Greece	2.8 (0.1)	1.2 (0.1)	2.4 (0.1)	0.6 (0.1)	0.9 (0.1)	2.6 (0.1)	0.4 (0.0)	1.3 (0.2)
Hong Kong	2.3 (0.2)	3.1 (0.2)	2.8 (0.2)	1.9 (0.1)	0.4 (0.1)	1.0 (0.1)	0.8 (0.1)	1.8 (0.2)
Hungary	2.7 (0.1)	2.2 (0.1)	3.7 (0.1)	1.8 (0.1)	0.8 (0.0)	2.1 (0.1)	0.7 (0.0)	2.3 (0.1)
Iceland	s 1.8 (0.2)	s 2.8 (0.2)	s 4.0 (0.2)	r 0.6 (0.1)	s 0.5 (0.0)	r 1.3 (0.2)	s 1.3 (0.1)	r 2.0 (0.2)
Iran, Islamic Rep.	2.5 (0.2)	1.8 (0.2)	2.0 (0.1)	0.9 (0.1)	0.7 (0.0)	0.51(0.1)	0.9 (0.1)	0.8 (0.1)
Ireland	r 2.1 (0.1)	s 1.7 (0.1)	r 2.3 (0.1)	r 0.8 (0.1)	r 0.3 (0.1)	r 0.8 (0.1)	r 0.8 (0.1)	r 1.1 (0.1)
Israel	r 3.4 (0.3)	s 2.1 (0.2)	r 3.5 (0.3)	s 1.1 (0.2)	s 0.7 (0.1)	s 3.3 (0.3)	s 1.2 (0.2)	r 1.6 (0.2)
Japan	1.8 (0.1)	1.7 (0.1)	3.0 (0.1)	2.0 (0.1)	0.5 (0.0)	1.7 (0.1)	1.3 (0.1)	2.4 (0.1)
Korea	1.9 (0.1)	1.7 (0.1)	2.4 (0.1)	1.9 (0.1)	0.4 (0.0)	1.7 (0.1)	1.1 (0.1)	1.9 (0.1)
Kuwait	r 2.8 (0.2)	r 2.1 (0.2)	r 2.1 (0.2)	s 0.4 (0.1)	r 0.5 (0.1)	s 0.9 (0.1)	r 1.3 (0.2)	r 0.8 (0.1)
Latvia (LSS)	r 2.3 (0.1)	r 1.6 (0.1)	r 3.1 (0.1)	r 1.5 (0.1)	r 0.6 (0.0)	r 1.2 (0.1)	r 0.4 (0.0)	r 1.4 (0.1)
Lithuania	r 1.5 (0.1)	r 2.0 (0.1)	r 2.6 (0.1)	r 1.6 (0.1)	r 0.8 (0.0)	r 2.3 (0.1)	r 0.8 (0.0)	r 0.7 (0.1)
Netherlands	3.8 (0.1)	r 1.1 (0.1)	3.0 (0.1)	r 1.3 (0.1)	0.6 (0.0)	1.2 (0.1)	r 0.5 (0.0)	1.4 (0.1)
New Zealand	2.3 (0.1)	2.1 (0.1)	3.0 (0.1)	1.2 (0.1)	0.4 (0.1)	1.3 (0.1)	1.0 (0.1)	2.6 (0.1)
Norway	2.1 (0.1)	1.6 (0.1)	3.4 (0.1)	0.7 (0.1)	0.6 (0.0)	0.5 (0.1)	0.8 (0.1)	1.7 (0.1)
Portugal	3.0 (0.1)	2.2 (0.1)	3.7 (0.1)	0.7 (0.1)	0.6 (0.0)	1.5 (0.1)	0.9 (0.1)	1.5 (0.1)
Romania	2.1 (0.1)	1.7 (0.1)	3.3 (0.1)	1.4 (0.1)	1.1 (0.0)	1.4 (0.1)	1.5 (0.1)	2.2 (0.1)
Russian Federation	2.1 (0.1)	2.0 (0.1)	3.1 (0.1)	1.9 (0.1)	1.0 (0.0)	2.8 (0.1)	0.9 (0.0)	1.9 (0.1)
Scotland	s 1.5 (0.1)	s 1.7 (0.1)	s 2.0 (0.1)	s 0.9 (0.1)	s 0.6 (0.1)	s 1.1 (0.1)	s 1.1 (0.1)	s 1.6 (0.1)
Singapore	3.3 (0.2)	4.0 (0.1)	3.1 (0.1)	1.4 (0.1)	0.4 (0.0)	1.3 (0.1)	1.2 (0.1)	2.3 (0.1)
Slovak Republic	2.3 (0.1)	1.6 (0.1)	3.5 (0.1)	1.2 (0.1)	0.6 (0.0)	0.9 (0.1)	1.1 (0.1)	1.1 (0.1)
Slovenia	r 2.2 (0.1)	r 1.2 (0.1)	r 3.4 (0.1)	r 1.2 (0.1)	r 1.1 (0.1)	r 2.2 (0.1)	r 0.6 (0.0)	r 1.6 (0.1)
Spain	2.2 (0.1)	1.5 (0.1)	1.8 (0.1)	0.9 (0.1)	1.1 (0.1)	1.6 (0.1)	0.8 (0.1)	1.7 (0.1)
Sweden	2.3 (0.1)	1.5 (0.1)	4.0 (0.1)	0.6 (0.0)	0.8 (0.0)	1.5 (0.1)	0.9 (0.0)	2.4 (0.1)
Switzerland	r 3.0 (0.1)	r 2.1 (0.1)	r 3.8 (0.1)	r 0.9 (0.1)	r 0.7 (0.1)	r 1.9 (0.1)	r 0.7 (0.0)	r 2.3 (0.1)
Thailand	s 2.7 (0.2)	s 2.4 (0.2)	s 2.3 (0.2)	s 1.3 (0.1)	s 0.6 (0.1)	s 1.6 (0.2)	s 1.4 (0.1)	s 1.8 (0.2)
United States	r 2.1 (0.1)	r 2.4 (0.1)	r 2.2 (0.1)	r 1.2 (0.1)	r 0.7 (0.1)	r 1.0 (0.1)	r 1.5 (0.1)	r 2.0 (0.1)

[1]Average hours based on: No time=0, Less Than 1 Hour=.5, 1-2 Hours=1.5; 3-4 Hours=3.5; More Than 4 Hours=5.
*Eighth grade in most countries; see Table 2 for more information about the grades tested in each country.
Countries shown in italics did not satisfy one or more guidelines for sample participation rates, age/grade specifications, or classroom sampling procedures (see Figure A.3). Background data for Bulgaria and South Africa are unavailable.
Because population coverage falls below 65%, Latvia is annotated LSS for Latvian Speaking Schools only.
( ) Standard errors appear in parentheses. Because results are rounded to the nearest whole number, some totals may appear inconsistent.
A dash (-) indicates data are not available.
An "r" indicates teacher response data available for 70-84% of students. An "s" indicates teacher response data available for 50-69% of students.
An "x" indicates teacher response data available for <50% of students.

SOURCE: IEA Third International Mathematics and Science Study (TIMSS), 1994-95.

Table 5.7

Teachers' Reports on How Often They Meet with Other Teachers in Their Subject Area To Discuss and Plan Curriculum or Teaching Approaches
Science - Upper Grade (Eighth Grade*)

Country		Percent of Students Taught by Teachers			
		Meeting Never or Once/Twice a Year	Meeting Monthly or Every Other Month	Meeting Once, Twice, or Three Times a Week	Meeting Almost Every Day
Australia	r	10 (2.0)	50 (3.6)	30 (3.2)	9 (2.3)
Austria	r	20 (2.5)	37 (3.0)	36 (3.1)	6 (1.9)
Belgium (Fl)		48 (5.6)	28 (4.2)	21 (3.5)	3 (1.2)
Belgium (Fr)	s	22 (4.2)	34 (5.6)	38 (5.2)	7 (2.4)
Canada		38 (2.9)	25 (3.5)	31 (3.8)	6 (1.7)
Colombia		24 (3.3)	30 (4.4)	42 (4.8)	4 (1.8)
Cyprus	r	4 (1.7)	6 (0.7)	67 (3.2)	22 (2.2)
Czech Republic		22 (3.2)	23 (2.5)	34 (3.4)	20 (2.3)
Denmark		- -	- -	- -	- -
England	s	8 (1.6)	41 (3.1)	51 (3.2)	0 (0.1)
France		45 (4.2)	22 (2.8)	29 (4.2)	4 (1.4)
Germany	s	32 (4.5)	31 (4.8)	22 (3.6)	15 (3.4)
Greece		43 (4.2)	26 (3.4)	26 (3.9)	6 (1.7)
Hong Kong		33 (5.3)	48 (5.9)	19 (4.3)	0 (0.0)
Hungary		9 (1.6)	16 (2.1)	39 (2.7)	35 (3.1)
Iceland	r	42 (6.1)	29 (7.0)	29 (8.0)	0 (0.0)
Iran, Islamic Rep.		18 (3.3)	37 (4.4)	34 (4.6)	11 (3.1)
Ireland	r	59 (4.3)	25 (4.1)	14 (3.1)	2 (0.9)
Israel	r	25 (6.9)	34 (9.5)	37 (8.6)	4 (2.6)
Japan		24 (3.4)	29 (3.9)	46 (3.7)	1 (1.0)
Korea		22 (3.0)	26 (3.6)	37 (4.1)	15 (3.1)
Kuwait	r	10 (4.5)	2 (1.1)	66 (8.3)	22 (7.3)
Latvia (LSS)	r	28 (2.5)	46 (3.0)	16 (2.3)	10 (1.9)
Lithuania		25 (2.5)	36 (2.7)	24 (2.4)	14 (1.7)
Netherlands		13 (2.5)	65 (3.9)	21 (3.1)	2 (0.9)
New Zealand		6 (1.8)	45 (4.1)	43 (4.0)	6 (2.1)
Norway		7 (2.3)	20 (3.5)	65 (4.0)	8 (2.0)
Portugal		8 (1.6)	69 (3.0)	18 (2.8)	5 (1.2)
Romania		12 (1.8)	58 (2.6)	14 (1.7)	16 (1.9)
Russian Federation		12 (1.9)	57 (2.7)	20 (2.6)	11 (2.1)
Scotland	s	7 (1.7)	12 (2.6)	74 (4.0)	8 (2.3)
Singapore		15 (3.8)	61 (4.6)	21 (4.1)	3 (1.4)
Slovak Republic		4 (1.5)	23 (3.6)	35 (4.0)	39 (4.6)
Slovenia	r	5 (1.8)	53 (3.6)	18 (2.8)	24 (2.9)
Spain		17 (2.9)	48 (4.4)	32 (4.0)	2 (1.2)
Sweden		9 (1.8)	19 (2.5)	46 (3.5)	26 (2.6)
Switzerland	r	36 (4.0)	32 (4.0)	30 (3.9)	2 (1.3)
Thailand	s	53 (6.1)	17 (4.3)	23 (5.2)	6 (3.1)
United States	r	37 (3.3)	31 (3.5)	26 (4.0)	6 (1.3)

*Eighth grade in most countries; see Table 2 for more information about the grades tested in each country.
Countries shown in italics did not satisfy one or more guidelines for sample participation rates, age/grade specifications, or classroom sampling procedures (see Figure A.3). Background data for Bulgaria and South Africa are unavailable.
Because population coverage falls below 65%, Latvia is annotated LSS for Latvian Speaking Schools only.
( ) Standard errors appear in parentheses. Because results are rounded to the nearest whole number, some totals may appear inconsistent.
A dash (-) indicates data are not available.
An "r" indicates teacher response data available for 70-84% of students. An "s" indicates teacher response data available for 50-69% of students.

SOURCE: IEA Third International Mathematics and Science Study (TIMSS), 1994-95.

How Are Science Classes Organized?

Table 5.8 presents teachers' reports about the size of eighth-grade science classes for the TIMSS countries. The data reveal rather large variation from country to country. Scotland appeared to have the smallest eighth-grade science classes, with 99% of the students in classes of 20 or fewer students. According to teachers, science classes were relatively small in a number of countries. For example, 90% or more of the students were in science classes of 30 or fewer students in Austria, Belgium (Flemish), Belgium (French), Denmark, France, Germany, Hungary, Iceland, Ireland, Lithuania, the Netherlands, Norway, Portugal, the Russian Federation, Scotland, Slovenia, and Switzerland. At the other end of the spectrum, 89% of the students in Korea were in science classes with more than 40 students. In Colombia, Hong Kong, Japan, Korea, and Singapore, 90% of the students were in classes with more than 30 students. Extensive research about class size in relation to achievement indicates that the existence of such a relationship is dependent on the situation. Dramatic reductions in class size can be related to gains in achievement, but the chief effects of smaller classes often are in relation to teacher attitudes and instructional behaviors. The TIMSS data illustrate the complexity of this issue. Across countries, three of the four highest-performing countries at the eighth grade–Singapore, Korea, and Japan–are among those with the largest science classes. Within countries, several show little or no relationship between achievement and class size, often because students mostly are in classes of similar size. Within others, there appears to be a curvilinear relationship, or those students with higher achievement appear to be in larger classes. In some countries, larger classes may represent the more usual situation for teaching science, with smaller classes used primarily for students needing remediation or for those students in the less advanced tracks.

Teachers can adopt a variety of organizational and interactive approaches in science class. Whole-class instruction can be very efficient, because it requires less time on management functions and provides more time for developing science concepts. Teachers can make presentations, conduct discussions, or demonstrate procedures and applications to all students simultaneously. Both whole-class and independent work have been standard features of science classrooms. Students also can benefit from the type of cooperative learning that occurs with effective use of small-group work. Because they can help each other, students in groups can often handle challenging situations beyond their individual capabilities. Further, the positive affective impact of working together mirrors the use of science in the workplace.

Figure 5.3 provides a pictorial view of the emphasis on individual, group, and whole class work as reported by the science teachers in the TIMSS countries. Because learning may be enhanced with teacher guidance and monitoring of individual and small-group activities, the frequency of lessons using each of these organizational approaches is shown both with and without assistance from the teacher. Internationally, teachers reported that working together as a class with the teacher teaching the whole class is a frequently used instructional approach. In most countries, 50% or more of the eighth-grade students were taught this way during most or every lesson. Students working individually with assistance from the teacher is also a popular

Table 5.8

Teachers' Reports on Average Size of Science Class Upper Grade (Eighth Grade*)

Country	1 - 20 Students		21 - 30 Students		31 - 40 Students		41 or More Students	
	Percent of Students	Mean Achievement	Percent of Students	Mean Achievement	Percent of Students	Mean Achievement	Percent of Students	Mean Achievement
Australia	x x	x x	x x	x x	x x	x x	x x	x x
Austria	r 17 (3.9)	568 (8.9)	81 (3.9)	561 (3.6)	1 (0.7)	~ ~	0 (0.0)	~ ~
Belgium (Fl)	r 45 (4.6)	550 (8.4)	53 (4.5)	560 (8.1)	2 (1.2)	~ ~	0 (0.0)	~ ~
Belgium (Fr)	s 42 (6.2)	489 (6.1)	57 (6.1)	484 (3.9)	1 (1.3)	~ ~	0 (0.0)	~ ~
Canada	s 10 (2.6)	520 (11.0)	62 (4.2)	540 (3.9)	25 (3.4)	535 (6.6)	3 (1.3)	533 (12.0)
Colombia	r 4 (1.7)	422 (9.8)	6 (2.4)	420 (21.6)	37 (4.3)	422 (5.2)	53 (4.5)	411 (4.2)
Cyprus	s 2 (0.1)	~ ~	45 (3.5)	460 (4.0)	53 (3.5)	458 (3.5)	0 (0.0)	~ ~
Czech Republic	r 11 (2.7)	552 (6.4)	78 (5.1)	576 (5.4)	11 (4.6)	590 (11.7)	0 (0.0)	~ ~
Denmark	s 62 (6.7)	481 (3.7)	38 (6.7)	485 (6.7)	0 (0.0)	~ ~	0 (0.0)	~ ~
England	x x	x x	x x	x x	x x	x x	x x	x x
France	16 (3.6)	490 (6.6)	83 (3.6)	501 (2.7)	1 (0.6)	~ ~	0 (0.0)	~ ~
Germany	s 20 (4.5)	520 (18.4)	73 (5.1)	536 (5.5)	6 (2.8)	587 (15.7)	0 (0.0)	~ ~
Greece	6 (1.8)	474 (7.0)	71 (3.9)	498 (2.6)	22 (3.3)	500 (4.9)	1 (0.9)	~ ~
Hong Kong	0 (0.0)	~ ~	1 (1.2)	~ ~	57 (6.5)	520 (7.5)	42 (6.5)	530 (7.9)
Hungary	40 (3.7)	548 (4.1)	56 (3.9)	555 (4.1)	4 (1.8)	569 (8.9)	0 (0.0)	~ ~
Iceland	s 38 (6.5)	480 (5.2)	59 (6.8)	486 (3.7)	0 (0.0)	~ ~	3 (2.4)	519 (0.0)
Iran, Islamic Rep.	r 3 (1.3)	467 (18.0)	23 (4.3)	475 (6.0)	52 (5.2)	472 (3.9)	22 (4.0)	462 (6.8)
Ireland	s 12 (3.0)	490 (19.4)	80 (4.4)	548 (5.4)	9 (3.2)	575 (13.0)	0 (0.0)	~ ~
Israel	s 11 (5.9)	532 (8.3)	30 (7.0)	533 (16.0)	47 (9.8)	544 (9.3)	12 (7.4)	466 (24.8)
Japan	0 (0.2)	~ ~	4 (1.4)	570 (6.6)	88 (2.0)	567 (1.6)	8 (1.5)	615 (10.2)
Korea	6 (1.8)	573 (9.0)	1 (0.7)	~ ~	5 (1.5)	536 (8.1)	89 (2.5)	566 (2.3)
Kuwait	r 0 (0.0)	~ ~	48 (6.8)	427 (5.4)	50 (6.5)	425 (7.3)	2 (2.1)	~ ~
Latvia (LSS)	s 37 (4.0)	485 (5.2)	47 (3.8)	488 (3.4)	10 (2.6)	483 (7.9)	6 (1.6)	477 (3.5)
Lithuania	r 38 (3.1)	467 (5.4)	59 (2.9)	484 (5.2)	1 (0.5)	~ ~	2 (1.0)	~ ~
Netherlands	r 15 (5.0)	498 (21.4)	75 (5.7)	567 (5.0)	10 (3.5)	615 (13.6)	0 (0.0)	~ ~
New Zealand	7 (1.8)	501 (12.4)	75 (3.5)	522 (5.7)	18 (3.0)	556 (8.0)	1 (0.0)	~ ~
Norway	s 27 (4.4)	519 (4.6)	72 (4.7)	526 (2.8)	2 (1.4)	~ ~	0 (0.0)	~ ~
Portugal	15 (2.9)	469 (4.0)	77 (3.8)	481 (2.8)	8 (2.5)	487 (9.7)	0 (0.4)	~ ~
Romania	20 (2.5)	476 (9.5)	52 (4.5)	474 (6.1)	25 (4.2)	510 (9.9)	2 (1.3)	~ ~
Russian Federation	15 (2.7)	523 (11.7)	76 (3.6)	539 (3.9)	9 (2.3)	546 (14.4)	0 (0.0)	~ ~
Scotland	s 99 (0.9)	520 (5.9)	1 (0.6)	~ ~	0 (0.0)	~ ~	1 (0.7)	~ ~
Singapore	0 (0.0)	~ ~	9 (2.4)	609 (15.7)	72 (4.2)	604 (7.3)	19 (4.0)	616 (7.7)
Slovak Republic	r 12 (3.1)	533 (13.9)	69 (4.8)	543 (4.2)	19 (4.3)	554 (10.1)	0 (0.0)	~ ~
Slovenia	r 14 (2.8)	554 (7.5)	81 (3.2)	558 (3.1)	5 (1.5)	575 (13.6)	0 (0.4)	~ ~
Spain	r 9 (2.5)	505 (8.3)	49 (4.0)	515 (3.4)	35 (4.2)	525 (3.8)	7 (2.4)	509 (6.3)
Sweden	x x	x x	x x	x x	x x	x x	x x	x x
Switzerland	s 50 (5.0)	513 (7.0)	47 (4.8)	530 (6.2)	3 (1.9)	551 (7.5)	0 (0.0)	~ ~
Thailand	x x	x x	x x	x x	x x	x x	x x	x x
United States	x x	x x	x x	x x	x x	x x	x x	x x

*Eighth grade in most countries; see Table 2 for more information about the grades tested in each country.
Countries shown in italics did not satisfy one or more guidelines for sample participation rates, age/grade specifications, or classroom sampling procedures (see Figure A.3). Background data for Bulgaria and South Africa are unavailable.
Because population coverage falls below 65%, Latvia is annotated LSS for Latvian Speaking Schools only.
( ) Standard errors appear in parentheses. Because results are rounded to the nearest whole number, some totals may appear inconsistent.
A tilde (~) indicates insufficient data to report achievement.
An "r" indicates teacher response data available for 70-84% of students. An "s" indicates teacher response data available for 50-69% of students.
An "x" indicates teacher response data available for <50% of students.

SOURCE: IEA Third International Mathematics and Science Study (TIMSS), 1994-95.

approach, as is working in pairs or small groups with teacher assistance. Working without teacher assistance is less common in most countries, although it does seem to be a feature of life in science classrooms in Canada, the Netherlands, and New Zealand.

Figure 5.3

Teachers' Reports About Classroom Organization During Science Lessons Upper Grade (Eighth Grade*)

Country	Percent of Students Whose Teachers Report Using Each Organizational Approach "Most or Every Lesson"					
	Work Together as a Class with Students Responding to One Another	Work Together as a Class with Teacher Teaching the Whole Class	Work Individually with Assistance from Teacher	Work Individually without Assistance from Teacher	Work in Pairs or Small Groups with Assistance from Teacher	Work in Pairs or Small Groups without Assistance from Teacher
Austria	r 3	r 65	r 13	r 3	r 18	r 12
Belgium (Fl)	r 11	r 62	r 19	r 6	r 13	r 7
Belgium (Fr)	s 11	s 53	s 24	s 8	s 8	s 4
Canada	s 17	r 28	r 26	r 23	r 33	s 24
Colombia	r 33	r 48	r 55	r 10	r 43	r 13
Cyprus	s 3	s 74	s 35	s 3	s 17	s 6
Czech Republic	11	70	r 46	15	14	4
Denmark	s 2	s 22	s 25	s 3	s 46	s 13
France	16	57	34	16	27	12
Germany	s 30	s 69	s 28	s 7	s 19	s 5
Greece	3	67	45	10	13	1
Hong Kong	12	45	35	2	44	13
Hungary	7	80	54	13	11	2
Iceland	s 1	r 35	r 30	r 9	r 16	r 6
Iran, Islamic Rep.	25	57	36	2	25	11
Ireland	s 7	s 62	s 25	s 6	s 20	s 6
Israel	s 17	r 41	r 30	r 15	r 32	r 18
Japan	19	79	12	8	12	6

*Eighth grade in most countries; see Table 2 for more information about the grades tested in each country.
Countries shown in italics did not satisfy one or more guidelines for sample participation rates, age/grade specifications, or classroom sampling procedures (see Figure A.3). Background data for Bulgaria and South Africa are unavailable.
Because population coverage falls below 65%, Latvia is annotated LSS for Latvian Speaking Schools only.
An "r" indicates teacher response data available for 70-84% of students. An "s" indicates teacher response data available for 50-69% of students.
Countries where data were not available or where teacher response data were available for <50% of students are omitted from the figure (Australia, England, Sweden, and the United States).

SOURCE: IEA Third International Mathematics and Science Study (TIMSS), 1994-95.

Figure 5.3 (Continued)

Teachers' Reports About Classroom Organization During Science Lessons
Upper Grade (Eighth Grade*)

Country	Percent of Students Whose Teachers Report Using Each Organizational Approach "Most or Every Lesson"					
	Work Together as a Class with Students Responding to One Another	Work Together as a Class with Teacher Teaching the Whole Class	Work Individually with Assistance from Teacher	Work Individually without Assistance from Teacher	Work in Pairs or Small Groups with Assistance from Teacher	Work in Pairs or Small Groups without Assistance from Teacher
Korea	34	83	28	8	15	3
Kuwait	r 9	r 46	r 45	r 0	r 36	r 2
Latvia (LSS)	s 25	s 84	s 59	s 32	s 24	s 8
Lithuania	r 16	r 60	r 57	r 22	r 26	r 8
Netherlands	r 5	r 63	r 36	r 23	r 25	r 18
New Zealand	15	41	33	26	44	20
Norway	s 24	s 62	s 23	s 1	s 23	s 4
Portugal	14	66	54	3	54	5
Romania	15	86	47	8	27	r 2
Russian Federation	9	68	43	21	13	7
Scotland	s 7	s 22	s 27	s 11	s 56	s 19
Singapore	12	59	41	17	40	19
Slovak Republic	r 48	r 64	r 45	r 15	r 3	r 1
Slovenia	r 7	r 65	r 57	r 19	r 34	r 13
Spain	r 14	r 65	r 46	r 14	r 18	r 7
Switzerland	s 3	s 56	s 21	s 6	s 30	8
Thailand	r 16	r 38	r 33	r 10	r 32	s 11

*Eighth grade in most countries; see Table 2 for more information about the grades tested in each country.
Countries shown in italics did not satisfy one or more guidelines for sample participation rates, age/grade specifications, or classroom sampling procedures (see Figure A.3). Background data for Bulgaria and South Africa are unavailable.
Because population coverage falls below 65%, Latvia is annotated LSS for Latvian Speaking Schools only.
An "r" indicates teacher response data available for 70-84% of students. An "s" indicates teacher response data available for 50-69% of students.
Countries where data were not available or where teacher response data were available for <50% of students are omitted from the figure (Australia, England, Sweden, and the United States).

SOURCE: IEA Third International Mathematics and Science Study (TIMSS), 1994-95.

What Activities Do Students Do in Their Science Lessons?

As shown in Table 5.9, science teachers in the participating countries generally reported heavier reliance on curriculum guides than textbooks in deciding which topics to teach. Only Japan, Korea, the Netherlands, and Thailand use textbooks more for this purpose. In contrast, in almost all countries the textbook was the major written source science teachers used in deciding how to present a topic to their classes. Internationally, the textbook appears to play a role in science classrooms in many countries. For nearly all students in all countries, teachers reported using a textbook in their science classes (see Figure 5.4).

The types of activities teachers asked eighth-grade students to do, however, varied from country to country. Teachers were asked how often they asked students to do reasoning tasks in science. The data in Table 5.10 reveal that such activities are very common in science classes, with the majority of students in all countries being asked to do some type of science reasoning task in most or every lesson. The activities TIMSS inquired about included explaining the reasoning behind an idea, using tables, charts or graphs to represent and analyze relationships, working on problems for which there is no immediately obvious solution, writing explanations about what was observed and why it happened, and putting events in order and giving a reason for the organization. In Cyprus, the Czech Republic, Hungary, Portugal, Romania, the Russian Federation, and the Slovak Republic, 90% or more of the students were asked to do at least one of these types of reasoning tasks in most or every lesson.

Students were asked about the frequency with which their teachers demonstrate an experiment or with which they themselves do an experiment or practical investigation in class. Since in almost half of the TIMSS countries science is taught not as an integrated subject but as individual science subjects (biology, chemistry, etc.), the student reports are presented to reflect this. According to students (Table 5.11), teacher demonstrations are common in almost all countries where science is taught as an integrated subject, and they are also common in chemistry and physics classes. Such demonstrations are reported much less frequently in biology and earth science classes. Countries with integrated science where students report high frequencies of teacher demonstrations usually also have high reported frequencies of student experiments or practical investigations, although there are some countries, notably Cyprus, Iran, Kuwait, and Thailand, where teacher demonstrations are reported as much more frequent than student practical work (see Table 5.12). In countries where science is taught as individual subjects, students reported more frequent teacher demonstrations than student practical work in most countries, particularly for chemistry and physics.

Students were also asked about the frequency with which they use things from everyday life in solving problems in science class (Table 5.13). Among countries with integrated science, more than half of the eighth-grade students in Canada, Colombia, Cyprus, England, Hong Kong, Iran, Scotland, Singapore, and the United States reported being asked to solve such problems on a frequent basis (pretty often or almost always). Using everyday things for science problems was reportedly less common in countries with individual science subjects, although more than half of the students in Latvia (LSS) reported that they do so frequently in all science subject classes (biology, chemistry, and physics).

Table 5.9

Teachers' Reports on Their Main Sources of Written Information When Deciding Which Topics to Teach and How to Present a Topic Science - Upper Grade (Eighth Grade*)[1]

Country	Percent of Students Taught by Teachers					
	Deciding Which Topics to Teach			Deciding How to Present a Topic		
	Curriculum Guide	Textbook	Examination Specifications	Curriculum Guide	Textbook	Examination Specifications
Australia	x x	x x	- -	x x	x x	- -
Austria	r 72 (2.8)	28 (2.8)	0 (0.2)	r 29 (3.3)	70 (3.2)	1 (0.6)
Belgium (Fl)	r 90 (3.7)	10 (3.7)	- -	r 13 (2.6)	87 (2.6)	- -
Belgium (Fr)	s 90 (4.5)	10 (4.5)	- -	s 8 (2.8)	92 (2.8)	- -
Canada	- -	- -	- -	- -	- -	- -
Colombia	r 68 (5.0)	30 (5.0)	2 (1.1)	r 34 (4.8)	64 (5.0)	2 (1.1)
Cyprus	s 89 (2.2)	9 (2.1)	2 (0.1)	s 36 (3.9)	62 (3.9)	2 (0.1)
Czech Republic	r 76 (2.8)	24 (2.8)	- -	r 8 (1.3)	92 (1.3)	- -
Denmark	- -	- -	- -	- -	- -	- -
England	- -	- -	- -	- -	- -	- -
France	94 (1.5)	5 (1.4)	2 (0.9)	32 (2.9)	68 (2.9)	0 (0.4)
Germany	s 88 (3.0)	12 (3.0)	- -	s 26 (5.0)	74 (5.0)	- -
Greece	71 (3.5)	29 (3.5)	- -	12 (3.1)	88 (3.1)	- -
Hong Kong	55 (4.9)	40 (4.9)	5 (2.5)	25 (4.3)	74 (4.5)	1 (1.3)
Hungary	78 (2.5)	19 (2.3)	4 (1.0)	25 (2.3)	73 (2.3)	2 (0.8)
Iceland	s 57 (8.1)	27 (7.0)	16 (3.7)	s 22 (6.9)	78 (6.9)	0 (0.0)
Iran, Islamic Rep.	r 49 (5.8)	48 (6.1)	3 (1.3)	r 36 (5.8)	51 (6.4)	14 (6.1)
Ireland	s 68 (4.9)	32 (4.9)	- -	s 16 (3.1)	84 (3.1)	- -
Israel	s 94 (4.4)	5 (3.5)	1 (1.4)	s 23 (8.1)	77 (8.1)	0 (0.0)
Japan	35 (4.3)	62 (4.4)	3 (1.4)	15 (3.2)	83 (3.2)	1 (0.9)
Korea	16 (2.9)	77 (3.7)	7 (2.2)	16 (2.8)	81 (2.9)	3 (1.6)
Kuwait	- -	- -	- -	- -	- -	- -
Latvia (LSS)	s 81 (2.2)	17 (2.1)	2 (0.7)	s 33 (2.7)	65 (2.8)	2 (0.8)
Lithuania	x x	x x	x x	x x	x x	x x
Netherlands	r 3 (1.1)	72 (3.5)	24 (3.4)	r 7 (1.8)	88 (2.3)	4 (1.4)
New Zealand	91 (2.5)	6 (2.0)	4 (1.7)	53 (4.6)	47 (4.6)	0 (0.0)
Norway	s 66 (4.6)	34 (4.6)	- -	s 11 (3.5)	89 (3.5)	- -
Portugal	94 (1.5)	6 (1.5)	- -	63 (3.6)	37 (3.6)	- -
Romania	93 (1.1)	4 (0.9)	3 (0.8)	35 (2.4)	61 (2.6)	4 (1.2)
Russian Federation	83 (2.9)	9 (1.7)	8 (1.9)	9 (1.9)	88 (2.0)	3 (1.2)
Scotland	s 68 (4.2)	24 (3.9)	8 (2.0)	s 49 (5.1)	47 (5.1)	4 (1.6)
Singapore	76 (4.0)	24 (4.0)	0 (0.0)	11 (2.7)	89 (2.7)	1 (0.4)
Slovak Republic	r 80 (4.4)	20 (4.4)	0 (0.0)	r 22 (3.8)	78 (3.8)	1 (0.8)
Slovenia	r 88 (2.2)	9 (2.0)	3 (1.1)	r 29 (2.8)	69 (2.9)	2 (0.9)
Spain	- -	- -	- -	- -	- -	- -
Sweden	x x	x x	- -	x x	x x	- -
Switzerland	x x	x x	x x	x x	x x	x x
Thailand	r 41 (6.7)	57 (6.4)	3 (1.6)	r 22 (5.6)	78 (5.6)	0 (0.0)
United States	x x	x x	x x	x x	x x	x x

*Eighth grade in most countries; see Table 2 for more information about the grades tested in each country.

[1]Curriculum Guides include national, regional, and school curriculum guides; Textbooks include teacher and student editions, as well as other resource books; and Examination Specifications include national and regional levels.

Countries shown in italics did not satisfy one or more guidelines for sample participation rates, age/grade specifications, or classroom sampling procedures (see Figure A.3). Background data for Bulgaria and South Africa are unavailable.

Because population coverage falls below 65%, Latvia is annotated LSS for Latvian Speaking Schools only.

( ) Standard errors appear in parentheses. Because results are rounded to the nearest whole number, some totals may appear inconsistent.

A dash (-) indicates data are not available.

An "r" indicates teacher response data available for 70-84% of students. An "s" indicates teacher response data available for 50-69% of students.

An "x" indicates teacher response data available for <50% of students.

SOURCE: IEA Third International Mathematics and Science Study (TIMSS), 1994-95.

Figure 5.4

Teachers' Reports About Using a Textbook in Teaching Science Upper Grade (Eighth Grade*)

Countries are classified by percentage of students whose teachers reported that they use a textbook in teaching their science class.

100%	95-99%	85-94%
r *Austria*	s *Germany*	r **Belgium(Flemish)**
s **Cyprus**	*Greece*	r **Canada**
Czech Republic	r **Hungary**	r *Colombia*
Hong Kong	s **Iceland**	**France**
r *Israel*	s **Ireland**	**Iran, Islamic Rep.**
Japan	**Korea**	
r **Lithuania**	r *Kuwait*	
Portugal	s **Latvia (LSS)**	
Romania	*Netherlands*	
Russian Federation	s **Norway**	
Singapore	r **Spain**	
r *Slovenia*	r *Thailand*	

Note: Twenty-four percent of the students in s Belgium(French), 70% in s Denmark, 71% in New Zealand, 84% in s Scotland, and 63% in s Switzerland had teachers who reported using a textbook in their science class.

*Eighth grade in most countries; see Table 2 for more information about the grades tested in each country.
Countries shown in italics did not satisfy one or more guidelines for sample participation rates, age/grade specifications, or classroom sampling procedures (see Figure A.3). Background data for Bulgaria and South Africa are unavailable.
Because population coverage falls below 65%, Latvia is annotated LSS for Latvian Speaking Schools only.
An "r" indicates teacher response data available for 70-84% of students. An "s" indicates teacher response data available for 50-69% of students.
Countries where data were not available or where teacher response data were available for <50% of students are omitted from the figure (Australia, England, Sweden, and the United States).
The Slovak Republic did not ask this question.

SOURCE: IEA Third International Mathematics and Science Study (TIMSS), 1994-95.

Table 5.10

Teachers' Reports on How Often They Ask Students To Do Reasoning Tasks[1] Science - Upper Grade (Eighth Grade*)

Country	Never or Almost Never		Some Lessons		Most Lessons		Every Lesson	
	Percent of Students	Mean Achievement	Percent of Students	Mean Achievement	Percent of Students	Mean Achievement	Percent of Students	Mean Achievement
Australia	x x	x x	x x	x x	x x	x x	x x	x x
Austria	r 1 (0.4)	~ ~	32 (3.9)	560 (4.5)	51 (3.6)	562 (4.6)	16 (2.6)	569 (7.4)
Belgium (Fl)	r 5 (3.1)	497 (66.9)	26 (3.0)	554 (5.3)	53 (4.7)	556 (6.9)	15 (3.5)	573 (6.0)
Belgium (Fr)	s 0 (0.0)	~ ~	22 (5.5)	481 (6.3)	55 (5.9)	484 (4.6)	23 (4.4)	485 (6.2)
Canada	r 0 (0.0)	~ ~	13 (2.1)	533 (8.3)	63 (3.7)	533 (4.4)	24 (3.5)	542 (6.8)
Colombia	r 0 (0.0)	~ ~	18 (4.7)	412 (22.1)	53 (5.1)	417 (4.3)	29 (4.0)	407 (6.0)
Cyprus	s 1 (1.3)	~ ~	4 (1.5)	445 (15.0)	54 (4.3)	460 (3.4)	41 (4.0)	458 (4.9)
Czech Republic	0 (0.0)	~ ~	4 (1.1)	549 (10.5)	60 (3.1)	576 (4.3)	36 (3.2)	576 (6.4)
Denmark	s 2 (1.6)	~ ~	49 (6.5)	479 (5.2)	46 (6.3)	480 (4.6)	3 (2.0)	458 (22.2)
England	s 0 (0.0)	~ ~	11 (1.9)	539 (13.4)	63 (3.1)	561 (5.9)	26 (2.9)	582 (10.3)
France	0 (0.0)	~ ~	23 (2.7)	503 (4.0)	56 (3.9)	496 (3.2)	21 (3.4)	505 (4.8)
Germany	s 0 (0.0)	~ ~	24 (3.9)	543 (12.4)	63 (4.2)	534 (6.3)	13 (3.0)	531 (16.2)
Greece	1 (0.7)	~ ~	19 (2.9)	498 (4.7)	55 (4.1)	497 (3.4)	25 (2.8)	497 (3.6)
Hong Kong	1 (1.2)	~ ~	21 (4.7)	510 (14.2)	50 (5.8)	525 (6.2)	27 (5.1)	522 (11.5)
Hungary	0 (0.3)	~ ~	4 (1.1)	540 (11.0)	63 (2.4)	553 (3.1)	33 (2.2)	555 (4.0)
Iceland	s 1 (0.7)	~ ~	35 (6.0)	486 (9.3)	58 (5.3)	489 (3.4)	6 (2.4)	480 (8.3)
Iran, Islamic Rep.	3 (2.6)	493 (3.7)	24 (4.5)	472 (5.4)	56 (5.1)	468 (4.0)	17 (4.1)	469 (5.3)
Ireland	s 0 (0.0)	~ ~	12 (2.6)	539 (12.6)	59 (4.6)	549 (6.7)	28 (4.5)	528 (11.6)
Israel	r 0 (0.0)	~ ~	11 (5.3)	541 (52.2)	45 (9.3)	538 (10.2)	44 (8.9)	515 (11.8)
Japan	0 (0.0)	~ ~	17 (3.3)	572 (3.7)	55 (4.5)	568 (3.0)	28 (3.5)	578 (3.6)
Korea	0 (0.3)	~ ~	12 (2.3)	560 (4.7)	62 (3.7)	567 (2.9)	25 (3.0)	562 (4.3)
Kuwait	r 0 (0.0)	~ ~	16 (5.5)	438 (3.0)	58 (6.5)	420 (4.4)	26 (5.1)	434 (12.9)
Latvia (LSS)	s 0 (0.0)	~ ~	11 (2.0)	482 (7.4)	71 (2.2)	486 (2.6)	18 (2.2)	486 (3.9)
Lithuania	r 0 (0.2)	~ ~	19 (1.9)	470 (6.2)	56 (2.4)	482 (4.5)	25 (1.9)	472 (4.9)
Netherlands	r 1 (0.2)	~ ~	31 (3.5)	541 (11.2)	52 (3.6)	569 (6.7)	16 (2.5)	581 (7.7)
New Zealand	0 (0.0)	~ ~	18 (3.1)	532 (11.7)	66 (3.9)	523 (5.4)	16 (3.0)	533 (12.3)
Norway	s 0 (0.0)	~ ~	52 (5.6)	520 (3.2)	45 (5.5)	531 (3.0)	2 (1.6)	~ ~
Portugal	0 (0.0)	~ ~	7 (1.6)	478 (4.8)	60 (3.2)	479 (3.1)	33 (3.2)	481 (3.2)
Romania	0 (0.0)	~ ~	4 (0.8)	466 (10.0)	29 (2.1)	482 (6.2)	67 (2.0)	489 (5.3)
Russian Federation	0 (0.0)	~ ~	16 (2.5)	536 (8.1)	56 (3.6)	537 (5.2)	28 (3.6)	540 (5.5)
Scotland	- -	- -	- -	- -	- -	- -	- -	- -
Singapore	0 (0.0)	~ ~	26 (3.9)	592 (8.2)	57 (4.6)	612 (8.5)	16 (3.6)	611 (12.0)
Slovak Republic	r 0 (0.0)	~ ~	0 (0.3)	~ ~	46 (5.1)	543 (5.8)	54 (5.1)	546 (5.1)
Slovenia	r 0 (0.0)	~ ~	17 (2.8)	560 (5.2)	71 (3.3)	558 (3.1)	12 (2.5)	548 (5.6)
Spain	r 0 (0.0)	~ ~	21 (4.0)	517 (4.6)	55 (3.9)	518 (2.7)	24 (4.5)	516 (4.9)
Sweden	x x	x x	x x	x x	x x	x x	x x	x x
Switzerland	s 0 (0.0)	~ ~	18 (4.0)	507 (14.2)	73 (4.1)	528 (4.9)	8 (2.9)	518 (13.8)
Thailand	r 0 (0.0)	~ ~	14 (4.6)	514 (14.7)	56 (6.0)	534 (6.1)	30 (5.0)	528 (6.2)
United States	x x	x x	x x	x x	x x	x x	x x	x x

[1]Based on most frequent response for: explain reasoning behind an idea; represent and analyze relationships using tables, charts or graphs; work on problems for which there is no immediately obvious method of solution; write explanations about what was observed and why it happened; and put events in order and give a reason for the organization.

*Eighth grade in most countries; see Table 2 for more information about the grades tested in each country.

Countries shown in italics did not satisfy one or more guidelines for sample participation rates, age/grade specifications, or classroom sampling procedures (see Figure A.3). Background data for Bulgaria and South Africa are unavailable.

Because population coverage falls below 65%, Latvia is annotated LSS for Latvian Speaking Schools only.

( ) Standard errors appear in parentheses. Because results are rounded to the nearest whole number, some totals may appear inconsistent.

A dash (-) indicates data are not available. A tilde (~) indicates insufficient data to report achievement.

An "r" indicates teacher response data available for 70-84% of students. An "s" indicates teacher response data available for 50-69% of students.

An "x" indicates teacher response data available for <50% of students.

SOURCE: IEA Third International Mathematics and Science Study (TIMSS), 1994-95.

Table 5.11

Students' Reports on the Frequency with Which Their Teacher Gives a Demonstration of an Experiment[1] - Science - Upper Grade (Eighth Grade*)

Country	Percent of Students Responding Pretty Often or Almost Always				
	Science (Integrated)	Science Subject Areas			
		Biology	Chemistry	Earth Science	Physics
Australia	75 (1.1)	. .	. .	. .	. .
Austria	68 (2.0)	. .	. .	. .	. .
Belgium (Fl)	. .	79 (1.7)	. .	18 (1.6)	x x
[2] **Belgium (Fr)**	s 62 (3.6)	x x	. .	. .	x x
Canada	73 (1.5)	. .	. .	. .	. .
Colombia	59 (1.9)	. .	. .	. .	. .
Cyprus	89 (0.7)	. .	. .	. .	. .
Czech Republic	. .	20 (2.0)	70 (2.5)	3 (0.4)	60 (2.4)
[3] *Denmark*	. .	32 (1.8)	. .	r 20 (1.4)	81 (1.5)
England	90 (0.9)	. .	. .	. .	. .
[4] **France**	. .	56 (1.9)	. .	. .	90 (1.1)
Germany	. .	30 (1.7)	s 76 (1.8)	. .	70 (1.6)
Greece	. .	. .	75 (1.4)	43 (1.5)	77 (1.5)
Hong Kong	91 (1.1)	. .	. .	. .	. .
Hungary	. .	18 (1.5)	80 (1.7)	9 (0.8)	68 (1.5)
Iceland	. .	33 (3.6)	x x	x x	s 72 (2.3)
Iran, Islamic Rep.	63 (2.3)	. .	. .	. .	. .
Ireland	84 (1.7)	. .	. .	. .	. .
Israel	73 (2.7)	. .	. .	. .	. .
Japan	66 (1.6)	. .	. .	. .	. .
Korea	42 (1.7)	. .	. .	. .	. .
Kuwait	81 (1.4)	. .	. .	. .	. .
Latvia (LSS)	. .	49 (1.9)	77 (1.6)	. .	73 (1.7)
Lithuania	. .	25 (1.6)	57 (2.1)	10 (0.9)	59 (1.9)
[5] *Netherlands*	. .	r 28 (2.2)	. .	6 (0.6)	53 (2.4)
New Zealand	79 (1.2)	. .	. .	. .	. .
Norway	71 (1.6)	. .	. .	. .	. .
Portugal	- -	- -	- -	- -	- -
Romania	. .	49 (1.3)	63 (1.7)	34 (1.4)	60 (1.6)
Russian Federation	. .	30 (1.5)	71 (1.9)	16 (1.4)	70 (1.6)
Scotland	89 (1.1)	. .	. .	. .	. .
Singapore	86 (1.0)	. .	. .	. .	. .
Slovak Republic	. .	29 (1.5)	64 (1.8)	12 (0.8)	58 (2.0)
Slovenia	. .	37 (2.0)	72 (1.7)	. .	61 (1.8)
Spain	28 (1.8)	. .	. .	. .	. .
Sweden	. .	61 (1.9)	s 90 (0.9)	r 21 (1.2)	r 83 (1.0)
Switzerland	51 (2.1)	. .	. .	. .	. .
Thailand	84 (1.3)	. .	. .	. .	. .
United States	68 (1.4)	. .	. .	. .	. .

[1]Countries administered either an integrated science or separate subject area form of the questionnaire. A dot (.) denotes questions not administered by design. Percentages for separate science subject areas are based only on those students taking each subject.
[2]Data for Belgium (Fr) are reported for students in both integrated science classes and separate biology and physics classes.
[3]Physics data for Denmark are for students taking physics/chemistry classes.
[4]Biology data for France are for students taking biology/geology classes; physics data are for students taking physics/chemistry classes.
[5]Physics data for the Netherlands include students in both physics classes and physics/chemistry classes.
*Eighth grade in most countries; see Table 2 for more information about the grades tested in each country.
Countries shown in italics did not satisfy one or more guidelines for sample participation rates, age/grade specifications, or classroom sampling procedures (see Figure A.3). Background data for Bulgaria and South Africa are unavailable.
Because population coverage falls below 65%, Latvia is annotated LSS for Latvian Speaking Schools only.
( ) Standard errors appear in parentheses. Because results are rounded to the nearest whole number, some totals may appear inconsistent.
A dash (–) indicates data are not available.
An "r" indicates a 70-84% student response rate. An "s" indicates a 50-69% student response rate.

SOURCE: IEA Third International Mathematics and Science Study (TIMSS), 1994-95.

Table 5.12

Students' Reports on Frequency of Doing an Experiment or Practical Investigation in Science Class[1] - Upper Grade (Eighth Grade*)

Country	Percent of Students Responding Pretty Often or Almost Always				
	Science (Integrated)	Science Subject Areas			
		Biology	Chemistry	Earth Science	Physics
Australia	77 (1.4)	. .	. .	. .	. .
Austria	33 (2.2)	. .	. .	. .	. .
[2] **Belgium (Fl)**	. .	43 (1.8)	. .	11 (1.1)	x x
Belgium (Fr)	s 36 (3.2)	x x	. .	. .	x x
Canada	70 (1.8)	. .	. .	. .	. .
Colombia	47 (1.9)	. .	. .	. .	. .
Cyprus	36 (1.0)	. .	. .	. .	. .
Czech Republic	. .	20 (1.6)	35 (2.2)	3 (0.4)	29 (2.0)
[3] *Denmark*	. .	32 (2.2)	. .	r 22 (1.4)	79 (1.3)
England	91 (0.6)	. .	. .	. .	. .
[4] **France**	. .	36 (2.0)	. .	. .	74 (2.0)
Germany	. .	21 (1.6)	s 48 (3.1)	. .	41 (2.1)
Greece	. .	. .	35 (1.7)	29 (1.6)	40 (1.7)
Hong Kong	83 (2.0)	. .	. .	. .	. .
Hungary	. .	7 (0.6)	20 (1.6)	6 (0.6)	20 (1.0)
Iceland	. .	32 (3.8)	x x	x x	s 74 (3.0)
Iran, Islamic Rep.	32 (1.4)	. .	. .	. .	. .
Ireland	61 (2.7)	. .	. .	. .	. .
Israel	53 (2.8)	. .	. .	. .	. .
Japan	77 (1.5)	. .	. .	. .	. .
Korea	33 (1.7)	. .	. .	. .	. .
Kuwait	47 (2.0)	. .	. .	. .	. .
Latvia (LSS)	. .	36 (1.7)	50 (2.3)	. .	46 (1.9)
Lithuania	. .	17 (1.8)	24 (1.6)	8 (0.6)	29 (1.6)
[5] *Netherlands*	. .	r 20 (2.6)	. .	5 (0.8)	49 (2.8)
New Zealand	81 (1.3)	. .	. .	. .	. .
Norway	66 (2.2)	. .	. .	. .	. .
[6] **Portugal**	. .	26 (1.5)	. .	. .	36 (1.7)
Romania	. .	34 (1.1)	49 (1.8)	32 (1.3)	49 (1.7)
Russian Federation	. .	17 (1.0)	45 (2.4)	12 (1.0)	44 (1.6)
Scotland	87 (0.9)	. .	. .	. .	. .
Singapore	85 (1.0)	. .	. .	. .	. .
Slovak Republic	. .	19 (1.1)	25 (1.5)	12 (0.7)	30 (1.5)
Slovenia	. .	15 (1.3)	25 (1.9)	. .	31 (1.6)
Spain	23 (1.6)	. .	. .	. .	. .
Sweden	. .	65 (1.8)	s 92 (0.8)	r 23 (1.1)	r 82 (1.3)
Switzerland	35 (1.7)	. .	. .	. .	. .
Thailand	55 (1.2)	. .	. .	. .	. .
United States	62 (1.7)	. .	. .	. .	. .

[1] Countries administered either an integrated science or separate subject area form of the questionnaire. A dot (.) denotes questions not administered by design. Percentages for separate science subject areas are based only on those students taking each subject.
[2] Data for Belgium (Fr) are reported for students in both integrated science classes and separate biology and physics classes.
[3] Physics data for Denmark are for students taking physics/chemistry classes.
[4] Biology data for France are for students taking biology/geology classes; physics data are for students taking physics/chemistry classes.
[5] Physics data for the Netherlands include students in both physics classes and physics/chemistry classes.
[6] Biology data for Portugal are for students taking natural science classes; physics data are for students taking physical science classes.
*Eighth grade in most countries; see Table 2 for more information about the grades tested in each country.
Countries shown in italics did not satisfy one or more guidelines for sample participation rates, age/grade specifications, or classroom sampling procedures (see Figure A.3). Background data for Bulgaria and South Africa are unavailable.
Because population coverage falls below 65%, Latvia is annotated LSS for Latvian Speaking Schools only.
( ) Standard errors appear in parentheses. Because results are rounded to the nearest whole number, some totals may appear inconsistent.
An "r" indicates a 70-84% student response rate. An "s" indicates a 50-69% student response rate. An "x" indicates a <50% student response rate.

SOURCE: IEA Third International Mathematics and Science Study (TIMSS), 1994-95.

Table 5.13

Students' Reports on Frequency of Using Things from Everyday Life in Solving Science Problems[1] - Upper Grade (Eighth Grade*)

Country	Percent of Students Responding Pretty Often or Almost Always				
	Science (Integrated)	Science Subject Areas			
		Biology	Chemistry	Earth Science	Physics
Australia	43 (0.8)	. .	. .	. .	. .
Austria	31 (1.0)	. .	. .	. .	. .
Belgium (Fl)	. .	44 (1.2)	. .	40 (1.2)	x x
2 Belgium (Fr)	x x	x x	. .	. .	x x
Canada	52 (1.1)	. .	. .	. .	. .
Colombia	52 (1.4)	. .	. .	. .	. .
Cyprus	65 (1.1)	. .	. .	. .	. .
Czech Republic	. .	33 (1.3)	31 (1.5)	35 (1.5)	39 (1.3)
3 *Denmark*	. .	23 (1.2)	. .	r 19 (1.1)	27 (1.2)
England	51 (1.2)	. .	. .	. .	. .
4 France	. .	41 (1.1)	. .	. .	51 (1.5)
Germany	. .	34 (1.5)	s 34 (1.7)	. .	37 (1.3)
Greece	. .	. .	48 (1.2)	52 (1.5)	65 (1.2)
Hong Kong	57 (1.5)	. .	. .	. .	. .
Hungary	. .	35 (1.4)	29 (1.2)	32 (1.3)	33 (1.1)
Iceland	. .	31 (2.2)	x x	x x	s 38 (1.9)
Iran, Islamic Rep.	53 (1.4)	. .	. .	. .	. .
Ireland	41 (1.2)	. .	. .	. .	. .
Israel	40 (2.0)	. .	. .	. .	. .
Japan	23 (0.9)	. .	. .	. .	. .
Korea	17 (0.8)	. .	. .	. .	. .
Kuwait	47 (2.0)	. .	. .	. .	. .
Latvia (LSS)	. .	65 (1.4)	73 (1.3)	. .	77 (1.1)
Lithuania	. .	24 (1.2)	30 (1.2)	22 (1.1)	44 (1.4)
5 *Netherlands*	. .	r 36 (1.5)	. .	31 (1.4)	31 (1.4)
New Zealand	48 (1.1)	. .	. .	. .	. .
Norway	31 (1.0)	. .	. .	. .	. .
6 Portugal	. .	35 (1.2)	. .	. .	43 (1.4)
Romania	. .	52 (1.2)	41 (1.3)	45 (1.4)	46 (1.1)
Russian Federation	. .	36 (2.7)	32 (2.0)	34 (1.8)	40 (1.8)
Scotland	57 (1.4)	. .	. .	. .	. .
Singapore	59 (1.1)	. .	. .	. .	. .
Slovak Republic	. .	35 (1.6)	30 (1.2)	40 (1.4)	31 (1.2)
Slovenia	. .	41 (1.7)	32 (1.2)	. .	24 (1.9)
Spain	44 (1.3)	. .	. .	. .	. .
Sweden	. .	37 (1.1)	s 43 (1.7)	r 33 (1.3)	r 48 (1.3)
Switzerland	40 (1.1)	. .	. .	. .	. .
Thailand	48 (1.3)	. .	. .	. .	. .
United States	51 (0.9)	. .	. .	. .	. .

[1]Countries administered either an integrated science or separate subject area form of the questionnaire. A dot (.) denotes questions not administered by design. Percentages for separate science subject areas are based only on those students taking each subject.
[2]Data for Belgium (Fr) are reported for students in both integrated science classes and separate biology and physics classes.
[3]Physics data for Denmark are for students taking physics/chemistry classes.
[4]Biology data for France are for students taking biology/geology classes; physics data are for students taking physics/chemistry classes.
[5]Physics data for the Netherlands include students in both physics classes and physics/chemistry classes.
[6]Biology data for Portugal are for students taking natural science classes; physics data are for students taking physical science classes.
*Eighth grade in most countries; see Table 2 for more information about the grades tested in each country.
Countries shown in italics did not satisfy one or more guidelines for sample participation rates, age/grade specifications, or classroom sampling procedures (see Figure A.3). Background data for Bulgaria and South Africa are unavailable.
Because population coverage falls below 65%, Latvia is annotated LSS for Latvian Speaking Schools only.
( ) Standard errors appear in parentheses. Because results are rounded to the nearest whole number, some totals may appear inconsistent.
An "r" indicates a 70-84% student response rate. An "s" indicates a 50-69% student response rate. An "x" indicates a <50% student response rate.

SOURCE: IEA Third International Mathematics and Science Study (TIMSS), 1994-95.

How Are Calculators and Computers Used?

As shown in Table 5.14, nearly all eighth-grade students reported having a calculator in the home, except in Iran (61%), Romania (62%), and Thailand (68%). Internationally, fewer students reported a computer in the home, even though more than three-fourths did so in Denmark, England, Iceland, Ireland, Israel, the Netherlands, and Scotland. Between 50% and 75% so reported in Australia, Austria, Belgium (Flemish), Belgium (French), Canada, France, Germany, Kuwait, New Zealand, Norway, Sweden, Switzerland, and the United States. Fewer than 20% of the students reported home computers in Colombia, Iran, Latvia (LSS), Romania, and Thailand.

Table 5.15 provides teachers' reports about how often calculators are used in eighth-grade science classes. Even though calculators appear to be widely available in most countries, teachers reported relatively low levels of calculator use in science classrooms. Only in Hungary, Kuwait, Latvia (LSS), Lithuania, the Russian Federation, and the Slovak Republic were the majority of students reported to use calculators as often as once or twice a week. The lowest levels of usage were reported in Japan and Korea, with more than 70% of students taught by teachers who reported that calculators are never or hardly ever used in their science classes. Although using calculators can take the drudgery out of mathematical computations in science class and free the learner to concentrate on higher-order problem-solving skills, another point of view is that permitting unrestricted use of calculators may damage students' mastery of basic computational skills.

As revealed in Table 5.16, teachers reported that students use calculators in science classes for a variety of purposes. Across countries, no single use appears to predominate, although routine computation, checking answers, and solving complex problems are frequent purposes in many countries.

Table 5.17 contains teachers' reports about how often computers are used in science class to solve exercises or problems. Such usage is reportedly quite rare, and only in Canada, Denmark, England, Iceland, Israel, Kuwait, Slovenia, and Switzerland did more than 20% of the students have teachers who reported at least some usage. Table 5.18 contains students' responses to a similar question, although expressed as the percentage of students using computers to solve problems in science class at least once in a while. Internationally, teachers and students agree that the computer is rarely used in most students' science lessons. Students reported moderate use of computers (more than 20% of the students in some lessons) in Austria, Canada, Cyprus, Denmark, England, Greece, Israel, New Zealand, Romania, the Russian Federation, Scotland, Slovenia, Sweden, and the United States.

Table 5.14

Students' Reports on Having a Calculator and Computer in the Home
Science - Upper Grade (Eighth Grade*)

Country	Calculator				Computer			
	Yes		No		Yes		No	
	Percent of Students	Mean Achievement	Percent of Students	Mean Achievement	Percent of Students	Mean Achievement	Percent of Students	Mean Achievement
Australia	97 (0.3)	548 (3.8)	3 (0.3)	467 (13.8)	73 (1.2)	554 (4.3)	27 (1.2)	525 (4.2)
Austria	100 (0.1)	558 (3.8)	0 (0.1)	~ ~	59 (1.5)	565 (4.0)	41 (1.5)	548 (4.7)
Belgium (Fl)	97 (0.8)	553 (4.0)	3 (0.8)	467 (11.4)	67 (1.3)	558 (4.2)	33 (1.3)	536 (5.3)
Belgium (Fr)	98 (0.3)	472 (2.9)	2 (0.3)	~ ~	60 (1.4)	481 (3.0)	40 (1.4)	457 (3.6)
Canada	98 (0.2)	533 (2.6)	2 (0.2)	~ ~	61 (1.3)	543 (2.5)	39 (1.3)	513 (3.1)
Colombia	88 (1.5)	415 (3.6)	12 (1.5)	389 (9.1)	11 (1.2)	431 (9.7)	89 (1.2)	409 (3.9)
Cyprus	96 (0.4)	466 (2.0)	4 (0.4)	403 (6.3)	39 (0.9)	472 (2.9)	61 (0.9)	459 (2.5)
Czech Republic	99 (0.2)	574 (4.3)	1 (0.2)	~ ~	36 (1.2)	593 (6.0)	64 (1.2)	563 (3.6)
Denmark	99 (0.3)	479 (3.1)	1 (0.3)	~ ~	76 (1.2)	484 (3.1)	24 (1.2)	464 (4.7)
England	99 (0.2)	554 (3.5)	1 (0.2)	~ ~	89 (0.8)	553 (3.7)	11 (0.8)	558 (6.5)
France	99 (0.2)	499 (2.6)	1 (0.2)	~ ~	50 (1.3)	504 (3.0)	50 (1.3)	492 (3.0)
Germany	99 (0.2)	532 (4.7)	1 (0.2)	~ ~	71 (1.0)	538 (4.6)	29 (1.0)	517 (6.4)
Greece	87 (0.6)	504 (2.2)	13 (0.6)	455 (3.7)	29 (1.0)	512 (4.3)	71 (1.0)	492 (2.1)
Hong Kong	99 (0.1)	524 (4.7)	1 (0.1)	~ ~	39 (1.9)	539 (5.0)	61 (1.9)	514 (4.9)
Hungary	97 (0.4)	556 (2.8)	3 (0.4)	496 (14.3)	37 (1.2)	581 (3.2)	63 (1.2)	539 (3.1)
Iceland	100 (0.1)	494 (4.1)	0 (0.1)	~ ~	77 (1.4)	494 (4.6)	23 (1.4)	491 (3.6)
Iran, Islamic Rep.	61 (1.8)	482 (2.8)	39 (1.8)	457 (3.6)	4 (0.4)	474 (11.3)	96 (0.4)	472 (2.4)
Ireland	97 (0.3)	540 (4.4)	3 (0.3)	506 (9.0)	78 (1.1)	542 (4.7)	22 (1.1)	530 (6.0)
Israel	99 (0.3)	529 (5.3)	1 (0.3)	~ ~	76 (2.1)	540 (5.8)	24 (2.1)	492 (4.6)
Japan	- -	- -	- -	- -	- -	- -	- -	- -
Korea	91 (0.5)	567 (2.0)	9 (0.5)	540 (5.5)	39 (1.2)	584 (2.7)	61 (1.2)	553 (2.2)
Kuwait	84 (1.4)	434 (3.6)	16 (1.4)	412 (6.0)	53 (2.1)	431 (5.4)	47 (2.1)	430 (3.3)
Latvia (LSS)	94 (0.5)	486 (2.7)	6 (0.5)	475 (5.9)	13 (0.9)	487 (5.3)	87 (0.9)	485 (2.6)
Lithuania	90 (1.0)	481 (3.5)	10 (1.0)	441 (6.4)	42 (1.4)	476 (3.9)	58 (1.4)	477 (4.1)
Netherlands	100 (0.1)	561 (5.2)	0 (0.1)	~ ~	85 (1.2)	563 (6.3)	15 (1.2)	547 (6.6)
New Zealand	99 (0.2)	528 (4.3)	1 (0.2)	~ ~	60 (1.3)	538 (4.8)	40 (1.3)	509 (4.8)
Norway	99 (0.2)	528 (1.9)	1 (0.2)	~ ~	64 (1.1)	534 (2.4)	36 (1.1)	516 (3.0)
Portugal	99 (0.2)	480 (2.3)	1 (0.2)	~ ~	39 (1.8)	493 (3.2)	61 (1.8)	471 (2.2)
Romania	62 (1.5)	495 (5.1)	38 (1.5)	473 (6.8)	19 (1.2)	504 (7.1)	81 (1.2)	482 (4.9)
Russian Federation	92 (0.8)	541 (3.8)	8 (0.8)	508 (8.8)	35 (1.5)	542 (4.7)	65 (1.5)	536 (4.7)
Scotland	98 (0.4)	520 (5.3)	2 (0.4)	~ ~	90 (0.6)	518 (5.3)	10 (0.6)	522 (8.6)
Singapore	100 (0.1)	608 (5.6)	0 (0.1)	~ ~	49 (1.5)	626 (6.2)	51 (1.5)	590 (5.4)
Slovak Republic	99 (0.2)	545 (3.2)	1 (0.2)	~ ~	31 (1.2)	561 (3.9)	69 (1.2)	537 (3.5)
Slovenia	98 (0.3)	561 (2.5)	2 (0.3)	~ ~	47 (1.3)	579 (3.2)	53 (1.3)	543 (2.9)
Spain	99 (0.2)	517 (1.7)	1 (0.2)	~ ~	42 (1.2)	528 (2.7)	58 (1.2)	509 (2.1)
Sweden	99 (0.1)	536 (2.9)	1 (0.1)	~ ~	60 (1.3)	547 (2.9)	40 (1.3)	518 (3.6)
Switzerland	99 (0.2)	523 (2.6)	1 (0.2)	~ ~	66 (1.2)	530 (2.9)	34 (1.2)	507 (3.2)
Thailand	68 (2.2)	528 (4.5)	32 (2.2)	520 (3.1)	4 (0.9)	542 (10.7)	96 (0.9)	525 (3.6)
United States	98 (0.3)	536 (4.6)	2 (0.3)	~ ~	59 (1.7)	555 (4.1)	41 (1.7)	506 (5.4)

*Eighth grade in most countries; see Table 2 for more information about the grades tested in each country.
Countries shown in italics did not satisfy one or more guidelines for sample participation rates, age/grade specifications, or classroom sampling procedures (see Figure A.3). Background data for Bulgaria and South Africa are unavailable.
Because population coverage falls below 65%, Latvia is annotated LSS for Latvian Speaking Schools only.
( ) Standard errors appear in parentheses. Because results are rounded to the nearest whole number, some totals may appear inconsistent.
A dash (-) indicates data are not available. A tilde (~) indicates insufficient data to report achievement.

SOURCE: IEA Third International Mathematics and Science Study (TIMSS), 1994-95.

Table 5.15

Teachers' Reports on Frequency of Students' Use of Calculators in Science Class[1] Upper Grade (Eighth Grade*)

Country	Never or Hardly Ever		Once or Twice a Month		Once or Twice a Week		Almost Every Day	
	Percent of Students	Mean Achievement	Percent of Students	Mean Achievement	Percent of Students	Mean Achievement	Percent of Students	Mean Achievement
Australia	x x	x x	x x	x x	x x	x x	x x	x x
Austria	r 61 (3.0)	563 (3.4)	32 (3.2)	561 (5.2)	4 (1.3)	566 (9.0)	3 (0.8)	557 (16.4)
Belgium (Fl)	r 61 (4.5)	550 (8.5)	14 (2.5)	572 (5.5)	9 (2.5)	557 (4.9)	16 (2.9)	560 (4.8)
Belgium (Fr)	s 31 (5.9)	479 (6.5)	37 (5.3)	481 (5.1)	9 (3.0)	506 (7.9)	23 (3.9)	486 (6.1)
Canada	r 16 (2.7)	532 (7.7)	38 (4.1)	536 (6.7)	21 (2.7)	538 (4.2)	25 (4.0)	539 (5.5)
Colombia	r 50 (5.2)	420 (4.8)	21 (3.8)	407 (6.6)	17 (5.0)	396 (18.1)	12 (3.1)	416 (13.1)
Cyprus	s 51 (3.9)	454 (3.5)	13 (2.5)	467 (8.9)	12 (3.1)	465 (8.4)	25 (3.7)	462 (5.2)
Czech Republic	r 22 (1.9)	572 (5.5)	30 (3.5)	582 (7.9)	31 (2.8)	572 (7.7)	17 (2.4)	575 (3.9)
Denmark	s 56 (5.8)	476 (4.9)	26 (5.3)	478 (6.1)	10 (3.8)	500 (10.8)	9 (3.6)	479 (6.0)
England	x x	x x	x x	x x	x x	x x	x x	x x
France	r 17 (2.4)	505 (5.0)	39 (3.6)	499 (3.5)	22 (2.4)	499 (4.4)	22 (2.8)	496 (3.8)
Germany	s 40 (4.5)	536 (7.3)	16 (3.2)	518 (14.2)	20 (3.5)	560 (9.2)	24 (3.6)	530 (12.5)
Greece	64 (4.0)	496 (2.7)	8 (1.9)	499 (6.0)	15 (2.7)	495 (5.8)	13 (2.5)	504 (5.3)
Hong Kong	59 (5.8)	525 (7.5)	24 (5.1)	516 (11.5)	5 (2.7)	488 (26.1)	12 (3.5)	542 (10.5)
Hungary	r 31 (2.9)	551 (4.2)	8 (1.5)	566 (6.9)	20 (2.0)	549 (4.1)	40 (3.3)	554 (5.4)
Iceland	s 31 (8.3)	489 (11.3)	35 (8.4)	484 (3.6)	17 (4.0)	488 (7.8)	17 (4.3)	486 (6.3)
Iran, Islamic Rep.	68 (5.3)	469 (3.3)	22 (4.7)	467 (4.3)	6 (1.7)	489 (7.0)	4 (1.9)	465 (7.3)
Ireland	s 54 (4.8)	536 (7.7)	28 (3.9)	547 (9.4)	12 (3.5)	567 (13.2)	6 (2.2)	539 (19.1)
Israel	s 53 (8.8)	535 (11.7)	35 (8.7)	510 (16.1)	4 (3.1)	514 (46.3)	8 (4.8)	535 (4.1)
Japan	91 (2.4)	570 (2.1)	9 (2.4)	580 (8.1)	0 (0.0)	~ ~	0 (0.5)	~ ~
Korea	73 (3.5)	568 (2.3)	12 (2.4)	555 (6.1)	11 (1.9)	556 (5.0)	4 (2.3)	575 (7.6)
Kuwait	r 16 (5.5)	419 (6.8)	24 (5.9)	443 (7.6)	30 (7.5)	418 (5.6)	29 (7.9)	425 (12.4)
Latvia (LSS)	s 27 (2.2)	488 (3.7)	18 (2.1)	483 (4.6)	27 (2.1)	488 (3.4)	29 (2.4)	480 (3.4)
Lithuania	r 35 (2.0)	476 (4.4)	10 (1.3)	472 (8.1)	21 (2.2)	475 (5.8)	34 (2.4)	479 (5.0)
Netherlands	34 (3.0)	548 (10.8)	35 (3.1)	562 (6.9)	22 (3.5)	586 (8.4)	9 (1.9)	561 (10.0)
New Zealand	30 (3.9)	511 (6.6)	40 (4.2)	528 (7.2)	21 (3.4)	549 (9.4)	9 (2.5)	515 (16.0)
Norway	s 35 (5.0)	522 (4.2)	34 (4.7)	530 (3.6)	15 (4.1)	527 (6.8)	17 (4.1)	518 (6.0)
Portugal	36 (2.1)	482 (2.9)	17 (2.2)	481 (3.7)	19 (2.5)	484 (4.7)	28 (2.0)	473 (3.8)
Romania	66 (2.3)	481 (5.3)	10 (1.3)	484 (7.3)	12 (1.5)	501 (9.3)	12 (1.6)	499 (8.5)
Russian Federation	40 (2.3)	531 (5.2)	6 (1.3)	530 (10.8)	32 (2.9)	533 (5.8)	22 (2.9)	549 (5.7)
Scotland	- -	- -	- -	- -	- -	- -	- -	- -
Singapore	19 (3.2)	601 (13.7)	31 (4.1)	604 (10.3)	17 (3.4)	598 (15.4)	32 (4.4)	623 (9.5)
Slovak Republic	r 1 (0.8)	~ ~	9 (2.9)	533 (13.9)	42 (4.6)	545 (5.9)	48 (5.0)	543 (5.6)
Slovenia	r 29 (2.2)	561 (3.1)	27 (2.7)	556 (5.4)	27 (2.7)	554 (3.3)	18 (2.2)	561 (4.7)
Spain	r 40 (4.3)	515 (3.7)	14 (3.6)	517 (6.1)	17 (3.4)	529 (3.9)	29 (4.3)	513 (3.9)
Sweden	x x	x x	x x	x x	x x	x x	x x	x x
Switzerland	x x	x x	x x	x x	x x	x x	x x	x x
Thailand	r 62 (6.0)	526 (5.8)	20 (4.7)	527 (9.0)	7 (3.5)	527 (14.8)	11 (4.1)	543 (13.0)
United States	x x	x x	x x	x x	x x	x x	x x	x x

[1]Based on most frequent response for: checking answers, test and exams, routine computations, solving complex problems, and exploring number concepts.
*Eighth grade in most countries; see Table 2 for more information about the grades tested in each country.
Countries shown in italics did not satisfy one or more guidelines for sample participation rates, age/grade specifications, or classroom sampling procedures (see Figure A.3). Background data for Bulgaria and South Africa are unavailable.
Because population coverage falls below 65%, Latvia is annotated LSS for Latvian Speaking Schools only.
( ) Standard errors appear in parentheses. Because results are rounded to the nearest whole number, some totals may appear inconsistent.
A dash (-) indicates data are not available. A tilde (~) indicates insufficient data to report achievement.
An "r" indicates teacher response data available for 70-84% of students. An "s" indicates teacher response data available for 50-69% of students.
An "x" indicates teacher response data available for <50% of students.

SOURCE: IEA Third International Mathematics and Science Study (TIMSS), 1994-95.

Table 5.16

Teachers' Reports on Ways in Which Calculators Are Used At Least Once or Twice a Week - Science - Upper Grade (Eighth Grade*)

Country	Percent of Students by Type of Use					
	Never or Hardly Ever Use Calculators	Checking Answers	Tests and Exams	Routine Computations	Solving Complex Problems	Exploring Number Concepts
Australia	x x	x x	x x	x x	x x	x x
Austria	r 61 (3.0)	r 5 (1.4)	r 2 (0.9)	r 5 (1.4)	r 3 (1.0)	r 2 (0.6)
Belgium (Fl)	r 61 (4.5)	r 17 (3.8)	r 14 (2.9)	r 20 (3.9)	r 20 (3.3)	r 8 (2.6)
Belgium (Fr)	s 31 (5.9)	s 27 (4.6)	s 23 (4.5)	s 29 (4.8)	s 23 (4.5)	s 12 (3.7)
Canada	r 16 (2.7)	r 34 (3.9)	r 23 (4.0)	r 39 (4.2)	r 32 (4.0)	s 21 (3.6)
Colombia	r 50 (5.2)	r 20 (5.1)	r 9 (2.7)	r 21 (5.4)	r 17 (3.6)	r 18 (3.5)
Cyprus	s 51 (3.9)	s 23 (4.1)	s 17 (3.4)	s 29 (3.5)	s 28 (4.0)	s 11 (2.3)
Czech Republic	r 22 (1.9)	r 39 (2.9)	r 17 (2.9)	r 37 (2.9)	r 29 (2.9)	r 11 (2.1)
Denmark	s 56 (5.8)	s 12 (4.4)	s 8 (3.7)	s 14 (4.6)	s 10 (3.4)	s 3 (2.2)
England	x x	x x	x x	x x	x x	x x
France	r 17 (2.4)	r 29 (3.7)	r 24 (3.4)	r 39 (3.1)	r 19 (3.3)	r 12 (3.1)
Germany	s 40 (4.5)	s 40 (4.7)	s 16 (4.4)	s 43 (4.8)	s 28 (4.6)	s 16 (4.5)
Greece	64 (4.0)	22 (3.5)	6 (1.9)	23 (3.3)	16 (2.8)	8 (2.2)
Hong Kong	59 (5.8)	5 (2.7)	8 (3.3)	16 (4.1)	7 (3.2)	6 (3.0)
Hungary	r 31 (2.9)	s 39 (3.1)	s 22 (2.8)	s 44 (3.2)	s 50 (3.1)	s 54 (3.5)
Iceland	s 31 (8.3)	s 27 (4.8)	s 19 (4.6)	s 32 (5.0)	s 30 (4.9)	s 20 (4.4)
Iran, Islamic Rep.	68 (5.3)	1 (0.9)	4 (1.9)	3 (1.8)	6 (1.8)	4 (1.5)
Ireland	s 54 (4.8)	s 12 (3.1)	s 4 (1.7)	s 15 (3.4)	s 7 (2.3)	s 2 (1.1)
Israel	s 53 (8.8)	s 7 (4.9)	s 8 (5.5)	s 13 (6.2)	s 9 (5.3)	s 6 (4.9)
Japan	91 (2.4)	0 (0.5)	0 (0.0)	0 (0.0)	0 (0.5)	0 (0.0)
Korea	73 (3.5)	5 (2.4)	5 (2.4)	10 (2.7)	8 (2.2)	8 (2.6)
Kuwait	r 16 (5.5)	r 40 (8.3)	r 27 (7.1)	r 53 (10.0)	r 43 (6.9)	r 38 (8.0)
Latvia (LSS)	s 27 (2.2)	s 44 (2.6)	s 25 (2.5)	s 55 (2.2)	s 38 (2.4)	s 14 (2.3)
Lithuania	r 35 (2.0)	s 48 (2.1)	s 16 (2.0)	s 49 (1.8)	s 46 (2.2)	s 15 (2.0)
Netherlands	34 (3.0)	23 (2.5)	13 (2.5)	r 28 (2.4)	r 14 (2.3)	r 5 (1.6)
New Zealand	30 (3.9)	6 (1.8)	5 (1.8)	27 (3.8)	11 (2.8)	6 (2.3)
Norway	s 35 (5.0)	s 24 (4.8)	s 14 (3.9)	s 27 (4.9)	- -	- -
Portugal	36 (2.1)	40 (2.2)	12 (1.9)	39 (2.0)	30 (2.5)	17 (2.1)
Romania	66 (2.3)	17 (1.8)	r 4 (0.9)	r 19 (1.7)	r 19 (1.8)	r 5 (1.0)
Russian Federation	40 (2.3)	44 (2.5)	14 (1.9)	50 (2.1)	43 (2.6)	27 (2.7)
Scotland	- -	- -	- -	- -	- -	- -
Singapore	19 (3.2)	42 (4.7)	33 (4.3)	39 (4.9)	38 (4.7)	31 (4.2)
Slovak Republic	r 1 (0.8)	r 70 (4.1)	r 29 (4.7)	r 81 (3.8)	r 60 (4.8)	r 59 (4.6)
Slovenia	r 29 (2.2)	r 30 (2.5)	r 12 (1.8)	r 34 (2.9)	r 28 (2.6)	r 15 (2.3)
Spain	r 40 (4.3)	r 33 (4.8)	r 13 (3.3)	r 34 (4.7)	r 36 (4.9)	r 19 (3.5)
Sweden	x x	x x	x x	x x	x x	x x
Switzerland	x x	x x	x x	x x	x x	x x
Thailand	r 62 (6.0)	s 8 (3.5)	s 0 (0.4)	r 14 (4.7)	s 17 (5.0)	s 11 (3.9)
United States	x x	x x	x x	x x	x x	x x

*Eighth grade in most countries; see Table 2 for more information about the grades tested in each country.
Countries shown in italics did not satisfy one or more guidelines for sample participation rates, age/grade specifications, or classroom sampling procedures (see Figure A.3). Background data for Bulgaria and South Africa are unavailable.
Because population coverage falls below 65%, Latvia is annotated LSS for Latvian Speaking Schools only.
( ) Standard errors appear in parentheses. Because results are rounded to the nearest whole number, some totals may appear inconsistent.
A dash (-) indicates data are not available.
An "r" indicates teacher response data available for 70-84% of students. An "s" indicates teacher response data available for 50-69% of students.
An "x" indicates teacher response data available for <50% of students.

SOURCE: IEA Third International Mathematics and Science Study (TIMSS), 1994-95.

Table 5.17

Teachers' Reports on Frequency of Using Computers in Science Class To Solve Exercises or Problems - Upper Grade (Eighth Grade*)

Country		Never or Almost Never		Some Lessons		Most or Every Lesson	
		Percent of Students	Mean Achievement	Percent of Students	Mean Achievement	Percent of Students	Mean Achievement
Australia		x x	x x	x x	x x	x x	x x
Austria	r	85 (2.6)	565 (3.1)	14 (2.6)	547 (7.1)	1 (0.2)	~ ~
Belgium (Fl)	r	98 (1.0)	555 (5.9)	2 (1.0)	~ ~	0 (0.0)	~ ~
Belgium (Fr)	s	95 (2.0)	483 (3.5)	5 (2.0)	491 (13.5)	0 (0.0)	~ ~
Canada	r	76 (3.3)	536 (2.9)	23 (3.4)	535 (9.9)	0 (0.4)	~ ~
Colombia	r	95 (2.5)	413 (4.5)	3 (1.4)	439 (51.1)	2 (2.1)	~ ~
Cyprus	s	92 (1.1)	456 (2.6)	8 (1.1)	483 (7.5)	0 (0.0)	~ ~
Czech Republic		93 (2.0)	573 (4.6)	6 (1.7)	603 (11.0)	2 (1.1)	~ ~
Denmark	s	63 (5.9)	482 (4.4)	35 (5.8)	475 (5.2)	2 (2.0)	~ ~
England	s	70 (3.3)	567 (6.9)	30 (3.3)	558 (7.3)	0 (0.0)	~ ~
France		97 (1.2)	499 (2.5)	3 (1.2)	508 (11.4)	0 (0.0)	~ ~
Germany	s	95 (1.8)	536 (6.2)	5 (1.8)	539 (23.1)	0 (0.0)	~ ~
Greece		93 (3.2)	498 (2.2)	6 (3.2)	481 (5.0)	0 (0.2)	~ ~
Hong Kong		95 (2.5)	523 (5.3)	4 (2.2)	487 (38.3)	1 (1.2)	~ ~
Hungary		- -	- -	- -	- -	- -	- -
Iceland	s	73 (6.1)	489 (4.5)	22 (6.0)	484 (4.0)	5 (1.7)	479 (9.2)
Iran, Islamic Rep.		99 (0.5)	469 (2.4)	1 (0.5)	~ ~	0 (0.0)	~ ~
Ireland	s	96 (1.4)	540 (6.0)	4 (1.4)	588 (14.8)	0 (0.0)	~ ~
Israel	r	75 (8.0)	538 (8.3)	24 (7.9)	498 (13.3)	1 (1.1)	~ ~
Japan		84 (2.8)	572 (2.0)	16 (2.8)	569 (5.8)	0 (0.0)	~ ~
Korea		96 (1.7)	566 (2.2)	4 (1.7)	555 (8.3)	0 (0.0)	~ ~
Kuwait	r	78 (7.7)	427 (4.5)	21 (7.6)	420 (7.5)	1 (0.9)	~ ~
Latvia (LSS)	s	91 (1.5)	485 (2.6)	6 (1.3)	483 (6.5)	3 (0.8)	479 (9.6)
Lithuania	r	96 (1.1)	477 (4.2)	3 (0.9)	482 (13.6)	1 (0.5)	~ ~
Netherlands	r	85 (2.6)	559 (7.4)	15 (2.6)	578 (7.9)	0 (0.0)	~ ~
New Zealand		90 (2.7)	526 (4.7)	10 (2.7)	527 (12.5)	0 (0.0)	~ ~
Norway	s	96 (1.9)	525 (2.3)	4 (1.9)	523 (12.8)	0 (0.0)	~ ~
Portugal		99 (0.5)	480 (2.5)	0 (0.3)	~ ~	0 (0.4)	~ ~
Romania	r	94 (1.3)	487 (4.7)	4 (1.1)	504 (11.9)	2 (0.7)	~ ~
Russian Federation		88 (1.7)	538 (4.6)	8 (1.5)	534 (8.0)	3 (1.0)	528 (15.1)
Scotland		- -	- -	- -	- -	- -	- -
Singapore		95 (1.5)	606 (5.8)	5 (1.5)	625 (22.3)	0 (0.0)	~ ~
Slovak Republic	r	96 (2.0)	546 (3.9)	4 (2.0)	514 (7.8)	0 (0.0)	~ ~
Slovenia	r	60 (3.1)	556 (3.5)	26 (3.1)	559 (4.3)	15 (2.2)	558 (5.3)
Spain	r	92 (2.7)	519 (2.1)	7 (2.5)	501 (8.6)	1 (0.9)	~ ~
Sweden		x x	x x	x x	x x	x x	x x
Switzerland	s	78 (4.3)	527 (4.9)	22 (4.3)	510 (12.7)	0 (0.0)	~ ~
Thailand	r	92 (3.6)	530 (5.3)	3 (2.2)	521 (15.5)	5 (2.9)	513 (8.2)
United States		x x	x x	x x	x x	x x	x x

*Eighth grade in most countries; see Table 2 for more information about the grades tested in each country.
Countries shown in italics did not satisfy one or more guidelines for sample participation rates, age/grade specifications, or classroom sampling procedures (see Figure A.3). Background data for Bulgaria and South Africa are unavailable.
Because population coverage falls below 65%, Latvia is annotated LSS for Latvian Speaking Schools only.
( ) Standard errors appear in parentheses. Because results are rounded to the nearest whole number, some totals may appear inconsistent.
A dash (-) indicates data are not available. A tilde (~) indicates insufficient data to report achievement.
An "r" indicates teacher response data available for 70-84% of students. An "s" indicates teacher response data available for 50-69% of students.
An "x" indicates teacher response data available for <50% of students.

SOURCE: IEA Third International Mathematics and Science Study (TIMSS), 1994-95.

Table 5.18

Students' Reports on Frequency of Using Computers in Science Class[1] Upper Grade (Eighth Grade*)

Country	Percent of Students Responding At Least Once in a While				
	Science (Integrated)	Science Subject Areas			
		Biology	Chemistry	Earth Science	Physics
Australia	16 (1.4)	. .	. .	. .	. .
Austria	23 (2.4)	. .	. .	. .	. .
Belgium (Fl)	. .	9 (1.1)	. .	8 (0.9)	x x
[2] **Belgium (Fr)**	x x	x x	. .	. .	x x
Canada	24 (1.5)	. .	. .	. .	. .
Colombia	6 (0.5)	. .	. .	. .	. .
Cyprus	23 (1.1)	. .	. .	. .	. .
Czech Republic	. .	2 (0.5)	5 (1.5)	6 (2.3)	6 (1.9)
[3] *Denmark*	. .	36 (2.9)	. .	r 39 (2.6)	17 (2.1)
England	36 (2.5)	. .	. .	. .	. .
[4] **France**	. .	8 (1.5)	. .	. .	12 (1.5)
Germany	. .	10 (0.9)	s 13 (1.6)	. .	15 (1.6)
Greece	. .	. .	22 (1.0)	23 (1.4)	24 (1.2)
Hong Kong	11 (0.9)	. .	. .	. .	. .
Hungary	. .	5 (0.5)	7 (0.9)	6 (0.6)	8 (0.8)
Iceland	. .	11 (2.5)	x x	x x	s 12 (2.4)
Iran, Islamic Rep.	9 (0.9)	. .	. .	. .	. .
Ireland	8 (1.3)	. .	. .	. .	. .
Israel	21 (4.0)	. .	. .	. .	. .
Japan	16 (2.4)	. .	. .	. .	. .
Korea	9 (0.8)	. .	. .	. .	. .
Kuwait	19 (1.8)	. .	. .	. .	. .
Latvia (LSS)	. .	3 (0.4)	5 (0.6)	. .	8 (1.3)
Lithuania	. .	4 (0.5)	6 (0.7)	6 (0.6)	8 (0.8)
[5] *Netherlands*	. .	r 11 (1.9)	. .	16 (2.6)	12 (1.7)
New Zealand	20 (2.2)	. .	. .	. .	. .
Norway	12 (1.3)	. .	. .	. .	. .
[6] **Portugal**	. .	4 (0.4)	. .	. .	7 (0.8)
Romania	. .	21 (1.0)	24 (1.1)	23 (1.1)	25 (1.3)
Russian Federation	. .	4 (0.8)	s 38 (1.9)	6 (1.0)	8 (1.0)
Scotland	32 (2.0)	. .	. .	. .	. .
Singapore	7 (1.3)	. .	. .	. .	. .
Slovak Republic	. .	2 (0.3)	4 (0.7)	3 (0.3)	5 (0.8)
Slovenia	. .	8 (0.8)	13 (0.9)	. .	20 (1.5)
Spain	9 (1.3)	. .	. .	. .	. .
Sweden	. .	18 (2.0)	s 17 (1.7)	r 25 (2.1)	r 23 (2.0)
Switzerland	13 (1.5)	. .	. .	. .	. .
Thailand	9 (1.0)	. .	. .	. .	. .
United States	35 (2.2)	. .	. .	. .	. .

[1]Countries administered either an integrated science or separate subject area form of the questionnaire. A dot (.) denotes questions not administered by design. Percentages for separate science subject areas are based only on those students taking each subject.
[2]Data for Belgium (Fr) are reported for students in both integrated science classes and separate biology and physics classes.
[3]Physics data for Denmark are for students taking physics/chemistry classes.
[4]Biology data for France are for students taking biology/geology classes; physics data are for students taking physics/chemistry classes.
[5]Physics data for the Netherlands include students in both physics classes and physics/chemistry classes.
[6]Biology data for Portugal are for students taking natural science classes; physics data are for students taking physical science classes.
*Eighth grade in most countries; see Table 2 for more information about the grades tested in each country.
Countries shown in italics did not satisfy one or more guidelines for sample participation rates, age/grade specifications, or classroom sampling procedures (see Figure A.3). Background data for Bulgaria and South Africa are unavailable.
Because population coverage falls below 65%, Latvia is annotated LSS for Latvian Speaking Schools only.
( ) Standard errors appear in parentheses. Because results are rounded to the nearest whole number, some totals may appear inconsistent.
An "r" indicates a 70-84% student response rate. An "s" indicates a 50-69% student response rate. An "x" indicates a <50% student response rate.

SOURCE: IEA Third International Mathematics and Science Study (TIMSS), 1994-95.

How Much Science Homework Are Students Assigned?

Although teachers often give students time to begin or review homework assignments in class, homework is generally considered a method of extending the time spent on regular classroom lessons. Table 5.19 presents teachers' reports about how often they assign science homework and the typical lengths of such assignments. Internationally, most eighth-grade students are assigned science homework at least once a week, although more than half of the students in Belgium (Flemish), Belgium (French), the Czech Republic, Denmark, Hong Kong, Japan, Korea, Scotland, and Slovenia are taught by teachers who reported that they assign homework less than once a week. Most typically, the majority of students were assigned up to 30 minutes of science homework once or twice a week. Students in Colombia, Cyprus, Greece and Iran are among those reporting most science homework, but even in those countries, less than 20% of students are taught by teachers who assign more than 30 minutes of science homework as often as three times a week.

Homework generally has its biggest impact when it is commented on and graded by teachers. Table 5.20 presents teachers' reports about their use of students' written science homework. In most countries, for at least 70% of the students, teachers reported at least sometimes, if not always, correcting homework assignments and returning those assignments to students. The exceptions were Austria, Germany, Hungary, Iran, Japan, the Netherlands, Norway, and the Slovak Republic.

Many teachers do not count homework directly in determining grades, using it more as a method to monitor students' understanding and correct misconceptions. In general for the TIMSS countries, teachers reported that science homework assignments contributed only sometimes to students' grades or marks. In some countries, however, it had even less impact on grades. According to their teachers, homework never or only rarely contributed to the grades for the majority of the students in Austria, the Czech Republic, Denmark, France, Hong Kong, Hungary, Ireland, Japan, Latvia (LSS), Lithuania, the Netherlands, Norway, Romania, Singapore, the Slovak Republic, Slovenia, Switzerland, and Thailand. At the other end of the continuum, teachers reported that homework always contributed to the grades for the majority of the students in Colombia, Kuwait, Portugal, the Russian Federation, and Spain.

Table 5.19

Teachers' Reports About the Amount of Science Homework Assigned
Upper Grade (Eighth Grade*)

Country	Percent of Students Taught by Teachers						
	Never Assigning Homework	Assigning Homework Less Than Once a Week		Assigning Homework Once or Twice a Week		Assigning Homework Three Times a Week or More Often	
		30 Minutes or Less	More Than 30 Minutes	30 Minutes or Less	More Than 30 Minutes	30 Minutes or Less	More Than 30 Minutes
Australia	x x	x x	x x	x x	x x	x x	x x
Austria	- -	- -	- -	- -	- -	- -	- -
Belgium (Fl)	r 16 (2.9)	72 (4.1)	4 (1.3)	7 (2.2)	0 (0.4)	1 (0.9)	0 (0.0)
Belgium (Fr)	s 4 (2.0)	57 (5.4)	4 (1.9)	31 (4.8)	2 (1.5)	2 (1.1)	1 (0.6)
Canada	r 4 (1.8)	16 (2.5)	4 (2.8)	47 (4.1)	8 (2.2)	18 (2.4)	2 (1.3)
Colombia	r 1 (1.4)	5 (2.1)	8 (2.2)	26 (4.1)	37 (5.2)	11 (3.0)	11 (3.0)
Cyprus	s 1 (1.3)	1 (0.6)	0 (0.0)	27 (3.6)	12 (3.1)	45 (4.6)	14 (3.8)
Czech Republic	r 4 (1.3)	75 (3.6)	0 (0.2)	21 (3.4)	0 (0.0)	0 (0.1)	0 (0.0)
Denmark	s 15 (4.7)	49 (6.4)	5 (3.2)	26 (5.6)	0 (0.0)	6 (2.7)	0 (0.0)
England	s 0 (0.0)	10 (2.1)	2 (0.8)	54 (3.3)	32 (3.0)	2 (1.4)	0 (0.1)
France	2 (0.9)	31 (3.6)	3 (1.2)	54 (3.6)	6 (1.5)	5 (1.5)	0 (0.0)
Germany	s 3 (1.5)	41 (4.1)	0 (0.4)	43 (3.8)	0 (0.4)	12 (2.8)	0 (0.0)
Greece	0 (0.0)	9 (2.3)	1 (0.9)	28 (3.1)	11 (3.4)	34 (3.5)	17 (3.1)
Hong Kong	1 (1.1)	37 (5.3)	21 (4.6)	36 (5.5)	4 (2.2)	1 (1.2)	0 (0.0)
Hungary	2 (0.7)	27 (2.3)	1 (0.4)	21 (2.3)	1 (0.5)	42 (2.5)	6 (1.2)
Iceland	s 3 (1.9)	23 (3.9)	2 (1.4)	49 (6.1)	12 (5.6)	11 (6.6)	0 (0.0)
Iran, Islamic Rep.	2 (1.3)	7 (3.1)	9 (3.3)	26 (5.8)	41 (5.4)	3 (1.1)	13 (2.8)
Ireland	s 0 (0.4)	5 (2.1)	0 (0.2)	34 (4.1)	4 (1.8)	53 (4.6)	4 (1.5)
Israel	r 0 (0.0)	19 (6.5)	0 (0.0)	48 (8.0)	13 (6.3)	18 (6.9)	3 (2.8)
Japan	10 (2.3)	55 (4.2)	14 (3.4)	12 (3.1)	5 (2.1)	4 (1.4)	0 (0.5)
Korea	2 (1.0)	39 (3.7)	11 (2.6)	29 (3.9)	10 (2.4)	8 (2.7)	0 (0.4)
Kuwait	r 0 (0.0)	0 (0.0)	0 (0.0)	20 (6.5)	3 (2.5)	68 (5.8)	9 (4.2)
Latvia (LSS)	s 1 (0.6)	23 (1.9)	1 (0.6)	58 (2.6)	3 (1.1)	14 (1.6)	1 (0.4)
Lithuania	r 1 (0.4)	19 (1.9)	0 (0.3)	62 (2.5)	4 (1.0)	13 (1.6)	1 (0.6)
Netherlands	r 0 (0.4)	11 (2.2)	0 (0.0)	76 (3.3)	3 (1.0)	9 (2.0)	1 (0.6)
New Zealand	0 (0.2)	12 (2.0)	2 (1.0)	54 (3.9)	2 (0.5)	30 (3.7)	0 (0.0)
Norway	s 0 (0.0)	11 (3.5)	1 (1.2)	65 (5.1)	9 (2.9)	14 (3.6)	0 (0.0)
Portugal	0 (0.2)	14 (2.4)	2 (0.9)	59 (3.0)	5 (1.2)	19 (2.7)	1 (0.8)
Romania	8 (1.2)	35 (2.3)	2 (0.6)	34 (2.0)	8 (1.3)	6 (1.2)	6 (1.0)
Russian Federation	0 (0.0)	1 (0.5)	0 (0.2)	65 (2.8)	16 (2.4)	12 (2.6)	6 (1.2)
Scotland	s 2 (1.4)	62 (4.8)	4 (1.7)	30 (4.5)	2 (1.3)	0 (0.2)	0 (0.0)
Singapore	0 (0.0)	14 (3.5)	3 (1.8)	49 (4.4)	28 (3.8)	6 (2.3)	0 (0.4)
Slovak Republic	r 2 (1.2)	37 (4.8)	0 (0.0)	59 (4.7)	0 (0.0)	2 (1.4)	0 (0.0)
Slovenia	r 3 (1.1)	56 (3.4)	2 (0.6)	37 (3.5)	2 (0.9)	0 (0.3)	0 (0.0)
Spain	r 0 (0.0)	8 (2.8)	4 (1.9)	45 (4.9)	5 (2.1)	30 (4.5)	8 (2.6)
Sweden	x x	x x	x x	x x	x x	x x	x x
Switzerland	s 4 (1.1)	43 (5.0)	3 (1.4)	38 (5.2)	3 (1.4)	8 (2.7)	1 (1.1)
Thailand	r 0 (0.0)	7 (3.0)	7 (3.4)	34 (6.4)	40 (6.7)	6 (2.8)	7 (3.0)
United States	x x	x x	x x	x x	x x	x x	x x

*Eighth grade in most countries; see Table 2 for more information about the grades tested in each country.
Countries shown in italics did not satisfy one or more guidelines for sample participation rates, age/grade specifications, or classroom sampling procedures (see Figure A.3). Background data for Bulgaria and South Africa are unavailable.
Because population coverage falls below 65%, Latvia is annotated LSS for Latvian Speaking Schools only.
( ) Standard errors appear in parentheses. Because results are rounded to the nearest whole number, some totals may appear inconsistent.
A dash (–) indicates data are unavailable.
An "r" indicates teacher response data available for 70-84% of students. An "s" indicates teacher response data available for 50-69% of students.
An "x" indicates teacher response data available for <50% of students.

SOURCE: IEA Third International Mathematics and Science Study (TIMSS), 1994-95.

Table 5.20

Teachers' Reports on Their Use of Students' Written Science Homework[1] Upper Grade (Eighth Grade*)

Country	Percent of Students Taught by Teachers: Collecting, Correcting and then Returning Assignments to Students				Using Homework to Contribute Towards Students' Grades or Marks			
	Never	Rarely	Sometimes	Always	Never	Rarely	Sometimes	Always
Australia	x x	x x	x x	x x	x x	x x	x x	x x
Austria	s 24 (3.1)	16 (2.7)	31 (2.9)	29 (3.8)	s 29 (3.8)	34 (4.1)	26 (3.7)	12 (2.7)
Belgium (Fl)	r 6 (2.0)	16 (4.0)	15 (3.3)	63 (4.7)	r 16 (4.0)	24 (6.1)	29 (4.1)	31 (5.0)
Belgium (Fr)	s 6 (2.6)	3 (1.9)	35 (5.9)	56 (6.4)	s 5 (2.8)	14 (3.9)	53 (6.2)	28 (5.1)
Canada	s 1 (0.7)	3 (1.7)	53 (5.2)	43 (5.1)	s 7 (2.2)	12 (2.2)	48 (3.9)	33 (3.6)
Colombia	r 0 (0.0)	1 (0.9)	14 (5.2)	85 (5.2)	r 1 (1.0)	5 (2.0)	40 (4.8)	54 (4.9)
Cyprus	s 5 (1.8)	15 (3.5)	51 (4.4)	29 (4.3)	s 0 (0.0)	6 (2.0)	46 (4.4)	49 (4.7)
Czech Republic	r 10 (1.9)	11 (2.1)	37 (3.4)	41 (3.1)	r 28 (3.6)	35 (3.5)	30 (3.2)	7 (1.3)
Denmark	s 14 (5.0)	8 (3.3)	31 (5.8)	46 (6.7)	s 41 (6.6)	17 (5.0)	29 (6.5)	13 (4.9)
England	s 1 (0.7)	2 (0.9)	31 (3.4)	66 (3.6)	s 3 (1.2)	8 (1.6)	45 (3.0)	44 (3.5)
France	7 (1.8)	18 (3.1)	45 (3.7)	30 (3.1)	25 (2.8)	28 (3.4)	39 (4.2)	8 (1.9)
Germany	s 3 (1.3)	28 (4.3)	56 (4.9)	13 (2.9)	s 17 (2.9)	22 (3.5)	52 (4.7)	9 (2.8)
Greece	6 (1.8)	17 (2.6)	43 (3.7)	34 (3.4)	2 (0.9)	12 (2.6)	41 (3.6)	45 (3.9)
Hong Kong	0 (0.0)	4 (2.3)	17 (3.7)	79 (3.8)	26 (5.3)	27 (5.1)	26 (5.0)	21 (5.1)
Hungary	14 (1.6)	32 (2.5)	39 (2.3)	15 (1.7)	16 (2.0)	39 (2.5)	34 (2.5)	11 (1.7)
Iceland	s 2 (1.4)	22 (7.2)	54 (7.6)	22 (4.0)	s 4 (3.1)	12 (4.5)	51 (8.1)	33 (6.8)
Iran, Islamic Rep.	17 (6.4)	22 (4.3)	26 (5.0)	35 (5.2)	9 (3.0)	25 (5.7)	43 (5.6)	23 (4.4)
Ireland	s 4 (1.9)	15 (3.2)	45 (4.7)	36 (4.3)	s 23 (3.9)	31 (4.3)	37 (4.5)	8 (2.6)
Israel	r 6 (4.4)	19 (6.8)	45 (8.8)	29 (6.3)	r 8 (4.5)	16 (5.4)	51 (8.9)	25 (5.8)
Japan	23 (4.4)	21 (3.6)	23 (3.9)	33 (4.5)	20 (3.2)	35 (3.8)	23 (3.8)	21 (3.6)
Korea	1 (0.7)	5 (2.2)	58 (4.0)	35 (3.6)	6 (1.8)	18 (3.0)	57 (3.9)	20 (3.0)
Kuwait	r 0 (0.0)	0 (0.0)	4 (2.9)	96 (2.9)	r 0 (0.0)	0 (0.0)	26 (6.9)	74 (6.9)
Latvia (LSS)	s 5 (1.2)	11 (1.7)	43 (2.3)	41 (2.5)	s 37 (3.2)	29 (3.0)	21 (2.1)	13 (1.7)
Lithuania	r 5 (1.1)	12 (1.5)	39 (2.3)	44 (2.1)	s 39 (2.7)	14 (2.0)	33 (2.6)	13 (2.3)
Netherlands	r 36 (3.0)	34 (2.8)	29 (3.3)	1 (0.7)	r 44 (3.2)	23 (2.9)	25 (3.6)	8 (1.7)
New Zealand	3 (1.3)	10 (2.5)	50 (3.9)	37 (3.9)	12 (2.7)	17 (2.9)	58 (3.5)	12 (2.6)
Norway	s 5 (2.4)	24 (4.6)	54 (5.6)	17 (4.1)	s 7 (2.8)	27 (4.7)	53 (4.8)	13 (3.8)
Portugal	5 (1.3)	18 (2.4)	46 (3.2)	30 (2.9)	1 (0.7)	4 (1.3)	37 (3.0)	57 (3.2)
Romania	r 9 (1.4)	11 (1.7)	33 (2.7)	47 (2.9)	r 12 (1.6)	18 (1.9)	46 (2.8)	24 (2.2)
Russian Federation	1 (0.5)	4 (1.0)	29 (2.9)	66 (2.8)	1 (0.5)	5 (0.8)	30 (2.2)	65 (2.5)
Scotland	- -	- -	- -	- -	- -	- -	- -	- -
Singapore	0 (0.0)	2 (1.5)	13 (3.2)	85 (3.2)	30 (4.3)	26 (3.7)	37 (4.8)	7 (2.8)
Slovak Republic	r 11 (3.2)	20 (4.3)	46 (5.1)	22 (3.7)	r 38 (4.5)	31 (4.6)	25 (4.2)	6 (2.2)
Slovenia	r 9 (1.8)	15 (2.3)	49 (3.4)	27 (2.9)	r 36 (3.6)	37 (3.5)	24 (3.0)	3 (1.1)
Spain	r 2 (1.3)	7 (2.3)	26 (4.3)	66 (4.3)	r 2 (1.7)	6 (2.3)	40 (4.2)	51 (4.5)
Sweden	x x	x x	x x	x x	x x	x x	x x	x x
Switzerland	s 8 (2.6)	18 (4.3)	51 (5.6)	22 (4.2)	s 28 (4.4)	35 (5.1)	35 (5.6)	2 (1.8)
Thailand	r 0 (0.0)	1 (0.5)	21 (5.2)	78 (5.2)	s 9 (3.9)	18 (4.5)	47 (6.6)	26 (5.4)
United States	x x	x x	x x	x x	x x	x x	x x	x x

[1]Based on those teachers who assign homework.

*Eighth grade in most countries; see Table 2 for more information about the grades tested in each country.

Countries shown in italics did not satisfy one or more guidelines for sample participation rates, age/grade specifications, or classroom sampling procedures (see Figure A.3). Background data for Bulgaria and South Africa are unavailable.

Because population coverage falls below 65%, Latvia is annotated LSS for Latvian Speaking Schools only.

( ) Standard errors appear in parentheses. Because results are rounded to the nearest whole number, some totals may appear inconsistent.

A dash (-) indicates data are not available.

An "r" indicates teacher response data available for 70-84% of students. An "s" indicates teacher response data available for 50-69% of students.

An "x" indicates teacher response data available for <50% of students.

SOURCE: IEA Third International Mathematics and Science Study (TIMSS), 1994-95.

What Assessment and Evaluation Procedures Do Teachers Use?

Teachers in participating countries were asked about the importance they place on different types of assessment and how they use assessment information. Their responses to these two questions are presented in Tables 5.21 and 5.22, respectively. The weight given each type of assessment varied greatly from country to country. The most heavily weighted type of assessment was teacher-made tests requiring explanations, observations of students, and students' responses in class. One or more of these assessment types was weighted heavily for 80% or more of the students in many European and Eastern European countries. In contrast, teachers were less in agreement about assessment approaches within Canada, England, Hong Kong, Ireland, Korea, New Zealand, and Thailand, where no type of assessment was weighted heavily for as many as 80% of the students. Internationally, the least weight reportedly was given to external standardized tests. In no participating country did as many as 80% of the eighth-grade students have science teachers who reported giving quite a lot or a great deal of weight to this type of assessment.

As might be anticipated, science teachers in most countries reported using assessment information to provide grades or marks, to provide student feedback, to diagnose learning problems, and to plan future lessons. Teachers in fewer countries reported considerable use of assessment information to report to parents or for the purpose of tracking or making program assignments.

As reported in Table 5.23, eighth-grade students reported quite a lot of testing in science classes. Among countries where science is taught as an integrated subject, the majority of the students reported having frequent (pretty often or almost always) quizzes and tests in Austria, Canada, Colombia, Cyprus, England, Hong Kong, Iran, Ireland, Kuwait, Singapore, Spain, Thailand, and the United States. Where the science subjects are taught separately, the majority reported frequent quizzes and tests in Belgium (Flemish), France, Germany, Greece, Lithuania, the Netherlands, Portugal, Romania, the Russian Federation, Slovenia, Spain, and Sweden. Countries with relatively little testing in science classes included Japan and Korea (integrated science), and the Czech Republic, Denmark, Hungary, Iceland, Latvia (LSS), and the Slovak Republic (separate science subjects).

Table 5.21

Teachers' Reports on the Types of Assessment Given "Quite A Lot" or "A Great Deal" of Weight in Assessing Students' Work in Science Class - Upper Grade (Eighth Grade*)

Country	Percent of Students Taught by Teachers Relying on Different Types of Assessment						
	External Standardized Tests	Teacher-Made Tests Requiring Explanations	Teacher-Made Objective Tests	Homework Assignments	Projects or Practical Exercises	Observations of Students	Students' Responses in Class
Australia	x x	x x	x x	x x	x x	x x	x x
Austria	r 5 (1.6)	r 74 (3.0)	r 20 (3.3)	s 20 (3.2)	r 41 (3.6)	r 97 (1.2)	r 84 (2.4)
Belgium (Fl)	r 11 (5.3)	r 92 (1.8)	r 28 (4.7)	r 20 (4.1)	r 39 (4.6)	r 48 (4.2)	r 50 (4.3)
Belgium (Fr)	s 6 (2.5)	s 84 (3.8)	s 33 (5.4)	s 41 (5.2)	s 34 (6.0)	s 67 (5.5)	s 61 (5.2)
Canada	r 8 (2.0)	r 75 (3.8)	r 49 (4.7)	r 50 (3.9)	r 76 (3.9)	r 36 (3.1)	r 32 (3.7)
Colombia	r 18 (3.7)	r 75 (4.3)	r 63 (4.0)	r 94 (2.1)	r 84 (3.0)	r 85 (3.0)	r 87 (3.4)
Cyprus	s 24 (4.3)	s 79 (3.4)	s 68 (4.0)	s 91 (2.6)	s 76 (4.1)	s 82 (3.4)	s 98 (1.5)
Czech Republic	r 40 (2.8)	93 (1.3)	r 37 (3.2)	10 (1.7)	r 48 (4.4)	r 72 (2.9)	94 (1.6)
Denmark	s 30 (5.5)	s 63 (5.9)	s 24 (5.6)	s 41 (5.9)	s 91 (3.1)	s 87 (4.2)	s 89 (3.7)
England	x x	s 68 (2.5)	x x	s 66 (2.6)	s 74 (2.4)	s 65 (2.9)	s 61 (3.2)
France	20 (2.6)	89 (2.1)	44 (3.7)	37 (3.7)	51 (3.7)	71 (3.6)	68 (3.9)
Germany	s 5 (2.5)	s 84 (3.5)	s 10 (2.4)	s 30 (4.4)	s 55 (4.7)	s 72 (4.9)	s 86 (2.3)
Greece	25 (3.5)	91 (2.0)	55 (4.1)	64 (3.9)	53 (4.4)	85 (2.5)	97 (1.5)
Hong Kong	22 (4.6)	49 (5.7)	78 (5.1)	53 (5.7)	41 (5.5)	43 (5.6)	43 (4.7)
Hungary	46 (2.8)	89 (1.8)	36 (2.3)	42 (2.8)	82 (2.1)	71 (2.4)	88 (1.7)
Iceland	s 5 (1.6)	s 94 (2.8)	s 55 (6.6)	s 87 (4.9)	s 48 (7.5)	s 42 (7.7)	s 43 (7.6)
Iran, Islamic Rep.	19 (3.6)	89 (2.9)	59 (6.0)	45 (5.3)	52 (5.0)	42 (5.6)	93 (2.1)
Ireland	s 28 (3.8)	s 69 (4.4)	s 32 (4.4)	s 67 (4.9)	s 63 (4.8)	s 69 (4.9)	s 76 (4.4)
Israel	s 21 (7.9)	r 69 (8.4)	r 92 (4.2)	r 35 (7.4)	r 48 (7.8)	r 60 (6.5)	r 71 (7.9)
Japan	16 (3.2)	72 (3.2)	45 (4.0)	44 (4.2)	88 (2.8)	79 (3.8)	69 (3.8)
Korea	s 23 (4.5)	s 41 (4.2)	s 41 (4.2)	s 16 (3.6)	s 55 (4.7)	s 38 (4.9)	s 38 (4.6)
Kuwait	r 22 (6.7)	r 84 (5.5)	r 90 (4.4)	r 67 (6.7)	r 52 (6.5)	r 67 (6.8)	r 85 (4.3)
Latvia (LSS)	s 62 (2.5)	s 81 (2.3)	s 65 (2.6)	s 74 (2.5)	s 89 (1.7)	s 80 (2.3)	s 97 (0.9)
Lithuania	s 15 (1.6)	s 48 (2.6)	s 29 (2.8)	s 36 (2.7)	s 41 (3.0)	s 36 (2.8)	s 82 (2.3)
Netherlands	r 60 (3.7)	r 90 (2.4)	r 64 (3.4)	r 11 (2.8)	r 25 (3.3)	r 17 (2.6)	r 14 (2.7)
New Zealand	10 (2.3)	63 (3.8)	56 (4.4)	30 (4.0)	66 (4.1)	53 (4.4)	36 (4.2)
Norway	s 6 (2.1)	s 95 (2.2)	s 8 (2.8)	s 56 (4.6)	s 68 (5.1)	s 68 (4.6)	s 74 (5.0)
Portugal	13 (2.0)	88 (1.9)	53 (2.9)	81 (2.5)	71 (2.9)	88 (2.1)	94 (1.6)
Romania	r 21 (2.2)	82 (1.8)	72 (2.1)	r 72 (2.3)	68 (2.1)	90 (1.3)	99 (0.6)
Russian Federation	- -	96 (1.3)	63 (2.9)	77 (2.9)	74 (3.0)	97 (1.1)	- -
Scotland	- -	- -	- -	- -	- -	- -	- -
Singapore	- -	80 (3.4)	61 (4.4)	48 (4.7)	77 (4.2)	47 (4.7)	46 (4.7)
Slovak Republic	r 76 (4.0)	r 97 (1.7)	r 24 (3.9)	r 27 (4.1)	r 76 (4.5)	r 93 (2.4)	r 99 (0.9)
Slovenia	r 46 (3.4)	r 89 (2.0)	r 29 (3.5)	r 39 (3.7)	r 76 (3.1)	r 76 (3.2)	r 88 (2.4)
Spain	r 8 (2.6)	r 97 (1.6)	r 43 (4.4)	r 76 (3.9)	r 62 (4.2)	r 88 (3.4)	r 92 (2.9)
Sweden	x x	x x	x x	x x	x x	x x	x x
Switzerland	s 11 (2.8)	s 88 (3.6)	s 20 (4.0)	s 13 (3.1)	s 46 (5.0)	s 54 (5.6)	s 61 (5.1)
Thailand	s 20 (5.1)	r 63 (5.9)	r 81 (4.5)	r 64 (5.7)	r 70 (5.7)	r 67 (5.7)	r 68 (5.8)
United States	x x	x x	x x	x x	x x	x x	x x

*Eighth grade in most countries; see Table 2 for more information about the grades tested in each country.

Countries shown in italics did not satisfy one or more guidelines for sample participation rates, age/grade specifications, or classroom sampling procedures (see Figure A.3). Background data for Bulgaria and South Africa are unavailable.

Because population coverage falls below 65%, Latvia is annotated LSS for Latvian Speaking Schools only.

( ) Standard errors appear in parentheses. Because results are rounded to the nearest whole number, some totals may appear inconsistent.

A dash (-) indicates data are not available.

An "r" indicates teacher response data available for 70-84% of students. An "s" indicates teacher response data available for 50-69% of students.

An "x" indicates teacher response data available for <50% of students.

SOURCE: IEA Third International Mathematics and Science Study (TIMSS), 1994-95.

Table 5.22

Teachers' Reports on Ways Assessment Information Is Used "Quite A Lot" or "A Great Deal" - Science - Upper Grade (Eighth Grade*)

Country	Percent of Students Taught by Teachers Using Assessment Information					
	To Provide Grades or Marks	To Provide Student Feedback	To Diagnose Learning Problems	To Report to Parents	To Assign Students to Programs or Tracks	To Plan for Future Lessons
Australia	x x	x x	x x	x x	x x	x x
Austria	- -	r 66 (3.3)	r 51 (3.2)	r 36 (4.3)	r 4 (1.2)	r 29 (3.0)
Belgium (Fl)	r 71 (3.6)	r 61 (5.1)	r 65 (4.8)	r 65 (4.1)	r 59 (5.0)	r 33 (5.0)
Belgium (Fr)	s 83 (4.4)	s 69 (6.2)	s 84 (5.2)	s 39 (5.4)	- -	s 73 (4.9)
Canada	r 90 (3.0)	r 82 (2.6)	r 55 (4.3)	r 78 (3.2)	s 29 (4.0)	r 59 (4.1)
Colombia	r 70 (4.5)	r 95 (2.0)	r 85 (3.4)	r 54 (4.8)	r 22 (4.4)	r 86 (3.4)
Cyprus	s 93 (2.0)	s 85 (2.9)	s 95 (2.4)	s 83 (3.0)	s 63 (4.8)	s 84 (3.2)
Czech Republic	94 (1.4)	r 92 (1.8)	97 (0.9)	r 53 (3.1)	r 19 (3.1)	r 79 (2.7)
Denmark	s 41 (5.5)	s 75 (5.7)	s 50 (6.0)	s 36 (6.2)	s 67 (6.1)	s 83 (5.0)
England	x x	x x	x x	x x	x x	x x
France	91 (1.8)	92 (1.9)	91 (1.7)	52 (3.4)	38 (3.8)	72 (3.4)
Germany	s 81 (3.4)	s 83 (3.5)	s 82 (3.5)	s 41 (4.4)	s 20 (3.6)	s 72 (4.1)
Greece	95 (1.7)	88 (2.6)	93 (2.0)	91 (2.1)	35 (4.3)	72 (3.5)
Hong Kong	73 (5.5)	64 (5.0)	74 (3.8)	13 (4.1)	5 (2.5)	63 (5.4)
Hungary	58 (2.6)	67 (2.4)	90 (1.7)	84 (1.9)	85 (1.7)	72 (2.1)
Iceland	s 73 (7.4)	s 67 (5.5)	s 55 (5.9)	s 43 (5.3)	s 6 (2.9)	s 70 (7.3)
Iran, Islamic Rep.	85 (3.4)	r 63 (4.6)	73 (5.7)	61 (4.6)	52 (5.6)	73 (3.8)
Ireland	s 60 (4.0)	s 81 (3.4)	s 77 (4.2)	s 70 (4.0)	s 31 (4.5)	s 75 (3.9)
Israel	r 85 (6.9)	s 74 (8.9)	r 82 (7.2)	s 78 (5.8)	r 59 (8.6)	r 91 (4.9)
Japan	79 (3.6)	68 (4.3)	64 (4.5)	15 (2.9)	16 (3.0)	54 (4.4)
Korea	44 (4.1)	34 (3.9)	50 (4.0)	6 (1.8)	4 (1.6)	41 (3.9)
Kuwait	r 83 (6.7)	r 69 (7.6)	r 76 (6.2)	r 47 (8.3)	r 76 (6.7)	r 83 (6.3)
Latvia (LSS)	s 93 (1.4)	s 91 (1.5)	s 92 (1.7)	s 22 (1.8)	s 47 (2.4)	s 91 (1.7)
Lithuania	r 80 (1.9)	r 55 (2.5)	r 56 (2.9)	r 42 (2.5)	r 35 (2.6)	r 73 (2.5)
Netherlands	r 91 (2.1)	r 57 (4.2)	r 42 (3.6)	r 55 (3.5)	r 58 (3.6)	r 42 (3.7)
New Zealand	91 (2.4)	83 (3.3)	59 (4.1)	84 (2.9)	21 (3.0)	58 (3.7)
Norway	s 70 (4.9)	s 63 (5.2)	s 24 (4.3)	s 15 (3.2)	s 15 (3.2)	s 61 (5.1)
Portugal	92 (1.9)	87 (1.9)	97 (1.1)	63 (3.3)	37 (3.0)	89 (1.9)
Romania	97 (0.8)	86 (1.9)	r 90 (1.3)	70 (2.3)	75 (2.2)	90 (1.6)
Russian Federation	94 (1.5)	81 (2.4)	95 (1.2)	29 (2.6)	77 (2.5)	95 (1.4)
Scotland	- -	- -	- -	- -	- -	- -
Singapore	76 (4.1)	88 (3.2)	82 (3.7)	33 (4.2)	31 (4.3)	73 (4.2)
Slovak Republic	r 80 (4.4)	r 85 (3.5)	r 83 (3.7)	r 63 (4.9)	r 13 (2.9)	r 76 (4.0)
Slovenia	r 66 (3.2)	r 95 (1.4)	r 87 (2.4)	r 61 (3.3)	r 30 (2.8)	r 83 (2.7)
Spain	r 95 (1.9)	r 89 (3.0)	r 92 (2.6)	r 91 (2.6)	r 64 (4.1)	r 90 (3.1)
Sweden	x x	x x	x x	x x	x x	x x
Switzerland	s 79 (4.4)	s 85 (3.8)	s 71 (4.5)	s 32 (4.8)	s 18 (4.0)	s 69 (5.1)
Thailand	r 73 (5.1)	r 84 (4.7)	r 86 (4.8)	r 47 (6.1)	r 76 (4.3)	r 88 (4.4)
United States	x x	x x	x x	x x	x x	x x

*Eighth grade in most countries; see Table 2 for more information about the grades tested in each country.
Countries shown in italics did not satisfy one or more guidelines for sample participation rates, age/grade specifications, or classroom sampling procedures (see Figure A.3). Background data for Bulgaria and South Africa are unavailable.
Because population coverage falls below 65%, Latvia is annotated LSS for Latvian Speaking Schools only.
( ) Standard errors appear in parentheses. Because results are rounded to the nearest whole number, some totals may appear inconsistent.
A dash (-) indicates data are not available.
An "r" indicates teacher response data available for 70-84% of students. An "s" indicates teacher response data available for 50-69% of students.
An "x" indicates teacher response data available for <50% of students.

SOURCE: IEA Third International Mathematics and Science Study (TIMSS), 1994-95.

Table 5.23

Students' Reports on Frequency of Having a Quiz or Test in Their Science Lessons[1] - Upper Grade (Eighth Grade*)

Country	Percent of Students Responding Pretty Often or Almost Always				
	Science (Integrated)	Science Subject Areas			
		Biology	Chemistry	Earth Science	Physics
Australia	44 (1.2)	. .	. .	. .	. .
Austria	75 (1.5)	. .	. .	. .	. .
Belgium (Fl)	. .	71 (2.0)	. .	68 (1.8)	x x
[2] Belgium (Fr)	x x	x x	. .	. .	x x
Canada	60 (1.4)	. .	. .	. .	. .
Colombia	75 (1.9)	. .	. .	. .	. .
Cyprus	78 (1.1)	. .	. .	. .	. .
Czech Republic	. .	32 (2.3)	37 (2.1)	30 (1.7)	34 (1.8)
[3] *Denmark*	. .	27 (1.9)	. .	r 32 (1.6)	48 (1.9)
England	54 (2.0)	. .	. .	. .	. .
[4] France	. .	67 (1.7)	. .	. .	83 (1.4)
Germany	. .	57 (2.2)	x x	. .	50 (2.1)
Greece	. .	. .	57 (1.3)	51 (1.2)	56 (1.2)
Hong Kong	62 (2.6)	. .	. .	. .	. .
Hungary	. .	21 (1.4)	25 (1.3)	19 (1.1)	24 (1.3)
Iceland	. .	16 (2.5)	x x	x x	x x
Iran, Islamic Rep.	66 (1.4)	. .	. .	. .	. .
Ireland	50 (1.5)	. .	. .	. .	. .
Israel	47 (2.9)	. .	. .	. .	. .
Japan	32 (2.2)	. .	. .	. .	. .
Korea	22 (1.3)	. .	. .	. .	. .
Kuwait	66 (1.9)	. .	. .	. .	. .
Latvia (LSS)	. .	26 (1.5)	20 (1.1)	. .	16 (1.1)
Lithuania	. .	55 (2.2)	67 (1.6)	50 (2.2)	69 (1.4)
[5] *Netherlands*	. .	r 54 (2.7)	. .	50 (2.5)	45 (1.9)
New Zealand	49 (1.7)	. .	. .	. .	. .
Norway	45 (1.7)	. .	. .	. .	. .
[6] Portugal	. .	57 (1.4)	. .	. .	53 (1.3)
Romania	. .	73 (1.3)	76 (1.2)	73 (1.4)	75 (1.1)
Russian Federation	. .	57 (2.1)	73 (1.4)	57 (1.1)	74 (1.0)
Scotland	46 (1.4)	. .	. .	. .	. .
Singapore	74 (1.4)	. .	. .	. .	. .
Slovak Republic	. .	30 (1.8)	48 (2.3)	29 (2.1)	38 (1.6)
Slovenia	. .	44 (1.9)	52 (1.9)	. .	53 (1.9)
Spain	75 (1.4)	. .	. .	. .	. .
Sweden	. .	60 (1.9)	x x	r 66 (1.5)	r 63 (2.0)
Switzerland	49 (1.4)	. .	. .	. .	. .
Thailand	62 (1.5)	. .	. .	. .	. .
United States	77 (1.4)	. .	. .	. .	. .

[1]Countries administered either an integrated science or separate subject area form of the questionnaire. A dot (.) denotes questions not administered by design. Percentages for separate science subject areas are based only on those students taking each subject.
[2]Data for Belgium (Fr) are reported for students in both integrated science classes and separate biology and physics classes.
[3]Physics data for Denmark are for students taking physics/chemistry classes.
[4]Biology data for France are for students taking biology/geology classes; physics data are for students taking physics/chemistry classes.
[5]Physics data for the Netherlands include students in both physics classes and physics/chemistry classes.
[6]Biology data for Portugal are for students taking natural science classes; physics data are for students taking physical science classes.
*Eighth grade in most countries; see Table 2 for more information about the grades tested in each country.
Countries shown in italics did not satisfy one or more guidelines for sample participation rates, age/grade specifications, or classroom sampling procedures (see Figure A.3). Background data for Bulgaria and South Africa are unavailable.
Because population coverage falls below 65%, Latvia is annotated LSS for Latvian Speaking Schools only.
( ) Standard errors appear in parentheses. Because results are rounded to the nearest whole number, some totals may appear inconsistent.
An "r" indicates a 70-84% student response rate. An "x" indicates a <50% student response rate.

SOURCE: IEA Third International Mathematics and Science Study (TIMSS), 1994-95.

Appendix A

Overview of TIMSS Procedures: Science Achievement Results for Seventh- and Eighth-Grade Students

History

TIMSS represents the continuation of a long series of studies conducted by the International Association for the Evaluation of Educational Achievement (IEA). Since its inception in 1959, the IEA has conducted more than 15 studies of cross-national achievement in curricular areas such as mathematics, science, language, civics, and reading. IEA conducted its First International Science Study (FISS) in 1970-71, and the Second International Science Study (SISS) in 1983-84. The First and Second International Mathematics Studies (FIMS and SIMS) were conducted in 1964 and 1980-82, respectively. Since the subjects of mathematics and science are related in many respects, the third studies were conducted together as an integrated effort.[1]

The number of participating countries and the inclusion of both mathematics and science resulted in TIMSS becoming the largest, most complex IEA study to date and the largest international study of educational achievement ever undertaken. Traditionally, IEA studies have systematically worked toward gaining more in-depth understanding of how various factors contribute to the overall outcomes of schooling. Particular emphasis has been given to refining our understanding of students' opportunity to learn as this opportunity becomes successively defined and implemented by curricular and instructional practices. In an effort to extend what had been learned from previous studies and provide contextual and explanatory information, the magnitude of TIMSS expanded beyond the already substantial task of measuring achievement in two subject areas to also include a thorough investigation of curriculum and how it is delivered in classrooms around the world.

The Components of TIMSS

Continuing the approach of previous IEA studies, TIMSS addressed three conceptual levels of curriculum. The **intended curriculum** is composed of the mathematics and science instructional and learning goals as defined at the system level. The **implemented curriculum** is the mathematics and science curriculum as interpreted by teachers and made available to students. The **attained curriculum** is the mathematics and science content that students have learned and their attitudes towards these subjects. To aid in meaningful interpretation and comparison of results, TIMSS

[1] Because a substantial amount of time has elapsed since earlier IEA studies in mathematics and science, curriculum and testing methods in these two subjects have undergone many changes. Since TIMSS has devoted considerable energy toward reflecting the most current educational and measurement practices, changes in items and methods as well as differences in the populations tested make comparisons of TIMSS results with those of previous studies very difficult. The focus of TIMSS is not on measuring achievement trends, but rather on providing up-to-date information about the current quality of education in mathematics and science.

also collected extensive information about the social and cultural contexts for learning, many of which are related to variation among different educational systems.

Even though slightly fewer countries completed all the steps necessary to have their data included in this report, nearly 50 countries participated in one or more of the various components of the TIMSS data collection effort, including the curriculum analysis. To gather information about the intended curriculum, mathematics and science specialists within each participating country worked section-by-section through curriculum guides, textbooks, and other curricular materials to categorize aspects of these materials in accordance with detailed specifications derived from the TIMSS mathematics and science curriculum frameworks.[2] Initial results from this component of TIMSS can be found in two companion volumes: *Many Visions, Many Aims: A Cross-National Investigation of Curricular Intention in School Mathematics* and *Many Visions, Many Aims: A Cross-National Investigation of Curricular Intentions in School Science.* [3] This component of TIMSS is conducted by researchers at Michigan State University.

To measure the attained curriculum, TIMSS tested more than half a million students in mathematics and science at five grade levels. TIMSS included testing at three separate populations:

Population 1. Students enrolled in the two adjacent grades that contained the largest proportion of 9-year-old students at the time of testing – third- and fourth-grade students in most countries.

Population 2. Students enrolled in the two adjacent grades that contained the largest proportion of 13-year-old students at the time of testing – seventh- and eighth-grade students in most countries.

Population 3. Students in their final year of secondary education. As an additional option, countries could test two special subgroups of these students:

1) Students taking advanced courses in mathematics,
2) Students taking physics.

Countries participating in the study were required to administer tests to the students in the two grades at Population 2, but could choose whether or not to participate at the other levels. In about half of the countries at Populations 1 and 2, subsets of the upper-grade students who completed the written tests also participated in a performance assessment. In the performance assessment, students engaged in a number of hands-on mathematics and science activities. The students designed experiments, tested

[2] Robitaille, D.F., McKnight, C., Schmidt, W., Britton, E., Raizen, S., and Nicol, C. (1993). *TIMSS Monograph No. 1: Curriculum Frameworks for Mathematics and Science.* Vancouver, B.C.: Pacific Educational Press.

[3] Schmidt, W.H., McKnight, C.C., Valverde, G. A., Houang, R.T., and Wiley, D. E. (in press). *Many Visions, Many Aims: A Cross-National Investigation of Curricular Intentions in School Mathematics.* Dordrecht, The Netherlands: Kluwer Academic Publishers. Schmidt, W.H., Raizen, S.A., Britton, E.D., Bianchi, L.J., and Wolfe, R.G., (in press). *Many Visions, Many Aims: A Cross-National Investigation of Curricular Intentions in School Science.* Dordrecht, The Netherlands: Kluwer Academic Publishers.

hypotheses, and recorded their findings. For example, in one task, students were asked to design and conduct a controlled experiment to measure the effect of water temperature on the rate at which tablets dissolve, requiring organization and interpretation of data to draw conclusions and explain results. Figure A.1 shows the countries that participated in the various components of TIMSS achievement testing.

TIMSS also administered a broad array of questionnaires to collect data about how the curriculum is implemented in classrooms, including the instructional practices used to deliver it. The questionnaires also were used to collect information about the social and cultural contexts for learning. Questionnaires were administered at the **country level** about decision-making and organizational features within their educational systems. The **students** who were tested answered questions pertaining to their attitudes towards mathematics and science, classroom activities, home background, and out-of-school activities. The mathematics and science **teachers** of sampled students responded to questions about teaching emphasis on the topics in the curriculum frameworks, instructional practices, textbook usage, professional training and education, and their views on mathematics and science. The heads of **schools** responded to questions about school staffing and resources, mathematics and science course offerings, and teacher support. In addition, a volume was compiled that presents descriptions of the educational systems of the participating countries.[4]

With its enormous array of data, TIMSS has numerous possibilities for policy-related research, focused studies related to students' understandings of mathematics and science subtopics and processes, and integrated analyses linking the various components of TIMSS. The initial round of reports is only the beginning of a number of research efforts and publications aimed at increasing our understanding of how mathematics and science education functions across countries, investigating what impacts student performance, and helping to improve mathematics and science education.

[4] Robitaille D.F. (in press). *National Contexts for Mathematics and Science Education: An Encyclopedia of the Education Systems Participating in TIMSS*. Vancouver, B.C.: Pacific Educational Press.

Figure A.1

Countries Participating in Additional Components of TIMSS Testing

Country	Population 1		Population 2		Population 3		
	Written Test	Performance Assessment	Written Test	Performance Assessment	Mathematics & Science Literacy	Advanced Mathematics	Physics
Argentina			●				
Australia	●	●	●	●	●	●	●
Austria	●		●		●	●	●
Belgium (Fl)			●				
Belgium (Fr)			●				
Bulgaria			●				
Canada	●	●	●	●	●	●	●
Colombia			●	●			
Cyprus	●	●	●	●	●	●	●
Czech Republic	●	●	●	●	●	●	●
Denmark			●	●	●	●	●
England	●		●	●			
France			●		●	●	●
Germany			●		●	●	●
Greece	●		●		●	●	●
Hong Kong	●	●	●	●			
Hungary	●		●		●		
Iceland	●		●		●		
Indonesia	●		●				
Iran, Islamic Rep.	●	●	●	●			
Ireland	●		●				
Israel	●	●	●	●	●	●	●
Italy	●		●		●		
Japan	●		●				●
Korea	●		●				
Kuwait	●		●				
Latvia	●		●				●
Lithuania			●		●	●	
Mexico	●		●		●	●	●
Netherlands	●		●		●		
New Zealand	●	●	●	●	●		
Norway	●		●	●	●		●
Philippines			●				
Portugal	●	●	●	●			
Romania			●	●			
Russian Federation			●		●	●	●
Scotland	●		●	●			
Singapore	●		●	●			
Slovak Republic			●				
Slovenia	●	●	●	●	●	●	●
South Africa			●		●		
Spain			●	●			
Sweden			●	●	●	●	●
Switzerland			●	●	●	●	●
Thailand	●		●				
United States	●	●	●	●	●	●	●

Developing the TIMSS Science Test

The TIMSS curriculum framework underlying the science tests at all three populations was developed by groups of science educators with input from the TIMSS National Research Coordinators (NRCs). As shown in Figure A.2, the science curriculum framework contains three dimensions or aspects. The **content** aspect represents the subject matter content of school science. The **performance expectations** aspect describes, in a non-hierarchical way, the many kinds of performances or behaviors that might be expected of students in school science. The **perspectives** aspect focuses on the development of students' attitudes, interest, and motivations in science.[5]

Working within the science curriculum framework, science test specifications were developed for Population 2 that included items representing a wide range of science topics and eliciting a range of skills from the students. The tests were developed through an international consensus involving input from experts in science and measurement specialists. The TIMSS Subject Matter Advisory Committee, including distinguished scholars from 10 countries, ensured that the test reflected current thinking and priorities in the sciences. The items underwent an iterative development and review process, with one of the pilot testing efforts involving 43 countries. Every effort was made to help ensure that the tests represented the curricula of the participating countries and that the items did not exhibit any bias towards or against particular countries, including modifying specifications in accordance with data from the curriculum analysis component, obtaining ratings of the items by subject-matter specialists within the participating countries, and conducting thorough statistical item analysis of data collected in the pilot testing. The final forms of the test were endorsed by the NRCs of the participating countries.[6] In addition, countries had an opportunity to match the content of the test to their curricula at the seventh and eighth grades. They identified items measuring topics not covered in their intended curriculum. The information from this Test-Curriculum Matching Analysis indicates that omitting such items has little effect on the overall pattern of results (see Appendix B).

Table A.1 presents the five content areas included in the Population 2 science test and the numbers of items and score points in each category. Distributions also are included for the five performance categories derived from the performance expectations aspect of the curriculum framework. Approximately one-fourth of the items were in the free-response format, requiring students to generate and write their own answers. Designed to represent approximately one-third of students' response time, some free-response questions asked for short answers while others required extended

[5] The complete TIMSS curriculum frameworks can be found in Robitaille, D.F. et al. (1993). *TIMSS Monograph No. 1: Curriculum Frameworks for Mathematics and Science.* Vancouver, B.C.: Pacific Educational Press.

[6] For a full discussion of the TIMSS test development effort, please see: Garden, R.A. and Orpwood, G. (1996). "TIMSS Test Development" in M.O. Martin and D.L. Kelly (eds.), *Third International Mathematics and Science Study Technical Report, Volume I.* Chestnut Hill, MA: Boston College; and Garden, R.A. (1996). "Development of the TIMSS Achievement Items" in D.F. Robitaille and R.A. Garden (eds.), *TIMSS Monograph No.2: Research Questions and Study Design.* Vancouver, B.C.: Pacific Educational Press.

Figure A.2

The Three Aspects and Major Categories of the Science Framework

Content

- Earth sciences
- Life sciences
- Physical sciences
- Science, technology, and mathematics
- History of science and technology
- Environmental issues
- Nature of science
- Science and other disciplines

Performance Expectations

- Understanding
- Theorizing, analyzing, and solving problems
- Using tools, routine procedures and science processes
- Investigating the natural world
- Communicating

Perspectives

- Attitudes
- Careers
- Participation
- Increasing interest
- Safety
- Habits of mind

Table A.1

Distribution of Science Items by Content Reporting Category and Performance Category - Population 2

Content Category	Percentage of Items	Total Number of Items	Number of Multiple-Choice Items	Number of Free-Response Items[1]	Number of Score Points[2]
Earth Science	16	22	17	5	24
Life Science	30	40	31	9	44
Physics	30	40	28	12	42
Chemistry	14	19	15	4	21
Environmental Issues and the Nature of Science	10	14	11	3	15

Performance Category	Percentage of Items	Total Number of Items	Number of Multiple-Choice Items	Number of Free-Response Items[1]	Number of Score Points[2]
Understanding Simple Information	40	55	53	2	55
Understanding Complex Information	29	39	29	10	41
Theorizing, Analyzing, and Solving Problems	21	28	9	19	36
Using Tools, Routine Procedures, and Science Processes	6	8	8	0	8
Investigating the Natural World	4	5	3	2	6

[1]Free-Response Items include both short-answer and extended-response types.
[2]In scoring the tests correct answers to most items were worth one point. However, responses to some constructed-response items were evaluated for partial credit with a fully correct answer awarded up to three points. In addition, some items had two parts. Thus, the number of score points exceeds the number of items in the test.

SOURCE: IEA Third International Mathematics and Science Study (TIMSS), 1994-95.

responses where students needed to show their work or provide explanations for their answers. The remaining questions used a multiple-choice format. In scoring the tests, correct answers to most questions were worth one point. Consistent with the approach of allotting students longer response time for the constructed-response questions than for multiple-choice questions, however, responses to some of these questions (particularly those requiring extended responses) were evaluated for partial credit with a fully correct answer being awarded two or even three points (see later section on scoring). This, in addition to the fact that several items had two parts, means that the total number of score points available for analysis somewhat exceeds the number of items included in the test.

The TIMSS instruments were prepared in English and translated into 30 additional languages. In addition, it sometimes was necessary to adapt the international versions for cultural purposes, including the 11 countries that tested in English. This process represented an enormous effort for the national centers, with many checks along the way. The translation effort included: (1) developing explicit guidelines for translation and cultural adaptation, (2) translation of the instruments by the national centers in accordance with the guidelines and using two or more independent translations, (3) consultation with subject-matter experts regarding cultural adaptations to ensure that the meaning and difficulty of items did not change, (4) verification of the quality of the translations by professional translators from an independent translation company, (5) corrections by the national centers in accordance with the suggestions made, (6) verification that corrections were implemented, and (7) a series of statistical checks after the testing to detect items that did not perform comparably across countries.[7]

[7] More details about the translation verification procedures can be found in Mullis, I.V.S., Kelly, D.L., and Haley, K. (1996). "Translation Verification Procedures" in M.O. Martin and I.V.S. Mullis (eds.), *Third International Mathematics and Science Study: Quality Assurance in Data Collection.* Chestnut Hill, MA: Boston College; and Maxwell, B. (1996). "Translation and Cultural Adaptation of the TIMSS Instruments" in M.O. Martin and D.L. Kelly (eds.), *Third International Mathematics and Science Study: Technical Report, Volume I.* Chestnut Hill, MA: Boston College.

TIMSS Test Design

Not all of the students in Population 2 responded to all of the science items. To ensure broad subject matter coverage without overburdening individual students, TIMSS used a rotated design that included both the mathematics and science items. Thus, the same students participated in both the mathematics and science testing. The TIMSS Population 2 test consisted of eight booklets, with each booklet requiring 90 minutes of student response time. In accordance with the design, the mathematics and science items were assembled into 26 different clusters (labeled A through Z). Eight of the clusters were designed to take students 12 minutes to complete; 10 of the clusters, 22 minutes; and 8 clusters, 10 minutes. In all, the design provided a total of 396 unique testing minutes, 198 for mathematics and 198 for science. Cluster A was a core cluster assigned to all booklets. The remaining clusters were assigned to the booklets in accordance with the rotated design so that representative samples of students responded to each cluster.[8]

Sample Implementation and Participation Rates

The selection of valid and efficient samples is crucial to the quality and success of an international comparative study such as TIMSS. The accuracy of the survey results depends on the quality of sampling information available and on the quality of the sampling activities themselves. For TIMSS, NRCs worked on all phases of sampling with staff from Statistics Canada. NRCs received training in how to select the school and student samples and in the use of the sampling software. In consultation with the TIMSS sampling referee (Keith Rust, WESTAT, Inc.), staff from Statistics Canada reviewed the national sampling plans, sampling data, sampling frames, and sample execution. This documentation was used by the International Study Center in consultation with Statistics Canada, the sampling referee, and the Technical Advisory Committee, to evaluate the quality of the samples.

In a few situations where it was not possible to implement TIMSS testing for the entire internationally desired definition of Population 2 (all students in the two adjacent grades with the greatest proportion of 13-year-olds), countries were permitted to define a national desired population that did not include part of the internationally desired population. Table A.2 shows any differences in coverage between the international and national desired populations. Most participants achieved 100% coverage (36 out of 42). The countries with less than 100% coverage are annotated in tables in this report. In some instances, countries, as a matter of practicality, needed to define their tested population according to the structure of school systems, but in Germany and Switzerland, parts of the country were simply unwilling to take part

[8] The design is fully documented in Adams, R. and Gonzalez, E. (1996). "Design of the TIMSS Achievement Instruments" in D.F. Robitaille and R.A. Garden (eds.), *TIMSS Monograph No. 2: Research Questions and Study Design*. Vancouver, B.C.: Pacific Education Press and Adams, R. and Gonzalez, E. (1996). "TIMSS Test Design" in M.O. Martin and D.L. Kelly (eds.), *Third International Mathematics and Science Study Technical Report, Volume I*. Chestnut Hill, MA: Boston College.

Table A.2

Coverage of TIMSS Target Population

The International Desired Population is defined as follows:
Population 2 - All students enrolled in the two adjacent grades with the largest proportion of 13-year-old students at the time of testing.

Country	International Desired Population		National Desired Population		
	Coverage	Notes on Coverage	School-Level Exclusions	Within-Sample Exclusions	Overall Exclusions
Australia	100%		0.2%	0.7%	0.8%
Austria	100%		2.9%	0.2%	3.1%
Belgium (Fl)	100%		3.8%	0.0%	3.8%
Belgium (Fr)	100%		4.5%	0.0%	4.5%
Bulgaria	100%		0.6%	0.0%	0.6%
Canada	100%		2.4%	2.1%	4.5%
Colombia	100%		3.8%	0.0%	3.8%
Cyprus	100%		0.0%	0.0%	0.0%
Czech Republic	100%		4.9%	0.0%	4.9%
Denmark	100%		0.0%	0.0%	0.0%
[2] England	100%		8.4%	2.9%	11.3%
France	100%		2.0%	0.0%	2.0%
[1] Germany	88%	15 of 16 regions*	8.8%	0.9%	9.7%
Greece	100%		1.5%	1.3%	2.8%
Hong Kong	100%		2.0%	0.0%	2.0%
Hungary	100%		3.8%	0.0%	3.8%
Iceland	100%		1.7%	2.9%	4.5%
Iran, Islamic Rep.	100%		0.3%	0.0%	0.3%
Ireland	100%		0.0%	0.4%	0.4%
[1] Israel	74%	Hebrew Public Education System	3.1%	0.0%	3.1%
Japan	100%		0.6%	0.0%	0.6%
Korea	100%		2.2%	1.6%	3.8%
Kuwait	100%		0.0%	0.0%	0.0%
[1] Latvia (LSS)	51%	Latvian-speaking schools	2.9%	0.0%	2.9%
[1] Lithuania	84%	Lithuanian-speaking schools	6.6%	0.0%	6.6%
Netherlands	100%		1.2%	0.0%	1.2%
New Zealand	100%		1.3%	0.4%	1.7%
Norway	100%		0.3%	1.9%	2.2%
Philippines	91%	2 provinces and autonomous regions excluded	6.5%	0.0%	6.5%
Portugal	100%		0.0%	0.3%	0.3%
Romania	100%		2.8%	0.0%	2.8%
Russian Federation	100%		6.1%	0.2%	6.3%
Scotland	100%		0.3%	1.9%	2.2%
Singapore	100%		4.6%	0.0%	4.6%
Slovak Republic	100%		7.4%	0.1%	7.4%
Slovenia	100%		2.4%	0.2%	2.6%
South Africa	100%		9.6%	0.0%	9.6%
Spain	100%		6.0%	2.7%	8.7%
Sweden	100%		0.0%	0.9%	0.9%
[1] Switzerland	86%	22 of 26 cantons	4.4%	0.8%	5.3%
Thailand	100%		6.2%	0.0%	6.2%
United States	100%		0.4%	1.7%	2.1%

[1]National Desired Population does not cover all of International Desired Population. Because coverage falls below 65%, Latvia is annotated LSS for Latvian Speaking Schools only.

[2]National Defined Population covers less than 90 percent of National Desired Population.

* One region (Baden-Wuerttemberg) did not participate.

SOURCE: IEA Third International Mathematics and Science Study (TIMSS), 1994-95.

in TIMSS. Because coverage fell below 65% for Latvia, the Latvian results have been labeled "Latvia (LSS)," for Latvian Speaking Schools, throughout the report.

Within the desired population, countries could define a population that excluded a small percent (less than 10%) of certain kinds of schools or students that would be very difficult or resource intensive to test (e. g., schools for students with special needs or schools that were very small or located in extremely remote areas). Table A.2 also shows that the degree of such exclusions was small. Only England exceeded the 10% limit, and this is annotated in the tables in this report.

Countries were required to test the two adjacent grades with the greatest proportion of 13-year-olds. Table A.3 presents, for each country, the percentage of 13-year-olds in the lower grade tested, the percentage in the upper grade, and the percentage in both the upper and lower grades combined.

Within countries, TIMSS used a two-stage sample design at Population 2, where the first stage involved selecting 150 public and private schools within each country. Within each school, the basic approach required countries to use random procedures to select one mathematics class at the eighth grade and one at the seventh grade (or the corresponding upper and lower grades in that country). All of the students in those two classes were to participate in the TIMSS testing. This approach was designed to yield a representative sample of 7,500 students per country, with approximately 3,750 students at each grade.[9] Typically, between 450 and 3,750 students responded to each item at each grade level, depending on the booklets in which the items were located.

Countries were required to obtain a participation rate of at least 85% of both the schools and the students, or a combined rate (the product of school and student participation) of 75%. Tables A.4 through A.8 present the participation rates and achieved sample sizes for the eighth and seventh grades.

[9] The sample design for TIMSS is described in detail in Foy, P., Rust, K. and Schleicher, A. (1996). "TIMSS Sample Design" in M.O. Martin and D.L. Kelly (eds.), *Third International Mathematics and Science Study Technical Report, Volume I*. Chestnut Hill, MA: Boston College.

Table A.3

Coverage of 13-Year-Old Students

Country	Percent of 13-Year-Olds in Lower Grade (Seventh Grade*)	Percent of 13-Year-Olds in Upper Grade (Eighth Grade*)	Percent of 13-Year-Olds in Both Grades
Australia	64	28	92
Austria	62	27	89
Belgium (Fl)	46	49	94
Belgium (Fr)	41	46	87
Bulgaria	58	37	95
Canada	48	43	91
Colombia	30	15	45
Cyprus	28	70	98
Czech Republic	73	17	90
Denmark	35	64	98
England	57	42	99
France	44	35	78
Germany	71	2	73
Greece	11	85	96
Hong Kong	44	46	90
Hungary	65	24	89
Iceland	16	83	100
Iran, Islamic Rep.	47	25	72
Ireland	69	17	86
Israel	–	–	–
Japan	91	9	100
Korea	70	28	98
Kuwait	–	–	–
Latvia (LSS)	60	26	86
Lithuania	64	26	90
Netherlands	59	31	90
New Zealand	52	47	99
Norway	43	57	100
Philippines	–	–	–
Portugal	44	32	76
Romania	67	9	76
Russian Federation	50	44	95
Scotland	24	75	99
Singapore	82	15	97
Slovak Republic	73	22	95
Slovenia	65	2	67
South Africa	36	20	55
Spain	46	39	85
Sweden	45	54	99
Switzerland	48	44	92
Thailand	58	20	78
United States	58	33	91

*Seventh and eighth grades in most countries; see Table 2 for more information about the grades tested in each country.
A dash (–) indicates data are unavailable. Israel and Kuwait did not test the lower (seventh) grade.

SOURCE: IEA Third International Mathematics and Science Study (TIMSS), 1994-95.

Table A.4

School Participation Rates and Sample Sizes - Upper Grade (Eighth Grade*)

Country	School Participation Before Replacement (Weighted Percentage)	School Participation After Replacement (Weighted Percentage)	Number of Schools in Original Sample	Number of Eligible Schools in Original Sample	Number of Schools in Original Sample That Participated	Number of Replacement Schools That Participated	Total Number of Schools That Participated
Australia	75	77	214	214	158	3	161
Austria	41	84	159	159	62	62	124
Belgium (Fl)	61	94	150	150	92	49	141
Belgium (Fr)	57	79	150	150	85	34	119
Bulgaria	72	74	167	167	111	4	115
Canada	90	91	413	388	363	1	364
Colombia	91	93	150	150	136	4	140
Cyprus	100	100	55	55	55	0	55
Czech Republic	96	100	150	149	143	6	149
Denmark	93	93	158	157	144	0	144
England	56	85	150	144	80	41	121
France	86	86	151	151	127	0	127
Germany	72	93	153	150	102	32	134
Greece	87	87	180	180	156	0	156
Hong Kong	82	82	105	104	85	0	85
Hungary	100	100	150	150	150	0	150
Iceland	98	98	161	132	129	0	129
Iran, Islamic Rep.	100	100	192	191	191	0	191
Ireland	84	89	150	149	125	7	132
Israel	45	46	100	100	45	1	46
Japan	92	95	158	158	146	5	151
Korea	100	100	150	150	150	0	150
Kuwait	100	100	69	69	69	0	69
Latvia (LSS)	83	83	170	169	140	1	141
Lithuania	96	96	151	151	145	0	145
Netherlands	24	63	150	150	36	59	95
New Zealand	91	99	150	150	137	12	149
Norway	91	97	150	150	136	10	146
Philippines	96 **	97 **	200	200	192	1	193
Portugal	95	95	150	150	142	0	142
Romania	94	94	176	176	163	0	163
Russian Federation	97	100	175	175	170	4	174
Scotland	79	83	153	153	119	8	127
Singapore	100	100	137	137	137	0	137
Slovak Republic	91	97	150	150	136	9	145
Slovenia	81	81	150	150	121	0	121
South Africa	60	64	180	180	107	7	114
Spain	96	100	155	154	147	6	153
Sweden	97	97	120	120	116	0	116
Switzerland	93	95	259	258	247	3	250
Thailand	99	99	150	150	147	0	147
United States	77	85	220	217	169	14	183

*Eighth grade in most countries; see Table 2 for more information about the grades tested in each country.
**Participation rates for the Philippines are unweighted.

SOURCE: IEA Third International Mathematics and Science Study (TIMSS), 1994-95.

Table A.5

Student Participation Rates and Sample Sizes - Upper Grade (Eighth Grade*)

Country	Within School Student Participation (Weighted Percentage)	Number of Sampled Students in Participating Schools	Number of Students Withdrawn from Class/School	Number of Students Excluded	Number of Students Eligible	Number of Students Absent	Total Number of Students Assessed
Australia	92	8027	63	61	7903	650	7253
Austria	95	2969	14	4	2951	178	2773
Belgium (Fl)	97	2979	1	0	2978	84	2894
Belgium (Fr)	91	2824	0	1	2823	232	2591
Bulgaria	86	2300	0	0	2300	327	1973
Canada	93	9240	134	206	8900	538	8362
Colombia	94	2843	6	0	2837	188	2649
Cyprus	97	3045	15	0	3030	107	2923
Czech Republic	92	3608	6	0	3602	275	3327
Denmark	93	2487	0	0	2487	190	2297
England	91	2015	37	60	1918	142	1776
France	95	3141	0	0	3141	143	2998
Germany	87	3318	0	35	3283	413	2870
Greece	97	4154	27	23	4104	114	3990
Hong Kong	98	3415	12	0	3403	64	3339
Hungary	87	3339	0	0	3339	427	2912
Iceland	90	2025	10	65	1950	177	1773
Iran, Islamic Rep.	98	3770	20	0	3750	56	3694
Ireland	91	3411	28	10	3373	297	3076
Israel	98	1453	6	0	1447	32	1415
Japan	95	5441	0	0	5441	300	5141
Korea	95	2998	31	0	2967	47	2920
Kuwait	83	1980	3	0	1977	322	1655
Latvia (LSS)	90	2705	19	0	2686	277	2409
Lithuania	87	2915	2	0	2913	388	2525
Netherlands	95	2112	14	1	2097	110	1987
New Zealand	94	4038	121	12	3905	222	3683
Norway	96	3482	26	49	3407	140	3267
Philippines	91 **	6586	93	0	6493	492	6001
Portugal	97	3589	70	13	3506	115	3391
Romania	96	3899	0	0	3899	174	3725
Russian Federation	95	4311	42	10	4259	237	4022
Scotland	88	3289	0	46	3243	380	2863
Singapore	95	4910	18	0	4892	248	4644
Slovak Republic	95	3718	5	3	3710	209	3501
Slovenia	95	2869	15	8	2846	138	2708
South Africa	97	4793	0	0	4793	302	4491
Spain	95	4198	27	102	4069	214	3855
Sweden	93	4483	71	28	4384	309	4075
Switzerland	98	4989	16	24	4949	94	4855
Thailand	100	5850	0	0	5850	0	5850
United States	92	8026	104	108	7814	727	7087

*Eighth grade in most countries; see Table 2 for more information about the grades tested in each country.
**Participation rates for the Philippines are unweighted.

SOURCE: IEA Third International Mathematics and Science Study (TIMSS), 1994-95.

Table A.6

School Participation Rates and Sample Sizes - Lower Grade (Seventh Grade*)

Country	School Participation Before Replacement (Weighted Percentage)	School Participation After Replacement (Weighted Percentage)	Number of Schools in Original Sample	Number of Eligible Schools in Original Sample	Number of Schools in Original Sample That Participated	Number of Replacement Schools That Participated	Total Number of Schools That Participated
Australia	75	76	214	213	156	3	159
Austria	43	86	159	159	63	62	125
Belgium (Fl)	61	93	150	150	91	49	140
Belgium (Fr)	57	80	150	150	85	35	120
Bulgaria	75	77	150	150	101	3	104
Canada	90	90	413	390	366	1	367
Colombia	91	93	150	150	136	4	140
Cyprus	100	100	55	55	55	0	55
Czech Republic	96	100	150	150	144	6	150
Denmark	88	88	158	154	137	0	137
England	57	85	150	145	81	41	122
France	87	87	151	151	126	0	126
Germany	70	90	153	153	101	31	132
Greece	87	87	180	180	156	0	156
Hong Kong	83	83	105	104	86	0	86
Hungary	99	99	150	150	149	0	149
Iceland	97	97	161	149	144	0	144
Iran, Islamic Rep.	100	100	192	192	192	0	192
Ireland	82	87	150	148	122	7	129
Israel	–	–	–	–	–	–	–
Japan	92	95	158	158	146	5	151
Korea	100	100	150	150	150	0	150
Kuwait	–	–	–	–	–	–	–
Latvia (LSS)	83	84	170	169	141	1	142
Lithuania	96	96	151	151	145	0	145
Netherlands	23	61	150	150	34	58	92
New Zealand	90	99	150	150	135	13	148
Norway	84	96	150	147	124	17	141
Philippines	97 **	97 **	200	200	194	0	194
Portugal	94	94	150	150	141	0	141
Romania	94	94	176	175	162	0	162
Russian Federation	97	100	175	175	170	4	174
Scotland	79	85	153	153	120	9	129
Singapore	100	100	137	137	137	0	137
Slovak Republic	91	97	150	150	136	9	145
Slovenia	81	81	150	150	122	0	122
South Africa	83	85	161	161	133	4	137
Spain	96	100	155	154	147	6	153
Sweden	96	96	160	160	154	0	154
Switzerland	90	94	217	217	200	6	206
Thailand	99	99	150	150	146	0	146
United States	77	84	220	214	165	14	179

*Seventh grade in most countries; see Table 2 for more information about the grades tested in each country.
**Participation rates for the Philippines are unweighted.
A dash (–) indicates data are unavailable. Israel and Kuwait did not test the lower grade.

SOURCE: IEA Third International Mathematics and Science Study (TIMSS), 1994-95.

Table A.7

Student Participation Rates and Sample Sizes - Lower Grade (Seventh Grade*)

Country	Within School Student Participation (Weighted Percentage)	Number of Sampled Students in Participating Schools	Number of Students Withdrawn from Class/School	Number of Students Excluded	Number of Students Eligible	Number of Students Absent	Total Number of Students Assessed
Australia	93	6067	26	21	6020	421	5599
Austria	95	3196	22	5	3169	156	3013
Belgium (Fl)	97	2857	3	0	2854	86	2768
Belgium (Fr)	95	2418	0	1	2417	125	2292
Bulgaria	87	2080	0	0	2080	282	1798
Canada	95	8962	89	248	8625	406	8219
Colombia	93	2840	2	0	2838	183	2655
Cyprus	98	3028	17	0	3011	82	2929
Czech Republic	92	3641	11	0	3630	285	3345
Denmark	86	2408	0	0	2408	335	2073
England	92	2031	31	67	1933	130	1803
France	95	3164	0	0	3164	148	3016
Germany	87	3388	0	37	3351	458	2893
Greece	97	4166	30	78	4058	127	3931
Hong Kong	98	3507	11	0	3496	83	3413
Hungary	94	3266	0	0	3266	200	3066
Iceland	92	2243	11	72	2160	203	1957
Iran, Islamic Rep.	99	3789	18	0	3771	36	3735
Ireland	91	3480	23	17	3440	313	3127
Israel	–	–	–	–	–	–	–
Japan	96	5337	0	0	5337	207	5130
Korea	94	2996	51	0	2945	38	2907
Kuwait	–	–	–	–	–	–	–
Latvia (LSS)	91	2853	7	0	2846	279	2567
Lithuania	89	2852	3	0	2849	318	2531
Netherlands	95	2220	23	0	2197	100	2097
New Zealand	95	3471	98	17	3356	172	3184
Norway	96	2629	8	53	2568	99	2469
Philippines	93 **	6283	29	1	6253	401	5852
Portugal	96	3594	80	4	3510	148	3362
Romania	95	3938	0	0	3938	192	3746
Russian Federation	96	4408	39	11	4358	220	4138
Scotland	90	3313	0	81	3232	319	2913
Singapore	98	3744	19	0	3725	84	3641
Slovak Republic	95	3797	10	3	3784	184	3600
Slovenia	95	3058	12	4	3042	144	2898
South Africa	96	5532	0	0	5532	231	5301
Spain	95	4087	38	116	3933	192	3741
Sweden	95	3055	27	36	2992	161	2831
Switzerland	99	4199	14	44	4141	56	4085
Thailand	100	5845	0	0	5845	0	5845
United States	94	4295	42	85	4168	282	3886

*Seventh grade in most countries; see Table 2 for more information about the grades tested in each country.
**Participation rates for the Philippines are unweighted.
A dash (–) indicates data are unavailable. Israel and Kuwait did not test the lower grade.

SOURCE: IEA Third International Mathematics and Science Study (TIMSS), 1994-95.

Table A.8

Overall Participation Rates
Upper and Lower Grades (Eighth and Seventh Grades*)

Country	Upper Grade		Lower Grade	
	Overall Participation Before Replacement (Weighted Percentage)	Overall Participation After Replacement (Weighted Percentage)	Overall Participation Before Replacement (Weighted Percentage)	Overall Participation After Replacement (Weighted Percentage)
Australia	69	70	69	71
Austria	39	80	41	82
Belgium (Fl)	59	91	59	91
Belgium (Fr)	52	72	54	76
Bulgaria	62	63	65	67
Canada	84	84	86	86
Colombia	85	87	84	86
Cyprus	97	97	98	98
Czech Republic	89	92	88	92
Denmark	86	86	76	76
England	51	77	52	78
France	82	82	82	82
Germany	63	81	61	78
Greece	84	84	84	84
Hong Kong	81	81	81	81
Hungary	87	87	93	93
Iceland	88	88	89	89
Iran, Islamic Rep.	98	98	99	99
Ireland	76	81	75	79
Israel	44	45	–	–
Japan	87	90	88	91
Korea	95	95	94	94
Kuwait	83	83	–	–
Latvia (LSS)	75	75	75	76
Lithuania	83	83	86	86
Netherlands	23	60	22	58
New Zealand	86	94	85	94
Norway	87	93	81	92
Philippines	87**	88**	90**	90**
Portugal	92	92	90	90
Romania	89	89	89	89
Russian Federation	93	95	93	95
Scotland	69	73	71	76
Singapore	95	95	98	98
Slovak Republic	86	91	86	92
Slovenia	77	77	77	77
South Africa	58	62	79	82
Spain	91	94	91	95
Sweden	90	90	91	91
Switzerland	92	94	89	93
Thailand	99	99	99	99
United States	71	78	72	79

*Seventh and eighth grades in most countries; see Table 2 for information about the grades tested in each country.
** Participation rates for the Philippines are unweighted.
A dash (–) indicates data are unavailable. Israel and Kuwait did not test the lower grade.

SOURCE: IEA Third International Mathematics and Science Study (TIMSS), 1994-95.

Indicating Compliance with Sampling Guidelines in the Report

Figure A.3 shows how countries have been grouped in tables reporting achievement results. Countries that achieved acceptable participation rates – 85% of both the schools and students, or a combined rate (the product of school and student participation) of 75% – with or without replacement schools, and that complied with the TIMSS guidelines for grade selection and classroom sampling are shown in the first panel of Figure A.3. Countries that met the guidelines only after including replacement schools are annotated. These countries (25 at the eighth grade and 27 at the seventh grade) appear in the tables in Chapters 1, 2, and 3 ordered by achievement.

Countries not reaching at least 50% school participation without the use of replacement schools, or that failed to reach the sampling participation standard even with the inclusion of replacement schools, are shown in the second panel of Figure A.3. These countries are presented in a separate section of the achievement tables in Chapters 1, 2, and 3 in alphabetical order, and are shown in tables in Chapters 4 and 5 in italics.

To provide a better curricular match, four countries (i.e., Colombia, Germany, Romania, and Slovenia) elected to test their seventh- and eighth-grade students even though that meant not testing the two grades with the most 13-year-olds and led to their students being somewhat older than in the other countries. These countries are also presented in a separate section of the achievement tables in Chapters 1, 2, and 3 in alphabetical order, and are shown in tables in Chapters 4 and 5 in italics.

For a variety of reasons, three countries (Denmark, Greece, and Thailand) did not comply with the guidelines for sampling classrooms. Their results are also presented in a separate section of the achievement tables in Chapters 1, 2, and 3 in alphabetical order, and are italicized in tables in Chapters 4 and 5. At the eighth grade, Israel, Kuwait, and South Africa also had difficulty complying with the classroom selection guidelines, but in addition had other difficulties (Kuwait tested a single grade with relatively few 13-year-olds; Israel and South Africa had low sampling participation rates), and so these countries are also presented in separate sections in tables in Chapters 1, 2, and 3, and are italicized in tables in Chapters 4 and 5. At the seventh grade, South Africa had a better sampling participation rate, and is presented in the same section of tables as Denmark, Greece and Thailand. Israel and Kuwait did not test at the seventh grade.

Because the Philippines was unable to document clearly the school sampling procedures used, its results are not presented in the main body of the report. A small set of results for the Philippines can be found in Appendix C.

Figure A.3

Countries Grouped for Reporting of Achievement According to Their Compliance with Guidelines for Sample Implementation and Participation Rates

Eighth Grade	Seventh Grade
Countries satisfying guidelines for sample participation rates, grade selection and sampling procedures	
† Belgium (Fl) Canada Cyprus Czech Republic †2 England France Hong Kong Hungary Iceland Iran, Islamic Rep. Ireland Japan Korea 1 Latvia 1 Lithuania New Zealand Norway Portugal Russian Federation Singapore Slovak Republic Spain Sweden 1 Switzerland † United States	† Belgium (Fr) † Belgium (Fl) Canada Cyprus Czech Republic †2 England France Hong Kong Hungary Iceland Iran, Islamic Rep. Ireland Japan Korea 1 Latvia (LSS) 1 Lithuania New Zealand Norway Portugal Russian Federation † Scotland Singapore Slovak Republic Spain Sweden 1 Switzerland † United States
Countries not satisfying guidelines for sample participation	
Australia Austria Belgium (Fr) Bulgaria Netherlands Scotland	Australia Austria Bulgaria Netherlands
Countries not meeting age/grade specifications (high percentage of older students)	
Colombia †1 Germany Romania Slovenia	Colombia †1 Germany Romania Slovenia
Countries with unapproved sampling procedures at the classroom level	
Denmark Greece Thailand	Denmark Greece 1 South Africa Thailand
Countries with unapproved sampling procedures at classroom level and not meeting other guidelines	
1 Israel Kuwait South Africa	
Countries with unapproved sampling procedures at school level	
3 Philippines	3 Philippines

†Met guidelines for sample participation rates only after replacement schools were included.

1 National Desired Population does not cover all of International Desired Population (see Table 1). Because coverage falls below 65%, Latvia is annotated LSS for Latvian Speaking Schools only.

2 National Defined Population covers less than 90 percent of National Desired Population (see Table 1).

3 TIMSS was unable to compute sampling weights for the Philippines. Selected unweighted achievement results for the Philippines are presented in Appendix C.

SOURCE: IEA Third International Mathematics and Science Study (TIMSS), 1994-95.

Data Collection

Each participating country was responsible for carrying out all aspects of the data collection, using standardized procedures developed for the study. Training manuals were developed for school coordinators and test administrators that explained procedures for receipt and distribution of materials as well as for the activities related to the testing sessions. The test administrator manuals covered procedures for test security, standardized scripts to regulate directions and timing, rules for answering students' questions, and steps to ensure that identification on the test booklets and questionnaires corresponded to the information on the forms used to track students.

Each country was responsible for conducting quality control procedures and describing this effort as part of the NRC's report documenting procedures used in the study. In addition, the International Study Center considered it essential to establish some method to monitor compliance with standardized procedures. NRCs were asked to nominate a person, such as a retired school teacher, to serve as quality control monitor for their countries, and in almost all cases, the International Study Center adopted the NRCs' first suggestion. The International Study Center developed manuals for the quality control monitors and briefed them in two-day training sessions about TIMSS, the responsibilities of the national centers in conducting the study, and their own roles and responsibilities.

The quality control monitors interviewed the NRCs about data collection plans and procedures. They also selected a sample of approximately 10 schools to visit where they observed testing sessions and interviewed school coordinators.[10] Quality control monitors observed test administrations and interviewed school coordinators in 37 countries, and interviewed school coordinators or test administrators in 3 additional countries.

The results of the interviews indicate that, in general, NRCs had prepared well for data collection and, despite the heavy demands of the schedule and shortages of resources, were in a position to conduct the data collection in an efficient and professional manner. Similarly, the TIMSS tests appeared to have been administered in compliance with international procedures, including the activities preliminary to the testing session, the activities during the testing sessions, and the school-level activities related to receiving, distributing, and returning materials from the national centers.

[10] The results of the interviews and observations by the quality control monitors are presented in Martin, M.O., Hoyle, C.D., and Gregory, K.D. (1996). "Monitoring the TIMSS Data Collection" and "Observing the TIMSS Test Administration" both in M.O. Martin and I.V.S. Mullis (eds.), *Third International Mathematics and Science Study: Quality Assurance in Data Collection.* Chestnut Hill, MA: Boston College.

Scoring the Free-Response Items

Because approximately one-third of the written test time was devoted to free-response items, TIMSS needed to develop procedures for reliably evaluating student responses within and across countries. Scoring utilized two-digit codes with rubrics specific to each item. Development of the rubrics was led by the Norwegian TIMSS national center. The first digit designates the correctness level of the response. The second digit, combined with the first digit, represents a diagnostic code used to identify specific types of approaches, strategies, or common errors and misconceptions. Although not specifically used in this report, analyses of responses based on the second digit should provide insight into ways to help students better understand science concepts and problem-solving approaches.

To meet the goal of implementing reliable scoring procedures based on the TIMSS rubrics, the International Study Center prepared guides containing the rubrics and explanations of how to implement them together with example student responses for the various rubric categories. These guides, together with more examples of student responses for practice in applying the rubrics, were used as a basis for an ambitious series of regional training sessions. The training sessions were designed to assist representatives of national centers who would then be responsible for training personnel in their respective countries to apply the two-digit codes reliably.[11]

To gather and document empirical information about the within-country agreement among scorers, TIMSS developed a procedure whereby systematic subsamples of approximately 10% of the students' responses were to be coded independently by two different readers. To provide information about the cross-country agreement among scorers, TIMSS conducted a special study at Population 2, where 39 scorers from 21 of the participating countries evaluated common sets of students' responses to more than half of the free-response items.

Table A.9 shows the average and range of the within-country exact percent of agreement between scorers on the free-response items in the Population 2 science test for 26 countries. Unfortunately, lack of resources precluded several countries from providing this information. A high percent of exact agreement was observed, with averages across the items for the correctness score ranging from 88% to 100% and an overall average of 95% across the 26 countries.

The cross-country coding reliability study involved 350 students' responses for each of 14 mathematics and 17 science items, totaling 10,850 responses in all. The responses were random samples from the within-country reliability samples from seven English-test countries: Australia, Canada, England, Ireland, New Zealand, Singapore, and

[11] The procedures used in the training sessions are documented in Mullis, I.V.S., Garden, R.A., and Jones, C.A. (1996). "Training for Scoring the TIMSS Free-Response Items" in M.O. Martin and D.L. Kelly (eds.), *Third International Mathematics and Science Study Technical Report, Volume I*. Chestnut Hill, MA: Boston College.

Table A.9

TIMSS Within-Country Free-Response Coding Reliability Data for Population 2 Science Items*

Country	Correctness Score Agreement			Diagnostic Score Agreement		
	Average of Exact Percent Agreement Across Items	Range of Exact Percent Agreement		Average of Exact Percent Agreement Across Items	Range of Exact Percent Agreement	
		Min	Max		Min	Max
Australia	91	69	99	78	48	97
Belgium (Fl)	100	95	100	98	82	100
Bulgaria	91	63	100	81	50	100
Canada	92	76	100	80	59	99
Colombia	97	83	100	91	73	100
Czech Republic	96	87	100	90	61	100
England	97	90	100	91	65	100
France	99	95	100	97	89	100
Germany	94	81	100	84	66	100
Hong Kong	94	72	100	87	56	100
Iceland	95	74	100	83	22	98
Iran, Islamic Rep.	88	67	100	73	33	99
Ireland	95	87	100	89	69	100
Japan	100	96	100	98	87	100
Netherlands	92	75	100	79	17	100
New Zealand	97	90	100	90	63	100
Norway	95	87	100	91	71	100
Portugal	96	88	100	91	75	100
Russian Federation	96	87	100	91	73	100
Scotland	89	73	99	74	52	96
Singapore	98	92	100	95	86	100
Slovak Republic	92	62	100	81	43	100
Spain	95	85	100	88	73	98
Sweden	94	80	100	83	54	99
Switzerland	98	93	100	93	85	99
United States	97	90	100	89	74	100
AVERAGE	95	82	100	87	63	99

*Based on 33 science items, including 4 multiple-part items.
Note: Percent agreement was computed separately for each part, and each part was treated as a separate item in computing averages and ranges.

SOURCE: IEA Third International Mathematics and Science Study (TIMSS), 1994-95.

the United States. The responses were presented to the scorers according to a rotated design whereby each response was coded by 7 to 18 different scorers. This design resulted in a large number of comparisons between coders, approximately 10,000 or more for each item.

Table A.10 presents the percent of exact agreement for the 17 science items and the scorers involved in the international study. For comparison purposes, it also shows the average and range of the percent of exact agreement for each of the items within the 26 countries submitting data about their scoring reliability. The percent of exact agreement for each science item was fairly high on the correctness score agreement. Most measures fell between 80% and 99%, although measures for three items were between 72% and 78%. In general, the average international correctness score agreement for the science items was not as high as the within-country agreement (86% as opposed to 94%), but results are acceptable, and to be expected given the nature of the science items and the nature of the international coding reliability study. The TIMSS data from the reliability studies indicate that scoring procedures were robust for the science items, especially for the correctness score used for the analyses in this report.[12]

[12] Details about the reliability studies can be found in Mullis, I.V.S. and Smith, T.A. (1996). "Quality Control Steps for Free-Response Scoring" in M.O. Martin and I.V.S. Mullis (eds.), *Third International Mathematics and Science Study: Quality Assurance in Data Collection*. Chestnut Hill, MA: Boston College.

Table A.10

Percent Exact Agreement for Coding of Science Items for International and Within-Country Reliability Studies

Item Label	Total Valid Comparisons in International Study	Correctness Score Agreement				Diagnostic Code Agreement			
		International Study	Within-Country Study			International Study	Within-Country Study		
			Average	Min	Max		Average	Min	Max
O10	9078	99	99	95	100	98	97	80	100
O17	46035	94	97	77	100	74	86	64	100
Q18	9150	93	96	81	100	85	91	54	100
K19	12600	93	95	83	100	67	80	52	99
P03	46050	92	97	88	100	78	88	58	100
K10	46050	91	96	90	100	79	91	79	99
[1] W01A	9150	90	95	83	100	71	87	67	99
[1] W01B	9150	89	95	87	100	77	89	74	98
R04	45930	89	96	90	100	70	84	65	98
P06	46050	88	93	74	100	74	87	64	100
O14	9150	88	96	86	100	83	91	65	100
R05	9122	86	95	86	100	72	87	61	100
O16	45930	86	95	81	100	59	80	53	96
Q17	46034	82	93	74	100	66	87	65	100
P05	9150	80	93	82	100	59	82	47	100
W02	46050	78	92	75	100	70	89	69	99
Q12	12600	75	91	74	100	51	78	55	100
R03	9129	72	90	70	100	50	82	59	100
AVERAGE SCIENCE ITEMS		86	94	81	100	70	86	62	99

[1]Two-part items; each part is analyzed separately.

SOURCE: IEA Third International Mathematics and Science Study (TIMSS), 1994-95.

Test Reliability

Table A.11 displays the science test reliability coefficient for each country for the lower and upper grades (usually seventh and eighth grades). This coefficient is the median KR-20 reliability across the eight test booklets. Median reliabilities in the lower grade ranged from 0.83 in the United States and the Philippines to 0.68 in Portugal and in the upper grade from 0.84 in Australia, Bulgaria, and the Philippines to 0.69 in Kuwait. The international median, shown in the last row of the table, is the median of the reliability coefficients for all countries. These international medians are 0.77 for the lower grade and 0.78 for the upper grade.

Data Processing

To ensure the availability of comparable, high quality data for analysis, TIMSS engaged in a rigorous set of quality control steps to create the international database.[13] TIMSS prepared manuals and software for countries to use in entering their data so the information would be in a standardized international format before being forwarded to the IEA Data Processing Center in Hamburg for creation of the international database. Upon arrival at the IEA Data Processing Center, the data from each country underwent an exhaustive cleaning process. The data-cleaning process involved several iterative steps and procedures designed to identify, document, and correct deviations from the international instruments, file structures, and coding schemes. This process also emphasized consistency of information within national data sets and appropriate linking among the many student, teacher, and school data files.

Throughout the process, the data were checked and double-checked by the IEA Data Processing Center, the International Study Center, and the national centers. The national centers were contacted regularly and given multiple opportunities to review the data for their countries. In conjunction with the Australian Council for Educational Research (ACER), the International Study Center conducted a review of items statistics for each of the cognitive items in each of the countries to identify poorly performing items. Twenty-one countries had one or more items deleted (in most cases, one). Usually the poor statistics (negative point-biserials for the key, large item-by-country interactions, and statistics indicating lack of fit with the model) were a result of translation, adaptation, or printing deviations.

[13] These steps are detailed in Jungclaus, H. and Bruneforth, M. (1996). "Data Consistency Checking Across Countries" in M.O. Martin and D.L. Kelly (eds.), *Third International Mathematics and Science Study Technical Report, Volume I*. Chestnut Hill, MA: Boston College.

Table A.11

Cronbach's Alpha Reliability Coefficients[1] - TIMSS Science Test Lower and Upper Grades (Seventh and Eighth Grades*)

Country	Lower Grade	Upper Grade
Australia	0.81	0.84
Austria	0.80	0.81
Belgium (Fl)	0.68	0.78
Belgium (Fr)	0.72	0.79
Bulgaria	0.81	0.84
Canada	0.79	0.78
Colombia	0.69	0.72
Cyprus	0.74	0.79
Czech Republic	0.75	0.78
Denmark	0.77	0.77
England	0.82	0.83
France	0.71	0.73
Germany	0.80	0.82
Greece	0.78	0.77
Hong Kong	0.78	0.78
Hungary	0.80	0.79
Iceland	0.74	0.75
Iran, Islamic Rep.	0.71	0.71
Ireland	0.78	0.82
Israel	–	0.83
Japan	0.76	0.79
Korea	0.79	0.79
Kuwait	–	0.69
Latvia (LSS)	0.74	0.76
Lithuania	0.75	0.75
Netherlands	0.74	0.76
New Zealand	0.80	0.82
Norway	0.77	0.78
Philippines	0.83	0.84
Portugal	0.68	0.75
Romania	0.81	0.82
Russian Federation	0.79	0.79
Scotland	0.79	0.82
Singapore	0.81	0.77
Slovak Republic	0.77	0.81
Slovenia	0.77	0.78
South Africa	0.78	0.82
Spain	0.75	0.73
Sweden	0.76	0.77
Switzerland	0.74	0.78
Thailand	0.70	0.72
United States	0.83	0.83
International Median	0.77	0.78

*Seventh and eighth grade in most countries; see Table 2 for more information about the grades tested in each country. Israel and Kuwait did not test the lower grade.

[1]The reliability coefficient for each country is the median KR-20 reliability across the eight test booklets. The international median is the median of the reliability coefficients for all countries.

SOURCE: IEA Third International Mathematics and Science Study (TIMSS), 1994-95.

IRT Scaling and Data Analysis

Two general analysis approaches were used for this report – item response theory scaling methods and average percent correct technology. The overall science results were summarized using an item response theory (IRT) scaling method (Rasch model). This scaling method produces a science score by averaging the responses of each student to the items which they took in a way that takes into account the difficulty of each item. The methodology used in TIMSS includes refinements that enable reliable scores to be produced even though individual students responded to relatively small subsets of the total science item pool. Analyses of the response patterns of students from participating countries indicated that, although the items in the test address a wide range of science content, the performance of the students across the items was sufficiently consistent that it could be usefully summarized in a single science score.

The IRT methodology was preferred for developing comparable estimates of performance for all students, since students answered different test items depending upon which of the eight test booklets they received. The IRT analysis provides a common scale on which performance can be compared across countries. In addition to providing a basis for estimating mean achievement, scale scores permit estimates of how students within countries vary and provide information on percentiles of performance. The scale was standardized using students from both the grades tested. When all participating countries and grades are treated equally, the TIMSS scale average is 500 and the standard deviation is 100. Since the countries varied in size, each country was reweighted to contribute equally to the mean and standard deviation of the scale. The average of the scale scores was constructed to be the average of the 41 means of participants that were available at the eighth grade and the 39 means at the seventh grade. The average and standard deviation of the scale scores are arbitrary and do not affect scale interpretations.

The analytic approach underlying the results in Chapters 2 and 3 of this report involved calculating the percentage of correct answers for each item for each participating country (as well as the percentages of different types of incorrect responses). The percents correct were averaged to summarize science performance overall and in each of the content areas for each country as a whole and by gender. For items with more than one part, each part was analyzed separately in calculating the average percents correct. Also, for items with more than one point awarded for full credit, the average percents correct reflect an average of the points received by students in each country. This was achieved by including the percent of students receiving one score point as well as the percentage receiving two score points and three score points in the calculations. Thus, the average percents correct are based on the number of score points rather than the number of items, per se. An exception to this is the international average percents correct reported for example items, where the values reflect the percent of students receiving full credit.

Estimating Sampling Error

Because the statistics presented in this report are estimates of national performance based on samples of students, rather than the values that could be calculated if every student in every country would have answered every question, it is important to have measures of the degree of uncertainty of the estimates. The jackknife procedure was used to estimate the standard error associated with each statistic presented in this report. The use of confidence intervals, based on the standard errors, provides a way to make inferences about the population means and proportions in a manner that reflects the uncertainty associated with the sample estimates. An estimated sample statistic plus or minus two standard errors represents a 95% confidence interval for the corresponding population result.

Appendix B

The Test-Curriculum Matching Analysis

When comparing student achievement across countries, it is important that the comparisons be as "fair" as possible. TIMSS has worked towards this goal in a number of ways, including providing detailed procedures for standardizing the population definitions, sampling, test translations, test administration, scoring, and database formation. Developing the TIMSS tests involved the interaction of experts in the sciences with representatives of the participating countries and testing specialists.[1] The National Research Coordinators (NRCs) from each country formally approved the TIMSS test, thus accepting it as being sufficiently fair to compare their students' science achievement with that of students from other countries.

Although the TIMSS test was developed to represent a set of agreed-upon science content areas, there are differences among the curricula of participating countries that result in various science topics being taught at different grades. To restrict test items not only to those topics in the curricula of all countries but also to those covered in the same sequence in all participating countries would severely limit test coverage and restrict the research questions about international differences that TIMSS is designed to address. The TIMSS tests, therefore, inevitably contain some items measuring topics unfamiliar to some students in some countries.

The Test-Curriculum Matching Analysis (TCMA) was developed and conducted to investigate the appropriateness of the TIMSS science test for seventh- and eighth-grade students in the participating countries, and to show how student performance for individual countries varied when based only on the test questions that were judged to be relevant to their own curriculum.[2]

To gather data about the extent to which the TIMSS tests were relevant to the curriculum of the participating countries, TIMSS asked the NRC of each country to report whether or not each item was in their country's intended curriculum at each of the two grades being tested. The NRC was asked to choose a person or persons who were very familiar with the curricula at the grades being tested to make the determination. Since an item might be in the curriculum for some but not all students in a country, an item was determined appropriate if it was in the intended curriculum for more than 50% of the students. The NRCs had considerable flexibility in selecting items and may have considered items inappropriate for other reasons. All participating countries except Thailand returned the information for analysis.

Tables B.1 and B.2 present the TCMA results for the eighth and seventh grades, respectively. The first row of each table indicates that at both grades the countries varied substantially in the number of items considered appropriate. At the eighth

1 See Appendix A for more information on the test development.

2 Because there also may be curriculum areas covered in some countries that are not covered by the TIMSS tests, the TCMA does not provide complete information about how well the TIMSS tests cover the curricula of the countries.

grade, more than half of the countries indicated that items representing three-quarters or more of the score points (110 out of a possible 146) were appropriate,[3] with the percent ranging from 100% in Spain, Iceland, and the United States to approximately 40% in Korea (59 score points) and French-speaking Belgium (58 score points). Fewer items were selected at the seventh grade, but nearly half of the countries selected at least 60%, with several selecting at least three-quarters of the score points. All items were selected at the seventh grade as well as the eighth grade in both the United States and Iceland. At the seventh grade there were also several countries, including Korea and Japan, which retained about 30% or less. That lower percentages of items were selected for the TCMA at the seventh grade is consistent with the instrument-development process, which put more emphasis on the upper-grade curriculum.

Since most countries indicated that some items were not included in their intended curricula at the two grades tested, the question becomes whether the inclusion of these items had any effect on the international performance comparisons.[4] The TCMA results provide a method for answering this question, providing evidence that it is reasonable to make cross-national comparisons on the basis of the TIMSS science test.

Each of the first columns in Tables B.1 and B.2 shows the overall average percent correct for each country (as discussed in Chapter 2 and reproduced here for convenience in making comparisons). The countries are presented in the order of their overall performance, from highest to lowest. To interpret these tables, reading across a row provides the average percent correct for the students in the country identified by that row on the items selected by each of the countries named across the top of the table. For example, at the eighth grade, Singapore, where the average percent correct was 72% on its own set of items, also had 72% for the items selected by Korea, 73% for those selected by Japan, 69% for those selected by the Czech Republic, and so forth. The column for a country shows how each of the other countries performed on the subset of items selected for its own students. Using the set of items selected by Hong Kong as an example, on average, 71% of these items were answered correctly by the Singaporean students, 65% by the Korean students, 66% by the Japanese, and so forth. The shaded diagonal elements in each table show how each country performed on the subset of items that it selected based on its own curriculum. Thus, the Hong Kong students themselves averaged 59% correct responses on the items identified by Hong Kong for the analysis.

[3] Of the 135 items in the test, some items were assigned more score points than others. In particular, some items had two parts, and some extended-response items were scored on a two-point scale and others on a three-point scale. The total number of score points available for analysis was 146. The TCMA uses the score points in order to give the same weight to items that they received in the test scoring.

[4] It should be noted that the performance levels presented in Tables B.1 and B.2 are based on average percents correct as was done in Chapter 2, which is different from the average scale scores that were presented in Chapter 1. The cost and delay of scaling would have been prohibitive for the TCMA analyses.

Table B.1 Test-Curriculum Matching Analysis Results - Science - Upper Grade (Eighth Grade*)

Average Percent Correct Based on Subsets of Items Specially Identified by Each Country as Addressing Its Curriculum (See Table B.3 for corresponding standard errors)

Instructions: Read ***across*** the row to compare that country's performance based on the test items included by each of the countries across the top.
Read ***down*** the column under a country name to compare the performance of the country down the left on the items included by the country listed on the top.
Read along the ***diagonal*** to compare performance for each different country based on its own decisions about the test items to include.

Country	*Average Percent Correct on All Items*	**Singapore**	**Korea**	**Japan**	**Czech Republic**	*Netherlands*	*Bulgaria*	*Slovenia*	*Austria*	**England**	**Hungary**	**Belgium (Fl)**	*Australia*	**Slovak Republic**	**Sweden**	**Canada**	**Ireland**	**United States**	**Russian Federation**	*Germany*	**New Zealand**	**Norway**	**Hong Kong**	*Israel*	**Switzerland**	**Spain**	*Scotland*	**France**	**Iceland**	*Greece*	*Denmark*	*Belgium (Fr)*	**Latvia (LSS)**	**Portugal**	*Romania*	**Lithuania**	**Iran, Islamic Rep.**	**Cyprus**	*Kuwait*	*Colombia*	*South Africa*
(Number of Score Points Included)	*146***	*109*	*59*	*86*	*136*	*102*	*112*	*140*	*131*	*124*	*129*	*98*	*133*	*129*	*125*	*121*	*90*	*146*	*96*	*129*	*126*	*111*	*68*	*102*	*105*	*146*	*97*	*73*	*146*	*111*	*70*	*58*	*113*	*133*	*99*	*120*	*87*	*78*	*131*	*112*	*74*
Singapore	70 (1.0)	72	72	73	69	72	70	69	70	71	69	69	70	70	71	71	72	70	70	70	72	70	71	71	72	70	71	71	70	71	72	70	68	70	71	71	69	72	70	72	73
Korea	66 (0.3)	66	67	68	66	67	66	66	66	66	65	67	65	66	66	67	67	66	68	66	67	67	65	66	68	66	67	67	66	65	67	67	65	65	65	68	65	66	66	67	65
Japan	65 (0.3)	66	65	70	65	68	66	66	67	66	65	66	65	66	66	67	66	65	68	66	67	66	66	66	68	65	67	65	65	65	68	67	65	65	65	67	65	66	66	65	66
Czech Republic	64 (0.8)	65	66	67	64	66	65	64	65	63	65	64	64	66	66	66	67	64	67	64	65	65	65	65	67	64	64	65	64	65	66	68	62	64	64	66	64	66	64	66	65
Netherlands	62 (1.0)	63	62	66	63	66	63	62	63	63	63	64	62	63	64	65	64	62	64	63	65	64	64	64	66	62	63	64	62	63	66	67	61	62	63	64	61	65	62	63	61
Bulgaria	62 (1.0)	64	65	65	62	64	64	62	63	61	62	61	61	63	63	62	63	62	66	62	62	63	62	62	65	62	61	64	62	62	64	62	60	62	63	64	61	64	61	64	64
Slovenia	62 (0.5)	62	63	64	62	63	62	62	63	61	62	63	61	63	63	63	63	62	64	62	63	63	62	62	65	62	62	64	62	62	63	66	60	61	60	64	61	63	61	63	63
Austria	61 (0.7)	63	65	65	61	63	62	62	63	61	62	61	61	63	63	63	64	61	64	62	63	63	63	62	64	61	61	63	61	63	64	64	59	61	62	63	62	64	61	63	62
England	61 (0.6)	62	62	63	62	64	61	61	62	62	62	63	61	62	62	64	63	61	62	61	64	63	63	62	64	61	62	61	61	63	64	63	59	61	61	63	61	64	61	63	61
Hungary	61 (0.6)	62	63	64	60	62	61	61	61	60	62	61	61	63	62	62	61	61	64	61	62	62	60	61	63	61	59	62	61	62	61	63	59	61	60	63	61	64	60	62	61
Belgium (Fl)	60 (1.1)	61	62	64	61	64	60	60	61	60	61	62	60	62	62	63	63	60	62	61	62	63	63	62	64	60	61	62	60	61	65	65	59	60	60	62	59	63	60	62	59
Australia	60 (0.7)	61	61	62	60	62	60	60	60	60	60	60	60	61	61	62	62	60	60	60	62	61	60	60	62	60	60	60	60	61	62	64	58	59	59	61	59	62	60	61	60
Slovak Republic	59 (0.6)	60	59	63	60	61	60	59	61	58	60	59	59	61	60	61	62	59	63	60	60	61	62	60	62	59	59	61	59	60	61	62	58	59	60	62	60	63	59	60	61
Sweden	59 (0.6)	58	60	63	59	61	59	59	59	58	59	58	59	60	61	60	60	59	61	59	61	61	60	60	63	59	60	61	59	59	62	63	57	58	59	61	58	61	59	60	59
Canada	59 (0.5)	59	58	61	59	61	59	59	59	59	59	59	59	59	60	61	61	59	60	59	61	60	60	60	62	59	59	59	59	60	61	62	58	58	58	61	57	61	58	60	59
Ireland	58 (0.9)	59	60	59	59	60	58	58	59	59	59	59	58	59	60	60	62	58	59	58	60	60	60	60	61	58	59	59	58	60	61	60	57	58	58	60	57	61	58	60	57
United States	58 (1.0)	59	60	60	58	60	58	58	59	59	59	59	58	59	60	60	61	58	59	58	60	60	59	59	61	58	58	60	58	59	62	63	57	58	57	60	56	61	58	60	58
Russian Federation	58 (0.8)	59	61	62	59	61	59	58	59	58	59	58	58	60	60	60	61	58	65	59	59	60	60	60	61	58	59	60	58	59	61	61	57	58	59	61	59	61	59	60	61
Germany	58 (1.0)	59	60	62	58	60	58	58	59	58	58	58	58	59	59	60	60	58	61	59	60	59	59	58	61	58	58	59	58	59	60	61	56	57	58	60	57	61	58	59	59
New Zealand	58 (0.8)	58	58	60	58	60	58	57	58	58	58	58	58	58	59	59	59	58	58	58	60	59	59	59	60	58	58	58	58	59	60	60	56	57	57	59	56	60	58	59	57
Norway	58 (0.4)	56	56	61	58	60	57	58	58	58	58	58	58	58	59	59	59	58	58	58	60	60	60	58	62	58	59	57	58	58	62	61	57	57	58	60	56	60	58	59	58
Hong Kong	58 (1.0)	59	58	61	58	60	59	58	59	58	57	57	57	58	59	59	59	58	61	58	60	58	59	58	61	58	58	60	58	58	59	62	56	57	57	59	57	59	57	60	60
Israel	57 (1.1)	57	57	60	57	59	57	57	58	56	58	58	57	58	58	58	59	57	58	57	58	58	58	58	59	57	57	57	57	58	60	60	55	57	57	59	56	61	57	58	56
Switzerland	56 (0.5)	57	56	60	56	59	56	57	57	56	57	57	56	58	58	59	57	56	58	57	58	58	58	57	60	56	56	57	56	57	59	60	55	56	57	58	56	59	56	58	56
Spain	56 (0.4)	56	57	58	56	57	56	56	57	55	56	56	55	57	56	57	57	56	57	55	57	58	56	56	57	56	55	55	56	57	58	58	53	55	55	57	55	59	55	57	55
Scotland	55 (1.0)	56	55	58	56	58	56	55	56	56	56	56	55	56	56	57	57	55	56	55	58	57	57	56	58	55	56	55	55	57	57	57	53	55	56	57	55	59	55	57	55
France	54 (0.6)	54	54	57	54	56	53	54	54	54	55	54	53	55	55	56	55	54	56	54	55	55	54	55	57	54	54	57	54	54	55	59	53	53	53	57	52	56	53	54	52
Iceland	52 (0.9)	51	51	55	52	55	53	52	53	52	52	53	51	53	53	54	52	52	54	53	55	55	53	53	55	52	52	52	52	52	55	57	51	51	52	54	51	55	52	53	51
Greece	52 (0.5)	53	53	54	52	53	53	52	53	52	53	52	52	53	53	53	53	52	53	52	53	53	53	53	54	52	52	52	52	54	52	53	50	52	52	54	52	55	52	54	54
Denmark	51 (0.6)	50	49	54	51	53	51	51	52	51	51	52	50	52	52	53	51	51	53	51	53	53	51	52	54	51	52	52	51	51	55	57	49	50	50	53	50	53	51	51	50
Belgium (Fr)	50 (0.7)	50	50	54	50	53	51	50	51	49	51	51	50	51	52	52	51	50	53	51	52	52	51	51	54	50	50	52	50	50	52	56	49	50	50	53	49	53	50	51	49
Latvia (LSS)	50 (0.6)	51	52	55	50	52	51	50	51	51	51	51	50	52	51	52	51	50	54	51	51	51	52	52	53	50	50	52	50	50	51	54	49	50	51	52	50	52	50	51	51
Portugal	50 (0.6)	51	53	53	50	52	50	50	51	50	51	49	50	51	51	51	52	50	52	50	51	51	49	50	52	50	49	52	50	51	52	54	48	50	49	52	49	54	50	52	49
Romania	50 (0.8)	51	52	52	50	51	50	50	51	49	50	51	50	52	50	51	52	50	54	50	50	51	49	50	51	50	48	52	50	49	52	52	47	50	48	51	50	51	49	52	51
Lithuania	49 (0.7)	50	51	53	49	51	50	49	50	48	50	49	49	51	50	50	51	49	55	49	49	50	50	50	51	49	49	51	49	49	50	53	47	49	50	52	49	50	49	50	51
Iran, Islamic Rep.	47 (0.6)	49	51	50	48	48	49	47	49	48	48	48	48	49	48	49	49	47	51	48	48	49	49	47	49	47	47	48	47	49	47	47	47	48	50	49	50	52	48	50	48
Cyprus	47 (0.4)	48	47	50	47	48	47	47	48	47	47	47	46	48	48	48	50	47	49	47	48	48	49	48	50	47	47	48	47	48	48	50	45	47	47	49	47	51	47	49	48
Kuwait	43 (0.9)	43	42	45	43	44	44	43	44	43	42	43	42	43	43	44	44	43	44	43	44	45	43	42	44	43	42	44	43	44	44	43	42	43	44	44	43	47	43	45	43
Colombia	39 (0.8)	39	40	41	39	40	39	39	40	39	39	40	39	39	39	40	41	39	40	38	40	40	39	40	41	39	39	39	39	40	42	41	36	39	38	40	38	41	38	41	39
South Africa	27 (1.3)	28	27	29	27	28	27	27	28	27	26	27	26	27	27	27	29	27	30	27	27	27	28	27	28	27	26	28	27	27	28	29	26	27	27	28	27	28	26	28	28
International Average	**55 (0.7)**	**56**	**56**	**59**	**56**	**58**	**56**	**56**	**56**	**56**	**56**	**56**	**55**	**57**	**57**	**57**	**57**	**55**	**58**	**56**	**57**	**57**	**57**	**56**	**58**	**55**	**56**	**57**	**55**	**56**	**58**	**58**	**54**	**55**	**56**	**57**	**55**	**58**	**55**	**57**	**56**

*Eighth grade in most countries; see Table 2 for more information about the grades tested in each country.

**Of the 135 items in the science test, some items had two parts and some extended-response items were scored on a two- or three-point scale, resulting in 146 total score points.

( ) Standard errors for the average percent of correct responses on all items appear in parentheses. Standard errors for scores based on subsets of items are provided in Table B.3.

Because results are rounded to the nearest whole number, some totals may appear inconsistent.

Countries shown in italics did not satisfy one or more guidelines for sample participation rates, age/grade specifications, or classroom sampling procedures (see Figure A.3 for details).

Because population coverage falls below 65% Latvia is annotated LSS for Latvian Speaking Schools only.

SOURCE: IEA Third International Mathematics and Science Study (TIMSS), 1994-95.

Table B.2 Test-Curriculum Matching Analysis Results - Science - Lower Grade (Seventh Grade*)

Average Percent Correct Based on Subsets of Items Specially Identified by Each Country as Addressing Its Curriculum (See Table B.4 for corresponding standard errors)

Instructions: Read ***across*** the row to compare that country's performance based on the test items included by each of the countries across the top.
Read ***down*** the column under a country name to compare the performance of the country down the left on the items included by the country listed on the top.
Read along the ***diagonal*** to compare performance for each different country based on its own decisions about the test items to include.

Country	Average Percent Correct on All Items	Singapore	Korea	Japan	Czech Republic	*Slovenia*	Belgium (Fl)	*Bulgaria*	*Netherlands*	England	Hungary	*Austria*	Slovak Republic	United States	Canada	*Australia*	Hong Kong	*Germany*	Ireland	Sweden	New Zealand	Norway	Switzerland	Russian Federation	Spain	Scotland	Iceland	France	Belgium (Fr)	*Romania*	*Greece*	*Denmark*	Iran, Islamic Rep.	Latvia (LSS)	Portugal	Cyprus	*Colombia*	Lithuania	*South Africa*
(Number of Score Points Included)	146**	83	43	45	108	132	46	105	34	104	98	52	111	146	78	94	32	88	60	86	110	92	36	49	132	49	146	26	23	91	72	20	48	46	81	29	79	108	26
Singapore	61 (1.2)	66	65	65	62	62	62	63	63	63	61	65	62	61	65	66	62	63	65	67	65	64	66	65	62	66	61	68	61	64	63	68	63	62	62	66	64	64	66
Korea	61 (0.4)	63	64	67	62	62	63	64	65	63	61	67	63	61	65	63	60	65	63	66	65	63	68	67	62	65	61	69	61	62	64	68	61	62	63	63	65	62	68
Japan	59 (0.3)	60	61	67	60	60	60	61	63	61	58	63	62	59	62	61	59	64	59	66	62	61	64	66	60	63	59	65	63	61	62	66	61	59	60	65	62	59	65
Czech Republic	58 (0.8)	60	61	64	61	59	60	61	63	59	59	64	62	58	60	60	55	63	62	65	62	61	63	64	59	59	58	65	65	62	61	62	62	57	59	59	63	61	61
Slovenia	57 (0.5)	59	60	61	58	58	59	58	60	57	58	61	60	57	58	59	55	61	62	62	59	60	63	62	57	59	57	65	65	59	59	60	61	57	59	58	61	59	61
Belgium (Fl)	57 (0.5)	58	58	60	59	58	60	58	65	58	59	61	60	57	61	59	59	62	60	66	61	63	66	63	59	61	57	61	64	59	62	66	63	57	59	58	64	59	58
Bulgaria	56 (1.0)	57	60	60	57	57	58	60	60	57	56	61	60	56	58	57	54	59	59	63	59	59	60	62	57	56	56	62	61	58	57	62	57	53	57	55	60	58	59
Netherlands	56 (0.7)	58	59	58	58	56	58	57	63	57	56	59	59	56	59	58	57	60	59	64	60	60	65	60	58	61	56	62	62	58	61	62	59	57	59	60	62	58	59
England	56 (0.6)	57	56	57	56	56	56	57	60	58	55	56	57	56	58	58	55	58	57	62	60	59	62	58	57	60	56	56	59	57	58	58	59	54	57	55	59	58	59
Hungary	56 (0.6)	57	57	57	57	56	56	57	61	55	56	59	58	56	56	58	52	59	59	60	58	58	60	62	56	53	56	60	60	58	57	61	59	52	56	51	60	58	57
Austria	55 (0.6)	58	56	58	55	56	57	56	60	55	56	60	59	55	57	57	53	59	58	62	59	59	62	59	56	55	55	60	63	59	58	59	59	54	57	57	60	58	58
Slovak Republic	54 (0.6)	56	58	61	57	54	55	56	58	55	55	60	58	54	55	56	53	59	59	60	57	58	60	61	55	56	54	61	58	57	56	59	59	54	55	54	58	56	57
United States	54 (1.1)	55	54	54	55	54	56	55	59	55	54	54	56	54	56	56	54	55	57	60	58	57	61	56	55	58	54	59	59	56	58	57	56	54	57	54	58	56	58
Canada	54 (0.5)	55	56	55	54	54	55	55	59	55	54	56	56	54	57	56	53	55	55	61	58	57	62	57	55	58	54	58	57	56	57	57	57	53	56	54	58	56	57
Australia	54 (0.7)	56	57	56	54	54	54	56	58	55	53	55	56	54	55	56	52	57	56	60	57	56	61	56	55	57	54	57	59	56	57	54	57	52	55	53	57	56	58
Hong Kong	53 (1.2)	56	57	57	54	54	56	56	60	55	52	58	54	53	56	55	54	56	55	60	57	55	61	59	54	58	53	60	60	55	55	54	55	52	54	51	56	54	61
Germany	53 (0.8)	55	55	57	53	54	54	55	58	53	53	57	56	53	55	55	51	57	55	60	57	56	60	57	54	52	53	59	60	55	56	58	56	51	54	53	58	55	56
Ireland	52 (0.7)	54	52	51	52	52	54	52	53	53	53	52	54	52	53	55	53	53	56	57	55	55	59	53	53	57	52	52	53	54	55	55	56	54	54	52	56	54	53
Sweden	51 (0.5)	53	53	56	53	52	52	53	57	53	52	54	53	51	54	53	50	56	54	59	56	56	60	56	53	53	51	55	59	53	55	58	53	52	53	54	57	53	54
New Zealand	50 (0.7)	52	50	51	51	50	50	52	54	52	50	51	52	50	52	53	50	53	51	56	55	54	58	51	52	53	50	53	54	52	54	52	53	50	52	51	55	52	52
Norway	50 (0.6)	51	53	54	52	51	50	52	57	51	50	52	53	50	53	52	49	54	53	58	54	55	59	54	52	52	50	52	55	52	55	58	53	50	52	52	56	52	52
Switzerland	50 (0.4)	53	52	54	50	51	52	51	55	51	51	55	53	50	52	52	49	55	53	57	54	54	60	55	52	52	50	56	56	52	53	55	54	50	52	51	56	51	52
Russian Federation	50 (0.8)	52	51	55	51	51	52	51	57	51	51	53	53	50	52	51	50	53	55	57	52	53	59	61	51	53	50	52	56	52	54	58	53	52	53	54	57	52	53
Spain	49 (0.4)	50	49	50	50	49	50	50	52	50	50	50	52	49	50	50	47	51	51	55	52	53	54	51	50	51	49	53	54	51	52	52	52	49	51	48	53	52	49
Scotland	48 (0.8)	50	50	50	49	48	49	50	51	50	48	49	50	48	51	51	49	50	50	54	52	52	55	50	49	53	48	50	51	50	50	49	51	46	49	46	52	50	52
Iceland	46 (0.6)	47	48	49	48	46	47	49	53	47	46	46	49	46	47	47	44	49	49	53	50	50	51	50	48	47	46	49	53	48	49	48	49	44	48	43	51	48	51
France	46 (0.6)	48	49	50	46	47	47	47	48	48	47	51	48	46	48	47	45	49	46	53	49	50	55	50	47	50	46	57	50	48	48	51	47	44	47	44	50	47	48
Belgium (Fr)	45 (0.7)	47	49	48	45	46	47	47	49	46	45	50	47	45	47	46	44	48	47	52	48	49	53	50	46	48	45	54	52	47	47	46	49	42	46	40	49	46	47
Romania	45 (0.7)	46	45	47	46	45	47	47	50	45	45	49	48	45	45	46	42	47	48	50	46	47	48	50	45	44	45	52	51	47	47	46	48	43	46	43	48	47	50
Greece	45 (0.5)	45	45	47	46	44	44	46	48	46	45	45	46	45	45	48	43	47	45	49	48	47	48	46	45	47	45	50	46	47	48	48	47	43	46	45	48	47	51
Denmark	44 (0.4)	45	46	49	45	44	45	46	50	45	44	48	47	44	47	45	42	49	45	53	47	48	53	51	45	46	44	48	52	46	48	52	47	41	46	44	49	45	47
Iran, Islamic Rep.	42 (0.6)	46	41	44	43	43	44	45	44	43	42	41	43	42	44	45	42	45	46	46	44	44	44	44	41	42	42	43	44	44	43	48	45	40	42	40	45	45	47
Latvia (LSS)	42 (0.5)	44	43	46	42	42	45	43	47	43	42	45	44	42	44	43	41	45	46	48	44	45	48	48	42	43	42	47	49	44	44	50	45	41	44	41	47	43	44
Portugal	41 (0.5)	43	41	42	41	41	42	42	43	41	41	44	44	41	42	42	37	43	45	47	44	44	45	45	42	43	41	47	44	42	44	47	45	42	45	42	46	44	42
Cyprus	40 (0.4)	43	42	43	40	40	42	41	42	42	41	44	42	40	42	42	40	42	43	45	42	43	45	43	40	45	40	47	43	43	42	48	44	40	41	44	43	42	45
Lithuania	38 (0.7)	40	39	44	37	38	41	39	42	39	38	42	40	38	40	38	36	41	42	44	40	40	45	46	38	40	38	41	44	40	40	45	40	38	40	38	44	39	43
Colombia	35 (0.7)	37	36	35	35	35	36	37	39	35	35	37	37	35	34	36	33	35	38	40	37	37	34	36	35	38	35	39	40	37	38	36	39	33	37	34	38	38	39
South Africa	26 (1.0)	27	27	28	26	25	27	26	28	26	25	27	27	26	25	26	26	27	29	29	27	27	27	30	26	26	26	28	27	27	27	26	27	25	26	25	27	27	30
International Average	**50 (0.7)**	**52**	**52**	**53**	**51**	**50**	**51**	**51**	**54**	**51**	**50**	**53**	**52**	**50**	**52**	**52**	**49**	**53**	**52**	**56**	**53**	**53**	**56**	**54**	**51**	**52**	**50**	**55**	**54**	**52**	**52**	**54**	**53**	**49**	**51**	**50**	**54**	**52**	**53**

*Seventh grade in most countries; see Table 2 for more information about the grades tested in each country.
**Of the 135 items in the science test, some items had two parts and some extended-response items were scored on a two- or three-point scale, resulting in 146 total score points.
( ) Standard errors for the average percent of correct responses on all items appear in parentheses. Standard errors for scores based on subsets of items are provided in Table B.4.
Because results are rounded to the nearest whole number, some totals may appear inconsistent.
Countries shown in italics did not satisfy one or more guidelines for sample participation rates, age/grade specifications, or classroom sampling procedures (see Figure A.3 for details).
Because population coverage falls below 65% Latvia is annotated LSS for Latvian Speaking Schools only.
SOURCE: IEA Third International Mathematics and Science Study (TIMSS), 1994-95.

The international averages of each country's selected items presented across the last row of the tables show that the selection of items for the participating countries varied somewhat in average difficulty, ranging from 55% to 59% at the eighth grade and from 49% to 56% at seventh grade. Despite these differences, the overall picture provided by both Tables B.1 and B.2 reveals that different item selections do not make a major difference in how well countries perform relative to each other. The items selected by some countries were more difficult than those selected by others. The relative performance of countries on the various item selections did vary somewhat, but generally not in a statistically significant manner.[5]

Comparing the diagonal element for a country with the overall average percentage correct shows the difference between performance on this subset of items and performance on the test as a whole. In general, there were only small increases in each country's performance on its own subset of items. To illustrate, the average percent correct for eighth-grade students in Singapore was 70%. The diagonal element shows that Singaporean students had about the same average percent correct (72%) based on the smaller set of items selected as relevant to the curriculum in Singapore as they did overall. In the eighth grade, most countries had a difference of less than 5 percentage points between the two performance measures, with the largest difference of 7% for the Russian Federation (65% compared to 58%). Performance differences between the entire TIMSS test and the subset of items selected for the TCMA were, in general, somewhat larger for seventh-grade students, including a few countries with an average performance that was about 10 percentage points higher on the subsets of items selected for the TCMA for their own students – Switzerland, France, and the Russian Federation. Even these increases are not particularly large, however, considering that France and Switzerland both selected less than one-quarter of the items at the seventh grade.

It is clear that the selection of items does not have a major effect on the general relationship among countries. Countries that had substantially higher or lower performance on the overall test in comparison to each other also had higher or lower relative performance on the different sets of items selected for the TCMA. For example, at the eighth grade, Singapore had the highest average percent correct on the test as a whole and on all of the different item selections, with Japan, Korea, and the Czech Republic among the four highest-performing countries in all cases. Although there are some changes in the ordering of countries based on the items selected for the TCMA, most of these differences are within the boundaries of sampling error. As the most extreme example, consider the 49 score points selected by the Russian Federation for the seventh grade. The Russian students did substantially better on these items than on the test as a whole, with 61% correct responses to these items, on average, compared to 50% average correct on the items on the test as a whole.

[5] Small differences in performance in these tables are not statistically significant. The standard errors for the estimated average percent correct statistics can found in Tables B.3 and B.4. We can say with 95% confidence that the value for the entire population will fall between the sample estimate plus or minus two standard errors.

However, all other countries also did better on these particular items, with an international average of 54% for the items selected by the Russian Federation compared with 50% on the test as a whole. Only 8 of the 22 countries that performed better than the Russian students on the overall test also did so on the items selected by the Russian Federation. However, 10 countries with the same or higher overall performance were within 5 percentage points of the Russian students on these items.

The TCMA results provide evidence that the TIMSS science test provides a reasonable basis for comparing achievement for the participating countries. This result is not unexpected, since making the test as fair as possible was a major consideration in test development. The fact that the majority of countries indicated that most items were appropriate for their students means that the different average percent correct estimates were based substantially on the same items. Insofar as countries rejected items that would be difficult for their own students, these items tended to be difficult for students in other countries as well. The analysis shows that omitting such items tends to improve the results for that country, but also tends to improve the results for all other countries, so that the overall pattern of results is largely unaffected.

Table B.3 Standard Errors for the Test-Curriculum Matching Analysis Results - Science - Upper Grade (Eighth Grade*)

See Table B.1 for the Test-Curriculum Matching Analysis Results

Instructions: Read ***across*** the row for the standard error for the score based on the test items included by each of the countries across the top.
Read ***down*** the column under a country name for the standard error for the score of the country down the left on the items included by the country listed on the top.
Read along the ***diagonal*** for the standard error for the score for each different country based on its own decisions about the test items to include.

Country	*Average Percent Correct on All Items*	Singapore	Korea	Japan	Czech Republic	*Netherlands*	*Bulgaria*	*Slovenia*	*Austria*	England	Hungary	Belgium (Fl)	*Australia*	Slovak Republic	Sweden	Canada	Ireland	United States	Russian Federation	*Germany*	New Zealand	Norway	Hong Kong	*Israel*	Switzerland	Spain	*Scotland*	France	Iceland	*Greece*	*Denmark*	*Belgium (Fr)*	Latvia (LSS)	Portugal	*Romania*	Lithuania	Iran, Islamic Rep.	Cyprus	*Kuwait*	*Colombia*	*South Africa*
(Number of Score Points Included)	*146***	*109*	*59*	*86*	*136*	*102*	*112*	*140*	*131*	*124*	*129*	*98*	*133*	*129*	*125*	*121*	*90*	*146*	*96*	*129*	*126*	*111*	*68*	*102*	*105*	*146*	*97*	*73*	*146*	*111*	*70*	*58*	*113*	*133*	*99*	*120*	*87*	*78*	*131*	*112*	*74*
Singapore	70 (1.0)	0.9	1.0	0.9	1.0	1.0	1.0	1.0	0.9	1.0	1.0	0.9	1.0	1.0	1.0	0.9	0.9	1.0	0.9	0.9	0.9	1.0	1.0	1.0	1.0	1.0	0.9	1.1	1.0	0.9	1.0	1.0	1.0	1.0	1.0	1.0	1.0	0.9	1.0	0.9	1.0
Korea	66 (0.4)	0.4	0.4	0.4	0.4	0.4	0.4	0.4	0.4	0.4	0.4	0.4	0.4	0.3	0.4	0.4	0.4	0.4	0.4	0.4	0.4	0.4	0.4	0.4	0.4	0.4	0.4	0.4	0.4	0.4	0.4	0.4	0.4	0.4	0.4	0.3	0.4	0.4	0.4	0.4	0.4
Japan	65 (0.3)	0.3	0.4	0.4	0.3	0.4	0.3	0.3	0.3	0.4	0.3	0.3	0.3	0.3	0.3	0.3	0.4	0.3	0.3	0.3	0.4	0.4	0.3	0.4	0.3	0.3	0.4	0.3	0.3	0.3	0.4	0.3	0.3	0.3	0.3	0.3	0.3	0.3	0.3	0.4	0.3
Czech Republic	64 (0.8)	0.9	0.9	0.8	0.8	0.8	0.8	0.9	0.8	0.9	0.8	0.9	0.9	0.9	0.8	0.8	0.8	0.8	0.8	0.8	0.8	0.8	0.8	0.8	0.8	0.8	0.9	0.9	0.8	0.8	0.8	0.8	0.9	0.9	0.9	0.8	0.9	0.9	0.8	0.9	0.9
Netherlands	62 (1.1)	1.1	1.1	1.1	1.1	1.1	1.0	1.0	1.0	1.1	1.0	1.2	1.1	1.0	1.1	1.2	1.0	1.1	0.9	1.1	1.1	1.1	1.1	1.1	1.1	1.1	1.1	1.1	1.1	1.0	1.3	1.1	1.0	1.1	1.0	1.1	1.0	1.1	1.1	1.1	0.9
Bulgaria	62 (1.0)	1.0	1.3	0.9	0.9	1.0	1.0	1.0	0.9	0.9	1.0	0.9	1.0	1.0	1.0	0.9	0.9	1.0	1.0	0.9	0.9	1.0	0.9	1.0	0.9	1.0	0.9	1.1	1.0	0.9	0.9	0.9	1.0	1.0	1.0	0.9	1.0	0.9	1.0	1.0	1.1
Slovenia	62 (0.5)	0.5	0.6	0.6	0.5	0.6	0.6	0.5	0.5	0.6	0.6	0.5	0.6	0.5	0.5	0.5	0.5	0.5	0.5	0.5	0.6	0.6	0.5	0.6	0.6	0.5	0.5	0.5	0.5	0.6	0.5	0.6	0.6	0.5	0.6	0.6	0.5	0.6	0.6	0.6	0.6
Austria	61 (0.7)	0.7	0.8	0.7	0.7	0.7	0.7	0.7	0.7	0.7	0.7	0.6	0.7	0.7	0.7	0.7	0.7	0.7	0.7	0.7	0.7	0.7	0.7	0.7	0.7	0.7	0.7	0.7	0.7	0.7	0.7	0.6	0.7	0.7	0.7	0.7	0.7	0.7	0.7	0.7	0.7
England	61 (0.6)	0.6	0.7	0.7	0.6	0.6	0.6	0.6	0.6	0.6	0.6	0.6	0.6	0.6	0.6	0.6	0.6	0.6	0.6	0.6	0.6	0.6	0.6	0.6	0.6	0.6	0.7	0.7	0.6	0.6	0.6	0.6	0.6	0.6	0.6	0.6	0.6	0.6	0.6	0.6	0.7
Hungary	61 (0.6)	0.6	0.6	0.6	0.6	0.6	0.6	0.6	0.6	0.6	0.6	0.6	0.6	0.6	0.6	0.6	0.6	0.6	0.5	0.6	0.6	0.6	0.6	0.6	0.6	0.6	0.6	0.6	0.6	0.6	0.6	0.6	0.6	0.6	0.6	0.6	0.6	0.6	0.6	0.6	0.7
Belgium (Fl)	60 (1.1)	1.1	1.2	1.1	1.2	1.1	1.1	1.1	1.1	1.2	1.1	1.1	1.1	1.2	1.2	1.1	1.2	1.1	1.1	1.2	1.2	1.2	1.1	1.2	1.2	1.1	1.2	1.1	1.1	1.2	1.0	1.2	1.1	1.0	1.1	1.2	1.2	1.1	1.2	1.2	1.2
Australia	60 (0.7)	0.7	0.8	0.7	0.7	0.8	0.7	0.7	0.7	0.7	0.7	0.7	0.7	0.7	0.8	0.7	0.7	0.7	0.7	0.7	0.7	0.7	0.7	0.8	0.8	0.7	0.7	0.8	0.7	0.7	0.7	0.7	0.8	0.7	0.7	0.7	0.7	0.7	0.7	0.8	0.7
Slovak Republic	59 (0.6)	0.6	0.6	0.6	0.6	0.6	0.6	0.6	0.6	0.6	0.6	0.6	0.6	0.6	0.6	0.6	0.6	0.6	0.6	0.6	0.6	0.6	0.6	0.6	0.6	0.6	0.6	0.6	0.6	0.6	0.6	0.6	0.6	0.6	0.6	0.6	0.6	0.6	0.6	0.6	0.6
Sweden	59 (0.6)	0.6	0.5	0.6	0.6	0.6	0.6	0.6	0.6	0.6	0.6	0.6	0.6	0.6	0.6	0.6	0.6	0.6	0.6	0.6	0.6	0.6	0.6	0.6	0.6	0.6	0.6	0.6	0.6	0.6	0.6	0.6	0.6	0.6	0.5	0.6	0.6	0.6	0.6	0.6	0.6
Canada	59 (0.5)	0.5	0.6	0.5	0.5	0.5	0.5	0.5	0.5	0.5	0.5	0.5	0.5	0.5	0.5	0.5	0.5	0.5	0.5	0.5	0.5	0.5	0.5	0.5	0.5	0.5	0.5	0.5	0.5	0.5	0.5	0.6	0.5	0.5	0.5	0.5	0.5	0.4	0.5	0.5	0.5
Ireland	58 (0.9)	0.9	1.0	0.9	0.9	0.9	0.9	0.9	0.9	0.9	0.9	0.9	0.9	0.9	0.9	0.9	1.0	0.9	0.9	0.9	0.9	0.9	1.0	0.9	0.9	0.9	0.9	0.9	0.9	0.9	1.0	0.9	0.9	0.9	0.9	0.9	0.9	0.9	0.9	0.9	0.9
United States	58 (1.0)	0.9	1.0	1.0	0.9	1.0	1.0	1.0	0.9	1.0	1.0	0.9	1.0	1.0	1.0	1.0	1.0	1.0	0.9	1.0	1.0	0.9	1.0	1.0	1.0	1.0	1.0	1.0	1.0	0.9	1.0	0.9	1.0	0.9	0.9	1.0	0.9	0.9	1.0	1.0	1.0
Russian Federation	58 (0.8)	0.8	0.9	0.8	0.7	0.7	0.8	0.8	0.8	0.7	0.8	0.6	0.8	0.7	0.7	0.7	0.7	0.8	0.7	0.8	0.7	0.7	0.7	0.8	0.7	0.8	0.7	0.8	0.8	0.8	0.7	0.7	0.8	0.8	0.8	0.7	0.8	0.8	0.8	0.7	0.8
Germany	58 (1.0)	1.0	1.1	1.1	1.0	1.0	1.0	1.0	1.0	1.0	1.0	1.0	1.0	1.0	1.0	1.0	1.0	1.0	1.0	1.0	1.0	1.0	1.0	1.1	1.0	1.0	1.0	1.1	1.0	1.0	1.0	1.0	1.0	1.0	1.0	1.0	1.0	1.0	1.0	1.0	1.0
New Zealand	58 (0.8)	0.9	0.9	0.9	0.8	0.9	0.8	0.9	0.8	0.9	0.8	0.8	0.9	0.8	0.8	0.8	0.8	0.8	0.8	0.8	0.9	0.8	0.9	0.9	0.9	0.8	0.8	0.9	0.8	0.8	0.9	0.9	0.9	0.9	0.8	0.9	0.8	0.8	0.8	0.9	0.9
Norway	58 (0.4)	0.4	0.5	0.4	0.4	0.4	0.4	0.4	0.4	0.4	0.4	0.4	0.4	0.4	0.4	0.4	0.4	0.4	0.4	0.4	0.4	0.4	0.4	0.4	0.4	0.4	0.4	0.4	0.4	0.4	0.4	0.4	0.4	0.4	0.4	0.4	0.4	0.4	0.4	0.4	0.4
Hong Kong	58 (1.0)	1.0	1.0	1.0	1.0	1.0	1.0	1.0	0.9	1.0	1.0	1.0	1.0	1.0	1.0	1.0	0.9	1.0	0.9	1.0	1.0	1.0	1.0	1.0	1.0	1.0	1.0	1.0	1.0	1.0	1.0	1.0	1.0	1.0	1.0	1.0	0.9	0.9	1.0	1.0	1.0
Israel	57 (1.1)	1.1	1.1	1.0	1.1	1.1	1.1	1.1	1.0	1.1	1.1	1.0	1.1	1.1	1.1	1.1	1.1	1.1	1.0	1.0	1.1	1.0	1.2	1.1	1.1	1.1	1.1	1.1	1.1	1.2	1.1	1.0	1.0	1.1	1.2	1.1	1.1	1.1	1.1	1.1	1.1
Switzerland	56 (0.5)	0.5	0.5	0.5	0.5	0.5	0.5	0.5	0.5	0.5	0.5	0.5	0.5	0.5	0.5	0.5	0.5	0.5	0.5	0.5	0.5	0.5	0.6	0.5	0.5	0.5	0.5	0.5	0.5	0.5	0.5	0.5	0.5	0.5	0.5	0.5	0.5	0.5	0.5	0.5	0.5
Spain	56 (0.4)	0.4	0.5	0.4	0.4	0.4	0.4	0.4	0.4	0.4	0.4	0.4	0.4	0.4	0.4	0.4	0.4	0.4	0.4	0.4	0.4	0.4	0.4	0.4	0.4	0.4	0.4	0.4	0.4	0.4	0.4	0.4	0.4	0.4	0.4	0.4	0.4	0.4	0.4	0.4	0.4
Scotland	55 (1.0)	1.0	1.1	1.0	1.0	1.0	1.0	1.0	1.0	1.0	1.0	0.9	1.0	1.0	1.0	1.0	1.0	1.0	0.9	1.0	1.0	1.0	1.0	1.0	1.0	1.0	1.0	1.1	1.0	1.0	1.0	1.0	1.0	1.0	1.0	1.0	1.0	1.0	1.0	1.0	1.0
France	54 (0.6)	0.6	0.7	0.7	0.6	0.6	0.6	0.6	0.6	0.6	0.6	0.6	0.6	0.6	0.6	0.6	0.7	0.6	0.6	0.6	0.6	0.6	0.6	0.7	0.6	0.6	0.6	0.6	0.6	0.6	0.6	0.7	0.6	0.6	0.6	0.6	0.6	0.6	0.6	0.6	0.6
Iceland	52 (0.9)	0.8	0.9	0.9	0.9	1.0	0.9	0.9	0.9	0.9	0.9	1.0	0.9	0.9	0.9	1.0	0.9	0.9	0.9	0.9	1.0	1.0	1.0	0.9	0.9	0.9	0.9	1.1	0.9	0.9	1.0	0.8	1.0	0.9	0.8	1.0	0.9	0.9	0.9	0.9	0.8
Greece	52 (0.5)	0.5	0.6	0.5	0.5	0.5	0.5	0.5	0.5	0.5	0.5	0.5	0.5	0.5	0.5	0.5	0.5	0.5	0.5	0.5	0.5	0.5	0.5	0.5	0.5	0.5	0.5	0.5	0.5	0.5	0.5	0.6	0.5	0.5	0.5	0.5	0.4	0.4	0.5	0.5	0.6
Denmark	51 (0.6)	0.6	0.6	0.6	0.5	0.5	0.6	0.5	0.6	0.6	0.6	0.6	0.5	0.5	0.6	0.6	0.5	0.6	0.6	0.6	0.6	0.5	0.6	0.6	0.5	0.6	0.6	0.6	0.6	0.6	0.6	0.7	0.6	0.6	0.5	0.6	0.6	0.6	0.6	0.5	0.6
Belgium (Fr)	50 (0.7)	0.6	0.7	0.7	0.7	0.7	0.7	0.7	0.7	0.7	0.7	0.7	0.7	0.7	0.7	0.7	0.6	0.7	0.6	0.7	0.7	0.7	0.7	0.7	0.7	0.7	0.7	0.7	0.7	0.7	0.8	0.8	0.7	0.7	0.7	0.7	0.6	0.7	0.7	0.7	0.7
Latvia (LSS)	50 (0.6)	0.6	0.6	0.6	0.6	0.6	0.6	0.6	0.6	0.6	0.6	0.6	0.6	0.6	0.6	0.6	0.6	0.6	0.6	0.6	0.6	0.6	0.6	0.6	0.6	0.6	0.6	0.6	0.6	0.6	0.6	0.6	0.6	0.6	0.6	0.6	0.6	0.6	0.6	0.6	0.6
Portugal	50 (0.6)	0.6	0.6	0.6	0.5	0.6	0.5	0.5	0.5	0.5	0.6	0.5	0.6	0.6	0.6	0.5	0.6	0.6	0.6	0.5	0.5	0.5	0.6	0.6	0.6	0.6	0.6	0.6	0.6	0.6	0.5	0.5	0.6	0.6	0.6	0.6	0.6	0.6	0.6	0.6	0.7
Romania	50 (0.8)	0.8	0.9	0.8	0.9	0.8	0.8	0.9	0.8	0.8	0.9	0.9	0.9	0.9	0.9	0.9	0.9	0.8	0.9	0.8	0.8	0.9	0.9	0.9	0.9	0.8	0.9	0.8	0.8	0.8	0.9	0.9	0.8	0.8	0.8	0.9	0.8	0.8	0.8	0.9	0.9
Lithuania	49 (0.7)	0.7	0.8	0.7	0.7	0.7	0.7	0.7	0.7	0.7	0.7	0.7	0.7	0.7	0.7	0.7	0.7	0.7	0.7	0.7	0.7	0.8	0.7	0.8	0.7	0.7	0.7	0.8	0.7	0.7	0.8	0.7	0.7	0.7	0.7	0.7	0.7	0.7	0.7	0.7	0.7
Iran, Islamic Rep.	47 (0.6)	0.6	0.6	0.7	0.6	0.6	0.6	0.6	0.6	0.6	0.6	0.6	0.6	0.6	0.6	0.6	0.6	0.6	0.6	0.5	0.6	0.6	0.6	0.6	0.6	0.6	0.6	0.6	0.6	0.6	0.6	0.6	0.6	0.6	0.6	0.6	0.6	0.6	0.6	0.6	0.6
Cyprus	47 (0.4)	0.4	0.5	0.4	0.4	0.4	0.4	0.4	0.4	0.4	0.4	0.4	0.4	0.4	0.4	0.4	0.5	0.4	0.3	0.4	0.4	0.4	0.4	0.5	0.4	0.4	0.5	0.4	0.4	0.5	0.4	0.5	0.4	0.4	0.4	0.4	0.4	0.5	0.4	0.4	0.4
Kuwait	43 (0.9)	1.0	1.0	1.1	0.8	1.0	0.9	0.9	0.9	1.0	0.9	0.8	0.9	0.9	0.9	0.9	0.9	0.9	0.9	0.9	0.9	1.0	0.8	0.9	0.9	0.9	0.9	1.0	0.9	0.9	0.8	0.9	1.0	0.9	0.9	1.0	0.9	1.0	0.9	1.0	1.0
Colombia	39 (0.8)	0.8	0.8	0.9	0.8	0.8	0.8	0.8	0.8	0.8	0.8	0.8	0.8	0.8	0.8	0.8	0.8	0.8	0.8	0.8	0.8	0.8	0.9	0.9	0.8	0.8	0.8	0.8	0.8	0.9	0.9	0.7	0.8	0.8	0.9	0.9	0.9	0.9	0.8	0.8	0.9
South Africa	27 (1.3)	1.3	1.2	1.4	1.2	1.3	1.3	1.3	1.3	1.3	1.3	1.3	1.3	1.3	1.3	1.3	1.3	1.3	1.2	1.3	1.4	1.3	1.4	1.3	1.3	1.3	1.3	1.2	1.3	1.4	1.3	1.2	1.2	1.3	1.3	1.3	1.3	1.4	1.3	1.3	1.3
International Average	**55 (0.7)**	**0.7**	**0.8**	**0.8**	**0.7**	**0.7**	**0.7**	**0.7**	**0.7**	**0.7**	**0.7**	**0.7**	**0.7**	**0.7**	**0.7**	**0.7**	**0.7**	**0.7**	**0.7**	**0.7**	**0.7**	**0.7**	**0.7**	**0.8**	**0.7**	**0.7**	**0.7**	**0.8**	**0.7**	**0.7**	**0.7**	**0.7**	**0.7**	**0.7**	**0.7**	**0.7**	**0.7**	**0.7**	**0.7**	**0.7**	**0.8**

*Eighth grade in most countries; see Table 2 for more information about the grades tested in each country.
**Of the 135 items in the science test, some items had two parts and some extended-response items were scored on a two- or three-point scale, resulting in 146 total score points.
( ) Standard errors for the average percent of correct responses on all items appear in parentheses. The matrix contains standard errors corresponding to the average percent of correct responses based on TCMA subsets of items, as displayed in Table B.1. Because results are rounded to the nearest whole number, some totals may appear inconsistent.
Countries shown in italics did not satisfy one or more guidelines for sample participation rates, age/grade specifications, or classroom sampling procedures (see Figure A.3 for details).
Because population coverage falls below 65% Latvia is annotated LSS for Latvian Speaking Schools only.
SOURCE: IEA Third International Mathematics and Science Study (TIMSS), 1994-95.

Table B.4 Standard Errors for the Test-Curriculum Matching Analysis Results - Science - Lower Grade (Seventh Grade*)

See Table B.3 for the Test-Curriculum Matching Analysis Results

Instructions: Read ***across*** the row for the standard error for the score based on the test items included by each of the countries across the top.
Read ***down*** the column under a country name for the standard error for the score of the country down the left on the items included by the country listed on the top.
Read along the ***diagonal*** for the standard error for the score for each different country based on its own decisions about the test items to include.

Country	*Average Percent Correct on All Items*	Singapore	Korea	Japan	Czech Republic	*Slovenia*	Belgium (Fl)	*Bulgaria*	*Netherlands*	England	Hungary	*Austria*	Slovak Republic	United States	Canada	*Australia*	Hong Kong	*Germany*	Ireland	Sweden	New Zealand	Norway	Switzerland	Russian Federation	Spain	Scotland	Iceland	France	Belgium (Fr)	*Romania*	*Greece*	*Denmark*	Iran, Islamic Rep.	Latvia (LSS)	Portugal	Cyprus	*Colombia*	Lithuania	*South Africa*
(Number of Score Points Included)	*146***	*83*	*44*	*46*	*108*	*132*	*45*	*106*	*34*	*105*	*98*	*53*	*111*	*146*	*79*	*94*	*33*	*88*	*60*	*86*	*110*	*93*	*36*	*49*	*132*	*50*	*146*	*26*	*23*	*92*	*72*	*20*	*48*	*46*	*81*	*29*	*79*	*109*	*26*
Singapore	61 (1.2)	1.3	1.3	1.3	1.3	1.2	1.3	1.2	1.4	1.3	1.2	1.3	1.2	1.2	1.3	1.4	1.3	1.3	1.2	1.2	1.2	1.2	1.3	1.1	1.2	1.3	1.2	1.5	1.3	1.2	1.3	1.4	1.2	1.3	1.3	1.4	1.3	1.2	1.3
Korea	61 (0.4)	0.4	0.5	0.4	0.4	0.4	0.5	0.4	0.6	0.4	0.4	0.5	0.4	0.4	0.5	0.5	0.5	0.4	0.4	0.4	0.4	0.4	0.5	0.5	0.4	0.5	0.4	0.6	0.6	0.4	0.5	0.7	0.5	0.5	0.4	0.6	0.4	0.4	0.5
Japan	59 (0.3)	0.3	0.4	0.4	0.3	0.3	0.3	0.3	0.4	0.3	0.3	0.3	0.3	0.3	0.4	0.3	0.4	0.3	0.3	0.3	0.3	0.3	0.4	0.4	0.3	0.4	0.3	0.4	0.5	0.3	0.3	0.4	0.3	0.4	0.3	0.4	0.3	0.3	0.4
Czech Republic	58 (0.8)	0.7	1.0	0.7	0.8	0.8	0.7	0.8	0.8	0.8	0.8	0.7	0.8	0.8	0.8	0.8	0.9	0.7	0.7	0.7	0.8	0.8	0.8	0.7	0.8	0.8	0.8	0.8	1.1	0.8	0.7	0.9	0.8	0.9	0.8	0.9	0.8	0.8	0.8
Slovenia	57 (0.5)	0.5	0.6	0.6	0.5	0.5	0.4	0.6	0.6	0.5	0.5	0.5	0.5	0.5	0.5	0.5	0.6	0.5	0.5	0.5	0.5	0.5	0.5	0.5	0.5	0.6	0.5	0.6	0.6	0.5	0.5	0.7	0.5	0.5	0.5	0.7	0.5	0.5	0.7
Belgium (Fl)	57 (0.5)	0.5	0.6	0.6	0.6	0.5	0.6	0.6	0.7	0.6	0.6	0.7	0.5	0.5	0.6	0.6	0.7	0.6	0.5	0.6	0.6	0.6	0.7	0.6	0.6	0.6	0.5	0.8	0.7	0.5	0.6	0.7	0.6	0.6	0.6	0.8	0.6	0.5	0.6
Bulgaria	56 (1.0)	1.0	1.1	1.1	1.0	1.0	1.1	1.1	1.1	1.0	1.0	1.2	0.9	1.0	1.0	1.0	1.1	1.0	1.0	1.0	0.9	1.0	1.0	1.0	1.0	1.2	1.0	1.2	1.4	0.9	1.0	1.1	1.0	1.0	0.9	1.0	1.0	1.0	1.1
Netherlands	56 (0.7)	0.7	0.9	0.8	0.7	0.7	0.8	0.7	0.9	0.7	0.8	0.8	0.7	0.7	0.8	0.8	0.9	0.8	0.7	0.8	0.8	0.8	1.0	0.8	0.8	0.8	0.7	0.9	1.0	0.7	0.9	1.1	0.9	0.9	0.9	1.0	0.9	0.7	0.8
England	56 (0.6)	0.6	0.7	0.7	0.6	0.6	0.6	0.6	0.7	0.6	0.6	0.6	0.7	0.6	0.6	0.7	0.7	0.6	0.7	0.6	0.6	0.6	0.8	0.7	0.6	0.7	0.6	0.8	0.7	0.6	0.7	0.8	0.6	0.7	0.7	0.8	0.7	0.7	0.7
Hungary	56 (0.6)	0.6	0.7	0.7	0.7	0.6	0.7	0.6	0.7	0.6	0.7	0.7	0.6	0.6	0.7	0.7	0.7	0.6	0.7	0.6	0.6	0.7	0.8	0.6	0.6	0.7	0.6	0.8	0.7	0.7	0.7	0.7	0.7	0.7	0.7	0.8	0.7	0.7	0.7
Austria	55 (0.6)	0.6	0.7	0.7	0.6	0.6	0.6	0.6	0.7	0.6	0.7	0.8	0.6	0.6	0.6	0.6	0.7	0.6	0.6	0.6	0.6	0.6	0.7	0.6	0.6	0.8	0.6	0.8	0.8	0.6	0.7	0.8	0.7	0.7	0.7	0.8	0.6	0.6	0.7
Slovak Republic	54 (0.6)	0.6	0.6	0.6	0.6	0.6	0.6	0.6	0.6	0.6	0.6	0.7	0.6	0.6	0.6	0.6	0.6	0.6	0.6	0.6	0.6	0.6	0.7	0.6	0.6	0.6	0.6	0.7	0.7	0.6	0.7	0.7	0.6	0.7	0.6	0.7	0.6	0.6	0.7
United States	54 (1.1)	1.0	1.1	1.1	1.1	1.0	1.1	1.0	1.1	1.1	1.1	1.1	1.1	1.1	1.1	1.1	1.2	1.0	1.1	1.1	1.1	1.1	1.2	1.1	1.1	1.2	1.1	1.2	1.0	1.1	1.1	1.3	1.1	1.2	1.1	1.3	1.1	1.0	1.1
Canada	54 (0.5)	0.5	0.6	0.5	0.5	0.5	0.6	0.5	0.7	0.5	0.5	0.6	0.5	0.5	0.6	0.5	0.7	0.5	0.5	0.5	0.5	0.5	0.6	0.6	0.5	0.6	0.5	0.6	0.8	0.5	0.5	0.7	0.5	0.5	0.5	0.6	0.5	0.5	0.7
Australia	54 (0.7)	0.7	0.7	0.7	0.7	0.7	0.7	0.7	0.7	0.7	0.7	0.7	0.7	0.7	0.7	0.7	0.7	0.7	0.7	0.6	0.7	0.6	0.7	0.7	0.7	0.7	0.7	0.7	0.8	0.6	0.7	0.7	0.7	0.7	0.7	0.7	0.7	0.7	0.7
Hong Kong	53 (1.2)	1.3	1.3	1.3	1.3	1.2	1.1	1.2	1.3	1.2	1.2	1.3	1.2	1.2	1.3	1.3	1.3	1.2	1.1	1.2	1.3	1.2	1.4	1.2	1.2	1.4	1.2	1.4	1.3	1.2	1.3	1.3	1.2	1.2	1.2	1.3	1.2	1.2	1.2
Germany	53 (0.8)	0.8	0.9	0.8	0.9	0.8	0.8	0.8	0.9	0.8	0.9	0.9	0.8	0.8	0.9	0.9	0.9	0.9	0.8	0.9	0.9	0.9	0.9	0.8	0.8	0.9	0.8	0.9	0.9	0.8	0.9	1.1	0.8	0.9	0.9	1.0	0.9	0.9	0.9
Ireland	52 (0.7)	0.7	0.7	0.7	0.7	0.7	0.7	0.7	0.9	0.7	0.7	0.7	0.7	0.7	0.8	0.8	0.8	0.7	0.7	0.7	0.7	0.7	0.8	0.7	0.7	0.8	0.7	0.9	0.9	0.7	0.8	0.8	0.7	0.7	0.7	0.8	0.7	0.7	0.7
Sweden	51 (0.5)	0.6	0.6	0.6	0.6	0.5	0.6	0.6	0.7	0.6	0.5	0.6	0.6	0.5	0.6	0.6	0.7	0.6	0.5	0.6	0.6	0.6	0.7	0.6	0.6	0.6	0.5	0.6	0.8	0.5	0.6	0.7	0.6	0.6	0.6	0.7	0.6	0.6	0.7
New Zealand	50 (0.7)	0.7	0.8	0.8	0.7	0.7	0.6	0.7	0.8	0.7	0.7	0.7	0.7	0.7	0.7	0.8	0.8	0.7	0.6	0.7	0.7	0.7	0.9	0.7	0.7	0.8	0.7	1.0	0.8	0.7	0.8	0.8	0.7	0.8	0.7	0.9	0.7	0.7	0.8
Norway	50 (0.6)	0.6	1.1	0.7	0.7	0.6	0.7	0.7	0.8	0.6	0.7	0.8	0.6	0.6	0.7	0.7	0.8	0.7	0.7	0.7	0.7	0.7	0.7	0.7	0.6	0.8	0.6	0.8	1.0	0.7	0.6	0.8	0.8	0.6	0.6	0.7	0.6	0.6	0.8
Switzerland	50 (0.4)	0.4	0.5	0.5	0.4	0.4	0.5	0.4	0.5	0.4	0.5	0.5	0.4	0.4	0.5	0.5	0.6	0.5	0.4	0.5	0.5	0.4	0.6	0.5	0.4	0.5	0.4	0.7	0.5	0.4	0.5	0.6	0.4	0.5	0.4	0.6	0.5	0.4	0.5
Russian Federation	50 (0.8)	0.8	0.8	0.7	0.8	0.8	0.9	0.8	0.8	0.7	0.8	0.9	0.8	0.8	0.7	0.8	0.9	0.8	0.8	0.8	0.8	0.8	0.8	0.7	0.8	0.8	0.8	1.0	0.9	0.8	0.8	1.0	0.9	0.7	0.7	0.8	0.7	0.8	1.0
Spain	49 (0.4)	0.4	0.5	0.5	0.4	0.4	0.5	0.5	0.5	0.4	0.5	0.5	0.4	0.4	0.4	0.5	0.5	0.5	0.5	0.5	0.5	0.5	0.5	0.4	0.4	0.5	0.4	0.5	0.6	0.5	0.5	0.6	0.5	0.6	0.5	0.6	0.4	0.4	0.6
Scotland	48 (0.8)	0.8	0.9	0.8	0.8	0.8	0.7	0.8	0.9	0.8	0.8	0.9	0.8	0.8	0.9	0.9	0.9	0.8	0.7	0.8	0.8	0.8	1.0	0.8	0.8	0.8	0.8	1.0	0.9	0.8	0.8	0.9	0.9	0.8	0.8	0.9	0.8	0.8	0.8
Iceland	46 (0.6)	0.7	0.7	0.8	0.7	0.7	0.8	0.7	0.9	0.7	0.7	0.9	0.6	0.6	0.8	0.7	0.8	0.7	0.7	0.7	0.7	0.7	0.8	0.7	0.7	0.8	0.6	0.8	0.7	0.7	0.6	0.8	0.7	0.7	0.6	0.9	0.7	0.7	0.8
France	46 (0.6)	0.6	0.7	0.7	0.6	0.6	0.6	0.6	0.7	0.6	0.6	0.7	0.6	0.6	0.6	0.6	0.6	0.6	0.6	0.6	0.6	0.6	0.8	0.6	0.6	0.6	0.6	0.8	0.8	0.6	0.7	0.8	0.6	0.7	0.6	0.8	0.6	0.6	0.7
Belgium (Fr)	45 (0.7)	0.6	0.7	0.8	0.6	0.7	0.7	0.6	0.8	0.7	0.7	0.9	0.7	0.7	0.7	0.7	0.7	0.7	0.7	0.7	0.7	0.7	0.9	0.7	0.7	0.8	0.7	0.8	0.8	0.6	0.8	1.0	0.7	0.8	0.7	0.9	0.7	0.6	0.8
Romania	45 (0.8)	0.7	0.8	0.8	0.8	0.8	0.8	0.8	0.8	0.7	0.8	0.8	0.8	0.8	0.8	0.8	0.8	0.8	0.8	0.8	0.8	0.7	0.8	0.9	0.8	0.8	0.8	0.9	0.8	0.8	0.8	0.9	0.8	0.8	0.8	0.9	0.8	0.8	0.8
Greece	45 (0.5)	0.5	0.6	0.6	0.5	0.5	0.6	0.6	0.6	0.6	0.6	0.6	0.6	0.5	0.6	0.6	0.6	0.5	0.5	0.6	0.6	0.6	0.7	0.6	0.5	0.6	0.5	0.7	0.7	0.6	0.6	0.7	0.6	0.6	0.6	0.7	0.6	0.5	0.7
Denmark	44 (0.4)	0.4	0.6	0.6	0.5	0.5	0.5	0.5	0.6	0.5	0.5	0.6	0.5	0.4	0.5	0.5	0.6	0.5	0.5	0.5	0.5	0.5	0.6	0.5	0.5	0.5	0.4	0.6	0.7	0.5	0.5	0.7	0.6	0.5	0.4	0.6	0.4	0.4	0.6
Iran, Islamic Rep.	42 (0.6)	0.6	0.9	0.8	0.6	0.7	0.6	0.6	0.6	0.7	0.7	0.6	0.7	0.6	0.7	0.7	0.8	0.6	0.6	0.7	0.8	0.6	0.9	0.6	0.6	0.8	0.6	0.7	0.7	0.7	0.8	0.8	0.6	0.7	0.7	0.9	0.7	0.6	0.7
Latvia (LSS)	42 (0.5)	0.6	0.6	0.6	0.6	0.5	0.7	0.6	0.6	0.5	0.6	0.6	0.5	0.5	0.6	0.6	0.6	0.6	0.5	0.6	0.6	0.6	0.7	0.5	0.5	0.6	0.5	0.8	0.7	0.5	0.6	0.7	0.6	0.6	0.6	0.7	0.6	0.5	0.8
Portugal	41 (0.5)	0.5	0.6	0.6	0.5	0.5	0.5	0.5	0.5	0.5	0.5	0.6	0.5	0.5	0.5	0.5	0.5	0.5	0.5	0.5	0.5	0.5	0.6	0.5	0.5	0.5	0.5	0.6	0.6	0.5	0.5	0.8	0.5	0.6	0.5	0.7	0.5	0.5	0.5
Cyprus	40 (0.4)	0.4	0.5	0.5	0.4	0.4	0.4	0.4	0.5	0.4	0.4	0.4	0.4	0.4	0.4	0.4	0.6	0.4	0.4	0.4	0.4	0.4	0.6	0.4	0.4	0.5	0.4	0.5	0.6	0.4	0.5	0.6	0.5	0.5	0.4	0.6	0.4	0.4	0.4
Lithuania	38 (0.7)	0.8	0.8	0.8	0.7	0.7	0.8	0.7	0.8	0.7	0.7	0.8	0.7	0.7	0.7	0.7	0.8	0.8	0.8	0.7	0.7	0.8	0.8	0.8	0.7	0.8	0.7	0.9	0.9	0.8	0.8	0.8	0.8	0.8	0.7	0.9	0.8	0.7	0.8
Colombia	35 (0.7)	0.6	0.9	0.7	0.7	0.7	0.7	0.7	0.8	0.7	0.7	0.7	0.8	0.7	0.8	0.8	0.8	0.6	0.8	0.8	0.8	0.7	0.8	0.8	0.7	0.8	0.7	0.7	1.0	0.8	0.8	1.0	1.0	0.6	0.7	1.0	0.8	0.8	0.6
South Africa	26 (1.0)	1.0	1.1	1.0	1.0	1.0	0.9	1.0	1.2	1.0	1.0	1.0	1.0	1.0	1.1	1.1	1.0	1.0	0.9	1.1	1.1	1.1	1.2	0.9	1.1	1.1	1.0	1.1	1.2	1.0	1.1	1.1	1.0	1.0	1.1	1.1	1.1	1.0	1.1
International Average	**50 (0.7)**	**0.7**	**0.8**	**0.7**	**0.7**	**0.7**	**0.7**	**0.7**	**0.7**	**0.7**	**0.7**	**0.7**	**0.7**	**0.7**	**0.7**	**0.7**	**0.8**	**0.7**	**0.7**	**0.7**	**0.7**	**0.7**	**0.8**	**0.7**	**0.7**	**0.7**	**0.7**	**0.8**	**0.8**	**0.7**	**0.7**	**0.8**	**0.7**	**0.7**	**0.7**	**0.8**	**0.7**	**0.7**	**0.7**

*Seventh grade in most countries; see Table 2 for more information about the grades tested in each country.

**Of the 135 items in the science test, some items had two parts and some extended-response items were scored on a two- or three-point scale, resulting in 146 total score points.

( ) Standard errors for the average percent of correct responses on all items appear in parentheses. The matrix contains standard errors corresponding to the average percent of correct responses based on TCMA subsets of items, as displayed in Table B.2. Because results are rounded to the nearest whole number, some totals may appear inconsistent.

Countries shown in italics did not satisfy one or more guidelines for sample participation rates, age/grade specifications, or classroom sampling procedures (see Figure A.3 for details).

Because population coverage falls below 65% Latvia is annotated LSS for Latvian Speaking Schools only.

SOURCE: IEA Third International Mathematics and Science Study (TIMSS), 1994-95.

Appendix C

Selected Science Achievement Results for the Philippines

Table C.1

Philippines - Selected Achievement Results in the Sciences - Unweighted Data

Distributions of Achievement in the Sciences - Seventh Grade

Mean	Years of Formal Schooling	Average Age	5th Percentile (Scale Score)	25th Percentile (Scale Score)	50th Percentile (Scale Score)	75th Percentile (Scale Score)	95th Percentile (Scale Score)
395 (2.8)	7	14.0	235 (1.5)	317 (2.7)	386 (4.0)	468 (4.9)	583 (5.2)

Distributions of Achievement in the Sciences - Sixth Grade

Mean	Years of Formal Schooling	Average Age	5th Percentile (Scale Score)	25th Percentile (Scale Score)	50th Percentile (Scale Score)	75th Percentile (Scale Score)	95th Percentile (Scale Score)
382 (1.8)	6	12.9	223 (4.1)	311 (4.9)	373 (2.8)	451 (3.1)	566 (1.6)

Gender Differences in Achievement in the Sciences - Seventh Grade

Boys Mean	Girls Mean	Difference
392 (3.1)	397 (2.8)	5 (4.2)

Gender Differences in Achievement in the Sciences - Sixth Grade

Boys Mean	Girls Mean	Difference
381 (2.3)	383 (1.8)	2 (2.9)

Percentages of Students Achieving International Marker Levels in the Sciences Seventh Grade

Top 10% Level	Top Quarter Level	Top Half Level
1 (0.1)	4 (0.3)	13 (0.7)

Percentages of Students Achieving International Marker Levels in the Sciences Sixth Grade

Top 10% Level	Top Quarter Level	Top Half Level
2 (0.1)	6 (0.2)	18 (0.5)

() Standard errors appear in parentheses. Because results are rounded to the nearest whole number, some totals may appear inconsistent.

SOURCE: IEA Third International Mathematics and Science Study (TIMSS), 1994-95.

Table C.1 (Continued)

Philippines - Selected Achievement Results in the Sciences - Unweighted Data

Average Percent Correct by Science Content Areas - Seventh Grade

Science Overall	Earth Science	Life Science	Physics	Chemistry	Environmental Issues & the Nature of Science
38 (0.5)	40 (0.6)	38 (0.5)	39 (0.5)	31 (0.5)	38 (0.5)

Average Percent Correct by Science Content Areas -Sixth Grade

Science Overall	Earth Science	Life Science	Physics	Chemistry	Environmental Issues & the Nature of Science
35 (0.3)	37 (0.4)	38 (0.4)	36 (0.3)	27 (0.3)	36 (0.5)

Average Percent Correct for Boys and Girls by Science Content Areas Seventh Grade

Science Overall		Earth Science		Life Science		Physics	
Boys	Girls	Boys	Girls	Boys	Girls	Boys	Girls
37 (0.6)	38 (0.5)	40 (0.6)	40 (0.6)	38 (0.6)	39 (0.5)	39 (0.6)	38 (0.5)

Chemistry		Environmental Issues & the Nature of Science	
Boys	Girls	Boys	Girls
31 (0.6)	31 (0.5)	36 (0.6)	40 (0.6)

Average Percent Correct for Boys and Girls by Science Content Areas Sixth Grade

Science Overall		Earth Science		Life Science		Physics	
Boys	Girls	Boys	Girls	Boys	Girls	Boys	Girls
35 (0.4)	36 (0.3)	37 (0.5)	37 (0.4)	37 (0.5)	39 (0.4)	37 (0.4)	35 (0.3)

Chemistry		Environmental Issues & the Nature of Science	
Boys	Girls	Boys	Girls
27 (0.4)	27 (0.4)	35 (0.6)	37 (0.5)

*Seventh or Eighth grades in most countries; see Table 2 for information about the grades tested in the Philippines.
() Standard errors appear in parentheses. Because results are rounded to the nearest whole number, some totals may appear inconsistent.

SOURCE: IEA Third International Mathematics and Science Study (TIMSS), 1994-95.

Appendix D

Selected Science Achievement Results for Denmark, Sweden, and Switzerland (German-Speaking) – Eighth Grade

Table D.1

Denmark - Selected Achievement Results in the Sciences

Distributions of Science Achievement - Eighth Grade

Mean	Years of Formal Schooling	Average Age	5th Percentile (Scale Score)	25th Percentile (Scale Score)	50th Percentile (Scale Score)	75th Percentile (Scale Score)	95th Percentile (Scale Score)
523 (3.3)	8	14.9	371 (6.5)	464 (5.1)	520 (4.5)	588 (4.0)	673 (4.9)

Gender Differences in Science Achievement - Eighth Grade

Boys Mean	Girls Mean	Difference
538 (3.9)	509 (4.0)	28 (5.5)

Percentages of Students Achieving International Marker Levels in Science Eighth Grade

Top 10% Level	Top Quarter Level	Top Half Level
4 (0.5)	14 (1.0)	35 (1.3)

Average Percent Correct by Science Content Areas - Eighth Grade

Science Overall	Earth Science	Life Science	Physics	Chemsitry	Environmental Issues & the Nature of Science
57 (0.7)	55 (0.8)	62 (0.8)	58 (0.7)	49 (0.9)	55 (1.2)

Average Percent Correct for Boys and Girls by Science Content Areas Eighth Grade

Science Overall		Earth Science		Life Science		Physics	
Boys	Girls	Boys	Girls	Boys	Girls	Boys	Girls
60 (0.8)	54 (0.8)	60 (0.9)	51 (1.1)	63 (0.9)	61 (1.0)	62 (0.9)	55 (0.9)

Chemistry		Environmental Issues & the Nature of Science	
Boys	Girls	Boys	Girls
54 (1.3)	45 (1.1)	56 (1.6)	55 (1.5)

() Standard errors appear in parentheses. Because results are rounded to the nearest whole number, some totals may appear inconsistent.

SOURCE: IEA Third International Mathematics and Science Study (TIMSS), 1994-95.

Table D.2

Sweden - Selected Achievement Results in the Sciences

Distributions of Science Achievement - Eighth Grade

Mean	Years of Formal Schooling	Average Age	5th Percentile (Scale Score)	25th Percentile (Scale Score)	50th Percentile (Scale Score)	75th Percentile (Scale Score)	95th Percentile (Scale Score)
570 (4.1)	8	14.9	419 (2.5)	507 (8.1)	566 (4.3)	637 (5.6)	724 (1.6)

Gender Differences in Science Achievement - Eighth Grade

Boys Mean	Girls Mean	Difference
574 (4.7)	567 (4.4)	7 (6.4)

Percentages of Students Achieving International Marker Levels in Science Eighth Grade

Top 10% Level	Top Quarter Level	Top Half Level
13 (1.0)	29 (1.4)	56 (2.1)

Average Percent Correct by Science Content Areas - Eighth Grade

Science Overall	Earth Science	Life Science	Physics	Chemsitry	Environmental Issues & the Nature of Science
64 (0.8)	64 (0.9)	69 (0.9)	63 (0.8)	63 (1.1)	57 (1.2)

Average Percent Correct for Boys and Girls by Science Content Areas Eighth Grade

Science Overall		Earth Science		Life Science		Physics	
Boys	Girls	Boys	Girls	Boys	Girls	Boys	Girls
65 (1.0)	63 (0.9)	66 (1.1)	62 (1.1)	68 (1.1)	70 (0.9)	65 (1.0)	61 (0.9)

Chemistry		Environmental Issues & the Nature of Science	
Boys	Girls	Boys	Girls
65 (1.4)	60 (1.2)	57 (1.5)	58 (1.6)

() Standard errors appear in parentheses. Because results are rounded to the nearest whole number, some totals may appear inconsistent.

SOURCE: IEA Third International Mathematics and Science Study (TIMSS), 1994-95.

Table D.3

Switzerland (German Speaking) - Selected Achievement Results in the Sciences

Distributions of Science Achievement - Eighth Grade

Mean	Years of Formal Schooling	Average Age	5th Percentile (Scale Score)	25th Percentile (Scale Score)	50th Percentile (Scale Score)	75th Percentile (Scale Score)	95th Percentile (Scale Score)
565 (3.1)	8	15.1	416 (4.8)	501 (2.1)	563 (4.3)	631 (3.8)	718 (5.2)

Gender Differences in Science Achievement - Eighth Grade

Boys Mean	Girls Mean	Difference
578 (4.0)	553 (3.7)	26 (5.4)

Percentages of Students Achieving International Marker Levels in Science Eighth Grade

Top 10% Level	Top Quarter Level	Top Half Level
11 (0.8)	28 (1.3)	54 (1.7)

Average Percent Correct by Science Content Areas - Eighth Grade

Science Overall	Earth Science	Life Science	Physics	Chemsitry	Environmental Issues & the Nature of Science
63 (0.5)	64 (0.7)	66 (0.6)	63 (0.6)	57 (0.8)	57 (1.1)

Average Percent Correct for Boys and Girls by Science Content Areas Eighth Grade

Science Overall		Earth Science		Life Science		Physics	
Boys	Girls	Boys	Girls	Boys	Girls	Boys	Girls
65 (0.7)	60 (0.7)	67 (1.0)	61 (0.9)	67 (0.7)	65 (0.7)	68 (0.7)	60 (0.9)

Chemistry		Environmental Issues & the Nature of Science	
Boys	Girls	Boys	Girls
62 (1.3)	53 (1.1)	58 (1.5)	55 (1.3)

() Standard errors appear in parentheses. Because results are rounded to the nearest whole number, some totals may appear inconsistent.

SOURCE: IEA Third International Mathematics and Science Study (TIMSS), 1994-95.

Appendix E

Percentiles and Standard Deviations of Science Achievement

Table E.1

Percentiles of Achievement in the Sciences Upper Grade (Eighth Grade*)

Country	5th Percentile	25th Percentile	50th Percentile	75th Percentile	95th Percentile
Australia	371 (6.6)	475 (4.6)	545 (6.5)	619 (3.9)	720 (1.4)
Austria	395 (6.0)	499 (4.1)	558 (3.7)	623 (6.0)	721 (2.6)
Belgium (Fl)	416 (5.3)	499 (6.6)	548 (4.9)	609 (4.5)	680 (1.4)
Belgium (Fr)	332 (5.4)	415 (3.9)	472 (5.3)	532 (4.5)	609 (5.7)
Bulgaria	386 (5.2)	488 (2.0)	560 (7.3)	641 (4.3)	747 (6.9)
Canada	380 (3.7)	472 (4.2)	529 (4.0)	594 (3.0)	685 (3.8)
Colombia	291 (8.3)	358 (6.4)	410 (5.8)	467 (8.8)	533 (2.6)
Cyprus	316 (1.4)	403 (2.8)	462 (3.0)	526 (2.9)	605 (4.2)
Czech Republic	438 (4.9)	513 (2.9)	570 (5.3)	634 (5.1)	716 (4.5)
Denmark	334 (5.4)	423 (3.8)	477 (3.6)	541 (3.2)	615 (3.0)
England	380 (2.0)	484 (5.2)	549 (5.9)	625 (4.7)	727 (6.7)
France	374 (3.9)	446 (4.6)	498 (3.9)	553 (3.1)	623 (4.6)
Germany	362 (9.3)	463 (6.6)	535 (8.5)	602 (4.2)	691 (5.5)
Greece	363 (3.8)	439 (2.3)	495 (2.2)	557 (3.0)	643 (1.4)
Hong Kong	376 (10.6)	467 (7.1)	524 (7.2)	583 (4.1)	669 (1.4)
Hungary	408 (6.1)	497 (5.2)	552 (4.2)	616 (4.2)	703 (2.5)
Iceland	363 (0.6)	442 (5.3)	491 (3.8)	555 (6.9)	623 (14.7)
Iran, Islamic Rep.	355 (4.3)	422 (2.5)	467 (2.8)	520 (2.3)	592 (6.8)
Ireland	383 (2.6)	471 (10.1)	536 (5.0)	605 (4.9)	694 (1.9)
Israel	356 (14.7)	460 (9.1)	526 (10.4)	591 (5.3)	694 (11.1)
Japan	421 (0.5)	514 (4.3)	573 (1.5)	632 (1.8)	715 (1.7)
Korea	408 (1.2)	504 (1.8)	564 (2.4)	629 (4.1)	719 (1.4)
Kuwait	316 (7.1)	380 (5.4)	427 (3.4)	484 (4.9)	551 (2.7)
Latvia (LSS)	353 (4.4)	432 (5.4)	482 (2.4)	540 (3.0)	625 (6.5)
Lithuania	346 (2.7)	421 (8.5)	476 (5.8)	533 (3.1)	613 (5.3)
Netherlands	419 (11.7)	505 (9.3)	561 (6.0)	619 (5.0)	701 (8.8)
New Zealand	364 (6.9)	458 (6.3)	524 (5.5)	594 (3.6)	692 (3.7)
Norway	385 (3.8)	470 (1.9)	526 (3.0)	588 (1.9)	671 (4.7)
Portugal	362 (4.4)	429 (1.1)	477 (1.4)	531 (2.1)	602 (5.3)
Romania	321 (3.8)	420 (8.5)	484 (5.2)	556 (6.7)	653 (6.6)
Russian Federation	386 (8.5)	474 (8.1)	535 (5.3)	606 (3.6)	697 (8.0)
Scotland	357 (7.7)	451 (4.3)	513 (6.7)	584 (6.3)	686 (6.2)
Singapore	457 (5.2)	541 (7.4)	603 (7.4)	674 (6.5)	768 (6.1)
Slovak Republic	396 (7.1)	484 (8.8)	543 (5.6)	607 (4.3)	696 (2.3)
Slovenia	421 (2.9)	501 (4.7)	556 (4.2)	620 (3.6)	709 (4.6)
South Africa	185 (2.8)	261 (4.7)	313 (3.6)	376 (9.2)	526 (15.3)
Spain	393 (4.0)	465 (1.7)	514 (2.9)	571 (3.1)	649 (3.3)
Sweden	386 (5.5)	476 (6.2)	533 (5.2)	598 (4.1)	686 (1.7)
Switzerland	371 (3.9)	460 (5.2)	524 (4.9)	587 (4.6)	669 (0.9)
Thailand	409 (2.3)	479 (4.5)	525 (5.6)	575 (4.8)	646 (4.2)
United States	359 (6.3)	465 (7.7)	537 (6.5)	608 (5.4)	705 (8.6)

*Eighth grade in most countries; see Table 2 for more information about the grades tested in each country.

() Standard errors appear in parentheses.

SOURCE: IEA Third International Mathematics and Science Study (TIMSS), 1994-95.

Table E.2

Percentiles of Achievement in the Sciences Lower Grade (Seventh Grade*)

Country	5th Percentile	25th Percentile	50th Percentile	75th Percentile	95th Percentile
Australia	339 (6.7)	437 (7.9)	504 (3.6)	576 (3.1)	676 (9.4)
Austria	368 (12.8)	460 (5.1)	521 (3.5)	583 (6.0)	671 (6.0)
Belgium (Fl)	412 (3.7)	480 (4.7)	526 (3.2)	579 (5.2)	648 (1.0)
Belgium (Fr)	312 (7.5)	391 (2.2)	443 (3.8)	494 (7.1)	572 (1.6)
Bulgaria	360 (8.6)	464 (2.6)	530 (7.4)	601 (7.8)	701 (10.5)
Canada	358 (8.6)	441 (3.1)	496 (1.6)	559 (4.0)	653 (4.4)
Colombia	271 (8.1)	338 (5.6)	386 (4.2)	439 (5.2)	505 (2.8)
Cyprus	279 (8.1)	364 (3.4)	422 (2.1)	480 (3.8)	559 (1.8)
Czech Republic	398 (2.7)	479 (5.3)	534 (6.3)	587 (7.4)	671 (9.6)
Denmark	298 (2.8)	386 (1.3)	436 (3.1)	501 (2.6)	581 (20.6)
England	342 (6.9)	444 (3.6)	511 (4.4)	584 (11.0)	678 (8.9)
France	330 (3.3)	402 (3.3)	453 (5.9)	502 (1.4)	574 (2.0)
Germany	345 (7.6)	439 (7.3)	499 (5.1)	564 (8.3)	655 (4.3)
Greece	306 (1.0)	389 (5.0)	448 (4.1)	510 (2.4)	593 (2.7)
Hong Kong	350 (8.9)	440 (5.3)	497 (7.3)	556 (4.0)	633 (5.1)
Hungary	363 (5.9)	458 (7.6)	519 (5.8)	581 (5.1)	668 (7.2)
Iceland	346 (3.5)	412 (5.9)	458 (3.4)	513 (4.0)	593 (1.5)
Iran, Islamic Rep.	324 (6.9)	387 (1.6)	433 (3.0)	486 (4.9)	557 (5.1)
Ireland	343 (5.4)	435 (6.1)	494 (5.1)	558 (7.4)	645 (6.4)
Japan	387 (3.8)	477 (1.1)	530 (2.3)	589 (2.7)	672 (6.6)
Korea	379 (8.4)	478 (5.1)	538 (2.1)	598 (4.0)	677 (9.5)
Latvia (LSS)	311 (5.2)	385 (4.2)	432 (2.2)	490 (3.6)	562 (4.8)
Lithuania	273 (3.2)	355 (5.1)	400 (4.3)	455 (4.7)	536 (2.8)
Netherlands	389 (5.4)	467 (5.9)	518 (4.0)	574 (4.6)	642 (5.6)
New Zealand	324 (6.6)	416 (7.7)	481 (5.6)	548 (3.2)	642 (9.7)
Norway	344 (2.3)	431 (5.5)	483 (4.4)	543 (4.2)	621 (11.0)
Portugal	317 (2.4)	381 (3.0)	425 (2.9)	476 (4.3)	549 (1.7)
Romania	290 (6.1)	384 (7.3)	450 (6.3)	523 (5.7)	614 (10.2)
Russian Federation	333 (8.0)	419 (5.9)	480 (5.7)	549 (6.6)	648 (11.7)
Scotland	323 (10.3)	407 (6.0)	465 (5.2)	534 (5.5)	631 (4.7)
Singapore	380 (8.1)	480 (11.2)	548 (9.9)	613 (7.7)	708 (4.1)
Slovak Republic	374 (3.8)	453 (8.5)	507 (3.4)	565 (5.0)	652 (6.2)
Slovenia	395 (9.1)	471 (1.7)	523 (3.7)	590 (2.7)	675 (6.0)
South Africa	178 (3.8)	258 (3.4)	310 (4.7)	369 (6.7)	486 (15.6)
Spain	350 (1.4)	422 (3.4)	474 (2.5)	532 (4.0)	612 (2.9)
Sweden	351 (4.6)	434 (3.9)	485 (3.0)	547 (9.0)	627 (1.5)
Switzerland	350 (3.8)	430 (3.5)	484 (3.2)	538 (3.1)	617 (4.3)
Thailand	379 (2.6)	448 (3.3)	492 (3.7)	542 (3.0)	605 (3.9)
United States	337 (9.5)	438 (10.7)	507 (7.3)	582 (6.8)	681 (7.2)

*Seventh grade in most countries; see Table 2 for more information about the grades tested in each country.

SOURCE: IEA Third International Mathematics and Science Study (TIMSS), 1994-95.

Table E.3

Standard Deviations of Achievement in the Sciences Upper Grade (Eighth Grade*)

Country	Overall		Boys		Girls	
	Mean	Standard Deviation	Mean	Standard Deviation	Mean	Standard Deviation
Australia	545 (3.9)	106	550 (5.2)	110	540 (4.1)	103
Austria	558 (3.7)	98	566 (4.0)	97	549 (4.6)	98
Belgium (Fl)	550 (4.2)	81	558 (6.0)	82	543 (5.8)	79
Belgium (Fr)	471 (2.8)	86	479 (4.8)	89	463 (2.9)	81
Bulgaria	565 (5.3)	111	– –	–	– –	–
Canada	531 (2.6)	93	537 (3.1)	95	525 (3.7)	89
Colombia	411 (4.1)	76	418 (7.3)	79	405 (4.6)	71
Cyprus	463 (1.9)	89	461 (2.2)	93	465 (2.7)	83
Czech Republic	574 (4.3)	87	586 (4.2)	87	562 (5.8)	85
Denmark	478 (3.1)	88	494 (3.6)	90	463 (3.9)	83
England	552 (3.3)	106	562 (5.6)	108	542 (4.2)	102
France	498 (2.5)	77	506 (2.7)	76	490 (3.3)	77
Germany	531 (4.8)	101	542 (5.9)	101	524 (4.9)	99
Greece	497 (2.2)	85	505 (2.6)	85	489 (3.1)	84
Hong Kong	522 (4.7)	89	535 (5.5)	90	507 (5.1)	86
Hungary	554 (2.8)	90	563 (3.1)	89	545 (3.4)	90
Iceland	494 (4.0)	79	501 (5.1)	83	486 (4.6)	74
Iran, Islamic Rep.	470 (2.4)	73	477 (3.8)	76	461 (3.2)	67
Ireland	538 (4.5)	96	544 (6.6)	99	532 (5.2)	92
Israel	524 (5.7)	104	545 (6.4)	103	512 (6.1)	98
Japan	571 (1.6)	90	579 (2.4)	93	562 (2.0)	86
Korea	565 (1.9)	94	576 (2.7)	95	551 (2.3)	91
Kuwait	430 (3.7)	74	– –	–	– –	–
Latvia (LSS)	485 (2.7)	81	492 (3.3)	82	478 (3.2)	79
Lithuania	476 (3.4)	81	484 (3.8)	81	470 (4.0)	81
Netherlands	560 (5.0)	85	570 (6.4)	85	550 (4.9)	83
New Zealand	525 (4.4)	100	538 (5.4)	103	512 (5.2)	95
Norway	527 (1.9)	87	534 (3.2)	91	520 (2.0)	83
Portugal	480 (2.3)	74	490 (2.8)	73	468 (2.7)	73
Romania	486 (4.7)	102	492 (5.3)	104	480 (5.0)	99
Russian Federation	538 (4.0)	95	544 (4.9)	97	533 (3.7)	93
Scotland	517 (5.1)	100	527 (6.4)	102	507 (4.7)	96
Singapore	607 (5.5)	95	612 (6.7)	95	603 (7.0)	95
Slovak Republic	544 (3.2)	92	552 (3.5)	92	537 (3.9)	92
Slovenia	560 (2.5)	88	573 (3.2)	89	548 (3.2)	85
South Africa	326 (6.6)	99	337 (9.5)	102	315 (6.0)	94
Spain	517 (1.7)	78	526 (2.1)	77	508 (2.3)	77
Sweden	535 (3.0)	90	543 (3.4)	91	528 (3.4)	89
Switzerland	522 (2.5)	91	529 (3.2)	94	514 (3.0)	87
Thailand	525 (3.7)	72	524 (3.9)	72	526 (4.3)	72
United States	534 (4.7)	106	539 (4.9)	110	530 (5.2)	101

*Eighth grade in most countries; see Table 2 for information about the grades tested in each country.
A dash (–) indicates data are not available.
( ) Standard errors appear in parentheses.

SOURCE: IEA Third International Mathematics and Science Study (TIMSS), 1994-95.

Table E.4

Standard Deviations of Achievement in the Sciences Lower Grade (Seventh Grade*)

Country	Overall		Boys		Girls	
	Mean	Standard Deviation	Mean	Standard Deviation	Mean	Standard Deviation
Australia	504 (3.6)	103	507 (5.2)	107	502 (4.0)	98
Austria	519 (3.1)	94	522 (4.3)	98	516 (4.1)	90
Belgium (Fl)	529 (2.6)	73	536 (3.3)	75	521 (3.1)	71
Belgium (Fr)	442 (3.0)	79	453 (3.6)	78	432 (3.5)	78
Bulgaria	531 (5.4)	103	– –	–	– –	–
Canada	499 (2.3)	90	505 (2.9)	94	493 (2.5)	84
Colombia	387 (3.2)	72	396 (3.8)	74	378 (4.4)	69
Cyprus	420 (1.8)	87	420 (2.8)	91	420 (2.6)	82
Czech Republic	533 (3.3)	82	543 (3.2)	82	523 (4.1)	80
Denmark	439 (2.1)	86	452 (3.0)	89	427 (2.8)	83
England	512 (3.5)	101	522 (5.6)	103	500 (4.6)	97
France	451 (2.6)	74	461 (3.1)	76	443 (3.0)	72
Germany	499 (4.1)	96	505 (4.9)	97	495 (4.5)	93
Greece	449 (2.6)	87	452 (3.2)	90	446 (2.8)	85
Hong Kong	495 (5.5)	86	503 (6.6)	88	485 (5.8)	83
Hungary	518 (3.2)	91	525 (3.9)	94	510 (3.4)	89
Iceland	462 (2.8)	75	468 (4.4)	77	456 (2.4)	73
Iran, Islamic Rep.	436 (2.6)	72	443 (2.9)	75	428 (4.1)	66
Ireland	495 (3.5)	91	504 (4.6)	91	487 (4.5)	90
Israel	– –	–	– –	–	– –	–
Japan	531 (1.9)	86	536 (2.6)	89	526 (1.9)	83
Korea	535 (2.1)	92	545 (2.8)	92	521 (3.2)	90
Kuwait	– –	–	– –	–	– –	–
Latvia (LSS)	435 (2.7)	78	440 (3.6)	81	430 (3.0)	74
Lithuania	403 (3.4)	79	405 (3.5)	81	401 (4.2)	77
Netherlands	517 (3.6)	79	523 (4.0)	80	512 (4.4)	78
New Zealand	481 (3.4)	97	489 (4.3)	100	472 (3.7)	92
Norway	483 (2.9)	85	489 (3.6)	88	477 (3.6)	81
Portugal	428 (2.1)	71	436 (2.4)	74	420 (2.4)	68
Romania	452 (4.4)	100	456 (4.7)	101	448 (4.9)	99
Russian Federation	484 (4.2)	94	493 (5.3)	99	475 (3.8)	89
Scotland	468 (3.8)	94	477 (4.4)	97	459 (4.1)	90
Singapore	545 (6.6)	100	548 (7.9)	102	541 (8.2)	98
Slovak Republic	510 (3.0)	85	520 (4.0)	86	499 (3.1)	82
Slovenia	530 (2.4)	86	539 (3.0)	86	521 (2.8)	85
South Africa	317 (5.3)	92	324 (6.4)	93	312 (5.2)	91
Spain	477 (2.1)	80	487 (2.9)	82	467 (2.3)	76
Sweden	488 (2.6)	84	493 (2.9)	87	484 (3.3)	81
Switzerland	484 (2.5)	82	492 (2.9)	83	475 (2.9)	80
Thailand	493 (3.0)	69	495 (3.3)	71	492 (3.5)	68
United States	508 (5.5)	105	514 (6.3)	109	502 (5.8)	100

*Seventh grade in most countries; see Table 2 for information about the grades tested in each country.
A dash (–) indicates data are not available. Israel and Kuwait did not test the lower grade.
( ) Standard errors appear in parentheses.

SOURCE: IEA Third International Mathematics and Science Study (TIMSS), 1994–95.

Appendix F

Acknowledgments

TIMSS was truly a collaborative effort among hundreds of individuals around the world. Staff from the national research centers, the international management, advisors, and funding agencies worked closely to design and implement the most ambitious study of international comparative achievement ever undertaken. TIMSS would not have been possible without the tireless efforts of all involved. Below, the individuals and organizations are acknowledged for their contributions. Given that implementing TIMSS has spanned more than seven years and involved so many people and organizations, this list may not pay heed to all who contributed throughout the life of the project. Any omission is inadvertent. TIMSS also acknowledges the students, teachers, and school principals who contributed their time and effort to the study. This report would not be possible without them.

MANAGEMENT AND OPERATIONS

Since 1993, TIMSS has been directed by the International Study Center at Boston College in the United States. Prior to this, the study was coordinated by the International Coordinating Center at the University of British Columbia in Canada. Although the study was directed centrally by the International Study Center and its staff members implemented various parts of TIMSS, important activities also were carried out in centers around the world. The data were processed centrally by the IEA Data Processing Center in Hamburg, Germany. Statistics Canada was responsible for collecting and evaluating the sampling documentation from each country and for calculating the sampling weights. The Australian Council for Educational Research conducted the scaling of the achievement data.

International Study Center (1993–)

Albert E. Beaton, International Study Director
Michael O. Martin, Deputy International Study Director
Ina V.S. Mullis, Co-Deputy International Study Director
Eugenio J. Gonzalez, Director of Operations and Data Analysis
Dana L. Kelly, Research Associate
Teresa A. Smith, Research Associate
Maryellen Harmon, Performance Assessment Coordinator
Robert Jin, Computer Programmer
William J. Crowley, Fiscal Administrator
Thomas M. Hoffmann, Art Director
Debora Galanti, Art Director (former)
Jonathan R. English, Systems Manager
José Rafael Nieto, Senior Production Specialist
Ann G.A. Tan, Conference Coordinator
Mary C. Howard, Office Supervisor
Cheryl L. Flaherty, Secretary

International Study Center (continued)

Diane Joyce, Secretary
Leanne Teixeira, Secretary (former)
Kelvin D. Gregory, Graduate Assistant
Kathleen A. Haley, Graduate Assistant
Craig D. Hoyle, Graduate Assistant

International Coordinating Center (1991-93)

David F. Robitaille, International Coordinator
Robert A. Garden, Deputy International Coordinator
Barry Anderson, Director of Operations
Beverley Maxwell, Director of Data Management

Statistics Canada

Pierre Foy, Senior Methodologist
Suzelle Giroux, Senior Methodologist
Jean Dumais, Senior Methodologist
Nancy Darcovich, Senior Methodologist
Marc Joncas, Senior Methodologist
Laurie Reedman, Junior Methodologist
Claudio Perez, Junior Methodologist

IEA Data Processing Center

Michael Bruneforth, Senior Researcher
Jedidiah Harris, Research Assistant
Dirk Hastedt, Senior Researcher
Heiko Jungclaus, Senior Researcher
Svenja Moeller, Research Assistant
Knut Schwippert, Senior Researcher
Jockel Wolff, Research Assistant

Australian Council for Educational Research

Raymond J. Adams, Principal Research Fellow
Margaret Wu, Research Fellow
Nikolai Volodin, Research Fellow
David Roberts, Research Officer
Greg Macaskill, Research Officer

FUNDING AGENCIES

Funding for the International Study Center was provided by the National Center for Education Statistics of the U.S. Department of Education, the U.S. National Science Foundation, and the International Association for the Evaluation for Educational Achievement. Eugene Owen and Lois Peak of the National Center for Education Statistics and Larry Suter of the National Science Foundation each played a crucial role in making TIMSS possible and for ensuring the quality of the study. Funding for the International Coordinating Center was provided by the Applied Research Branch of the Strategic Policy Group of the Canadian Ministry of Human Resources Development. This initial source of funding was vital to initiate the TIMSS project. Tjeerd Plomp, Chair of the IEA and of the TIMSS Steering Committee, has been a constant source of support throughout TIMSS. It should be noted that each country provided its own funding for the implementation of the study at the national level.

NATIONAL RESEARCH COORDINATORS

The TIMSS National Research Coordinators and their staff had the enormous task of implementing the TIMSS design in their countries. This required obtaining funding for the project; participating in the development of the instruments and procedures; conducting field tests; participating in and conducting training sessions; translating the instruments and procedural manuals into the local language; selecting the sample of schools and students; working with the schools to arrange for the testing; arranging for data collection, coding, and data entry; preparing the data files for submission to the IEA Data Processing Center; contributing to the development of the international reports; and preparing national reports. The way in which the national centers operated and the resources that were available varied considerably across the TIMSS countries. In some countries, the tasks were conducted centrally, while in others, various components were subcontracted to other organizations. In some countries, resources were more than adequate, while in others, the national centers were operating with limited resources. Of course, across the life of the project, some NRCs have changed. This list attempts to include all past NRCs who served for a significant period of time as well as all the present NRCs. All of the TIMSS National Research Coordinators and their staff members are to be commended for their professionalism and their dedication in conducting all aspects of TIMSS.

Argentina
Carlos Mansilla
Universidad del Chaco
Av. Italia 350
3500 Resistencia
Chaco, Argentina

Australia
Jan Lokan
Raymond Adams *
Australian Council for Educational Research
19 Prospect Hill
Private Bag 55
Camberwell, Victoria 3124
Australia

* Past National Research Coordinator.

Austria
Guenter Haider
Austrian IEA Research Centre
Universität Salzburg
Akademiestraße 26/2
A-5020 Salzburg, Austria

Belgium (Flemish)
Christiane Brusselmans-Dehairs
Rijksuniversiteit Ghent
Vakgroep Onderwijskunde &
The Ministry of Education
Henri Dunantlaan 2
B-9000 Ghent, Belgium

Belgium (French)
Georges Henry
Christian Monseur
Universite de Liège
B32 Sart-Tilman
4000 Liège 1, Belgium

Bulgaria
Kiril Bankov
Foundation for Research, Communication,
Education and Informatics
Tzarigradsko Shausse 125, Bl. 5
1113 Sofia, Bulgaria

Canada
Alan Taylor
Applied Research & Evaluation Services
University of British Columbia
2125 Main Mall
Vancouver, B.C. V6T 1Z4
Canada

Colombia
Carlos Jairo Diaz
Universidad del Valle
Facultad de Ciencias
Multitaller de Materiales Didacticos
Ciudad Universitaria Meléndez
Apartado Aereo 25360
Cali, Colombia

Cyprus
Constantinos Papanastasiou
Department of Education
University of Cyprus
Kallipoleos 75
P.O. Box 537
Nicosia 133, Cyprus

Czech Republic
Jana Strakova
Vladislav Tomasek
Institute for Information on Education
Senovazne Nam. 26
111 21 Praha 1, Czech Republic

Denmark
Peter Weng
Peter Allerup
Borge Prien*
The Danish National Institute for
Educational Research
28 Hermodsgade
Dk-2200 Copenhagen N, Denmark

England
Wendy Keys
Derek Foxman*
National Foundation for
Educational Research
The Mere, Upton Park
Slough, Berkshire SL1 2DQ
England

France
Anne Servant
Ministère de l'Education
Nationale 142, rue du Bac
75007 Paris, France

Josette Le Coq*
Centre International d'Etudes
Pédagogiques (CIEP)
1 Avenue Léon Journault
93211 Sèvres, France

Germany
Rainer Lehmann
Humboldt-Universitaet zu Berlin
Institut Fuer Allgemeine
Erziehungswissenschaft
Geschwister-Scholl-Str. 6
10099 Berlin, Germany

Juergen Baumert
Max-Planck Institute for Human
Development and Education
Lentzeallee 94
14191 Berlin, Germany

Manfred Lehrke
Universität Kiel
IPN Olshausen Str. 62
24098 Kiel, Germany

Greece
Georgia Kontongiannopoulou-Polydorides
Joseph Solomon
University of Athens
Department of Education
Ippokratous Str. 35
106 80 Athens, Greece

Hong Kong
Frederick Leung
Nancy Law
The University of Hong Kong
Department of Curriculum Studies
Pokfulam Road, Hong Kong

Hungary
Péter Vari
National Institute of Public Education
Centre for Evaluation Studies
Dorottya U. 8, P.O. Box 120
1051 Budapest, Hungary

Iceland
Einar Gudmundsson
Institute for Educational Research
Department of Educational Testing
and Measurement
Surdgata 39
101 Reykjavik, Iceland

Indonesia
Jahja Umar
Ministry of Education and Culture
Examination Development Center
Jalan Gunung Sahari - 4
Jakarta 10000, Indonesia

Ireland
Deirdre Stuart
Michael Martin*
Educational Research Centre
St. Patrick's College
Drumcondra
Dublin 9, Ireland

Iran, Islamic Republic
Ali Reza Kiamanesh
Ministry of Education
Center for Educational Research
Iranshahr Shomali Avenue
Teheran 15875, Iran

Israel
Pinchas Tamir
The Hebrew University
Israel Science Teaching Center
Jerusalem 91904, Israel

Italy
Anna Maria Caputo
Ministero della Pubblica Istruzione
Centro Europeo dell'Educazione
Villa Falconieri
00044 Frascati, Italy

Japan
Masao Miyake
Eizo Nagasaki
National Institute for Educational Research
6-5-22 Shimomeguro
Meguro-Ku, Tokyo 153, Japan

Korea
Jingyu Kim
Hyung Im*
National Board of Educational Evaluation
Evaluation Research Division
Chungdam-2 Dong 15-1, Kangnam-Ku
Seoul 135-102, Korea

Kuwait
Mansour Hussein
Ministry of Education
P. O. Box 7
Safat 13001, Kuwait

Latvia
Andrejs Geske
University of Latvia
Faculty of Education & Psychology
Jurmalas Gatve 74/76, Rm. 204a
Riga, Lv-1083, Latvia

Lithuania
Algirdas Zabulionis
University of Vilnius
Faculty of Mathematics
Naugarduko 24
2006 Vilnius, Lithuania

Mexico
Fernando Córdova Calderón
Director de Evaluación de Politicas y
Sistemas Educativos
Netzahualcoyotl #127 2ndo Piso
Colonia Centro
Mexico 1, D.F., Mexico

Netherlands
Wilmad Kuiper
Anja Knuver
Klaas Bos
University of Twente
Faculty of Educational Science
and Technology
Department of Curriculum
P.O. Box 217
7500 AE Enschede, Netherlands

New Zealand
Hans Wagemaker
Steve May
Ministry of Education
Research Section
45-47 Pipitea Street
Wellington, New Zealand

Norway
Svein Lie
University of Oslo
SLS Postboks 1099
Blindern 0316
Oslo 3, Norway

Gard Brekke
Alf Andersensv 13
3670 Notodden, Norway

Philippines
Milagros Ibe
University of the Philippines
Institute for Science and Mathematics
Education Development
Diliman, Quezon City
Philippines

Ester Ogena
Science Education Institute
Department of Science and Technology
Bicutan, Taquig
Metro Manila 1604, Philippines

Portugal
Gertrudes Amaro
Ministerio da Educacao
Instituto de Inovação Educacional
Rua Artilharia Um 105
1070 Lisboa, Portugal

Romania
Gabriela Noveanu
Institute for Educational Sciences
Evaluation and Forecasting Division
Str. Stirbei Voda 37
70732-Bucharest, Romania

Russian Federation
Galina Kovalyova
The Russian Academy of Education
Institute of General Secondary School
Ul. Pogodinskaya 8
Moscow 119905, Russian Federation

Scotland
Brian Semple
Scottish Office, Education &
Industry Department
Victoria Quay
Edinburgh, E86 6QQ
Scotland

Singapore
Chan Siew Eng
Research and Evaluation Branch
Block A Belvedere Building
Ministry of Education
Kay Siang Road
Singapore 248922

Slovak Republic
Maria Berova
Vladimir Burjan*
SPU-National Institute for Education
Pluhova 8
P.O. Box 26
830 00 Bratislava
Slovak Republic

Slovenia
Marjan Setinc
Pedagoski Institut Pri Univerzi v Ljubljana
Gerbiceva 62, P.O. Box 76
61111 Ljubljana, Slovenia

South Africa
Derek Gray
Human Sciences Research Council
134 Pretorius Street
Private Bag X41
Pretoria 0001, South Africa

Spain
José Antonio Lopez Varona
Instituto Nacional de Calidad y Evaluación
C/San Fernando del Jarama No. 14
28071 Madrid, Spain

Sweden
Ingemar Wedman
Anna Hofslagare
Kjell Gisselberg*
Umeå University
Department of Educational Measurement
S-901 87 Umeå, Sweden

Switzerland
Erich Ramseier
Amt Für Bildungsforschung der
Erziehungsdirektion des Kantons Bern
Sulgeneck Straße 70
Ch-3005 Bern, Switzerland

Thailand
Suwaporn Semheng
Institute for the Promotion of Teaching
Science and Technology
924 Sukhumvit Road
Bangkok 10110, Thailand

United States
William Schmidt
Michigan State University
Department of Educational Psychology
463 Erikson Hall
East Lansing, MI 48824-1034
United States

TIMSS ADVISORY COMMITTEES

The International Study Center was supported in its work by several advisory committees. The International Steering Committee provided guidance to the International Study Director on policy issues and general direction of the study. The TIMSS Technical Advisory Committee provided guidance on issues related to design, sampling, instrument construction, analysis, and reporting, ensuring that the TIMSS methodologies and procedures were technically sound. The Subject Matter Advisory Committee ensured that current thinking in mathematics and science education were addressed by TIMSS, and was instrumental in the development of the TIMSS tests. The Free-Response Item Coding Committee developed the coding rubrics for the free-response items. The Performance Assessment Committee worked with the Performance Assessment Coordinator to develop the TIMSS performance assessment. The Quality Assurance Committee helped to develop the quality assurance program.

INTERNATIONAL STEERING COMMITTEE

Tjeerd Plomp (Chair), The Netherlands
Lars Ingelstam, Sweden
Daniel Levine, United States
Senta Raizen, United States
David Robitaille, Canada
Toshio Sawada, Japan
Benny Suprapto Brotosiswojo, Indonesia
William Schmidt, United States

Technical Advisory Committee

Raymond Adams, Australia
Pierre Foy, Canada
Andreas Schleicher, Germany
William Schmidt, United States
Trevor Williams, United States

Sampling Referee

Keith Rust, United States

Subject Area Coordinators

Robert Garden, New Zealand (Mathematics)
Graham Orpwood, Canada (Science)

Special Mathematics Consultant

Chancey Jones

Subject Matter Advisory Committee

Svein Lie (Chair), Norway
Antoine Bodin, France
Peter Fensham, Australia
Robert Garden, New Zealand
Geoffrey Howson, England
Curtis McKnight, United States
Graham Orpwood, Canada
Senta Raizen, United States
David Robitaille, Canada
Pinchas Tamir, Israel
Alan Taylor, Canada
Ken Travers, United States
Theo Wubbels, The Netherlands

Free-Response Item Coding Committee

Svein Lie (Chair), Norway
Vladimir Burjan, Slovak Republic
Kjell Gisselberg, Sweden
Galina Kovalyova, Russian Federation
Nancy Law, Hong Kong
Josette Le Coq, France
Jan Lokan, Australia
Curtis McKnight, United States
Graham Orpwood, Canada
Senta Raizen, United States
Alan Taylor, Canada
Peter Weng, Denmark
Algirdas Zabulionis, Lithuania

Performance Assessment Committee

Derek Foxman, England
Robert Garden, New Zealand
Per Morten Kind, Norway
Svein Lie, Norway
Jan Lokan, Australia
Graham Orpwood, Canada

Quality Control Committee

Jules Goodison, United States
Hans Pelgrum, The Netherlands
Ken Ross, Australia

Editorial Committee

David F. Robitaille (Chair), Canada
Albert Beaton, International Study Director
Paul Black, England
Svein Lie, Norway
Rev. Ben Nebres, Philippines
Judith Torney-Purta, United States
Ken Travers, United States
Theo Wubbels, The Netherlands

Cover Design by Thomas Hoffmann